RELIGION AND THE CULTURE WARS

Religious Forces in the Modern Political World
General Editor Allen D. Hertzke, The Carl Albert Center,
University of Oklahoma at Norman

Religious Forces in the Modern Political World features books on religious forces in politics, both in the United States and abroad. The authors examine the complex interplay between religious faith and politics in the modern world, emphasizing its impact on contemporary political developments. This new series spans a diverse range of methodological interpretations, philosophical approaches, and substantive concerns. Titles include:

God at the Grass Roots: The Christian Right in the 1994 Elections
    edited by Mark J. Rozell, Mary Washington College, and Clyde
    Wilcox, Georgetown University
Let Justice Roll: Prophetic Challenges in Religion, Politics, and Society
    edited by Neal Riemer, Drew University
Churches of the Poor: The Pentecostal Church in Central America
    by Anne M. Hallum, Stetson University
*The Right and the Righteous: The Christian Right Confronts the
Republican Party*
    by Duane Murray Oldfield, Boston College
Religion and the Culture Wars: Dispatches from the Front
    by John C. Green, University of Akron; James L. Guth, Furman
    University; Corwin E. Smidt, Calvin College; and Lyman A.
    Kellstedt, Wheaton College

RELIGION AND THE CULTURE WARS

Dispatches from the Front

John C. Green
James L. Guth
Corwin E. Smidt
and
Lyman A. Kellstedt

ROWMAN & LITTLEFIELD PUBLISHERS, INC.
Lanham • Boulder • New York • London

ROWMAN & LITTLEFIELD PUBLISHERS, INC.

Published in the United States of America
by Rowman & Littlefield Publishers, Inc.
4720 Boston Way, Lanham, Maryland 20706

3 Henrietta Street
London WC2E 8LU, England

British Cataloging in Publication Information Available

Library of Congress Cataloging-in-Publication Data

Religion and the culture wars : dispatches from the front / by
John C. Green . . . [et al.].
p.   cm. — (Religious forces in the modern political world)
Includes bibliographical references and index.
1. Christianity and politics—United States—History—20th
century.   2. Christianity and culture—United States—History—20th
century.   3. United States—Church history—20th century.   4. United
States—Politics and government—1945–1989.   5. United States—
Politics and government—1989–1993.   6. United States—Politics and
government—1993–   I. Green, John Clifford, 1953– . II. Series.
BR526.R45 1996   320.5′5′0973—dc20   96-15997   CIP

ISBN 0–8476–8267–6 (cloth: alk. paper)
ISBN 0–8476–8268–4 (pbk: alk. paper)

Printed in the United States of America

♾ ™ The paper used in this publication meets the minimum requirements of
American National Standard for Information Sciences—Permanence of
Paper for Printed Library Materials, ANSI Z39.48–1984.

Dedicated to four deeply religious women

Char Kellstedt
Marilyn Smidt
Cydelle Guth
Lynn Green

Contents

List of Illustrations   xi

Preface   xv

Acknowledgments   xxi

1   Introduction: Religion and the Culture Wars   1

Part I. The Christian Right

2   The Politics of the Christian Right   7
James L. Guth

3   The Moralizing Minority: Christian Right Support among
Political Contributors   30
James L. Guth and John C. Green

4   A Look at the "Invisible Army": Pat Robertson's 1988
Activist Corps   44
John C. Green

5   Onward Christian Soldiers: Religious Activist Groups in
American Politics   62
*James L. Guth, John C. Green, Lyman A. Kellstedt, and
Corwin E. Smidt*

Part II. Religion and Political Activists

6   The Christian Right in the Republican Party: The Case of Pat
Robertson's Supporters   86
John C. Green and James L. Guth

7 Faith and Election: The Christian Right in Congressional
   Campaigns 1978–1988   103
   John C. Green, James L. Guth, and Kevin Hill

8 Politics in a New Key: Religiosity and Participation among
   Political Activists   117
   James L. Guth and John C. Green

9 The Bully Pulpit: Southern Baptist Clergy and Political
   Activism 1980–92   146
   James L. Guth

Part III. Evangelical Voters

10 Grasping the Essentials: The Social Embodiment of Religion
   and Political Behavior   174
   *Lyman A. Kellstedt, John C. Green, James L. Guth, and
   Corwin E. Smidt*

11 Measuring Fundamentalism: An Analysis of Different
   Operational Strategies   193
   Lyman Kellstedt and Corwin Smidt

12 The Spirit-Filled Movements and American Politics   219
   *Corwin E. Smidt, John C. Green, Lyman A. Kellstedt, and
   James L. Guth*

13 The Puzzle of Evangelical Protestantism: Core, Periphery,
   and Political Behavior   240
   *Lyman A. Kellstedt, John C. Green, Corwin E. Smidt, and
   James L. Guth*

Part IV. Religion and Political Behavior

14 Religious Voting Blocs in the 1992 Election: The Year of
   the Evangelical?   267
   *Lyman A. Kellstedt, John C. Green, James L. Guth, and
   Corwin E. Smidt*

15 Has Godot Finally Arrived? Religion and Realignment   291
   *Lyman A. Kellstedt, John C. Green, James L. Guth, and
   Corwin E. Smidt*

16 The Political Relevance of Religion: The Correlates of
Mobilization　300
*James L. Guth, John C. Green, Lyman A. Kellstedt, and
Corwin E. Smidt*

17 Religion and Foreign Policy Attitudes: The Case of
Christian Zionism　330
*James L. Guth, Cleveland R. Fraser, John C. Green, Lyman
A. Kellstedt, and Corwin E. Smidt*

Index　361

About the Authors　369

Illustrations

Figures

3.1 Support for Moral Majority 39
4.1 The Deployment of the "Invisible Army" 56
8.1 Average Participation Rates, Secular and Religious Donors 126
8.2 High Participation Rates, Secular and Religious Donors 126

Tables

3.1 Support for Moral Majority among PAC and Party Donors 34
3.2 Support for Moral Majority: Status, Religious, and Ideological Variables 37
4.1 Robertson's Christian Soldiers: A Demographic Profile 48
4.2 Characteristics of Robertson's Supporters 50
4.3 Robertson's Clergy Supporters 51
4.4 Robertson 1988 Activists Demography by ZIP Code 54
4.5 Robertson 1988 Activists Demography by County 57
5.1 Religious Characteristics of Group Activists 69
5.2 Social and Political Theology of Group Activists 72
5.3 Political Agendas of Group Activists 74
5.4 Political Attitudes and Identifications of Group Activists 76
5.5 Ideology: Proximities and Ideological Clusters of Group Activists 77
5.6 Sources of Information for Group Activists 79
5.7 Political Activities Undertaken by Group Activists 81
6.1 Issue Salience 90
6.2 Opinion Cleavages 91
6.3 Religiosity and Demography 93
6.4 Partisan Attachments 95

6.5   GOP Factionalism   97
7.1   Christian Right (CR) Activism in Congressional
      Campaigns   109
8.1   Political Participation, 1980 Election   124
8.2   Political Activism in the 1980 Election   128
8.3   Issue Salience, Extreme Opinion and Partisan Evaluation   129
8.4   Information, Organizations and Movements   131
8.5   Region, Residence, Age and Ethnicity   133
8.6   Education   134
8.7   Occupation, Income and Gender   135
9.1   Approval of Types of Political Activities by Southern
      Baptist Clergy   150
9.2   Career Political Activities of Southern Baptist Clergy   153
9.3   Election Year Activities of Southern Baptist Clergy   155
9.4   Personal Resources and Activism, Baptist Clergy   159
9.5   Ideological Influences on Activism, Baptist Clergy   161
9.6   Organizational Influences on Activism, Baptist Clergy   165
9.7   Combined Model: Influences on Activism, Baptist Clergy   167
10.1 A Classification of Affiliation Responses   180
10.2 Religious Tradition and Political Behavior   182
10.3 Religious Commitment and Political Behavior   184
10.4 Religious Tradition and Religious Commitment   185
10.5 Religious Tradition, Religious Commitment, and Political
      Behavior   186
11.1 Fundamentalism and Sociodemographic Characteristics   202
11.2 Measures of Fundamentalism and Criterion Variables   204
11.3 Fundamentalism and Religiosity   205
11.4 Fundamentalism and Separatist Orientation   207
11.5 Fundamentalism and Self-Classification   208
11.6 Fundamentalism and Attitudes toward Abortion   210
11.7 Fundamentalism Measures and Four Criterion Variables   212
12.1 The Distribution of Spirit-Filled Christians   224
12.2 Religious Affiliation and Measures of Spirit-Filled
      Movements   226
12.3 Distribution of the Spirit-Filled by Religious Tradition   228
12.4 Issue Positions and Cohesion Levels   230
12.5 Partisanship of the Spirit-Filled   232
12.6 Relative Level of Politicization among the Spirit-Filled   235
13.1 Evangelical Traits and Political Variables   251
13.2 Combined Evangelical Traits and Political Variables   253
13.3 Varieties of Evangelicalism and Political Variables   256

14.1   Religious Tradition, Church Attendance and Political
        Behavior, 1960 and 1980   271
14.2   Religious Tradition, Church Attendance and Political
        Behavior, Spring 1992   274
14.3   Religious Tradition, Church Attendance and Issue Position,
        Spring 1992   276
14.4   Religious Tradition, Church Attendance and Political
        Behavior, Election Day 1992   278
14.5   Religious Tradition, Church Attendance and Issue
        Positions, Election Day 1992   279
14.6   Religious Tradition, Church Attendance and Political
        Behavior, Fall 1992   282
14.7   Religious Tradition, Church Attendance and Issue Position,
        Fall 1992   283
15.1   Religious Groups, Voting and Partisanship in the 1994
        Elections   292
15.2   Percentage Voting Republican   295
16.1   Sociodemographic Influences on Political Relevance of
        Religion   305
16.2   Agenda and Issue Influences on Political Relevance of
        Religion   308
16.3   Cognitive Influences on Political Relevance of Religion   313
16.4   Organizational Influences on Political Relevance of
        Religion   317
16.5   Combined Model for the Political Relevance of Religion   319
16.6   Partial Correlations between Orthodoxy and Political
        Variables   322
17.1   Protestant Clergy's Support for Israel   340
17.2   Clerical Activists' Support for Israel   343
17.3   Lay Activists' Support for Israel   344
17.4   Evangelical Activists' Support for Israel   347
17.5   Party Contributors' Support for Israel   349
17.6   American Public's Support for Israel   352

Preface

While searching for a suitable title for this book, a colleague suggested, only half in jest, "the greatest hits of the gang of four." The "gang of four" is the nickname regularly applied to the principal authors of this volume, Kellstedt, Smidt, Guth, and Green, who have collaborated for almost a decade in the study of religion and politics. We have been given other nicknames as well, ranging from "the knights of the woeful countenance" to the "evangelical mafia."

Kidding aside (where we generally give as good as we get), these nicknames reveal the ambivalence with which many colleagues view our work and the study of religion and politics in general. Some scholars simply do not think religion matters politically and wonder why we are wasting our effort and their time on an unimportant topic. Others are deeply suspicious of religion and offended by most, if not all, of its connections to politics, believing that religion should be a private matter. Still others believe we are simply projecting our own religious beliefs in the guise of social science.

We take the nicknames as compliments and the ambivalence of our colleagues as a good omen. We firmly believe that our empirical work will help persuade skeptics that religion does, in fact, matter in politics. Suspicion of religion is hardly a reason for rejecting research on the topic. Indeed, the more fulsome the challenge of politicized religion, more fully it should be studied. Our own religious backgrounds are a source of insight in our work, much as race is for some African American scholars, but certainly do not determine our conclusions.

This last point touches on the interesting question of how scholars choose their subjects. How was it that we came to study religion and politics, which is hardly a popular topic in our discipline? Each of us can best answer the question in his own words.

Bud Kellstedt. My interest in religion and politics was not what first led me into political science. I came from a family that was only nominally religious, but very political. My father was a great fan of that perennial candidate, Harold Stassen; my older brother ran for public office while I was still a teenager, and I can remember working in his campaigns. Given this family background, it is not surprising that I became a political scientist with interests in voting behavior and political participation.

I was raised in the First Presbyterian Church of Peoria, Illinois, which was made up of folks who wore navy blue suits and expensive dresses in order to be properly attired for lunch at "the club" after the Sunday service. I never heard the gospel of Jesus Christ proclaimed loudly, forthrightly, or consistently, and so I quit going as a teenager. When I got married, I joined my wife's denomination, the American Lutheran Church, where we spent the first twelve years of our marriage.

In 1970, my wife and I had what we would call a religious conversion experience that moved us in a more evangelical direction, and we began attending the Western Springs Baptist Church (Illinois), the only church Billy Graham ever pastored. It was in this loving church among wonderful people that I began thinking about the links between religion and politics. This speculation filtered into my scholarly interests in political participation and survey research: the literature on these topics had very little to say about religion, and I wondered why.

It took a move to Wheaton College (an independent evangelical college) in 1981 to turn my attention to religion and politics in a serious manner. I began with an effort to conceptualize and measure "evangelicalism" for the purpose of understanding the political behavior of this community, then a topic of considerable interest both in the country at large and at Wheaton itself. Much to my dismay, I found theologians and historians to be as wanting in this area as political scientists and survey researchers. And as they say, "the rest is history."

Corwin Smidt. My interest in religion and politics originated in the 1960 presidential election. As a junior high school student, I watched the televised coverage of each party's convention nearly "from gavel to gavel." Being the son of a Protestant minister (Reformed Church in America) in Iowa, I remember discussing John F. Kennedy's Catholicism and the role of religion in public life. Later I spent a year at New Brunswick Theological Seminary, not with the purpose of becoming a pastor, but because I was interested in theology. I eventually came to teach at Calvin College (a Christian Reformed school) for many of the same reasons.

In graduate school and my initial years as a political scientist, I focused on standard topics, including party identification, political socialization, and campaign finance. It was only with the election of Ronald Reagan in 1980 and the growing attention to the Moral Majority that I began to systematically focus on the connections between religion and electoral politics. My attention was prompted in part by scholarly and journalistic confusion over the difference between "evangelicals" and "fundamentalists," and the tendency to lump all religious people together as the latter. Obviously, with such errors in classification, any analyses of the links between religion and politics would be faulty. There was clearly a need for better research, and I set out to address the need.

At the same time, there was a growing network of scholars working on these questions. This network developed as scholars concerned with religion and politics encountered a lack of interest in the profession at large, and sought out each other for mutual support and assistance. These colleagues have been important in promoting continued research.

Jim Guth. My interest in religion and politics arose from familiarity with the traditional ethno-religious underpinning of political alignments. For example, in the Wisconsin of my youth, Catholics were almost invariably Democrats, German Lutherans were split in partisan affiliation, and Norwegians were mostly Republicans, though of a distinctly Progressive variety. Although I was raised a Baptist, my family was at the convergence of several of these religio-political streams, including German freethinking radicalism, Methodist pietism, and Seventh-Day Adventist escapism.

However, with the Kennedy nomination in 1960 and, even more, the Goldwater campaign of 1964, I noticed a swelling Republican enthusiasm among the evangelical faithful. Occasional field trips from high school to rallies of the Christian Anti-Communist Crusade also whetted my interest in the connection between religion and political life. Thus, I began to perceive (although I couldn't give it a name) the transition from "ethno-religious" to "culture war" politics. I found it all endlessly fascinating.

In graduate school, I discovered that religion had long been a part of politics. Perhaps the most formative influence for me was Michael Walzer's seminar on early modern political thought, and especially his own book, *The Revolution of the Saints*. When I began teaching at Furman University (then a Southern Baptist school), I decided to do a comparative course on the politics of religious movements, ranging from the Puritans to the abolitionists to liberation theology. I was thus well prepared to study the "new" Christian Right when it appeared in the late 1970s. In addition, years spent worshiping in a variety of Baptist congregations put me at one focal point of conservative Protestantism, but also in contact with other, more liberal (if minority), currents of opinion. I became convinced that religion was a legitimate object of study for political scientists, whatever the discipline as a whole might think.

John Green. Given my background, it is remarkable that I would be interested in religion as a subject of scholarly study. When I was born, my father was a fledgling Methodist minister in rural Oklahoma. He soon became disillusioned with the ministry, partly because of its stifling social conformity and partly because of its limited worldview, and eventually he became a research scientist with the federal government. His work led us to many parts of the United States, and overseas, including a ten-year sojourn in Peru.

My experience of living in many places was complemented by the atmosphere of our household, which combined a relentless curiosity with a deep, if unorthodox, spirituality. Such an environment bred an intense interest in politics, ranging from presidential elections to foreign affairs. Indeed, the family dinner table was the equivalent of a graduate seminar on politics. It was only natural, then, that I became a political scientist.

My interest in religion came much later. I was teaching at Furman University just as the "new" Christian Right appeared on the political scene. I joined with colleagues to study the movement, fully expecting it to fade quickly, given the conventional wisdom about the role of religion in politics. When the movement didn't disappear, but persisted and expanded, I found myself drawing on my diverse background to find out why. On the one hand, the strong connection between religion and politics suddenly seemed obvious—so much so that I wondered how the conventional wisdom had missed it. On the other hand, the Christian Right seemed different from past links between religion and politics, suggesting that something new was afoot. This puzzle fit well with my interests in parties, campaigns, and grassroots politics.

The "gang of four" began as two "gangs of two" in the early 1980s: Kellstedt and Smidt joined forces out of a web of college and personal connections (Smidt's brother-in-law teaches at Wheaton, Kellstedt's son attended Calvin), while Guth and Green worked together at Furman University (a partnership that continued after Green moved to the University of Akron in 1987). By the late 1980s, common interests brought all four together to work on a series of projects.

Collaborations of this sort are somewhat unusual in academics, where most incentives are focused on individual achievement. While joint work has its frustrations, it also has many rewards, including enhanced productivity, comradeship, and great fun. All these features are well illustrated in our "Disquisition on Measurement Error," produced after a particularly grueling week of work:

Kellstedt: Measurement error is sin.

Smidt: Measurement error is predestined and is only overcome by the grace of God.

Guth: A stereotype is truth with measurement error.

Green: What is a little measurement error among friends?

Of course, all scholarship is part of a broader collaboration. In this regard, we owe much to other colleagues, especially Cleveland Fraser, Kevin Hill, Margaret Poloma, James Penning, Paul Kellstedt, Jesse Marquette, Clyde Wilcox, Ted Jelen, Ken Wald, David Leege, Matthew Moen, and Hubert Morken, many of whom belong to the Religion and Politics section of the American Political Science Association. To Allen Herztke, who first proposed this volume, we owe a double thanks, which extends to Jon Sisk, Steve Wrinn, and Julie Kirsch at Rowman & Littlefield. Special appreciation goes to Joel Carpenter and the Pew Charitable Trusts, and to our respective institutions: Wheaton College and the Institute for the Study of American Evangelicals; Calvin College and the Calvin Center for Christian Scholarship; Furman University and Furman Advantage Program; the University of Akron and the Ray Bliss Institute of Applied Politics. More than anything else, it was the love and patience of our families that made this work possible and for which we are immensely grateful.

Acknowledgments

We would like to thank the publishers who graciously gave us their permission to reprint the following material in *Religion and the Culture Wars*.

Chapter 2, "The Politics of the Christian Right" by James L. Guth originally appeared in *Interest Group Politics*, 1st ed., ed. Allan Cigler and Burdett Loomis (Washington, D.C.: CQ Press, 1983), 60–83.

Chapter 3, "The Moralizing Minority: Christian Right Support among Political Contributors" by James L. Guth and John C. Green originally appeared in *Social Science Quarterly* 68, no. 3: 598–610. Permission granted by the University of Texas Press.

Chapter 5, "Onward Christian Soldiers: Religious Activist Groups in American Politics" by James L. Guth, John C. Green, Lyman A. Kellstedt, and Corwin E. Smidt originally appeared in *Interest Group Politics*, 4st ed., ed. Allan Cigler and Burdett Loomis (Washington, D.C.: CQ Press, 1994), 55–76.

Chapter 6, "The Christian Right in the Republican Party: The Case of Pat Robertson's Supporters" by John C. Green and James L. Guth originally appeared in *Journal of Politics* 50, no. 1 (February 1988): 150–165. Permission granted by the University of Texas Press.

Chapter 7, "Faith and Election: The Christian Right in Congressional Campaigns 1978–1988" by John C. Green, James L. Guth, and Kevin Hill originally appeared in *Journal of Politics* 55, no. 1 (February 1993): 80–91. Permission granted by the University of Texas Press.

Chapter 8, "Politics in a New Key: Religiosity and Participation among Political Activists" by James L. Guth and John C. Green originally appeared in *Western Political Quarterly* 43, no. 1 (March 1990): 153–79. Permission granted by the University of Utah.

Chapter 11, "Measuring Fundamentalism: An Analysis of Different Operational Strategies" by Lyman Kellstedt and Corwin Smidt originally appeared in *Journal for the Scientific Study of Religion* 30, no. 3 (1991): 259–78.

Chapter 14, "Religious Voting Blocs in the 1992 Election: The Year of the Evangelical? by Lyman A. Kellstedt, John C. Green, James L. Guth, and Corwin E. Smidt originally appeared in *Sociology Review* 55, no. 3 (Fall 1994):307–26.

Chapter 15, "Has Godot Finally Arrived? Religion and Realignment" by Lyman A. Kellstedt, John C. Green, James L. Guth, and Corwin E. Smidt originally appeared in *The Public Perspective* 6, no. 4 (June/July 1995): 18–22. © *The Public Perspective*, a publication of the Roper Center for Public Opinion Research, University of Connecticut, Storrs. Reprinted by permission.

1

Introduction:
Religion and the Culture Wars

Cultural conflict has become a critical element of American politics as the twentieth century draws to a close, with religion playing a central role in often-bitter confrontations over issues ranging from abortion to public education. While these kinds of disputes are hardly new in American history, the reappearance of "political religion" after 1980 took many observers by surprise.

The term "culture wars" has been widely adopted to describe such conflicts, and it captures both the amazement of observers and the fervor of protagonists. Most fully described by Hunter (1991) in his book by the same name, this military metaphor evokes images of irreconcilable conflict over basic values. Hunter saw the rise of two new and rival coalitions undergirding this combat, with an "orthodox" alliance of traditionalists from many religious backgrounds facing a "progressive" alliance of religious modernists and secularists of equally diverse origins. These alliances were observed mostly among political leaders and activists, but their possible expansion to the general public was recognized. Beyond this empirical claim, Hunter's work was haunted by a dark specter: the concern that such deep-seated disputes would eventually erupt into violence—a possibility that is certainly consistent with religious-based conflict in other times and places.

While social scientists were hardly immune to the popularity of the culture wars metaphor, it has also been met with a degree of skepticism. Some scholars doubted the existance of orthodox and progressive alliances in politics, while others found the grim tone of Hunter's forecasts

1

to be a great exaggeration of the real-life situation (cf. Horton 1994; Kellstedt et al. 1994).

The sixteen essays in this book provide some hard evidence on the linkage between religion and politics implicit in the image of culture wars. Written between 1980 and 1996, in the midst of the recent expansion of religious-based politics, these research reports have the character of "dispatches from the front," assessing the phenomenon as it unfolded. Employing different theoretical perspectives, methodologies, and sources of data, they define, measure, and describe critical elements of American religion and their relationship to political attitudes and behavior.

When taken as a whole, these essays provide a mixed assessment of the culture wars metaphor. Some of the evidence supports Hunter's view of the character of religio-political conflict. Religion is indeed a potent factor in political alignments and has become more so in recent times; the outlines of something like orthodox and progressive alliances are clearly evident. These patterns are strongest among political activists, but also appear in the public. However, much of this evidence also points to the limitations of the culture wars imagery: these emerging religious-based coalitions are complex and nuanced, and do not extend to all issues or social groups; the potential for cooperation is at least as great as for conflict.

This collection is divided into four sections of four chapters each. The first two sections report on religion and political activists, beginning with the Christian Right, and then considering the movement's relationship to the broader activist corps. The final two sections turn to the mass public, initially focusing on evangelical Protestants, and eventually looking at the links between religion and political behavior more broadly.

The Christian Right

Although the attraction of the culture wars metaphor comes from the possibility of an orthodox alliance, only one element of such a coalition has been fully activated: the Christian Right and evangelical Protestants. The Christian Right is a social movement located principally among evangelicals, dedicated to restoring traditional values in public policy. Beginning in the late 1970s, it has grown in size and sophistication so that by the mid-1990s it exercises influence in national politics, especially by mobilizing evangelical religious voters on behalf of Republican candidates (cf. Green 1995).

The first four chapters of this book report on Christian Right activists, beginning with the origins of the movement and progressing chronologically to the present day. Chapter 2 is one of the original essays published on the movement, focusing on the Moral Majority and related organizations and cataloging the movement's strengths and weaknesses. Written in the context of wild claims about both the movement's power and its imminent demise, the essay accurately predicted that the Christian Right would survive in a modest form.

The next two essays further document the early movement's strengths and weaknesses. Chapter 3 investigates support for the Moral Majority in a national sample of political activists, finding Christian Rightists to be a "moralizing minority": a small but potent constituency of social issue conservatives. This situation is further demonstrated in chapter 4 which reviews the "invisible army" of Pat Robertson's 1988 bid for the Republican presidential nomination. These data reveal the sources of the Christian Coalition, founded by Robertson in 1989 out of the remnants of his campaign.

Chapter 5 moves into the 1990s, comparing contemporary Christian Right activists to their counterparts on the "religious left." These data make an important point: religion can be a source of liberal politics, even among evangelicals. But strikingly different religious values and worldviews separate the Christian Right from the Christian Left. Of equal importance, these activists merge respectively with broader conservative and liberal alignments in politics. These groups are clearly potential contenders in culture wars, although the mainstream character of their activities militates against the breakdown of civil politics (cf. Green et al. 1994b; Smidt et al. 1994).

Religion and Political Activists

The next four chapters investigate the relationship of the Christian Right and other religious conservatives to broader liberal and conservative alignments. Chapter 6 compares Christian Rightists to their counterparts in the GOP, finding some sharp differences on issues and political style, much as the culture wars metaphor would suggest. But there is also evidence that the movement is in the "right" party, sharing many attitudes with the Republican regulars and showing every prospect of becoming socialized to routine party politics. A similar pattern emerges from chapter 7, which reports on the involvement of the Christian Right in congressional campaigns from 1978 to 1988. While the movement did back some extreme candidates with little success, it more commonly—

and successfully—operated as part of a broader Republican coalition, a pattern that reached full flower in the 1994 elections.

The integration of the Christian Right into the GOP suggests a deeper link between religion and political alignments. Chapter 8 documents a wide-spread "reformation" that has been under way in the nation's activist corps for some time, with Republicans increasingly characterized by a broadly defined "religious right" and Democrats by a combination of a "secular left" and a "religious left" (cf. Green, Guth, and Fraser 1991). Indeed, the latter is the most active, reflecting the historic commitment of theological liberals to political action on behalf of the "social gospel" (cf. Guth et al. 1991).

However, theological conservatives are catching up with their liberal counterparts politically, as is demonstrated in chapter 9, a longitudinal analysis of Southern Baptist clergy between 1980 and 1992. This large and influential body of evangelical clergy has become increasingly active and Republican in a region where Southern Baptists are a major cultural force. Crucial to this change has been the development of a new social theology, a "civic gospel" that connects conservative theology to political action. The mobilization of liberal and conservative church bodies into left- and right-wing alignments is also consistent with the culture wars metaphor. But the interest of church institutions in order and stability are likely to encourage conventional rather than disruptive politics.

Evangelical Voters

What about the targets of the Christian Right, evangelical voters? The next four chapters are concerned with defining and measuring religion in the mass public, with a special emphasis on evangelicals. When scholars first sought to study the potential constituency of the Christian Right, and indeed of broader religio-political alignments as well, they encountered poorly developed measures of religion that generated weak and contradictory results. Chapter 10 responds to these problems with an exposition of two concepts, religious tradition and religious commitment. These concepts are a useful first step in studying the links between religion and politics at the mass level, thus testing the usefulness of the culture wars metaphor (cf. Leege and Kellstedt 1993).

One benefit of defining religious traditions with precision is the identification of churches in the evangelical Protestant tradition, about which there has been much confusion (Kellstedt and Green 1993). But Evangelicalism can be defined in ways other than church affiliation, including beliefs, practices, and participation in religious movements. In fact, Evangelicals are best known for their religious movements, and the next chapters explore the three most important of these: fundamentalism, the "spirit-filled" movements (Pentecostals and charismatics), and Evangelicalism. These movements are the primary constituencies of the Christian Right (cf. Smidt 1993).

Religion and Political Behavior

The last four chapters apply the results of the previous chapters to political behavior, with chapters 14 and 15 considering the 1992 and 1994 elections, respectively. The analysis of religious voting blocs in 1992 reveals the dramatic shift of evangelical Protestants to the Republican Party. Even in the midst of a major electoral debacle, evangelicals were the GOP's strongest constituency, where they were joined by more traditional mainline Protestants and Catholics. Secular voters played a similar role in Bill Clinton's winning coalition, along with less traditional mainliners and Catholics. Thus, the outlines of the orthodox and progressive alliances were clearly visible, although not as well developed as the images of culture wars suggest (Green et al. 1994). The 1994 elections show the further development of such religio-political alignments, particularly on the orthodox side.

The final two essays consider other aspects of religion and political behavior. Chapter 16 explores the extent to which voters consciously perceive their own religious beliefs to be relevant to their politics. Such religious relevance is strongly related to religious commitment and traditional beliefs, and also the mobilizing efforts of religious organizations, including those associated with the Christian Right and Left. As the culture wars metaphor implies, religious relevance is high among evangelicals, but it is much lower among mainliners and Catholics. Thus, the orthodox alliance extends only so far. Chapter 17 concludes the book with a detailed look at "Christian Zionism," support for the state of Israel among activists and the mass public, suggesting the power of religious beliefs in shaping political attitudes (cf. Guth et al. 1995).

References

Green, John C. 1994. "The Christian Right and the 1994 Election: An Overview." In *God at the Grassroots*, ed. Mark J. Rozell and Clyde Wilcox. Lanham, Md.: Rowman & Littlefield.

Green, John C., James L. Guth, and Cleveland Fraser. 1991. "Apostles and Apostates? Religion and Politics among Political Activists." In *The Bible and the Ballot Box*, ed. James L. Guth and John C. Green. Boulder, Colo.: Westview Press.

Green, John C., James L. Guth, Lyman A. Kellstedt, and Corwin E. Smidt. 1994a. "Uncivil Challenges? Support for Civil Liberties among Religious Activists." *Journal of Political Science* 22:25–50.

Green, John C., James L. Guth, Lyman A. Kellstedt, and Corwin E. Smidt. 1994b. "Murphy Brown Revisited: The Social Issues in the 1992 Election." In *Disciples and Democracy*, ed. Michael Cromartie. Grand Rapids, Mich.: Eerdmans Press.

Guth, James L., John C. Green, Corwin E. Smidt, and Margaret Poloma. 1991. "Pulpits and Politics: The Protestant Clergy in the 1988 Election." In *The Bible and the Ballot Box*, ed. James L. Guth and John C. Green. Boulder, Colo.: Westview Press.

Guth, James L., John C. Green, Lyman A. Kellstedt, and Corwin E. Smidt. 1995. "Faith and the Environment: Religious Beliefs and Attitudes on Environmental Policy." *American Journal of Political Science* 39:364–382.

Horton, Michael. 1994. *Beyond Culture Wars*. Chicago: Moody Press.

Hunter, James Davison. 1991. *Culture Wars*. New York: Basic Books.

Kellstedt, Lyman A., and John C. Green. 1993. "Knowing God's Many People: Religious Denomination and Political Behavior." In *Rediscovering the Impact of Religion on Political Behavior*, ed. David C. Leege and Lyman A. Kellstedt. Armonk, N.Y.: Sharpe.

Kellstedt, Lyman A., John C. Green, James L. Guth, and Corwin E. Smidt. 1994. "It's the Culture Stupid! 1992 and Our Political Future." *First Things*. April:28–33.

Leege, David C., and Lyman A. Kellstedt. eds. 1993. *Rediscovering the Impact of Religion on Political Behavior*. Armonk, N.Y.: Sharpe.

Smidt, Corwin E. 1993. "Evangelicals in American Politics: 1976–1988." In *No Longer Exiles*, ed. Michael Cromartie. Washington, D.C.: Ethics and Public Policy Center.

Smidt, Corwin E., Lyman A. Kellstedt, John C. Green, and James L. Guth. 1994. "The Characteristics of Religious Group Activists." In *Christian Political Activism at the Crossroads*, ed. William Stevenson. Lanham, Md.: University Press of America.

2

The Politics of the Christian Right

James L. Guth

Few political movements have enjoyed as much notoriety in recent years as the "New Christian Right." Organizations such as Christian Voice, Religious Roundtable, and Moral Majority have appeared, seemingly out of nowhere, actively lobbied Congress on behalf of antiabortion, school prayer, and "profamily" proposals, supported political candidates from the local to federal level, and sponsored massive voter registration and "education" drives.

Of course, religion has often played an important part in American politics. Christians have joined both sides of many historic battles, including those over slavery, prohibition, America's wars, civil rights, and social reform. Indeed, many historians now argue that religion rather than social class has been the chief determinant of party cleavages for most of American history. And although "liberal" churches and clergymen often have appeared in the forefront of twentieth-century activism, conservatives also have mobilized on occasion, as lobbying by the Women's Christian Temperance Union on behalf of Prohibition reminds us.[1] What is "new" about the "New Christian Right" is its apparent success in building grass-roots support for all-out political activism on a wide range of conservative issues.

To many professional observers of politics and religion, this forceful reassertion of religious values is surprising. Social scientists often assume that "secularization" (that is, the declining strength of religious beliefs and institutions) is an inevitable result of the process of economic and political modernization, with its accompanying industrialization, urbanization, and social mobility. And yet, secularization is often met by resistance; indeed, rapid modernization often creates tensions within the sectors of traditional society most severely affected, with sometimes explosive results—as the Ayatollah Khomeini's Moslem "fundamentalists" demonstrated late in 1978. That the current American religious militance is located primarily in the rapidly "modernizing" Sun Belt hints that the strains of transition from rural, traditionalist society to modernity may lie at the roots of the movement.

Rapid mobilization of traditional rural populations into industrial society often gives rise to "cultural defense movements." Organized groups appear to defend old values, which may be embodied in time-honored institutions (or sometimes in new ones), centered around religion, the family, or locality—all of which are perceived as under attack. Scholars have analyzed some of the conditions under which such movements appear, exercise a degree of power, and either fade away or become a part of modern politics. Although such work generally has focused on "developing nations," many of the insights also are applicable to "developing regions" within "modernized" societies.[2] In this vein, three major sets of questions present themselves. First, why has American conservative Protestantism given rise to this type of political activism now? Second, what are the chief components of the Christian Right? What issue concerns, strategies, and political alliances are characteristic of the movement? Finally, what is the future for the Christian Right?

The Rise of the "Christian Right"

Theories concerning the Christian Right's origins are as numerous as its observers. Journalists and scholars have seen the Right emerging out of fundamentalist or evangelical religion, the political malaise of the Vietnam and Watergate eras, a renewal of white racism, or a struggle between a "New Class" of symbol manipulators and older business elites. Some or all of these interpretations may have an element of truth, but they hardly account for the movement's timing.[3] After all, most of these elements have been present for some time; continuous attempts to forge conservative believers into a political bloc have been made since the 1950s, all without success. Why, then, the coalescence of Christian Right groups in 1979?

Here the literature on modernization can be of some help. Cultural defense movements often appear at the conjunction of several economic, social, and political developments: a degree of social mobility creating a new political constituency, the growth of "indigenous" leadership and communication networks, and, most important, a threat to the traditional values, beliefs, and institutions of that constituency, often from a "secularizing" (or at least secular) political elite. In broad form, that is exactly what has happened here. Industrialization and urbanization have created a new "evangelical" constituency, traversed by intricate new organization and communication networks. This group is then activated by "trigger issues" involving outside threats to its religious values and institutions. And, as often happens during modernization, the resulting reaction has been used by both religious and secular conservative entrepreneurs to add to their own power.

The New Evangelical Constituency

Protestant evangelicalism has always been a prominent feature of the South, rural Midwest, and other "underdeveloped" parts of the United States. But recently many observers have detected an evangelical "revival," suggesting variously that "born-again" Christians are becoming more numerous, that members of "mainline" denominations such as Episcopalians, Presbyterians, and Methodists are deserting in large numbers to theologically more conservative churches, and (perhaps as a result) that evangelical churches are growing rapidly and their members are becoming more visible and active.

Do these trends really exist? In the absence of detailed, long-term studies of religious affiliations and attitudes, it is difficult to say. Estimates of American evangelicals range from 20 million to 90 million or more, depending upon the definition used. If theological orthodoxy and Biblical literalism are the keys, a very substantial number of Americans (perhaps even a narrow majority) are "evangelicals." If a "born-again" experience of Christ's presence is added as a third criterion, the number drops substantially. If an "evangelical" must also "witness" (proselytize) to others, only about a fifth of American adults qualify. Whatever definition is adopted may not correspond with older meanings (for example, in the Lutheran or Reformed traditions) or with self-identification by believers themselves. Furthermore, any definition will combine under a single label groups with little in common: fundamentalists, neoevangelicals, charismatics, pietists, and others whose ethnic backgrounds and religious beliefs may push them in very different political directions (or in no direction at all).[4]

Despite such difficulties, one can try to sort out survey findings. Are evangelical Christians becoming more numerous? In fact, most Americans (including the unchurched) are quite orthodox, but seem not to have become more so. Whether "born-again" experiences exceed those of 10 or 15 years ago is not clear, although "charismatics"—those who "speak in tongues" and engage in other "spirit-filled" practices—seem to be more numerous. The decline in overall religious observation beginning in the 1950s has been halted for a time, at least among most age groups, but in many ways religion plays a less important part in American life than at any time since the advent of scientific polling.

If there is little evidence of a massive increase in evangelical numbers, many theologically conservative churches do seem to be growing, although the reasons are subject to dispute. The fastest growth is in the small fundamentalist sects, rather than in the giant Southern Baptist Convention, which has expanded more slowly and seems to have reached a plateau. Does such growth represent massive "switching" from declining "liberal," mainline denominations into conservative bodies? Apparently not. The Southern Baptist expansion is due largely to higher birth rates and successful "socialization" of those "born Baptist," while the sects attract converts (mostly from other sects) and also benefit from higher birth rates. Thus, the "evangelical revival" is mostly "homegrown"; there is little realignment of Christians out of liberal denominations into evangelical ones.

Whatever their numbers, evangelicals have become more visible and active. Very likely this change is due to recent upward mobility. Although Gallup's "core evangelicals" (literalist, "born-again," witnessing believers) are still more likely than nonevangelicals to be rural, poorly educated, female, black, and in lower status occupations, among white male evangelicals these differences almost disappear. Political scientist John Stephens Hendricks' careful analysis of Survey Research Center and National Opinion Research Center data from 1960 to 1976 has demonstrated graphically that from a position far below that of mainline Protestants in education, income, and self-identified middle-class status, the evangelicals have almost pulled even, paralleling the movement upward of American Catholics. The new visibility of evangelicals, then, may be attributed in large part to the increased wealth, growing community involvement, and greater organizational skills that come with upward mobility.[5]

What Binds Them. Evangelicals, then, would seem an attractive target for political mobilization. Whether they possess a common social and political ideology which might foster such a development is less clear. Protestant evangelicals and other conservative Christians share a constellation of attitudes based on localism, conventional moral standards, traditionalist family values, and vocal "Americanism," all of which distinguish them from more liberal Christians and nonbelievers. Whether this conservative consensus extends to classic "New Deal" economic issues is uncertain, despite the intuitive appeal of equating religious and social traditionalism with political conservatism. With some exceptions, studies of evangelicals' political views have found that "they look like everyone else"—except on social and "moral" issues, of course. The political alignment of evangelical voters, then, may depend on the relative salience of social and economic issues during any particular period—and on the choices offered by contending political forces.[6]

The Clerical Leadership. Evangelical ministers, on the other hand, are a more promising target. Their numbers have grown (both absolutely and relatively) thanks to high attrition among liberal clergy after 1970, burgeoning enrollment in conservative seminaries (almost 20 percent of divinity students attend Southern Baptist seminaries alone), and greater job availability in conservative denominations. Consequently, young ministers today are actually more conservative theologically than their elders, a reversal of the classic pattern. Inasmuch as clergymen show more systematic linkage between their theological and political views— "attitude constraint"—than do laymen, these trends have augmented the ranks of potential conservative activists. ("Attitude constraint," in social science parlance, is an indication of the degree to which opinion in one sphere predicts or reflects that in another. If one is conservative on theological issues, one's political views may likely be conservative or otherwise compatible.) Evangelical ministers, like their congregants, are now better educated and better off, possessing the resources necessary for political influence. Their centrality in Christian Right organization and strategy suggests that ministers, rather than evangelical laymen, constitute the movement's core.

Although the clerics may bring only a few laymen with them into conservative activism, they do not face the resistance encountered by the "New Breed" of the 1960s, whose civil rights and antiwar activities affronted the sensibilities of middle-class, conservative parishioners. During that era, most evangelical ministers—whose beliefs were often more in line with their congregations than they are today—eschewed politics, largely because of their own "otherworldly" theology. Now, however, some conservative ministers may be expected to engage in political activism. A November 1980 study of Southern Baptist pastors by the author showed that more than 25 percent (mostly conservatives) felt "encouraged" to be active by the laity, 17 percent (mainly political moderates) felt "discouraged," and the rest felt free to participate or not as they chose. How widespread such positive congregational attitudes may be is still conjectural, but the flood of conservative clerical activism suggests that the pattern is no longer rare.[7]

Still, many (if not most) evangelical ministers remain stolidly apolitical. Considerable evidence exists that only one group of evangelicals—"fundamentalists"—have responded with alacrity to the Right's call. For example, the Rev. Jerry Falwell, founder and president of Moral Majority, has conceded that despite efforts to broaden his base, the most "aggressive leaders in Moral Majority are fundamentalist pastors." Fundamentalists are distinguished from the rest of the evangelical community by rigor of belief in Biblical "inerrancy," preference for "confrontation" over penetration of society, and refusal to cooperate with believers not sharing these traits. But their most distinctive characteristic is militance; Falwell notes that "fundamentalists like me were taught to fight before we were taught to read and write." Fundamentalist ministers—and, if John Hendricks is correct, some fundamentalist laymen—do share the same comprehensive social, economic, and political conservatism espoused by Moral Majority. They are the "Vanguard of the Christian Right"—but not necessarily the entire army.[8]

Networks and "Trigger Issues"

By the mid-1970s, a significant new political constituency had appeared, ready to defend "Christian values." Yet it still required an activating mechanism. Evangelicals had long been ignored politically not only because of their geographical, social, and economic isolation, but because they were located in dozens of sects and denominations, differed sharply on some religious questions, and followed many different prophets. Carl F. H. Henry, a "neoevangelical" church father, could lament as recently as 1976 that "evangelical churches in America lack a cohesive integrating structure, leader, or publication that can swiftly coordinate their energies." Even the narrower fundamentalist movement, according to Falwell, "was so fragmented and diversified that it was impossible to describe it, categorize it, or even understand it."[9]

A unifying structure soon appeared: the "electronic church." By 1978, TV evangelists and religious entrepreneurs such as Jerry Falwell, Pat Robertson, Jim Bakker, Oral Roberts, James Robison, Rex Humbard, and others had established vast audiences, pushed their church services and Christian talk shows onto hundreds of stations, fostered their own TV and radio networks, and encouraged "all-Christian" local channels.

In the process, they established extensive two-way communications with their viewers, built computerized mailing lists, and honed sophisticated fund-raising techniques. By January 1980, religious broadcasters claimed audiences in the millions, hundreds of thousands of regular contributors, and bulging treasuries. Although both the evangelists and reporters often exaggerated the size and wealth of this new religious empire, even less-than-astute politicians could recognize all the necessary parts for a political machine. But despite evident personal interest in politics—and repeated nudges from conservative politicos—the TV evangelists explicitly forswore politics in favor of "soul-winning."[10]

Entering Politics. What, then, finally prompted them to abandon the apolitical stance of modern American evangelicalism? In brief, the actions of secular political authorities threatened the institutional interests of the evangelists and the social and moral sensibilities of their followers—sensibilities which were increasingly embodied in "alternative institutions," such as TV and radio stations, Christian schools, and evangelical business networks. Such threats simultaneously motivated both to fight for reversal of government policy, with almost synergistic effects.

On their part, the evangelists perceived threats from the federal government: a possible Federal Communications Commission (FCC) ban on more licenses for Christian TV and radio stations or limits on commercial "air time"; FCC enforcement of "fairness" provisions due to their political statements (such as James Robison's fiery broadcast attack on "gay rights"); and repeated inquiries of the Securities and Exchange Commission (SEC), the Internal Revenue Service (IRS), and other Federal agencies into fund raising by Falwell, Bakker, Humbard, and others. That the evangelists' political debut followed these assaults on their institutional interests is not coincidental.

Traditions to Uphold. The evangelists' viewers proved loyal defenders when called on—over three million sent letters and postcards to protest the supposed FCC "gag." Yet other government policies were more threatening to traditionalist beliefs and values: the passage of the Equal Rights Amendment (ERA) by Congress and ratification by many states; the "gay rights" movement; local struggles over pornography and school textbooks; and the 1973 Supreme Court decision on abortion. All these issues aroused evangelical—especially fundamentalist—clergy and lay activists to fight "secularization" of public policy, as local networks developed all over the country, especially in the South and Midwest.

However, provocative as these organizational focal points were, they paled beside the secularists' "assault on the Christian school."

Christian schools were an institutional embodiment of the fundamentalists' social and moral concerns. Deriving a large boost from the desegregation clashes of the 1960s and early 1970s, such schools expanded to areas far removed from minority populations, as parents sick about the absence of discipline, "moral education," the "three Rs," and God from the public schools took advantage of their rising prosperity to create these "alternative institutions." For many, these schools (usually affiliated with a fundamentalist church) represented their best hope of passing traditional values on to their children. In any case, by 1980 more than 16,000 Christian elementary schools had appeared and the movement showed no appreciable loss of momentum as it began to expand to the high school level.

The investment of enormous financial and emotional capital in these schools by evangelical parents, pastors, and teachers lent a bitter edge to recurring battles with state authorities over facilities, teacher qualifications, textbooks, and accountability to education agencies. For such parents it appeared that secular elites had not only pushed religious and traditional moral values out of public schools, but were trying to purge them from the private institutions where they had taken refuge. Even more threatening than state action was a 1978 IRS plan to stiffen nondiscrimination requirements for tax-exempt private schools.

Structure from Adversity. Such confrontations spawned much of the Christian Right's infrastructure, as parents' networks, legal defense funds, and lobbying groups mushroomed. Jerry Falwell himself has blamed federal "harrassment" of his Lynchburg, Virginia, Christian Academy for pushing him into public life, and school controversies provided a real political baptism for many other Christian Rightists. Robert Billings, for example, came to his post as Moral Majority's first legislative director fresh from success in orchestrating the lobbying against the IRS proposal; Ronald Godwin, Moral Majority's executive director, moved directly from Pensacola (Florida) Christian College. The same has been true at the state and local levels, where the Right's early organization building depended heavily on Christian school connections. The continuing emphasis on preservation and expansion of the Christian school points to its importance in both the Right's ideology and organization.[11]

Thus, threats to traditionalist values, and more important, to institutions in which those values were embedded, simultaneously spurred political action by the TV evangelists and supplied them with a partially mobilized constituency. As they increased the political content of their broadcasts, described the successes of local evangelical militants, and encouraged viewers to take action themselves, they advanced their own fortunes and the movement's. All that remained to complete the politicization process was some prompting and help from the outside.

The Role of Secular Conservatives

During the modernization process, secular conservatives often play a key role in the rise of cultural defense movements. Not only do they find the traditionalist values espoused by the religionists of at least nostalgic appeal, but they often sense that their grip on power or hope for it lies in the ability to direct these movements for their own purposes.

The history of the Christian Right is no exception. Secular "New Right" political strategists such as Richard Viguerie, Howard Phillips, and Paul Weyrich had been impressed with the evangelicals' potential at least since 1976, when Southern Baptist Jimmy Carter was the apparent beneficiary of their votes. Gary Jarmin, then with the American Conservative Union, noted that "the beauty of it is that we don't have to organize these voters. They already have their own television networks, publications, schools, meeting places, and respected leaders who are sympathetic to our goals."[12] So, late in 1978, New Right leaders set about recruiting the evangelicals. Viguerie provided his mass-mailing expertise, Robert Billings joined Falwell to set up Moral Majority, Gary Jarmin moved to Christian Voice, and Conservative Caucus field organizer Edward McAteer created the Religious Roundtable.

Were the New Right leaders manipulating the Christian activists or merely fostering a mutually beneficial alliance? It is true that the so-called Gang of Four—Viguerie, Phillips, Weyrich, and Terry Dolan of the National Conservative Political Action Committee (NCPAC)—share neither the religious affiliations (three are Catholic, one Jewish) nor all of the "life style" values of those they hoped to organize, but they do hold the same positions on abortion, ERA, private schools, and gay rights. And many Christian Right leaders at times have defined "moral" issues so broadly as to incorporate the New Right's economic and foreign policy stances. Both sides have sought to nurture mutuality through personnel ties, information exchange, and discussion groups such as the "Kingston" and "Library Court" meetings, which bring together leaders and lobbyists from most New Right organizations.

Congressional conservatives were equally helpful, as New Right heroes such as Sens. Orrin Hatch, R-Utah; James McClure, R-Idaho; Roger Jepsen, R-Iowa; and Gordon Humphrey, R-N.H.; joined House members Larry McDonald, D-Ga.; Daniel Crane, R-Ill.; and Robert Dornan, R-Calif., on the "advisory board" of Christian Voice. But the key figure in showing the Christian Right the political ropes was Republican Sen. Jesse Helms of North Carolina, a Southern Baptist. Helms introduced their lobbyists to his colleagues, advised Moral Majority on organization strategy, and assisted in fund-raising efforts. Some of this aid took unusual forms, such as a sample sermon written by Helms' strategists—to be included in a packet of materials urging ministers to endorse Moral Majority's anointed candidates. Whatever the original relationship between the New and Christian Rights, the ties have remained strong.[13]

Organizations and Strategies

By November 1980, the Christian Right still had many characteristics of a social movement; it was a loose and poorly articulated collection of almost a dozen TV evangelists, renegade mainline clergymen, nascent lobbies, ill-defined constituencies, and numerous "organizations." Nevertheless, a clearer internal structure was appearing as Christian Voice, the Roundtable, and, especially, Moral Majority emerged into national prominence and drew religious activists from local and smaller organizations.

Organizations

Christian Voice appeared first, launched in January 1979 by California ministers Robert Grant and Richard Zone as an extension of several West Coast antigay, antipornography groups. Voice's policy board included several well-known fundamentalist pastors, as well as actor-singer-theologian Pat Boone. By mid-1980 its mailing list contained the names of 150,000 laymen and 37,000 ministers—including 3,000 Catholic priests and some Mormons—but failed to reach the founders' early projection of one million. Voice claimed members from 37 denominations, but most activists came from independent Bible, Baptist, and Assemblies of God churches, located primarily in the West and Southwest and, to a lesser extent, the Southeast.

At first Christian Voice was heavily dependent upon TV evangelist Pat Robertson's daily "700 Club" program for exposure. The show provided access to the hundred or more stations tied directly to the Christian

Broadcasting Network. (Some observers speculated that Robertson's backing was calculated to undercut TV rival Jerry Falwell's Moral Majority.) Besides such radio and TV appeals, Voice also sought money and members through direct mailings supervised by Jerry Hunsinger, a former United Methodist minister, who also handled accounts for Falwell, Robert Schuller ("Hour of Power"), and Moral Majority.

Conceived originally as a broad vehicle for political activism by the TV evangelists, Moral Majority actually took shape as Jerry Falwell's personal instrument. Since its founding in July 1979, Majority has been led by Falwell, a shifting collage of independent Baptists, and a few militantly conservative Southern Baptists and Presbyterians. Robert Billings, a Bob Jones University[14] graduate, was executive director and lobbyist before joining Ronald Reagan's presidential campaign. He also served for a time on Christian Voice's policy committee, joining Hunsinger as an early link between the two groups. Using Falwell's computer lists of prime "Old Time Gospel Hour" contributors, Majority raised a third of its projected 1980 budget of $3 million within a month in the fall of 1979. Meanwhile, Falwell conducted "I Love America" rallies across the country (usually on statehouse steps with friendly politicos as honored guests) and set up state chapters. By November 1980 he claimed 47 such units. But real organizations, dominated by ministers, existed in only about 18, mostly Sun Belt, states. Both national and state organizations attracted members primarily from independent Baptist churches (especially from the Baptist Bible Fellowship and the Southwide Baptist Fellowship), small fundamentalist sects, and a few conservatives from larger denominations.

The Religious Roundtable was specially designed to appeal to conservative clergymen uncomfortable with either Christian Voice or Moral Majority. Edward McAteer, a Southern Baptist field organizer for the Conservative Caucus, brought leading religious conservatives together with secular New Right luminaries such as Paul Weyrich, Howard Phillips, Terry Dolan, and Phyllis Schlafly as a preliminary to a vast effort to instruct ministers in the art of politics. The best publicized of the Roundtable's "workshops" was an August 1980 extravaganza in Dallas, where ministers heard from every major New Right figure, many of the TV preachers, Southern Baptist president Bailey Smith, and, of course, Ronald Reagan, who enthusiastically endorsed the Roundtable's efforts. Although McAteer did the mundane organizational work, much of the Roundtable's early fervor was generated by its vice president, Southern Baptist TV evangelist James Robison, who had become a prominent figure in lobbying for congressional action to overturn the

Supreme Court's 1962 and 1963 decisions prohibiting state-sponsored prayer and Bible reading in public schools.[15]

Lobbying: Issues and Strategies

Despite general agreement on policy and overlapping activities, the various Christian Right groups (including smaller or specialized organizations such as the National Christian Action Coalition) emphasized somewhat different issues. Still, all shared a common lobbying strategy: to focus attention on "moral" issues, activate fundamentalist ministers, and count on them to mobilize their congregations to flood targeted legislators with mail and phone calls. Christian Voice stimulated a mountain of anti-SALT II mail in late 1979, over 115,000 letters to the IRS (with Majority's help) protesting "harrassment" of Christian schools, and some antiabortion mail, while Moral Majority whipped up support for Senator Helms's school prayer bills and against legislation that would have set up a federal program to study and prevent "domestic violence" such as wife beating and child abuse. Their experience with Christian Right politics led many legislators to conclude "if their ability to generate mail is at all indicative of their political power, we are in trouble."[16]

The Christian Right's direct lobbying was much less impressive, due to inexperience and, at times, naiveté. Moral Majority misdirected much energy behind Senator Paul Laxalt's catch-all "Family Protection Act," a compendium of virtually every New Right social policy objective that has languished in Congress since 1979. Whether because of increasing sophistication or greater member interest, Majority eventually shifted to the school prayer bill, but failed to dislodge it from a hostile House Judiciary Committee, thanks to a massive countercampaign by mainline denominations, conservative and liberal alike, which opposed it as a violation of the First Amendment clause prohibiting the establishment of a state religion.

In its early forays, Christian Voice devoted more attention to votes on seemingly secular issues, votes which were nevertheless used to calculate legislators' "Morality Rating." In addition to school prayers, IRS rulings on Christian schools, and abortion, Voice lobbied on other issues, rating members of Congress on their support for restoration of the U.S. defense treaty with Taiwan and "parental rights" at home, and on their opposition to establishment of the Department of Education, economic sanctions against Rhodesia, busing, and behavioral research funding. The "findings" created quite a stir in the press and on Capitol Hill, where several evangelical liberals (including some ministers) flunked the exam, while Rep. Richard Kelly, R-Fla., convicted in 1981 of taking bribes in the FBI's Abscam investigation, hit 100%. Gary Jarmin's subsequent explanation that the scores were not intended to convey any judgment on a legislator's personal morality did little to quiet the furor—or to prevent Voice from issuing an updated version just prior to the 1980 elections.[17]

Electoral Strategies

These ratings were designed not only to generate grass-roots pressure on recalcitrant legislators, but also to single them out for punishment by evangelical voters. Although all three major groups envisioned electoral involvement from the start, the disappointments of their maiden lobbying efforts in 1979 and 1980 no doubt solidified their resolve to acquire political clout.

While the Christian Right's electoral plans went through several phases in 1980, clergymen remained at the center. Jerry Falwell summed up the Right's approach in his repeated admonitions to sympathetic ministers: "What can you do from the pulpit? You can register people to vote. You can explain the issues to them. And you can endorse candidates, right there in church on Sunday morning."[18] This strategy reflected both organizational imperatives—the movement's heavy reliance on clerical activists—and certain assumptions about evangelicals: that they had higher nonvoting rates than other Americans and were especially susceptible to pastoral guidance. As Robert Billings put it, "People want leadership. They don't want to think for themselves."[19]

The Christian Right's participation in the 1980 congressional races was fairly selective. Although Moral Majority toyed with recruiting candidates who were "pro-life, pro-American—free enterprise, etcetera—pro-Bible morality and pro-family,"[20] all three groups quickly adopted the New Right strategy of "targeting" prominent liberal and moderate legislators for defeat: Sens. Robert Packwood, R-Ore.; Frank Church, D-Idaho; Birch Bayh, D-Ind.; George McGovern, D.-S.D.; John Culver, D-Iowa; and a few others, and several House members from marginal, conservative districts (see Chapter 2). During the primaries, Moral Majority was credited with mobilizing enough voters to help defeat Sen. Donald Stewart, D-Ala., and, more surprisingly, Rep. John Buchanan, R-Ala., a Southern Baptist minister who failed to adopt the Christian Right's school prayer policy with sufficient single mindedness. Buchanan's defeat not only sent a shiver of political fear through Capitol Hill, but encouraged the fundamentalists to expect even greater victories in November.[21]

The National Effort. The Christian Right also tested the presidential waters early, gearing up to defeat fellow evangelical Jimmy Carter, perceived on a wide range of issues as much too liberal. Initially, the Right's leaders were unenthusiastic about Ronald Reagan, who lacked previous identification with either the beliefs or life style of Protestant fundamentalists. Californian Richard Zone of Christian Voice summed up their dilemma: "Reagan was not the best Christian who ever walked the face of the earth, but we really didn't have a choice." The lack of options derived not only from early elimination of Philip Crane and John Connally, two favorites of the Christian Right leaders, but also from evident grass-roots fundamentalist enthusiasm for Reagan. Indeed, in several states Christian Right activists not only helped push the Reagan bandwagon, but entrenched themselves within the GOP. At the Republican National Convention in Detroit, the evangelicals—almost all Reagan delegates—were a much-noticed presence. Indeed some journalists claimed a majority of the delegates were Christian Rightists. And although they failed to block Reagan's choice of George Bush for the vice-presidential nomination (preferring a Rightist such as Senator Helms), they did shove party policy a long way to the right, especially on social issues such as abortion, ERA, and school prayer. If the Republican platform had not been etched in stone, one delegate announced, "it ought to be. It's right down the line an evangelical platform."

During the fall election campaign, Republican strategists met with Christian Right leaders to discuss their contribution to the "community of shared values" Reagan hoped to make the basis of a new partisan alignment. Both concurred that the Right's greatest contribution would come in educating and mobilizing previously uninvolved evangelicals. And Moral Majority, Roundtable, and Christian Voice conducted extensive registration and education programs, usually under church auspices, concentrated in states where favorite candidates or targeted liberals were on the ballot. Moral Majority alone claimed to have registered at least four million new voters. In any case, after the election Christian Right leaders claimed partial credit for Reagan's victory, for the defeat of several prominent liberals, and for the election of Sens. Jeremiah Denton, R-Ala.; Senator Donald Nickles, R-Okla.; and Senator John East, R-N.C.[22]

How Much Muscle? To what extent was the Christian Right due credit for these 1980 results? Although pollster Louis Harris's instant analysis seemed to support the Right's own claims, subsequent study of evidence from polls, academic surveys, and the politicians themselves suggests that political scientists Seymour Martin Lipset and Earl Raab are probably correct: evangelical voters may have switched from Carter to Reagan in large numbers, but they did so for the same economic and foreign policy reasons that led equally large (or perhaps larger) numbers of other voters to switch. Nor did the Christian Right's strategy really "jell": very few ministers (even Moral Majority members) actually used their pulpits to push candidates, parishioners were not inclined to honor such requests when they were made, and, in general, the Christian Right failed to impress the electorate. Thus, in 1980, the Right demonstrated the same capacities as other narrow-gauged interest groups: it mobilized enough activists to influence some statewide and local races, especially in low-visibility, low-turnout, primaries and caucuses; raised modest sums for favored candidates (Christian Voice gathered in more than $200,000 while Moral Majority collected a mere $25,000)[23]; and added a few new voters to the conservative totals. These real but limited accomplishments are consistent with the interpretation suggested above: across-the-board political conservatism is characteristic only of fundamentalist ministers and a few militant laymen. Outrages to tradition in the Sun Belt and elsewhere had been sufficient to generate masses of television devotees, but nothing like the fundamentalist revolt in Iran or even a phalanx of loyal Christian voters. There is little evidence of a massive new commitment of evangelicals as a whole to the ranks of Republicans or ideological conservatives.[24]

Postelection developments buttress this conclusion. The Christian Right remained much in evidence but fulfilled neither the hopes of its friends nor the fears of its foes. The three major groups underwent rather different organizational transformations. Christian Voice lost many of its leaders, as its two founders moved on to other endeavors and several congressional "advisory board" members resigned in protest over the "Morality Rating." Roundtable announced a campaign to build local chapters, but served primarily as a platform for Edward McAteer's conservative pronouncements, as vice president James Robison resigned and other leading participants lost interest. Moral Majority, on the other hand, became almost a household word, at least among clergymen and politicians. Although a striking number of voters had not heard of the group even by the summer of 1981, Majority enjoyed growing revenues, increasing membership, and proliferating state and local units.

But, despite the accession of a "friendly" administration and conservative Congress, the Christian Right logged few political successes. The movement's leaders failed to get "top priority" status for abortion, school prayer, tuition tax credit, and other vital proposals in Congress.

They received only a few token federal appointments, and, in a most embarrassing episode, failed to muster any Senate opposition to the nomination of Sandra Day O'Connor to the Supreme Court. The former Arizona state senator had been targeted for her ambiguous stands on abortion.

Their few victories tended to be symbolic ones: defeat of a District of Columbia ordinance liberalizing sex laws, convincing some sponsors and the networks to reduce sex and violence on TV, and winning a formal Senate endorsement of school prayer. At least one "victory" was counterproductive: Reagan's clumsy effort to placate the Christian Right by loosening the tight IRS nondiscrimination rules for private schools produced such a political outcry from civil rights organizations, public interest groups, and legislators (many of them Republican) that the president backtracked, saying that he had only intended to ask Congress to "legalize" the IRS interpretation. Some local advances on gay rights, textbook and library censorship, pornography, and "creationism" were offset by defeats elsewhere. All in all, if the Christian Right expected to transform the face of American politics, this change was hardly evident by mid-1982.[25]

The Future of the Christian Right

What, then, are the Christian Right's long-term prospects? The developments fostering the movement are likely to persist or even intensify for a time. Continuing upward mobility may provide an even larger corps of potential evangelical activists, especially among the clergy, given the growing self-selection of conservatives to the ministry. At the top, the electronic church will probably remain—despite having reached the natural limits of its market—given the technological possibilities of "narrowcasting." Nor will the "trigger issues" vanish. Not only does government continue to affront believers' sensibilities on issues such as abortion, pornography, school prayer, and gay rights, but it intrudes more and more upon the institutionalized inculcators of those values— schools and churches. As a result, Christian colleges are expanding rapidly, providing higher education for the products of both private and public schools in an effort to offset or preclude the "liberalizing" effects of secular institutions. As church-state expert John M. Swomley, Jr., has pointed out, even mainline churches are joining their conservative competitors in resisting "government regulations that impinge on the free exercise of religion."[26]

This presents the Christian Right with a strategic choice: should it focus on moral and institutional concerns that unite many conservative believers, both lay and clerical, fundamentalist and mainline? Or should it cast its lot with the secular New Right's economic and foreign policy priorities, thus pleasing fundamentalist ideologues and gaining allies outside the fold, but antagonizing more moderate religious groups? Christian Voice has leaned hard toward the New Right option (and seemingly lost) while Moral Majority appears (at times) to be concentrating on the moral values and institutional interests of conservative churchmen. Assuming that the Christian Right chooses this latter strategy— which would involve downplaying, if not jettisoning, New Right ties—what are the primary obstacles to success?

The first barrier will be the residual antipolitical bias of evangelical religion, which for decades has stressed the futility (or even sinfulness) of trying to reform society rather than save souls. As one respondent to the author's survey of Southern Baptist pastors put it, "our nation and government are part of the world. I cannot waste God's time by trying to influence for God, that which is irrepairably [*sic*] set against God and his Kingdom." Or, in the words of another, "we have better things to do—like soul-winning." Although the press focused in 1980 and 1981 on the political mobilization of some TV evangelists and local fundamentalist ministers, many conservative Christians at both levels chose the old apolitical, otherworldly preoccupations, a decision that reflected organizational as well as theological considerations. As TV pastor Rex Humbard observed, "If I backed a Republican for president, what about all the Democrats in my audience?" Even Jerry Falwell felt the weight of tradition; during the campaign thousands of viewers took themselves off his mailing lists and, according to Nielsen viewer ratings, he lost part of his audience, a fact that both Falwell and his critics attributed to his political involvement.[27]

Besides evangelical resistance to politicization, the Christian Right may be hurt by internal disunity. Personal rivalries among the TV ministers, doctrinal divisions among the movement's leaders, and pure organizational competition for a static market may prevent harmony. And even among the Christian Right's hard core of fundamentalists, differences in strategy may surface. During the 1980 election campaign, for example, Bob Jones II, one of the most political of traditional fundamentalists, attacked Falwell as "the most dangerous man in America so far as Biblical Christianity is concerned." This attack was prompted by Jones's belief that Falwell's politicking had led him to stray from preaching the Gospel and that his pragmatic determination to rally "Jews, Catholics, Protestants, and nothings" for moral causes was a violation of the historic fundamentalist principle of not being "unequally yoked with unbelievers." (Nor did it help that Falwell has made deep inroads into the large national network of Bob Jones–trained fundamentalist ministers, who have kept money and students flowing back to their alma mater for 30 years.)

Such omens, against a past filled with internecine evangelical bloodletting, do not bode well for the Right. Even in the halcyon early days, one or more prominent figures were typically absent from Christian Right spectaculars, whether the Robertson-sponsored "Washington for Jesus" rally in April 1980 or less-publicized ventures such as Pat Boone's TV special for Cambodian relief earlier that year. Still, the early determination not to let theological, personal, and organizational differences impede political cooperation held through 1980, but began to dissolve after the election. As William Elder of the Southern Baptist Convention's Christian Life Commission observed in early 1981, "all the old interlocking harmony is gone. They are disassociating themselves from each other, searching to get individual attention." Ultimately, of course, the Christian Right groups may develop a division of labor to avoid conflict and facilitate cooperation (see Chapter 14). Even a certain degree of rivalry might benefit the movement, by mobilizing the evangelical community more completely than any single organization could. Christian Voice might accommodate the charismatics, Moral Majority bring in most fundamentalists, and Roundtable attract upscale conservative ministers.[28]

Will the Christian Right be able to reach beyond its fundamentalist core to forge a "grand alliance" with other conservative religionists? Already the Right has made extensive overtures to Catholics: Robertson and Bakker feature conservative Catholics (especially charismatics) on their broadcasts, and both Christian Voice and Moral Majority make much of their numerous Catholic adherents. (Majority says that 30 percent of its contributions come from Catholics.) By early 1981, Christian Right activists had joined "prolife" lobbies opposing abortion and Moral Majority worked alongside Catholic bishops for tuition tax credits for private school parents. But similar moral views and parallel institutional interests may not suffice to overcome the Catholic hierarchy's suspicions of fundamentalism's latent anti-Catholicism or of the Christian Right's economic conservatism and foreign policy militarism. Black evangelicals will be even more difficult to attract, for similar reasons. Although *Moral Majority Report*—sent to over 400,000 clergymen, church members, and opinion leaders each month—features regular columns by black conservatives such as Rev. E. V. Hill and economist

Walter Williams, favorable response from blacks has hardly been comparable even to that from individual Catholics.[29]

Above all, the Christian Right will have to infiltrate or at least activate the larger evangelical denominations. This task will not be easy, despite the growing political involvement of such churches. The National Association of Evangelicals (NAE), an alliance of smaller denominations and individual evangelical churches, has established its own Washington office, set up a "legislative alert" system, and cautiously cooperated with selected Christian Right initiatives—except for electoral activities—but has counseled more moderation and less stridency. And, despite its basically conservative complexion, the NAE also harbors political moderates (plus a few "evangelical leftists") who want more action on hunger, racism, poverty, and human rights—a minority bolstered by Billy Graham's recent calls for a new evangelical commitment to social justice, disarmament, and simple "Christian" lifestyles. The NAE has also deplored Moral Majority's tendency to "shoot from the lip," as in a bitter split over the religious lobbies' posture toward revisions in the federal criminal code.[30]

Even more critical to the Right is the 14-million-member Southern Baptist Convention (SBC), the nation's largest Protestant denomination. The SBC boasts four of the five largest U.S. seminaries, a big religious publishing house, and an enormous denominational bureaucracy.

While Southern Baptists share the Right's issue concerns, the movement faces staunch opposition within the SBC from a coalition of political liberals (entrenched in the Christian Life Commission and Baptist Joint Committee), Convention bureaucrats, and traditionalist leaders. Each group has its own concerns: the CLC objects to "Moral Majority politics" as a violation of historic Baptist principles on separation of church and state and as a horrid example of "civil religion"; Convention staff members abhor the Right's pledges to purge denominational agencies of theological "liberals"; and traditionalists fear that sectarian exclusiveness will hurt the SBC's missions (funded through the denomination's multimillion dollar "Cooperative Program," which collects money from churches throughout the United States for all SBC institutions). This resistance (and that of many local pastors) is intensified by the identification of Jerry Falwell and other Rightists with the schismatic independent Baptists who have plagued the SBC for decades. Many SBC officials have felt that the money Falwell draws from grass-roots Southern Baptists might otherwise have gone into local churches or to the Cooperative Program. That the churches of some prominent SBC Rightists have neglected the Program in favor of independent endeavors such as schools, Bible colleges, or TV ministries has only fueled suspicions.

Yet, despite some recent successes at the SBC's annual meetings, the Christian Right is not in a strong position to take over the Convention. Most of its supporters are drawn from among ministers with farm backgrounds, modest educational advancement, and working-class churches—all of which are becoming rarer in the increasingly urban, middle-class denomination.[31]

If the Christian Right cannot capture established organizations, control over its core constituency becomes even more pressing. During its early days, the Right depended on access to both the electronic church and secular press to marshal its rank-and-file forces; Falwell served as "stage manager" for the Christian Right, shifting the spotlight (and presumably grass-roots pressure) from issue to issue. By early 1981, however, the Right was attempting to move, in the words of Moral Majority's Ronald Godwin, "from the media period to the organizational period." Creating disciplined cadres has not been an easy job. Moral Majority has had to allow local enthusiasts considerable autonomy, accustomed as they are to the independence of their fundamentalist churches. This has often resulted in serious embarrassment to the national office: a Maryland chapter's drive to ban anatomically explicit gingerbread men; repeated anti-Semitic remarks by local leaders; California activists' proposal to make homosexuality a capital offense; and the resignation of the New York chapter's president over Falwell's refusal to take on an issue "more important than abortion, homosexuality, or the arms race"—the *Reader's Digest* condensation of the Bible. Thus, Moral Majority and other Right groups may have to depend upon fundamentalist true believers who demand (as the price of their adherence) actions which preclude any alliance building with more moderate religious forces. One indication of such dependence may be Moral Majority's fund-raising difficulties when it tones down its "Sodom-and-Gomorrah-are-coming," crisis-of-the-week style appeals.[32]

Finally, the Right's impact also will depend upon the strength of the resistance from secular organizations, liberal interest groups, and mainline churches. Over the past three years, the press has teemed with accounts of counterorganization, full of familiar names such as the National Council of Churches, Norman Lear, Common Cause, the American Civil Liberties Union, the NAACP, and many others. And politicians, even friendly ones, sometimes react adversely to Christian Right claims to exclusive moral insights. Such resistance may swell or shrink depending upon the Right's ability to compromise at times and to see some moral ambiguity in political questions.[33]

The most likely prospect is that the Christian Right will survive, but in relatively modest form. The continuing penetration of government into the lives and institutions of believers will provide both the motive and the occasion for activism, higher levels of education and income will supply the resources, and modern communications technology will provide the machinery. Over the long-run, however, the further inroads of higher education, urbanization, and social and goegraphical mobility may constrict the Right's potential clientele. As with cultural defense movements elsewhere, the Right's appeal may be strongest to the "first modernized generation," traditional believers caught in the throes of transition to urban life.

The Christian Right, then, is the product of a particular historical period and conjunction of events in social development, reflecting a massive amount of change in a very few decades. That period is now past; the best the Right can do is maintain a small organized voice, speaking for traditional values.

Notes

1. Robert Kelley, *The Cultural Pattern in American Politics* (New York: Alfred A. Knopf, 1979).

2. See Bryan Wilson, "Return of the Sacred," *Journal for the Scientific Study of Religion* 18 (September 1979). For analysis of the relationships between political modernization and religion, see Donald E. Smith, *Religion and Political Development* (Boston: Little, Brown & Co., 1970) and Smith, *Religion and Political Modernization* (New Haven, Conn.: Yale University Press, 1974).

3. See James E. Woods, "Religious Fundamentalism and the New Right," *Journal of Church and State* 22 (Autumn 1980): 409–421, and Peter Berger, "The Class Struggle in American Religion," *Christian Century*, February 25, 1981, 194–199.

4. See "Who and Where Are the Evangelicals?" *Christianity Today*, December 21, 1979, 17–19, and Cullen Murphy, "Protestantism and the Evangelicals," *The Wilson Quarterly* (Autumn 1981): 105–166.

5. See The Gallup Organization, Inc., "Religion in America, 1981"; James R. Kluegel, "Denominational Mobility," *Journal for the Scientific Study of Religion* 19 (March 1980): 36–39; and John Stephen Hendricks, "Religious and Political Fundamentalism," (Ph.D. diss., University of Michigan, 1977).

6. For the differences between believers and others, see Wade Clark Roof and Dean R. Hoge, "Church Involvement in America," *Review of Religious Research* 21 (Supplement, 1980): 405–426. For a review of studies on the linkage between religious and political conservatism, see Robert Wuthnow, "Religious Commitment and Conservatism: In Search of an Elusive Relationship," in *Religion*

in Sociological Perspective, ed. Charles Glock (Belmont, Calif.: Wadsworth, 1973), 117–132.

7. See Jeffrey K. Hadden, *The Gathering Storm in the Churches* (Garden City, N.Y.: Anchor Press, 1970) and Harold Quinley, *The Prophetic Clergy* (New York: John Wiley & Sons, 1974). The Southern Baptist study cited is by the author and reported in "The Southern Baptist Clergy: Vanguard of the Christian Right?," in *The New Christian Right,* ed. Robert Liebman and Robert Wuthnow (Hawthorne, N.Y.: Aldine Publishing Co., 1983).

8. "An Interview with the Lone Ranger of American Fundamentalism," *Christianity Today,* September 4, 1981, 22–27.

9. Carl F. H. Henry, "Signs of Evangelical Disunity," *Christianity Today,* April 9, 1976, 33–34, and "The Fundamentalist Phenomenon," *Christianity Today,* September 4, 1981, 30–31.

10. Jeffrey K. Hadden and Charles Swann, *Prime Time Preachers* (Reading, Mass.: Addison-Wesley, 1981).

11. B. Drummond Ayres, Jr., "Private Schools Provoking Church-State Conflict," *New York Times,* April 28, 1978, 1; "IRS Pins 'Badge of Doubt' on Tax-Exempt Private Schools," *Christianity Today,* January 5, 1979, 42–44; Dudley Clendinen, " 'Christian New Right's' Rush to Power," *New York Times,* August 18, 1980, B7.

12. "Preachers in Politics," *U.S. News and World Report,* September 24, 1979, 37–41.

13. Clendinen, " 'Christian New Right's' Rush to Power," and Edward E. Plowman, "Is Morality All Right?" *Christianity Today,* November 2, 1979, 76–85.

14. Bob Jones University is an unaccredited fundamentalist institution in Greenville, S.C. The university has been engaged in a protracted battle with the Internal Revenue Service over its tax-exempt status. The IRS argued that the school discriminates against blacks. In 1982 the Supreme Court agreed to hear the case; meanwhile the Reagan administration attempted to reverse IRS policy, creating a political furor.

15. John Herbers, "Ultraconservative Evangelicals a Surging New Force in Politics," *New York Times,* August 17, 1980, 1; Clendinen, " 'Christian New Right's' Rush to Power," and Plowman, "Is Morality All Right?"

16. Lisa Myers, "Evangelicals Flexing New-Found Muscle," *Washington Star,* June 30, 1980.

17. Plowman, "Is Morality All Right?"; Myers, "Evangelicals Flexing New-Found Muscle"; Ted Moser, "If Jesus Were a Congressman," *Christian Century,* August 15 and 22, 1979, 781–782; and "Evangelical Group Disagrees with 276 in Congress," *New York Times,* September 8, 1981, 8.

18. George Vecsey, "Militant Television Preachers Try to Weld Fundamentalist Christians' Political Power," *New York Times,* January 21, 1980, A21.

19. Lisa Myers, "Evangelicals Making Plans for Coming Battles at Polls," *Washington Star,* July 1, 1980.

20. "The New Lobbies Solicit Endorsement from the Pulpit," *Christianity Today*, March 21, 1980, 48.

21. See Myers, "Evangelicals Making Plans for Coming Battles at the Polls"; Vecsey, "Militant Television Preachers Try to Weld Fundamentalist Christians' Political Power"; and "Evangelical Group Quietly Upsets Alabama Primary," *New York Times*, September 8, 1980, 8.

22. See Maxwell Glen, "The Electronic Ministers Listen to the Gospel According to the Candidates," *National Journal*, December 22, 1979, 2142–2145; Kathy Sawyer and Robert Kaiser, "Evangelicals Flock to GOP Standards," *Washington Post*, July 16, 1980; and Kathy Sawyer, "Linking Politics and Religion," *Washington Post*, August 24, 1980.

23. FEC data is available from several sources. See Morton Mintz, "Evangelical Groups Plan November 2 Political Appeal at Churches," *Washington Post*, October 5, 1980.

24. See Seymour Martin Lipset and Earl Raab, "The Elections and the Evangelicals," *Commentary*, March 1981, 15–18, and Albert Menendez, "Religion at the Polls, 1980," *Church & State* (December 1980): 140.

25. Barry Sussman and Bill Peterson, "Moral Majority Is Growing in Recognition, But It Remains Unknown to Half of Public," *Washington Post*, June 13, 1981, A2; Linda Greenhouse, "New Right Loses on Judge but Gains New Zeal," *New York Times*, September 17, 1981; and Nadine Cohodas, "Emphasis on the Economy Kept Divisive Social Issues on a Back Burner in 1981," *Congressional Quarterly Weekly Report*, January 2, 1982, 3–5.

26. John M. Swomley, Jr., "The Decade Ahead in Church-State Issues," *Christian Century*, February 25, 1981, 199–203.

27. William Martin, "The Birth of a Media Myth," *Atlantic*, June, 1981, 7–16.

28. William H. Elder, III, "Politics and the New Right—Toward 1984," *Report from the Capital*, March 1981, 10–11.

29. Kenneth Baker, "Catholics and Moral Majority," *Moral Majority Report*, April 20, 1981, 6; Marjorie Hunter, "Tuition Tax Credits Backed At Hearing," *New York Times*, June 5, 1981, 8; Sheila Rule, "Blacks Told to Oppose Evangelicals," *New York Times*, September 29, 1980, 7.

30. John Maust, "Preaching the Gospel and the Bill of Rights," *Christianity Today*, April 6, 1979, 44–45, and Richard V. Pierard, "An Innocent in Babylon," *Christian Century*, February 25, 1981, 190–191. The feud between the NAE and Moral Majority is discussed in Beth Spring, "Moral Majority Aims at Criminal Code," *Christianity Today*, February 19, 1982, 49–50.

31. Richard Marius, "The War Between the Baptists," *Esquire*, December 1981, 46–55, and Kenneth Briggs, "Baptists Calm Their Quarrel and Affirm U.S. Pluralism," *New York Times*, June 12, 1981, 9.

32. Tom Minnery, "The Man Behind the Mask: Bandit or Crusader," *Christianity Today*, September 4, 1981, 28–29.

33. For some very helpful articles on the opposition to the Christian Right, see The Data Center, *The New Right: Readings and Commentary*, vol. 4 (Oakland, Calif.: The Data Center, 1981), 546–604.

3

The Moralizing Minority: Christian Right Support among Political Contributors

James L. Guth
John C. Green

Most studies of the Christian Right echo at least half the common bumper sticker: "The Moral Majority Is Neither." Few Americans, even among the religious, identify with Jerry Falwell's organization (Lipset and Raab, 1981; Shupe and Stacey, 1983; Buell and Sigelman, 1985). Scholars have paid less attention, however, to Christian Right inroads among political activists. Yet what Rogin (1967) calls "the political stratum" is at least as vital as the mass public for assessing a movement's power. Such a focus is particularly relevant here, as the Christian Right may not be a mass movement at all, but "in large part an elite phenomenon" (Lienesch, 1982: 407).

In this article, we assess the extent, location, and sources of support for the best-known Christian Right organization, the Moral Majority, among a large and critically important group of activists: contributors to national parties and political action committees (PACs). Not only are donors a broad cross-section of the political stratum, but PACs have been a vehicle for recent conservative movements. We find that support for the Moral Majority is explained best by activists' political attitudes, rather than by demographic or religious characteristics, though these contribute to a fuller explanation. Our findings suggest that the Christian Right's influence derives from its strategic position as a "moralizing minority" within broader conservative coalitions.

Explanations of Moral Majority Support

Although most theoretical perspectives on the Moral Majority are concerned with mass publics, these can be extended to political activists with only minor modifications. We have sorted demographic, religious, and attitudinal variables into status politics, religious mobilization, and ideological congruence explanations, respectively. While each emphasizes different traits which predispose activists toward the Moral Majority, they are not mutually exclusive and overlap significantly. As we shall see, a full explanation of Moral Majority support draws on insights from all three perspectives.

1. Status Politics Explanations. Some scholars see the Christian Right emerging from social groups uncomfortable with the economic, social, or symbolic transformations of modernity (Johnson and Bullock, 1986). These people are subject to stress ("social dislocations," "status anxiety," or "cultural strain"), leading them to embrace reactionary politics. Although status politics explanations are notoriously difficult to test (Polsby, 1963), if they apply here, Moral Majority proximity should peak among demographic groups identified by Lipset and Raab (1970:460–82) as inclined toward the "Quondam Complex": older citizens; southerners; WASPs; rural and small town residents; the poorly educated; the geographically and socially mobile; products of large, traditional families; and those with declining personal fortunes.

While status politics theorists emphasize demography, some include organizational and attitudinal variables: conservative religious affiliations and beliefs, intolerance, and distrust in social and political institutions (Lipset and Raab, 1970:446, 468; Patel, Pilant, and Rose, 1985). Since others see such factors as independent sources of Moral Majority support, we discuss them as part of explanations stressing the Christian Right's organizational and ideological origins.

2. Religious Mobilization Explanations. Not surprisingly, other observers find the Christian Right rooted in growing religious conservatism or the expansion of "fundamentalist" or "evangelical" denominations. In mass studies, Biblical literalism, salience of religion, and religious involvement all correlate with Moral Majority sympathies (Buell and Sigelman, 1985; Miller and Wattenberg, 1984). From a resource mobilization perspective, the Moral Majority was created through independent fundamentalist and parachurch organizations, outside major denominations but drawing on existing religious networks (Liebman, 1983). Thus, Moral Majority supporters should take religion seriously, be active in churches, belong to fundamentalist Protestant sects and—as a result—distrust "organized" (mainline) religion.

3. Ideological Congruence Explanations. Finally, many analysts see the Christian Right tied primarily to ideological or partisan values. These explanations take varied forms. Some scholars have reformulated the status politics argument into a "symbolic politics" perspective, which has right-wing movements arising from conflict over "life-style" or "family" issues, such as abortion, ERA, gay rights, and school prayer (Fairbanks, 1981). For others, social traditionalism is coupled with economic libertarianism and militant anti-Communism in a broader conservatism (Himmelstein, 1983). These ideological perspectives are often accompanied by disgust with politics-as-usual: rightists are politically intolerant and distrust most political and social institutions (Wilcox, 1983 14–16). Thus, Moral Majorityism should derive from social, economic, and foreign policy conservatism, buttressed by intolerance and cynicism.

Extent and Location of Moral Majority Support

Our data are drawn from a 1982–83 mail survey of a stratified random sample of contributors to 60 party, ideological, and interest group PACs.[1] In total, 2,683 usable questionnaires were returned for a response rate of 52 percent, superior to that in other studies of contributors (cf. Brown, Hedges, and Powell, 1980). Analysis of response rates by type of PAC, region of residence, and size of contribution reveals no significant response bias, although Republican party and conservative PAC donors had a slightly higher response rate than their Democratic and liberal counterparts.

We used a ten-page, 350-item form designed to elicit political attitudes, affiliations, and demographic information. Support for the Christian Right was measured by a proximity question asking how "close" donors felt to the Moral Majority, using a five-point scale ranging from "very close" to "very far." Although Falwell's organization is only one element of the Christian Right, his activities have "made the Moral Majority a byword for the entire New Christian Right" (Buell and Sigelman, 1985:427). Using the Moral Majority as our target also permits comparisons with thermometer items from the 1980 and 1984 Center for Political Studies' National Election Studies.

Although our proximity measure and the CPS thermometer rating (recoded into quintiles) differ somewhat, they produce very similar estimates of Moral Majority support: about one-fifth of each sample reported feeling either "very close" or "close" or, in the mass public, "warm" toward the organization. (Interestingly, "membership" is also comparable: about 1 percent of both donors and the CPS respondents reported contributing to the Moral Majority or other Christian Right group.) Despite similar levels of support, opposition is much stronger among activists: 61 percent of donors reported feeling "far" or "very far" from the Moral Majority, compared with 40 and 44 percent for 1980 and 1984 CPS respondents, respectively. As we might expect, indifference is rarer among activists (20 percent), than within the CPS samples (40 and 36 percent).

The Moral Majority's size may matter less than its location. Supporters are concentrated in conservative PACs, including both those with obvious religious ties, such as the Eagle Forum and Right to Life committees, and more secular groups, such as the gun owners and pro-defense PACs. They also make up a substantial minority of business and Republican donors, but are far outnumbered there by opponents. Democratic, labor union, and liberal PAC donors are uniformly hostile. Not surprisingly, proximity to the Moral Majority is highly correlated with ratings for other New Right groups and leaders, such as Phyllis Schlafly ($r = .62$), Right to Life (.60), John Birch Society (.56), and the National Rifle Association (.55), but is related more weakly to backing for the mainstream conservatism of Barry Goldwater (.42) and the Chamber of Commerce (.33). As expected, Moral Majoritarians feel distant from liberal groups and leaders: ACLU ($-.47$), Ralph Nader ($-.36$), Sierra Club ($-.32$), AFL-CIO ($-.29$), and Common Cause ($-.28$).

Neither voters nor activists necessarily match their sentiments toward the Moral Majority with adherence to its agenda. Simpson (1983) has argued that Falwell's lobby is less popular among voters than its "core platform" of conservative stances on abortion, homosexuality, women's rights, and school prayer. For activists, the opposite is true. Although proximity and platform support are strongly correlated ($r = .65$), more donors feel close to the Moral Majority than hold conservative views on all four issues (table 3.1). Indeed, only half the Christian Right PAC donors endorse the entire platform! (For most activists, the Christian Right's abortion stance is the least popular.) Thus, while contributors exhibit considerable ideological constraint, linking issues to organizational assessments, their evaluations are as much "coalitional" as substantive: conservatives endorse other conservative groups because of broad ideological compatibility and customary electoral and legislative alliances. Thus, while Simpson saw large public constituencies ripe for mobilization on these "core" issues, we find no untapped corps of activists available to do the job.

TABLE 3.1
Support for Moral Majority among PAC and Party Donors

| | Response Category Percentages | | | (N) | |
	Feel Close to Moral Majority	Net Close (Close − Far)	Support Core Platform[a]	Weighted[b]	Raw
Christian Right	93%	+93%	50%	(15)	(34)
Gun owners	71	+47	25	(24)	(43)
Eagle Forum	68	+62	26	(17)	(33)
Conservative third party	61	+50	33	(10)	(47)
NCPAC	56	+35	29	(148)	(66)
Right to Life	54	+47	57	(12)	(34)
Pro-defense	52	+41	32	(15)	(44)
Congressional Club	46	+15	21	(140)	(86)
Other New Right	41	+12	20	(310)	(204)
Economic conservatives	37	−3	19	(26)	(64)
Business	28	−14	15	(399)	(86)
Old Right	28	−17	19	(100)	(129)
Republican party	25	−24	14	(1,655)	(278)
All contributors	19	−42	11	(2,683)	
Labor	11	−69	5	(352)	(90)
Democratic party	10	−68	3	(340)	(295)
Jesse Jackson	5	−73	4	(22)	(51)
Jewish PACs	4	−83	0	(21)	(31)
Democratic candidates	1	−84	1	(155)	(218)
Libertarian party	0	−84	0	(31)	(72)
Feminist	0	−90	0	(59)	(142)
Liberal PACs	0	−95	0	(202)	(360)
John Anderson	0	−95	0	(211)	(298)
Gun control	0	−97	0	(14)	(39)

[a] Conservative stands on abortion, school prayer, the Equal Rights Amendment, and gay rights.

[b] Because donors to smaller PACs were overrepresented in the survey, the sample was weighted according to the amount of money raised in the 1981–82 election cycle. All analyses below were performed with unweighted data with similar results. (For additional information, see Green and Guth [1986].)

Sources of Moral Majority Support

By now it should come as no surprise that ideological variables predict Moral Majority support better than religious mobilization and status politics indicators. Moral Majority sympathies are strongly tied to conservatism on the "platform" issues of school prayer, abortion, ERA, and gay rights.[2] But several other measures are also linked to pro-Majority sentiment: self-identified ideology, defense spending, the Panama Canal treaties, a balanced budget amendment, partisan identification, and conservative positions on almost every issue included. Intolerance is an important correlate, while measures of cynicism (distrust and pessimism) are far weaker. Hence, the Moral Majority attracts those sharing conservative values, especially on social issues, but extending to other domains as well.

Perhaps this primacy of political ideology is not surprising, as campaign contributors by definition engage in politics, but scholars and journalists have too often seen the Christian Right as the intrusion of narrow religious concerns into the public arena. Among our respondents, this is clearly not the case. Thus, activists differ sharply from the mass public, where Buell and Sigelman (1985) found religiosity the best predictor of Moral Majority sentiment. Our religious measures, while clearly related to Moral Majority support, do not match the influence of ideology. Although religious activists are more likely than their secular counterparts to feel close to the Moral Majority, a great many religious donors do not identify with the organization.

In fact, a detailed breakdown by denomination shows that the Moral Majority has not begun to mobilize the full potential constituency of religious conservatives. Falwell's group receives overwhelmingly positive ratings only from a few fundamentalist sects—the independent Baptists, the various "Bible" churches, Christian Reformed churches, and Mormons. Other theological conservatives, such as the Southern Baptists, Assemblies of God, Churches of Christ, and Lutheran Church–Missouri Synod, are either indifferent, or in most cases opposed, to the Moral Majority. The organization draws no backing whatever from socially conservative activists among Roman Catholics, Orthodox Jews, or Eastern Orthodox. Thus, the Moral Majority has not yet transcended its sectarian origins and activated the entire "religious right."

While our contributors differ from the mass public in expected ways (they are older, wealthier, better educated, and more often male), they do show substantial variation on many demographic measures. And, although the correlations are modest, status politics variables operate in the expected direction: Moral Majority support peaks among those from traditional (and larger) families, the South and rural areas, older age cohorts, Northern European ancestry, and the upwardly (but not downwardly) mobile. Supporters also have fewer years of schooling, attended less prestigious colleges, and majored in applied subjects. Income, change in personal fortunes, occupation, and geographic mobility, however, show absolutely no relationship (data not shown). Ironically, demographic variables actually perform better in this well-educated and high-status corps of activists than similar measures do in mass samples (Buell and Sigelman, 1985), but the results reconfirm the inadequacy of the original status politics formulations (Lienesch, 1982).

Indeed, the status politics thesis does not really even fit donors to Christian Right PACs. While many were born and live in the South, they are relatively young, urban, well educated, highly mobile, and not likely to belong to large, traditional families. Most are affluent ministers in fundamentalist Protestant denominations or are wealthy business and professional laity. Although considerably more religious than the average contributor, their real distinction is a thoroughgoing and adamant conservatism on most social issues.

Multiple regression confirms the Moral Majority's ideological basis. As the partial betas in table 3.2 indicate, abortion, school prayer, gay rights, and self-identified ideology are most closely related to variance in Moral Majority scores, holding other predictors constant. A few other issues, political intolerance, and cynicism make smaller contributions. Only a handful of religious and status measures survive the regression with modest coefficients: adherence to a strict moral code, distrust of organized religion, and religious salience remain, as well as the length and type of education. These results parallel Conover's (1983) finding that social issues overshadow status concerns as predictors of New Right activism.

Mobilizing Moral Majority Supporters

Discovering that social conservatism is the best predictor of Moral Majority support pushes the question one step back: what accounts for such traditionalism? Perhaps status and religious traits identified by earlier theorists underlie the social conservatism which contributes to Moral Majority support. These variables, then, should be included in a more complex model of Moral Majority support. The work of Roof and Hoge (1980) presents a plausible causal sequence: status or demographic variables influence religiosity, which in turn affects social and political ideology. The path diagram in figure 3.1 exhibits the coefficients for the hypothesized relationships and calculations of both direct and indirect effects of each set of variables. (To make the path model more manageable, the original variables were reduced through a factor analysis.)[3]

The path model basically supports our conclusions. The status factors

TABLE 3.2
Support for the Moral Majority: Status, Religious, and Ideological Variables

		Beta
Status Politics		
Level of education	−.29*	−.06*
College major	−.23*	−.03*
Traditional family	.21*	.01
Size of place	.19*	.02
Region of residence	.17*	.02
Age	.16*	−.01
Ethnicity	.13*	.02
Quality of college	−.13*	−.03*
Number of children	.08*	.00
Upward mobility	.05*	.01
Religious Mobilization		
Follow God's will	.38*	.06*
Denomination	.36*	.02
Strict moral code	.34*	.11*
Distrust organized religion	.17*	.09*
Church involvement	.15*	.01
Ideological Congruence		
School prayer	.57*	.15*
Abortion	.54*	.23*
Gay rights	.53*	.13*
Ideology	.50*	.11*
Panama Canal	.49*	.09*
Defense spending	.49*	.05*
Equal Rights Amendment	.47*	.04*
Balanced budget amendment	.47*	.03*
State welfare	.43*	.06*
Marijuana laws	.42*	.02
Party identification	.42*	.01
Business regulation	.39*	.02
National health insurance	.37*	.02
Support SALT	.36*	.02
Tuition tax credits	.35*	.03*
Unemployment vs. inflation	.29*	.03
Support dictators	.21*	.07*
Intolerance	.36*	.08*
Social distrust	.12*	.04*
Pessimism for country	.08*	.01
Political distrust	.05*	.02
Adjusted R^2	—	.54

NOTE: For coding of variables see footnote 2.

*$p < .05$.

have their greatest impact on religiosity and only indirectly on the ideological variables or Moral Majority support. Two partial exceptions occur. Traditional family status is significantly related to economic conservatism, a theoretically unexpected finding. Education has, as expected, a direct (and negative) influence on religiosity, but also directly reduces intolerance and social conservatism, while having a modest direct impact on Moral Majority support. As hypothesized, religiosity acts primarily as an intervening variable, producing social and economic conservatism, intolerance, and cynicism—all contributing to Moral Majority orientation.

The total effects, direct and indirect, of all factors are also shown in figure 3.1. The indirect effects of status variables are always at least twice their direct impacts, rivaling the direct contributions of religiosity, intolerance, and cynicism. Education is clearly the most important status factor, approaching the total influence of religiosity and exceeding that of economic conservatism. Religiosity, like education, ranks high in total impact largely because of its effects on social conservatism, which is, by far, the most important factor. Thus, demography and religiosity predispose activists toward traditional social values. But it is these values that mobilize Moral Majority activists, whatever their background.

The Moralizing Minority

Instead of the "Liberty Federation," Jerry Falwell might have renamed his organization the "Moralizing Minority." Mobilized primarily by social issues, Moral Majority supporters are a distinct minority among both activists and voters. Nevertheless, they are concentrated in large and powerful conservative PACs and have strategic access to the GOP, where they have become a critical element in the "coalition of minorities" which has raised the Republican party to near-majority status.

Our evidence, in conjunction with the work of other scholars, helps explain the failures and successes of Christian Right groups. Quite clearly, these organizations have failed to mobilize large sectors of the electorate or a majority of political activists. Indeed, the Moral Majority, with its sectarian Protestant genesis and strident rhetoric, has not even rallied most religious conservatives (cf. Guth and Green, 1986). Where mass support is required for influence, the Moral Majority has had limited impact, whether in presidential or congressional elections, issue referenda, or legislative forums (see Lipset and Raab, 1981; Pierard, 1985; Johnson and Tamney, 1985; and Wald, 1987: chap. 6). Indeed,

FIGURE 3.1
Support for the Moral Majority: Path Model for PAC and Party Donors

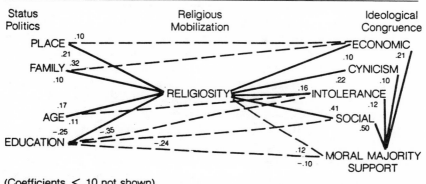

(Coefficients < .10 not shown)

	Factor Scores		
	Direct Impact	Indirect Impact	Total Impact
Status Politics			
FAMILY	(.05)[a]	.11	.17
PLACE	(.03)	.09	.12
AGE	(.03)	.07	.10
EDUCATION	−.10	−.25	−.35
Religious Mobilization			
RELIGIOSITY	.12	.27	.39
Ideological Congruence			
ECONOMIC ISSUES	.21	—	.21
CYNICISM	.10	—	.10
INTOLERANCE	.12	—	.12
SOCIAL ISSUES	.50	—	.50

[a]Coefficients not shown in figure 3.1 are given in parentheses.

where the Christian Right groups have claimed victories, as on religious access to public schools or further restrictions on abortion, it has been a part of a broader religious coalition, including more moderate and powerful allies (cf. Hertzke, 1986).

It is precisely in less public contexts where the mobilization of volunteers, money, and enthusiasm really counts, that the Christian Right has had substantial impact. The recent "infiltration" of such activists into local, state, and national Republican organizations is a good illustration (Gurwitt, 1986). By and large, this influx has been welcomed by secular activists, seeking to harness the religious enthusiasts to a larger conservative cause. The real question is whether the process can be reversed: might a Christian Right leader, such as Pat Robertson, use the movement's strategic position to manipulate larger political institutions? Robertson's evident early success in raising money and mobilizing volunteers suggests this possibility, but preliminary polls demonstrate that he shares typical Christian Right liabilities: a very narrow public base and limited support within the Christian religious community (Shribman, 1986).

Our findings are also an important reminder of the primacy of politics. The Christian Right is one more manifestation of a militant conservatism constantly percolating among activists. And, as in the case of earlier conservative movements, ideological congruence provides a better explanation of why people join than does status politics, which often implies individual dysfunction, or than resource mobilization, which begs the question of why social networks are activated (Ealy, 1978). Indeed, demographic and organizational correlates of such movements may be as much the result as the cause of ideological mobilization. If nothing else, the "Moralizing Minority" illustrates the importance of ideas among political activists.

Notes

1. The sample was drawn primarily from donors to ideological PACs, chosen on the basis of three criteria. First, we included the "Top Ten" nonconnected PACs, six conservative and four liberal, in the 1981–82 election cycle (see Sabato, 1984:21). Second, we chose the largest and most visible "single-issue" PACs on both sides of major controversies, such as abortion, women's rights, and gun control, as well as important "minor" party and candidate movements (cf. Table 1). Finally, to represent more traditional activists, we sampled national Democratic and Republican party committees, as well as prominent business and labor "peak association" PACs including the U.S. Chamber of Commerce, the Business and Industry Political Action Committee, AFL-CIO COPE, and the National Education Association PAC. As federal election law requires PACs to report only contributors of $200 or more per election cycle, our sample consists of larger donors. (For more details, see Green and Guth, 1986.)

2. Although most of our measures are ordinal in nature, we have followed Labovitz (1970) in treating them as interval variables to take advantage of more powerful, sensitive, and clearly interpretable statistical techniques. The variables and their coding were as follows: traditional family (1 = no employed mother or

wife, no divorce in family; 0 otherwise); region (1 = South; 0 = non-South); size of place (1 = metropolitan, 3 = rural; age (1 = under 35; 4 = over 65); ethnicity (1 = Northern European; 0 = non-Northern European); college major (1 = social science or humanities; 0 = not social science or humanities); quality of school (1 = highly selective; 0 = not highly selective); level of education (1 = less than high school; 5 = post graduate work); upward mobility (1 = occupation much lower than father's; 5 = occupation much higher); number of children (1 = 0 to 1; 3 = 5 or more); God's will (1 = not at all important; 3 = very important); strict moral code (1 = not at all important; 3 = very important); denomination (1 = none; 4 = fundamentalist Christian); distrust organized religion (1 = trust a great deal; 3 = hardly any trust); church involvement (1 = none; 3 = very active); specific issue question variables (1 = most liberal; 5 = most conservative); partisanship (1 = strong Democrat; 7 = strong Republican); self-identified ideology (1 = extremely liberal; 7 = extremely conservative); intolerance, an additive index of three items measuring intolerance for political expression by groups identified by the respondent as "dangerous" (1 = highly tolerant; 4 = highly intolerant); political distrust (1 = trust federal government "almost always"; 3 = trust federal government "hardly ever" or "never"); pessimism for country (1 = very optimistic; 3 = not optimistic); social distrust (1 = trust leaders of at least 10 of 22 listed social institutions "a great deal"; 3 = trust leaders of 4 or fewer of these institutions "a great deal)."

3. Loadings for the Status Politics, Religious Mobilization, and Ideological Congruence factor scores were produced in separate analyses. All factors had eigenvalues of at least 1.0 and all factor loadings were at least .20. Grouped variables loading on each factor were PLACE (region of residence, size of place, ethnicity); FAMILY (traditional family, number of children); AGE; EDUCATION (level of education, college major, quality of school); RELIGIOSITY (God's will, strict moral issues, partisanship); CYNICISM (political distrust, social distrust, pessimism for country); INTOLERANCE; SOCIAL (all social and foreign policy issues, ideology).

References

Brown, Clifford W., Jr., Roman B. Hedges, and Linda W. Powell. 1980. "Modes of Elite Participation: Contributors to the 1972 Presidential Candidates," *American Journal of Political Science,* 24 (May):259–90.

Buell, Emmett H., and Lee Sigelman. 1985. "An Army That Meets Every Sunday? Popular Support for the Moral Majority in 1980," *Social Science Quarterly,* 66 (June):427–34.

Conover, Pamela Johnston. 1983. "The Mobilization of the New Right: A Test of Various Explanations," *Western Political Quarterly,* 36 (December):632–49.

Ealy, Steven D. 1978. "Political Science and the Study of the Radical Right," *Intercollegiate Review,* 1978 (Fall):25–32.

Fairbanks, James D. 1981. "The Evangelical Right: The Beginnings of Another Symbolic Crusade?" Paper presented at the annual meeting of the American Political Science Association, New York, 3–6 September.

Green, John C., and James Guth. 1986. "Big Bucks and Petty Cash: Party and Interest Group Activists in American Politics," in Allan Cigler and Burdett Loomis, eds., *Interest Group Politics* (Washington, D.C.: Congressional Quarterly Press): pp. 91–113.

Gurwitt, Rob. 1986. "1986 Elections Generate GOP Power Struggle," *Congressional Quarterly Weekly Report*, 44 (12 April):802–7.

Guth, James L., and John Green. 1986. "Faith and Politics: Religion and Ideology among Political Contributors," *American Politics Quarterly*, 14 (July):186–99.

Hertzke, Allen D. 1986. "Religious Lobbies and Policy-Making on Church-State Relations." Paper presented at the annual meeting of the Midwest Political Science Association, Chicago, 10–12 April.

Himmelstein, Jerome. 1983. "The New Right," in Robert C. Liebman and Robert Wuthnow, eds., *The New Christian Right* (New York: Aldine): pp. 13–30.

Johnson, Loch, and Charles S. Bullock III. 1986. "The New Religious Right and the 1980 Congressional Elections," in Benjamin Ginsberg and Alan Stone, eds., *Do Elections Matter?* (Armonk, N.Y.: M. E. Sharpe): pp. 148–63.

Johnson, Stephen D., and Joseph B. Tamney. 1985. "The Christian Right and the 1984 Presidential Election," *Review of Religious Research*, 27 (December):124–33.

Labovitz, Sanford. 1970. "The Assignment of Numbers to Rank Order Categories," *American Sociological Review*, 35 (June):515–24.

Liebman, Robert C. 1983. "Mobilizing the Moral Majority," in Robert C. Liebman and Robert Wuthnow, eds., *The New Christian Right* (New York: Aldine): pp. 50–73.

Lienesch, Michael. 1982. "Christian Conservatism as a Political Movement," *Political Science Quarterly*, 97 (Fall):403–25.

Lipset, Seymour Martin, and Earl Raab. 1970. *The Politics of Unreason: Right-Wing Extremism in America, 1790–1970* (Harper & Row: New York).

———. 1981. "The Election and the Evangelicals," *Commentary*, 71 (March):25–31.

Miller, Arthur H., and Martin P. Wattenberg. 1984. "Politics from the Pulpit: Religiosity and the 1980 Elections," *Public Opinion Quarterly*, 48 (Spring): 301–17.

Patel, Kant, Denny Pilant, and Gary L. Rose. 1985. "Christian Conservatism: A Study in Alienation and Life Style Concerns," *Journal of Political Science*, 12 (Spring):17–30.

Pierard, Richard V. 1985. "Religion and the 1984 Election Campaign," *Review of Religious Research*, 27 (December):98–114.

Polsby, Nelson. 1963. "Toward an Explanation of McCarthyism," in Nelson W.

Polsby, Robert A. Dentler, and Paul A. Smith, eds., *Politics and Social Life* (Boston: Houghton Mifflin): pp. 809–24.

Rogin, Michael Paul. 1967. *The Intellectuals and McCarthy: The Radical Specter* (Cambridge: MIT Press).

Roof, Wade Clark, and Dean R. Hoge. 1980. "Church Involvement in America: Social Factors Affecting Membership and Participation," *Review of Religious Research*, 21 (Supplement):405–26.

Sabato, Larry. 1984. *PAC Power: Inside the World of Political Action Committees* (New York: Norton).

Shribman, David. 1986. "Michigan Results Expose Weakness of Robertson," *Wall Street Journal*, 7 August, p. 46.

Shupe, Anson, and William Stacey. 1983. "The Moral Majority Constituency," in Robert C. Liebman and Robert Wuthnow, eds., *The New Christian Right* (New York: Aldine): pp. 104–16.

Simpson, John H. 1983. "Moral Issues and Status Politics," in Robert C. Liebman and Robert Wuthnow, eds., *The New Christian Right* (New York: Aldine): pp. 188–205.

Wald, Kenneth. 1987. *Religion and Politics in the United States* (New York: St. Martin's).

Wilcox, Clyde. 1983. "The Ohio Moral Majority: A Case Study of the New Christian Right." Paper presented at the 1983 annual meeting of the American Political Science Association, Chicago, 1–4 September.

4

A Look at the "Invisible Army": Pat Robertson's 1988 Activist Corps

John C. Green

Both American elections and evangelical Protestantism have a rich history of military metaphors (Jensen 1980). From "campaigns" waged by "battalions" of party regulars to "Christian soldiers" marching as to war wielding the "Sword of the Lord," these institutions of mass persuasion have in common militant zeal and grassroots organizing. Thus, it is hardly surprising that the best-known conjunction of electioneering and Evangelicalism in recent times, Reverend Marion "Pat" Robertson's 1988 campaign for the Republican presidential nomination, would be referred to as an army, if only an "invisible" one.

In 1988, the "invisible army" was a term of both ridicule and pride. For journalists and Robertson's many opponents, the label captured the improbability of his campaign (Reid 1988). But to Robertson and his supporters, the term implied hidden strength and the prospects for unexpected victory (Reid 1987). To some extent, both points of view were confirmed by events: while Robertson's army was largely invisible at the polls (Oldfield 1996), the size of his activist following surprised journalists and shocked opponents (Hertzke 1993).

These results suggest two ways in which Robertson's campaign might be described as an army. Many observers expected it to be a conventional army, with division after division of disciplined lower-class and rural voters, marshaled by ministers and marched to the polls to vote "Christian." However, Robertson's campaign is better described as an unconventional or irregular army. Such dispersed and mobile forces do not so much marshal voters as concentrate legions of activists against political elites. This kind of activity has become common in presidential nomination campaigns (Polsby 1983), but such insurgencies against party and church elites have a long history. Evangelicals have often been in the forefront of both kinds of efforts (Reichley 1985).

Pat Robertson mustered an impressive unconventional army of activists in the 1988 campaign, one that was not so much invisible as located in unexpected places. To begin with, these Christian soldiers were largely middle-class members of the spirit-filled movements, charismatics and Pentecostals, a narrow slice of evangelical Protestantism (Hunter 1983). Thus, the cadre was unrepresentative of evangelicalism as a whole but not strikingly different from the GOP regulars. "Spirit-filled" churches and clergy played a crucial but indirect role in amassing these forces, generating an unusual deployment: The invisible army was largely located in middle-class, urban communities that were already trending Republican in the 1980s. These findings help explain the strengths and weaknesses of the Christian Right in 1988 and afterward.

The Christian Right and Presidential Politics

With the advent of the "new" Christian Right in the late 1970s, some observers expected something like Robertson's presidential bid because of the religious resources available to the movement (Hadden and Shupe 1988). Indeed, the Christian Right seemed to have all the ingredients necessary for a successful campaign in the highly permeable and complex presidential nomination process. In the parlance of campaign consultants, the movement had an extensive "fund-raising and activist base" with which to support an extensive "ground game" at the "grassroots" and an effective "air game" in the media "tree tops," both directed at mobilizing a large "electoral constituency" in caucuses and primaries. Robertson himself gave ample notice of this possibility in his 1979 boast: "We have enough votes to run the country. . . . And when the people say 'we've had enough,' we are going to take over the country" (Hadden and Swann 1981:161).

Robertson, like other Christian Right leaders, was deeply enmeshed in evangelical church and parachurch networks that offered access to financial supporters and grassroots activists. Groups like the Moral Majority and Christian Voice had already attracted hundreds of thousands of backers from television ministries and social issues agitation in the 1970s (Jorstad 1990:57–65). Robertson's own operation, the Christian Broadcasting Network, including his popular *700 Club* program, was among the largest and most prosperous of the television ministries. In 1986, it had an estimated annual viewership of 16 million, some 2.4 million financial contributions, of which perhaps 1 million were committed "associates," generating total revenues of $230 million (Hadden and Shupe 1988; Babcock 1987; Hoover 1985). Robertson also founded a political group, the Freedom Council, which joined in Christian Right's efforts from 1981 to 1987 (Babcock 1988). In addition, Robertson's organizations tapped an element of Evangelicalism that was still largely unmobilized, Pentecostals and particularly charismatics, and had special appeal to middle-class people in these churches (Hoover 1988).

Scholars were quick to point out that there were large obstacles to the full mobilization of these resources (cf. Wald 1987:202–6). First, the Christian Right was not particularly efficient at collecting resources (Latus 1983; 1984), and, press reports notwithstanding, the existing groups were quite weak at the grassroots (Hadden et al. 1987). The movement was deeply divided on religious grounds, including long-standing tensions between fundamentalists and the spirit-filled (Wilcox 1992). Moreover, many of these deeply religious people were not particularly interested in politics (Jelen 1991), religious broadcasting was not particularly influential on political matters (Gaddy 1984; Mobley 1984), and the audiences were not particularly Republican in orientation (Horsfield 1984:111–25). And although Evangelicals were increasingly voting Republican, whether they were ready to support a "Christian" candidate for the White House was unclear (Kellstedt, Smidt, and Kellstedt 1991).

The Robertson campaign certainly made extraordinary efforts to overcome these obstacles (cf. Runkel 1989). For example, Robertson first undertook a massive drive to collect 3 million signatures. The actual number collected is in some doubt (Reid 1989), but the drive did identify likely *political* supporters from among Robertson's religious constituency. He also established a "leadership" political action committee, the Committee for Freedom, to test-market fund-raising appeals and campaign themes (Babcock 1987). Although much of this activity produced few votes in the primaries and eventually raised legal questions, these efforts overcome the apolitical bias of many spirit-filled Evangelicals (Oldfield 1996). The task before us is to sketch out the results of these efforts.

Data and Methods

We will use several sources of information to map the invisible army. The most extensive of these are the individual donations to Robertson's presidential fund-raising committee, Americans for Robertson, between September 1, 1986, and June 30, 1988, available from the Federal Election Commission (FEC). By law, these records include an itemized listing of all individuals giving a total of $200 in the two-year election cycle. A unique identification code was assigned to each individual donor, and then the amount, date, and ZIP code of each donation were computerized for statistical analysis. Because such a large proportion of Robertson's donors were unitemized (less than the $200 threshold), a separate study was conducted of a random sample of five thousand individuals from the Public Financing Threshold records at the FEC. To study the context of these donations, we will employ the 1980 Census of Population and Housing, aggregated by ZIP code and county (ICPSR 1987), county-level data from the 1980 Glenmary survey churches and church membership (Quinn et al. 1982), and county-level data on the audience size of the *700 Club* obtained from Arbitron television ratings (see Tweedie 1977–78).

This kind of aggregate analysis tells us little about the characteristics or attitudes of Robertson's supporters, and for this purpose, we will make references to three surveys of activists. First, we will report results from a mail survey of Robertson campaign contributors conducted in 1987 (see Green and Guth 1988). Second, the Robertson campaign published a list of 358 delegates and alternates to the 1988 Republican National Convention that had supported Robertson, although most were formally committed to George Bush. This list was surveyed by mail in the summer of 1989 with a response rate of 50 percent, excluding undeliverable mail (169 usable cases). Third, the campaign also published a list of 351 ministers who supported the campaign. The affiliations of nearly all of these clergy were ascertained by documentary means, and 120 individuals were interviewed by telephone in the summer of 1989.[1]

Reviewing the "Christian Soldiers"

What were Robertson's "Christian soldiers" like? A good place to begin is by describing the characteristics of the "privates" and "lieutenants" of the invisible army, based on surveys of Robertson's campaign contributors and convention delegates, respectively. Although contributors and delegates may not fully represent the Christian Right activist corps, they are a reasonable proxy (cf. Green and Guth 1986). Table 4.1 reports on the demography of these activists.

First, the invisible army had a definite Sun Belt bias, with almost two-fifths of the donors located in the South and one-quarter in the West,

TABLE 4.1
Robertson's Christian Soldiers: A Demographic Profile

	Donors (144)	Delegates (169)
N of Cases		
% Urban Residence	59%	70%
% Mobility	58%	62%
% South	38%	35%
% West	24%	46%
% Some college or college degree	72%	96%
% Income over $40,000	63%	75%
% Sales and Technical occupations	56%	45%
% Female	41%	41%
% Over 50 years old	62%	38%
Denomination:		
% Nondenominational	32%	49%
% Other non-evangelical	27%	16%
% Pentecostal	23%	17%
% Other Evangelical	18%	16%
Religious Identity:		
% Charismatic/Pentecostal	69%	58%
% Evangelical/fundamentalist	21%	20%
% Others	10%	22%
Attend Church Weekly or more	90%	na
Christian Broadcasting "Important"	62%	na

where most resided in urban places, including both small cities and major metropolitan areas. These activists were fairly mobile, with more than one-half having moved in the previous ten years. And they were solidly middle-class: some three-fifths of the donors had at least some college education, over one-half enjoyed family incomes of $40,000 or more, and more than one-half had sales, technical, or middle-management jobs. The Robertson delegates showed these same patterns to an even greater extent, with the exception that a larger number hailed from Western states.

So the invisible army was staffed and led by middle-class people, just the kind of folk who make up the political strata in American politics and are especially common in Republican circles (Verba and Nie 1972). However, both the donors and delegates lagged behind the extraordinarily high social status of the "regular" Republicans, and they were more female and somewhat younger as well (Guth and Green 1989). Age is another characteristic in which the donors and delegates differ: the latter were substantially younger.

The distinguishing feature of these Christian soldiers was, of course, religion. One-third of the donors came from nondenominational or independent churches, followed by one-quarter from churches outside the evangelical tradition, the lion's share of which were charismatics in mainline Protestant churches. Another one-quarter were Pentecostals, and just under one-fifth, a variety of other Evangelicals. Overall, more than two-thirds of the donors identified themselves as charismatic or Pentecostal; about one-fifth, as evangelical or fundamentalist; and one-tenth, in other ways. Not surprisingly, these people were deeply religious, as evidenced by very high levels of church attendance; most also reported religious broadcasting as an "important" source of political information.

The delegates showed similar patterns, with some modest differences. Almost one-half belonged to nondenominational churches, another sixth each to mainline, Pentecostal, and other evangelical churches. Although self-identified charismatics and Pentecostals also dominated the delegates, the religious identities were somewhat more diverse. (Questions on church attendance and religious broadcasting were not asked of the delegates, but extensive write-in comments strongly suggest these delegates paralleled the donors in this regard as well.) Thus, the invisible army was recruited from a narrow slice of the evangelical community—the one most closely linked to Robertson's ministry in social and religious terms.

It is these religious characteristics that generate the trademark conservatism of the Christian Right, and Robertson's activists were no exception. For example, more than four-fifths of the donors took the most conservative positions on abortion, school prayer, and regulation of pornography; one-half identified social and moral issues as the "most serious problem" facing the nation; and two-fifths labeled themselves as "extremely conservative." In these regards, Robertson's backers differed from the Republican regulars. But in other respects, they were remarkably similar: these Christian soldiers were quite conservative on economic and foreign policy issues and nearly as committed to the GOP, reporting, for example, a great willingness to support the eventual 1988 nominee (Green and Guth 1988; Guth and Green 1989).

All of these findings are supported by the perceptions of the Robertson's delegates. Table 4.2 reports the extent to which the delegates regarded a list of descriptions of the invisible army as "very accurate." To begin with, almost three-quarters believed "people with traditional values" was a good description, followed by "viewers of the *700 Club*" with just under one-third and charismatic/Pentecostals at about one-quarter. "Other religious people" garnered about one-sixth of the respondents and "evangelicals/fundamentalists" gleaned one-tenth, with the rest of the options in single digits, including "clergy and churches," "single-issue activists," "people moving up financially," and "less affluent people."

The Quartermasters of the Invisible Army

An interesting point that emerges from table 4.2 is the *political* rather than *religious* emphasis of Robertson's activist corps. This point is illustrated by the fact that clergy and religious workers made up less than

TABLE 4.2
Characteristics of Robertson's Supporters: Reports from Delegates
(N = 169)

% "A very accurate description of Robertson's Supporters"	
People with traditional values	74%
Viewers of the *700 Club*	31%
Charismatics/Pentecostals	26%
Other "religious people"	14%
Evangelicals	10%
Fundamentalists	10%
Clergy and Churches	8%
"Single-issue" activists	5%
"People moving up financially"	5%
"Less affluent people"	2%

3 percent of the donors and 8 percent of the delegates. In some respects, these numbers reflect the small number of clergy relative to their congregations. It also reveals the limitations of clergy as political actors. Churches frequently restrict the direct political activities of clergy, and the evangelical clergy have a tradition of political quiescence. In addition, as with other people, numerous factors beyond religion influence the politics of preachers. In fact, many Christian Right leaders, such as Jerry Falwell, backed other Republican candidates for the 1988 GOP nomination (Jorstad 1990).

Other evidence from the 1988 election supports these points. First, the evangelical clergy were not particularly supportive of Robertson. Just over one-quarter of a national sample of Assemblies of God ministers and about one-tenth of a similar sample of Southern Baptist ministers backed him in the primaries. In both denominations, George Bush was the favorite. Antipolitical sentiments of the laity and "otherworldly" theology helped explain this lack of support (Guth et al. 1991). Many ministers rejected Robertson because he had no real chance of winning (Langenbach and Green 1992). Indeed, to the extent Robertson saw the core of his campaign as clergy, like many of the early Christian Right organizations, then the campaign's core was hollow.

All of these points are supported by evidence from the clergy identified as campaign supporters, the affiliations of which are listed in table 4.3 (each column adds to 100 percent). Overall, some four-fifths of these people were ordained clergy, and 70 percent of these were in the parish

TABLE 4.3
Robertson's Clergy Supporters: Organizational Affiliations
(N = 340)

CLERGY	83%	MINISTRY:			
		PARISH	70%		
				Nondenominational	43%
				Pentecostal	43%
				Other evangelical	17%
		PARACHURCH	30%		
				Charismatic	63%
				Other evangelical	37%
LAITY	17%	GROUP:			
		Religious	53%		
		Political	47%		

ministry. Among these parish clergy, equal numbers came from nondenominational (mostly charismatic) and Pentecostal churches and a smattering from other evangelical churches (also mostly independent).

Telephone interviews with these ministers revealed several salient features:

1. Nearly all felt unrestricted by the attitudes of their congregations
   regarding political activity—some because they had founded the
   church they pastored, others because of the political homogeneity
   of their congregation. The lack of denominational constraints mattered as well.
2. Nearly all were younger and aggressively political, interpreting
   traditional theology to require the maintenance of a good social
   order.
3. Nearly all believed either that the Robertson campaign had had
   good prospects in 1988 or that it would advance the broader cause
   of the Christian Right.
4. Nearly all saw the informal and indirect recruitment of lay activists
   as their *single* most important contribution to the campaign.

Thirty percent of the clergy listed worked in evangelical parachurch
ministries, the largest portion tied to spirit-filled organizations, like
Robertson's own Christian Broadcasting Network. Just under one-fifth
of the entire list were not actually clergy but evangelical laity employed
in a host of religious and political groups. The individuals outside the
parish ministry were far less involved in the campaign, limiting their
activities to the public endorsement of Robertson, which may also have
contributed to the recruitment of Christian soldiers.

Taken together, these findings suggest that clergy and churches served
as "quartermasters" of the invisible army, but were not themselves
"frontline" or even "rear echelon" troops. Overall, Robertson's activist
corps was made up of middle-class, spirit-filled laity mobilized to pursue
political goals.

Counting the Troops

Robertson mobilized impressive resources in 1988, which are best illustrated by his fund-raising: $19.4 million from individual donations of

$1,000 or less during the preprimary and primary seasons. Only Vice President George Bush, the eventual Republican nominee, raised more funds—$22.3 million from individuals—and Robertson's closest ideological competitor, Congressman Jack Kemp, raised $9.9 million from individuals.

The general characteristics of Robertson's itemized donations reveal his constituency's distinctiveness. First, the modal ($19.88) and mean ($106) donations were quite small. Second, the mean number of donations per person was four, producing an average total contribution of $339, with only 4 percent giving the legal maximum of $1,000. Third, the survey of unitemized donors suggests that they were of the same character as the itemized ones, with the key difference being the number of donations made. For instance, the modal donation was the same; the mean, $26; the average number of donations, two; and the mean amount per person, $69. Comparable figures for itemized donations to Bush were a mode of $550 and a mean of $695; and to Kemp, a mode of $150 and a mean of $363.

From these figures, we can estimate the total number of donors to the Robertson campaign. First, the itemized donations aggregate to some 25,500 individuals. Second, by dividing total unitemized funds ($8.78 million) by the average unitemized donation per person ($69), we arrive at some 127,250 donors. Third, when added together these figures generate some 152,750 individuals, which, allowing for campaign hyperbole, resemble the post-election estimates of "not quite 200,000" donors by Robertson campaign officials (Runkel 1989:187). A similar analysis of the Bush and Kemp campaigns suggests that they probably had a total of 60,000 and 30,000 donors, respectively, or roughly one-half and one-quarter the size of Robertson's total. Thus, the invisible army substantially outnumbered Robertson's GOP rivals, no mean feat for a maiden political campaign.

These data fit well the evidence on Christian Broadcasting Network donors, whose mean contributions were small and multiple donations common (Gerbner et al. 1984). Robertson did not, however, exploit his religious constituency particularly well. The funds raised from individuals amounted to only 6 percent of the contributions to the Christian Broadcasting Network in 1986, and the number of donors was only about 15 percent of the estimated size of his ministry's core "associates." These figures strongly suggest that the invisible army was difficult to muster and costly to provision, which underscores the problems of transferring religious resources to politics.

The Invisible Army in Quarters

The geographic and social locations of political activists are as important as their numbers and attitudes. To study the distribution and social context of the invisible army, the donor data were aggregated by ZIP code. While ZIP codes do not have intrinsic political meaning, commercial direct-mail marketers have discovered that important demographic and behavioral regularities are captured by them (Weiss 1988).

Robertson's 25,500 itemized donors aggregate to 7,450 ZIP codes (15 percent of the total nationwide), a geographic spread greater than that for other Republican presidential candidates. Table 4.4 (first column) reports the correlations between the number of donors per ZIP code and key demographic traits. First, note that the number of donors is positively correlated with total population and with the proportion that is

TABLE 4.4
Robertson 1988 Activists Demography by ZIP Code
(N = 7,450)

	PEARSON'S R	BETA WEIGHTS
Total Population	.26*	.06
% Urban	.19*	.11*
% Mobile	.12*	.70*
% South	.24*	.13*
% West	.15*	.10*
% Some college or college degree	.17*	.10*
% Income $50,000 or more	.12*	.02
% Sales and technical occupations	.13*	.16*
% Home owners	.37*	.21*
% Over 50 years of age	.30*	.22*
% Female	.20*	.15*
R^2	—	.44

* p<.05
Source: 1980 Census of Housing and Population by ZIP code.

urban, mobile (having moved in the previous decade), and residing in the South or West. Second, measures of middle-class status also show positive correlations: moderate levels of education (at least some college), midlevel family incomes ($40,000 or more), sales and technical occupations, and home ownership. The population over fifty years of age and the number of women are positively associated as well.

Multiple-regression analysis reveals a more striking pattern (table 4.4, second column). The most important variable is the mobile population, and then the proportion of population over fifty, female, home owning, with sales and technical occupations, and with at least some college education. Location in the West and South and urban population show more modest positive relationships. Oddly enough, total population is not significant, perhaps reflecting the highly skewed distribution of donors across ZIP codes.

These findings strongly suggest that the invisible army was quartered in middle-class suburban communities, largely but not exclusively in the Sun Belt. Thus, the invisible army was deployed among people of similar demography.

The Invisible Army in the Field

Unfortunately, we have no information on religious affiliation or broadcasting by ZIP code, so the donor data were again aggregated, this time to the county level. Of course, counties are key political units and are thus relevant in any event. Aggregating the 7,540 ZIP codes yields Robertson donors in 1,753 counties (57 percent of the total nationwide). Figure 4.1 illustrates the raw distribution of the invisible army. For purposes of presentation, Figure 4.1 does not control for population, but such a control does not eliminate these patterns, and the raw geographic distributions make a very important point: the deployment of the invisible army closely paralleled the distribution of the population.

The largest number of counties had no itemized donors (though perhaps some unitemized ones), followed by those with one to five donors. Both these kinds of counties were largely rural and were as likely to be found in the Northeast and Midwest as in the South or Southwest. However, even in these "outposts," most of the donors lived in urban places. Larger concentrations of donors—intermediate and major "encampments"—were found in major metropolitan areas, substantially but

FIGURE 4.1
The Deployment of the "Invisible Army"
Robertson's 1988 Donors by County

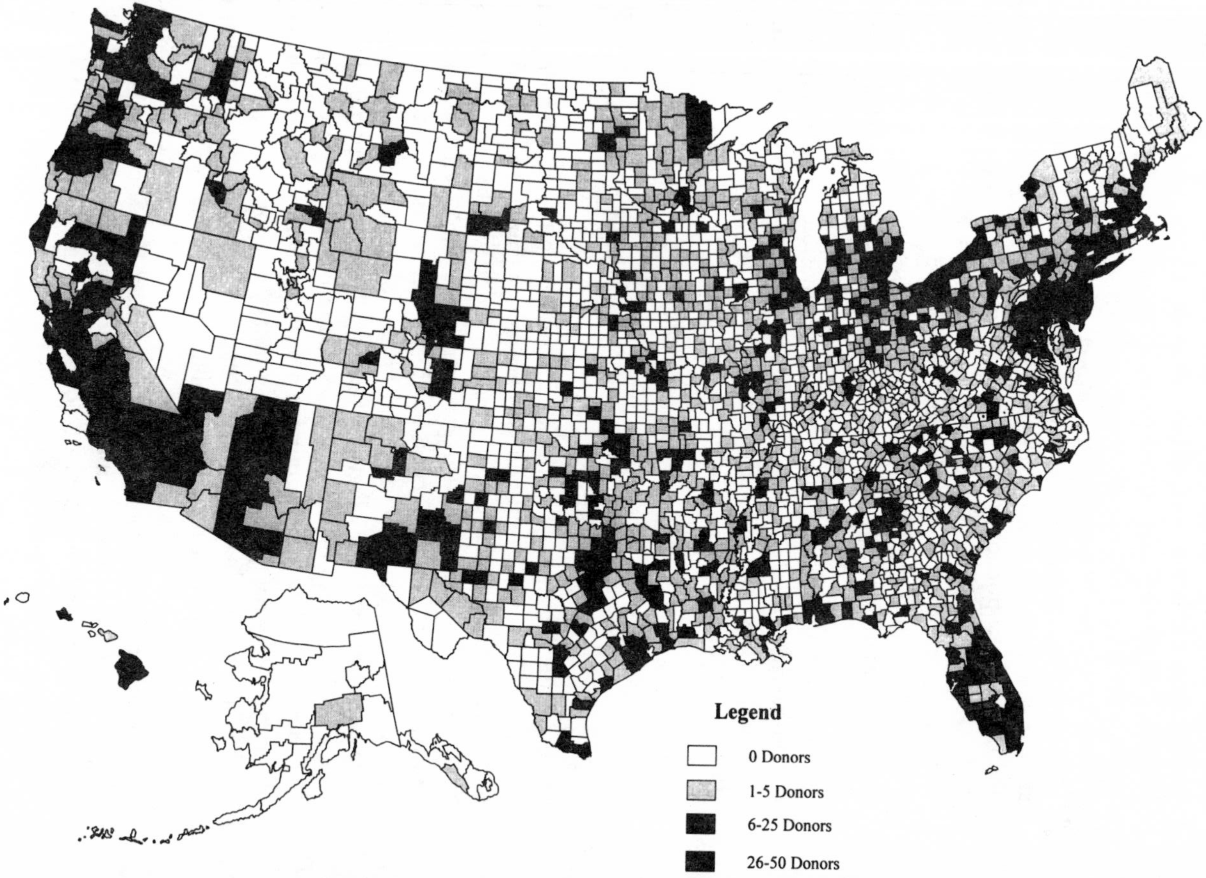

Legend

☐ 0 Donors

▨ 1-5 Donors

■ 6-25 Donors

■ 26-50 Donors

not exclusively in the South and Southwest. Note, for instance, the concentrations of donors in the Northeast corridor and industrial Midwest. The top ten encampments were near Los Angeles, Phoenix, Dallas, Chicago, Houston, Pittsburgh, Seattle, Atlanta, Washington, D.C., and Tampa. In fact, the Sun Belt bias of the invisible army results almost entirely from the large number of donors from major metropolitan areas.

Table 4.5 (first column) repeats many of the same findings as table 4.4 at the bivariate level, although age and gender are not significant (and not shown). The religion data available at the county level are quite interest-

TABLE 4.5
Robertson 1988 Activists Demography by County
(N = 1,753)

	PEARSON'S R	BETA WEIGHTS
Total Population	.52*	.41*
% Urban	.21*	.08*
% Mobile	.44*	.17*
% South	.20*	.08*
% West	.15*	.06
% Some college or college degree	.20*	.13*
% Income $50,000 or more	.22*	.13*
% Sales and technical occupations	.24*	.12*
% Home owners	.40*	.10*
Number of Churches		
Charismatic/Pentecostal	.62*	.42*
Fundamentalist	.50*	-.06
Evangelical	.46*	.13*
Mainline Protestant	.25*	.03
Roman Catholic	.40*	-.09
Evangelical population	.30*	-.12*
700 Club viewers	.23*	.12*
R^2	—	.75

* $p < .05$ or better
Sources: 1980 Census of Population and Housing; 1980 Census of Churches and Church Members; Arbitron Ratings.

ing. As might be expected, the number of donors is positively correlated with the number of spirit-filled, fundamentalist, and evangelical churches; the total evangelical population; and the *700 Club* audience size. But, interestingly, the invisible army is also positively associated with the number of mainline Protestant and Catholic churches. These data suggest that the invisible army was concentrated in areas of some religious diversity.

A multiple-regression analysis of the county-level data also produces more striking results (table 4.5, second column). The most important variable is the number of spirit-filled churches, followed by total population, the number of other evangelical churches, and the *700 Club* audience size. However, a negative correlation occurs for the total evangelical population. Although the coefficients are not statistically significant, the number of fundamentalist, mainline, and Catholic churches also show negative associations. These findings reveal the narrowness of the invisible army. The middle-class demography revealed in the ZIP code analysis remains important at the county level, though attenuated in strength.

Thus, the invisible army was largely the product of spirit-filled church and parachurch networks and middle-class, urban communities. These are just the kinds of communities that have been identified as major battlegrounds between modern secular culture and traditional religious values (Green, Guth, and Hill 1993).

"Converting" the Faithful to Politics

Taken together, these findings help account for several features of the 1988 campaign. First, Robertson's large activist corps was invisible to many journalists and rival politicians because it was located where least expected: in urban settings and among middle-class, spirit-filled people. In contrast, Robertson's troops were few and scattered in rural areas and among lower-class groups, where they were most expected. Within the campaign, Robertson must have been impressed by the hidden strength of this mainstream deployment.

These patterns also help explain why the campaign could overrun party caucuses but failed to generate primary votes. Robertson had enough activists for major grassroots efforts in middle-class communities, but he lacked a critical mass of activists in the more culturally congenial rural heartland. Indeed, an analysis of the impact of Robertson's resources in key caucus and primary outcomes support this point: the invisible army was well equipped to fight party elites but poorly situated to mobilize the evangelical voters as a whole (Green 1993).

As scholars anticipated, major obstacles to the mobilization of the invisible army indeed arose: inefficiency, religious particularism, and the limitations of converting church resources into politics. The forces that mustered the invisible army virtually guaranteed that it would be an unconventional one, well suited to participating in a broader conservative coalition but largely incapable of winning campaigns on its own. So, the invisible army was both an organizational triumph and a political failure. The implication of these mixed results is clear: if it is to exercise influence in Republican politics, the Christian Right must build broad-based political organizations at the grass roots.

If the Robertson campaign was any indication, then, the Christian Right is both a potent and self-limiting movement. Although it will certainly continue to play a major role in the Republican Party, it is unlikely to dominate the GOP in the near future. By the same token, however, the kind of activist base described here cannot be ignored. Indeed, the most lasting effects of the 1988 campaign may be within the GOP itself, where many of Robertson's lieutenants—and privates—are now actively involved. If nothing else, these activists will help ensure that the Christian Right is never again invisible in electoral politics.

Note

1. These lists were generously made available by Sara Diamond, whose books (1989; 1995) are an excellent source of information on the Christian Right.

References

Babcock, Charles R. 1987. "Charity Begins at Home . . . and Ends at Campaign Headquarters." *Washington Post National Weekly Edition* 5(3):12–13.

———. 1988. "Robertson's 1986 Records Are Finally in the Hands of the IRS." *Washington Post National Weekly Edition* 5(26):14.

Diamond, Sara. 1989. *Spiritual Warfare: The Politics of the Christian Right.* Boston: South End.

———. 1995. *Roads to Dominion: Right-Wing Movements and Political Power in the United States.* New York: Guilford.

Gaddy, Gary D. 1984. "The Power of the Religious Media: Religious Broadcast Use and the Role of Religious Organizations in Public Affairs." *Review of Religious Research* 25:289–301.

Gerbner, George, Larry Gross, Stewart Hoover, Michael Morgan, Nancy Signo-rielli, Robert Wuthnow, and Harry Coutgno. 1984. *Religion and Television.* New York: Committee on Electronic Church Research.

Green, John C. 1993. "Pat Robertson and the Latest Crusade: Religious Re-sources and the 1988 Presidential Campaign." *Social Science Quarterly* 74:157–68.

Green, John C., and James L. Guth. 1986. "Big Bucks and Petty Cash: Party and Interest Group Activists in American Politics." In *Interest Group Politics,* 2nd ed., ed. Allan Cigler and Burdett Loomis. Washington, D.C.: CQ Press.

———. 1988. "The Christian Right in the Republican Party: The Case of Pat Robertson's Supporters." *Journal of Politics* 50:150–65.

Green, John C., James L. Guth, and Kevin Hill. 1993. "Faith and Election: The Christian Right in Congressional Campaigns 1978–1988." *Journal of Politics* 55:80–91.

Guth, James L., and John C. Green. 1989. "God and the GOP: Varieties of Religiosity among Political Contributors." In *Religion in American Political Behavior,* ed. Ted G. Jelen. New York: Praeger.

Guth, James L., John C. Green, Corwin E. Smidt, and Margaret Poloma. 1991. "Pulpits and Politics: The Protestant Clergy in the 1988 Election." In *The Bible and the Ballot Box,* ed. James L. Guth and John C. Green. Boulder, Colo.: Westview.

Hadden, Jeffrey K., and Anson Shupe. 1988. *Televangelism: Power and Politics on God's Frontier.* New York: Holt.

Hadden, Jefferey K., Anson Shupe, James Hawdon, and Kenneth Martin. 1987. "Why Jerry Falwell Killed the Moral Majority." In *The God Pumpers: Religion in the Electronic Age,* ed. Marshall W. Browne and Ray C. Browne. Bowling Green, Ohio: Bowling Green Popular Press.

Hadden, Jeffrey K., and Charles E. Swann. 1981. *The Prime Time Preachers.* Reading, Mass.: Addison-Wesley.

Hertzke, Allen D. 1993. *Echoes of Discontent.* Washington, D.C.: CQ Press.

Hoover, Stewart M. 1985. "The 700 Club as Religion and as Television." Ph.D. dissertation, University of Pennsylvania, Penn.

———. 1988. *Mass Media Religion: Social Sources of the Electronic Church.* Beverly Hills, Calif.: Sage.

Horsfield, Peter G. 1984. *Religious Television: The American Experience.* New York: Longman.

Hunter, James D. 1983. *American Evangelicalism.* New Brunswick, N.J.: Rutgers University Press.

ICPSR (Inter-university Consortium for Political and Social Research) 1987. "Census of Population and Housing, 1980 (United States): Summary Tape File 3." Washington, D.C.: U.S. Department of Commerce, Bureau of the Census.

Jelen, Ted G. 1991. *The Political Mobilization of Religious Beliefs.* New York: Praeger.

Jensen, Richard. 1980. "Armies, Admen and Crusaders." *Public Opinion* 3:44–53.

Jorstad, Erling. 1990. *Holding Fast/Pressing On: Religion in America in the 1980s.* New York: Praeger.

Kellstedt, Lyman A., Corwin E. Smidt, and Paul M. Kellstedt. 1991. "Religious Tradition, Denomination, and Commitment: White Protestants and the 1988 Elections." In *The Bible and the Ballot Box,* ed. James L. Guth and John C. Green. Boulder, Colo.: Westview Press.

Langenbach, Lisa, and John C. Green. 1992. "Hollow Core: Evangelical Clergy and the 1988 Robertson Campaign." *Polity* 25:147–58.

Latus, Margaret A. 1983. "Ideological PACs and Political Action," in Robert C. Liebman and Robert Wuthnow, eds., *The New Christian Right.* New York: Aldine.

———. 1984. "Mobilizing Christians for Political Action: Campaigning with God on Your Side." In *New Christian Politics,* ed. David G. Bromley and Anson Shupe. Macon, Ga.: Mercer University Press.

Mobley, G. Melton. 1984. "The Political Influence of Television Ministers." *Review of Religious Research* 25:314–20.

Oldfield, Duane. 1996. *The Right and the Righteous: The Christian Right Confronts the Republican Party.* Lanham, Md.: Rowman & Littlefield.

Polsby, Nelson. 1983. *Consequences of Reform.* New York: Oxford University Press.

Quinn, Bernard, Herman Anderson, Martin Bradley, Paul Goetting, and Peggy Shriver. 1982. *Churches and Church Membership in the United States 1980.* Atlanta: Glenmary Research Center.

Reichley, A. James. 1985. *Religion in American Public Life.* Washington, D.C.: Brookings Institution.

Reid, T. R. 1987. "Robertson's Christian Soldiers Are Marching to a Political Fray." *Washington Post National Weekly Edition* 4(50):16.

———. 1988. "A Serious Contender Get Serious Scrutiny." *Washington Post National Weekly Edition.* 5(17):14–15.

———. 1989. "Pat Robertson's Invisible Army." *Washington Post National Weekly Edition* 6(8):14.

Runkel, David R. 1989. *Campaign for President: The Managers Look at '88.* Dover, Mass.: Auburn House.

Tweedie, Stephen W. 1977–78. "Viewing the Bible Belt." *Journal of Popular Culture* 11:865–76.

Verba Sidney, and Norman H. Nie. 1972. *Participation in America.* New York: Harper & Row.

Wald, Kenneth D. 1987. *Religion and Politics in the United States.* New York: St. Martin's.

Weiss, Michael J. 1988. *The Clustering of America.* New York: Harper & Row.

Wilcox, Clyde. 1992. *God's Warriors: The Christian Right in Twentieth Century America.* Baltimore: Johns Hopkins University Press.

Onward Christian Soldiers: Religious Activist Groups in American Politics

James L. Guth
John C. Green
Lyman A. Kellstedt
Corwin E. Smidt

Religious organizations have always been enmeshed in American politics, from the days when colonial clergy blessed the American Revolution to the 1960s when Protestant, Catholic, and Jewish leaders fought for civil rights. Throughout most of American history, according to many historians, the interlocked dimensions of ethnicity and faith have been the main ingredients of party politics.[1]

Although God's people were not strangers in the lobbies of Caesar, the advent of the Moral Majority in 1979 stunned scholars and pundits alike. Historically apolitical, evangelical Protestants were entering the political arena, and doing so in a fashion more reminiscent of secular interest groups than other religious organizations. When the Moral Majority folded a decade later, a host of larger and more sophisticated successors remained on the scene.[2] These organizations were part of broader institutional changes taking place in American politics and religion.

The Rise of Religious Citizen Groups

The last thirty years have witnessed a remarkable profusion of citizen groups of all kinds. The rapid expansion of the middle class generated a large pool of activists with the interests, resources, and opportunities to pursue public-policy goals independent of political parties and economic interest groups. Many of these activists were less concerned with New Deal economic issues than with new questions such as minority rights, women's rights, environmental policy, and consumer protection. The continued nationalization of economic and cultural life, as well as government's growing penetration into matters once left to local communities, heightened interest in organizing. At the same time, new tools for mobilization—such as computerized direct mail and radio and television solicitation—became available. These could reach millions of like-minded people across the country. The combination of novel issues and new techniques enabled political entrepreneurs to mobilize members, financial resources, and expertise into citizen groups. Religious constituencies were no exception to the general trend.[3]

Two important changes in American religion furthered the rise of religious citizen groups. These were the decline of centralized denominations and the shifting balance of power within Protestantism. For most of American history, denominations were the basic building blocks of religious life and the institutional connection to national politics. Ethnic ties, lifestyle concerns, and philosophical worldviews generated social and political ideologies that bound the denominations to one political party or another. During the twentieth century, white mainline Protestants—Congregationalists, Episcopalians, Presbyterians, and Methodists—constituted the religious core of the Republican party. Members of the mainline denominations shared a common northern European ancestry, a nineteenth-century impulse for moral and social reform (as revealed, for example, in the abolition and temperance movements), and support for unfettered capitalism, at least among more affluent church members.

In contrast, Catholics were the backbone of the Democratic party in the North. The Democratic party better accommodated their more mixed European heritages and expressed their philosophical preference for "personal liberty" during Prohibition and for New Deal social welfare programs. White southern Protestants, another element of the Democratic coalition, were tied to the party of the former Confederacy by Civil War memories and racial attitudes. Despite some convergence with their northern Protestant kin on moral questions, the oft-impoverished southern Protestants' economic interests were better represented by Roosevelt's New Deal than by Republican business conservatism. So most Southern Baptists, many Southern Methodists, and other theologically conservative Protestants were yoked with their religious archenemies, the Catholics, in the Democratic coalition, along with Jews and other cultural "outgroups."[4]

More recently, however, these historic alliances began to break up. First, major denominations experienced deep divisions, over theology and politics.[5] Just as general farm organizations, labor federations, and peak associations in the business world (such as the U.S. Chamber of Commerce) lost influence to specialized commodity groups, unions, and trade associations, denominations have often failed in aggregating the religious views and policy interests of diverse constituencies. For example, mainline Protestant elites who endorsed liberal Democratic domestic programs and dovish foreign policies often became "generals without armies," with little supporting fire from their predominantly conservative Republican laity. Similarly, in the 1980s, the Catholic bishops' policies on nuclear war, the economy, and abortion elicited vocal dissent from both liberal and conservative Catholics, depending on the issue. Such conflicts often led the warring forces to seek other avenues for political expression.[6]

Shifts in the balance of power within Protestantism also fostered citizen-group politics. By the 1960s the numerical and cultural dominance of mainline Protestant churches was fading as steep membership losses beset their high-status congregations, further undermining the "progressive" political witness of these theologically liberal denominations and their umbrella organization, the National Council of Churches. At the same time, theologically conservative evangelical Protestants prospered, both in numbers and, especially, in social status. In the process, their own umbrella organization, the National Association of Evangelicals, gained in visibility and prestige.[7]

This new prominence confronted evangelicals with hard choices. Traditionally dedicated to "soul winning," they were now tempted to "go political," as school prayer, abortion, gay rights, and other moral issues hit the national agenda. For those so inclined, however, there were limits to the political utility of existing agencies. Local evangelical clergy often refused to add political dimensions to their ministry, as did many national leaders. The evangelical community was still divided into distinct theological camps, including fundamentalists, charismatics, Pentecostals, and neo-evangelicals, who often found cooperation difficult. Evangelicals were scattered in dozens of denominations, movements, and nondenominational churches, often with little or no national organization.[8] Thus, the new political vitality of a self-confident evangelical community struggled to find an effective outlet.

By the 1970s, ready constituencies of religious activists sought new vehicles for political action. Like members of other middle-class citizen groups, liberal and conservative Christians had formulated rival ideologies containing competing critiques of American society, programs for action, and rationales for collective effort.[9] For liberal Christians (primarily mainline Protestants and Catholics), the key issues were disarmament, world hunger, and social justice, while for conservatives (including many evangelicals), school prayer, abortion, and gay rights were crucial. Emulating the founders of other citizen groups, ambitious entrepreneurs used new techniques to exploit salient issues and mobilize preexisting religious networks, producing a rich variety of organizations. Although liberal Christians were not unrepresented, most of the new citizen groups were conservative.[10]

Most of the new citizen groups of the 1970s faced resistance from established political organizations. The new religious groups aroused extraordinary controversy. Secular (and culturally liberal) interests attacked any overt expression of religious values in politics, while other critics expressed narrower concerns, worrying that the new groups might violate the "separation of church and state" by imposing sectarian views on policy or some sort of "religious test" for public office. Even some who welcomed religious people into the public square worried about "undemocratic" traits such as political intolerance.[11] Finally, religious leaders themselves feared that politics would dilute the churches' spirituality, destroy their internal harmony, and debase their moral authority.[12]

Resistance to the new religious groups was intensified by recognition of their potential power. Their greatest strength lay in their large membership, which not only supplied money for lobbying and campaign work by group leaders, but also constituted a vast reservoir of potential activists. Religious beliefs provide many citizens with a powerful source of direction; clear priorities and policy stances orient them in the political process. Religious people are enmeshed in webs of local churches, channels of religious information, and networks of religious associations that make them readily accessible for mobilization. Finally, active churchgoers often have organizational experiences—such as speaking in public, leading committees, and managing budgets—that are almost directly transferrable to politics.[13] Thus equipped, the new groups brought formidable institutional and personal resources into the political fray.

A Profile of the Organization

Our 1990–91 Religious Activist Survey included 5,002 members of eight religious interest groups. In this chapter, we report the results of our study of members of five organizations: Concerned Women for America (CWA), Americans for the Republic (AFR), Focus on the Family (Focus), JustLife, and Bread for the World (BFW). Although these constitute a fair cross section of citizen religious lobbies, and the factors that influence their members also shape many other religious organizations, we make no claim that they are strictly representative of the range of such groups.[14] The first three groups are conservative to varying degrees and are often considered part of the so-called Christian Right, whereas the last two organizations are liberal, representing a less-publicized "Christian Left." As we shall see, Right and Left groups differ sharply in their theologies, social philosophies, political ideologies, and public activities.

Concerned Women for America (CWA)

Founded in 1979 by Beverly LaHaye, wife of fundamentalist minister and author Tim LaHaye, CWA is a stuanchly antifeminist women's group that concentrates on "profamily" issues. CWA began as groups of neighborhood church women who met to pray for the country, and its one thousand local units in forty-nine states are still called "Prayer Action Chapters." While CWA claims almost six hundred thousand members—far more than its feminist rival, the National Organization for Women (NOW)—its active membership is probably only modestly larger than that of NOW. CWA publishes the monthly *Family Voice,* has a daily radio program broadcast on Christian stations across the country, and maintains a well-staffed lobbying and legal affairs office in Washington, D.C.

Americans for the Republic (AFR)

Modeled on Ronald Reagan's "Citizens for the Republic," AFR was created as a political action committee (PAC) to support religious broadcaster Marion "Pat" Robertson's 1988 GOP presidential bid by attracting hundreds of thousands of small contributors, primarily from among Pentecostal and charismatic Christians. Although in a sense AFR was nothing more than a list of Robertson donors, it was also a repository for activists from previous Robertson organizations (such as the Freedom Council and the Committee for Freedom) and the base from which he created the Christian Coalition in 1989. The Coalition is a grassroots organization with more than 450,000 members and almost one thousand chapters located in all fifty states. The Coalition staff, led by executive director Ralph Reed, organizes local chapters, trains activists and potential candidates, and supplies materials for mobilizing voters, such as candidate "score cards." Many observers credited the Coalition with a key role in writing the 1992 GOP platform and in getting conservative Christians to the polls in support of Republican candidates. The Coalition participated in the purported "capture" of some state and local Republican parties by Christian Right forces. Headquartered in Virginia Beach, the Coalition also maintains a Washington lobbying office and publishes a monthly paper, the *Christian American*. A related Robertson group, the American Center for Law and Justice, litigates for conservative causes, and Robertson still uses his *700 Club* TV program to advance his political agenda.

Focus on the Family (Focus)

Founded and led by popular radio psychologist and evangelical layman James Dobson, Focus has several hundred thousand members and is headquartered in a mammoth, well-equipped office complex in Colorado Springs. Dobson's radio program is broadcast on eighteen hundred stations throughout the country and has the third largest daily audience of any radio program, ranking behind only Paul Harvey and Rush Limbaugh. Focus receives more than two hundred thousand letters from listeners monthly and twelve hundred phone calls each day. The group publishes several magazines for segments of its membership; more than 267,000 members pay $15 a year for the political monthly, *Citizen*. Political training seminars are routinely offered to interested subscribers, but few local chapters have appeared. Focus is associated with several state-level research units on family policy and for a time had a Washington lobbying arm, the Family Research Council, headed by former Reagan staffer Gary Bauer. Focus later dropped the tie because of tax concerns. Although Dobson tries to keep his distance from the Christian Right, Focus has been embroiled in local battles over school curricula and gay rights. California, Colorado, Texas, Michigan, Pennsylvania, and North Carolina have especially strong state units.

JustLife PAC

Formed in 1986 by seminary professor and best-selling author Ron Sider and other "progressive" evangelical leaders, JustLife PAC promoted a "seamless garment of life ethic." The group backed antiabortion candidates but only if they also took liberal "profile" stances on social justice and militarism issues. Recruited by direct mail appeals, donors numbered more than five thousand by 1990, when JustLife assisted fifty-four candidates. It also produced a newsletter, compiled candidate score cards, and lobbied on Capitol Hill. As anticipated by JustLife's founders, contributors were primarily evangelical Protestants and Catholics. Just-Life tried to develop local chapters but with little success, and in 1993, as a result of increasing financial difficulties, the group disbanded.

Bread for the World (BFW)

Founded in 1973 by Arthur Simon, a Lutheran pastor and brother of U.S. senator Paul Simon, BFW focuses on national hunger policy. BFW's forty thousand members live in virtually every congressional district and receive a monthly newsletter to keep them abreast of Washington policy issues. BFW members engage in grassroots lobbying, such as calling, writing, or visiting public officials. Besides its large Washington office, BFW's hundreds of local chapters are often connected to Catholic parishes and Methodist and other mainline Protestant churches, which in effect serve as sponsors. BFW has a reputation for particular clout on hunger issues.

On the surface, members of these groups look like typical political activists: they are older, predominantly white, better educated, and have higher-status occupations and incomes than the population at large.[15] Their religious interests aside, they are just the sort of people who participate regularly and exercise influence in American politics. Nevertheless, there are important differences among them. The conservatives are not as highly educated as their liberal rivals: fewer than one-half of the members of CWA, AFR, and Focus have college degrees, whereas nearly nine-tenths of BFW and JustLife members do. Educational differences are reflected in occupation as well, with the conservatives including more business managers, clerical and skilled workers, and homemakers, whereas the liberals draw heavily from traditional professions such as law, medicine, education, and the clergy. CWA, AFR, and Focus members tend to live in the South and West; JustLife and BFW members are concentrated in the Northeast and Midwest. All groups draw disproportionately from rural areas, small towns, and suburbs, rather than major metropolitan areas. Women are numerous in all five groups but are the majority in the conservative organizations.

The Religious Basis: Beliefs, Denominations, Networks

As their histories suggest, all five groups are rooted in religious communities, but in different ones. CWA, AFR, and Focus are composed almost entirely of evangelical Protestants (table 5.1). In contrast, JustLife drew a majority from among Catholics, with evangelical and mainline Protestants constituting substantial minorities. BFW is predominantly mainline Protestant, with a significant Catholic minority.

Even more revealing are specific denominational patterns (for which the data are not shown in the table). In all three conservative groups, nondenominational evangelicals are most numerous, followed by Baptists, Pentecostals and, at a distance, by Holiness denominations, such as the Nazarenes. Thus, all three recruit from movements with strong local churches but minimal national organization (and a history of eschewing politics). On the liberal side, Protestants in JustLife and Bread differ. Those in JustLife come from Reformed (Calvinistic) backgrounds, such as conservative Presbyterians and the Christian Reformed Church, as well as from Anabaptist churches like the Mennonites. (Calvinists differ

TABLE 5.1
Religious Characteristics of Group Activists (in percent)

	CWA	AFR	FOCUS	JL	BFW
Religious tradition					
Evangelical Protestant	86	79	81	28	13
Mainline Protestant	10	16	12	18	54
Roman Catholic	3	4	7	52	32
Other	1	1	0	2	2
Religious beliefs					
High doctrinal orthodoxy	81	79	80	28	15
High fundamentalist	67	63	59	5	1
Self-identification					
Evangelical	77	69	68	40	29
Fundamentalist	62	52	51	4	3
Charismatic/Pentecostal	37	75	27	16	7
Mainline/liberal/ecumen'l	9	14	17	72	88
Religious involvement					
Church attendance					
Attend more than weekly	69	61	59	47	35
Attend once a week	26	27	31	42	47
"Very active" in church	43	34	41	42	43
Religion at center of life	80	66	67	63	49
All/most friends in same church	53	45	48	33	40
Member of parachurch group	59	57	45	52	40

Source: 1990 Religious Activist Survey conducted by authors.

from other evangelicals in their historic affinity for politics, while Anabaptist pacifism sometimes generates antiwar and foreign policy involvement.) BFW's Protestants are mostly mainline: Lutherans (perhaps reflecting founder Simon's role), Presbyterians, United Methodists, and Episcopalians, in that order. Thus, BFW typifies the religious coalition on the liberal side of the civil rights, nuclear freeze, and environmental movements.

The religious beliefs and identifications of group members vary greatly. CWA, AFR, and Focus members hold very orthodox Christian beliefs (such as the deity of Jesus, His virgin birth, and His resurrection), while JustLife and BFW adherents are less orthodox. The same pattern appears on a scale of fundamentalism (including items on Biblical literalism, the second coming of Christ, and the historicity of Adam and Eve, among others).

Most conservatives have entered the Christian community by a sudden "born-again" experience, whereas most JustLife and BFW members eschew the term or see it as representing gradual nurture in the church. Asked to select shorthand religious labels, majorities in the conservative groups think of themselves as both "evangelical" and "fundamentalist" Christians. But they differ significantly on two other identifications: most AFR members are either "charismatic" or "Pentecostal" (or both), whereas the proportion of both is much lower in CWA and, especially, Focus. Thus, the religious similarity of the three groups must be sharply qualified: the AFR's reliance on charismatics and Pentecostals divides the Robertson movement from the wider evangelical constituency, which is better represented in groups such as Focus. Although significant minorities in JustLife and BFW are also "evangelicals," most prefer "mainline," "liberal," or "ecumenical" labels.

Not surprisingly, general religious measures do not differentiate the groups very well. Almost all activists are church members, attend services regularly, and regard religion as very important. About half of each group also report that all or most of their friends attend their own church, suggesting intense social ties to the congregation. Many are also members of other religious entities (often called "parachurch groups"), including devotional organizations, mission societies, and charities. Although faith may be a little more central psychologically to conservatives, their advantage in actual involvement is not very large.

On the whole, Christian conservatives and Christian liberals inhabit different religious worlds, sharing little but commitment to faith and church—and the dense social and organizational networks that facilitate political mobilization.

The Role of Religion in Politics

If historians are correct, these religious differences have shaped the way activists connect their faith and public policy. Perhaps the fundamental question has been that of religion's role in transforming society. Evangelicals long ago adopted an individualistic theory of social change. Because evil springs from the depravity of the human heart, society can be improved only by the religious conversion and reform of the individual, rather than by altering social and governmental institutions. In contrast, both Catholics, with a communitarian social theology, and mainline Protestants, influenced by the social gospel of the Progressive Era, have held a more optimistic view of human nature, one that admits the possibility of bettering society by reforming institutions.[16]

These varying "social theologies" have had clear implications for politics. As evangelicals emphasized salvation in the next world, the priority of converting sinners, and the separation of true Christians from corrupt worldly institutions (including most churches), they rejected "getting involved in politics."[17] Catholics, mainline Protestants, and the Reformed churches, on the other hand, remained open to politics as an avenue for social betterment.

Of course, the Christian Right's growth suggests some change in contemporary evangelical attitudes, at least among activists. To discover how our respondents see those issues, we asked several questions about the political roles of religion, churches and clergy, and grassroots Christians (table 5.2). Conservatives remain staunchly individualistic in theory, arguing that the church should inculcate personal morality rather than fight for social justice and should strive to change human hearts rather than social institutions. In this view, social problems such as poverty result from personal inadequacies and will disappear if enough people are converted to true faith. JustLife and BFW members, though still hoping for individual transformation, are more sympathetic to communitarian views and institutional solutions, understandings justified by the historic social theologies of their traditions.

Despite the continuing individualism of evangelical social theology, important changes have occurred in attitudes about politics. Large majorities in all organizations think Christians ought to cooperate in politics, even if they differ in theology. At least some of the distaste that evangelicals historically have felt for other religious traditions (and sometimes for each other) has clearly dissipated. Less surprising is the willingness of "ecumenical" Christians in JustLife and BFW to cooperate. All five groups also have a solid consensus concerning the clergy's involve-

TABLE 5.2
Social and Political Theology of Group Activists (in percent)

	CWA	AFR	FOCUS	JL	BFW
Percentage agreeing with assertion					
Role of church					
The church should...					
Focus on individual morality	57	72	63	12	11
Focus on morality and justice	39	25	30	51	45
Focus on social justice	4	3	7	37	44
Change hearts	84	90	86	42	33
Change hearts and institutions	13	5	10	38	39
Change social institutions	3	5	4	20	28
If people were converted, social ills would disappear	71	82	69	32	28
Cause of poverty					
Poverty is due to ...					
Individual inadequacies	36	45	27	3	3
Inadequacies and social factors	41	34	36	21	18
Social factors	23	21	37	76	79
Christians in politics					
Cooperate even if theology differs	91	89	82	94	91
Approve clergy in campaigns	76	75	59	65	68
Churches should be free to lobby	69	59	62	73	73
Religion has "great deal" of influence on my politics	84	73	59	56	43
Religious views of candidates very important to me	77	65	72	25	25
Christians need not compromise	81	84	80	57	59
There is only one correct Christian view	65	69	53	20	10
U.S. needs Christian party	39	53	46	13	12
Position on "political tolerance scale" High political tolerance	43	36	41	68	64

Source: 1990 Religious Activist Survey conducted by authors.

ment in political campaigns and lobbying by churches. Indeed, if national polls are correct, activists approve such activity far more often than do average Americans.[18]

On the linkage between religious beliefs and political choices, however, activists differ. Conservatives now see a strong connection between their faith and political activities, whereas liberals mix religious motivations with other considerations. Conservatives deny that political success inevitably requires compromise of principle, whereas many liberals admit the possibility. In a similar vein, CWA, AFR, and Focus members often see only one "Christian" view on most issues, while JustLife and BFW members sense more religious ambiguity in politics. Finally, many conservatives think the United States needs a Christian party, although some disagreed with the question's premise, arguing that the nation already had one—the GOP! Few JustLife or BFW members want a religious party system.

These last findings suggest that some conservative activists may, in fact, be intolerant of political rivals. Table 5.2 concludes with direct evidence on this point. Using a technique developed by political scientist John Sullivan and others,[19] we asked respondents to name the "most dangerous group" in America, and then asked if members of that group should be allowed to speak in public, demonstrate, teach in public schools, and run for office. We also asked if the government should outlaw the group or tap their telephones. Combining answers into a single scale produces a strong test of tolerance. As expected, activists usually saw political foes as "most dangerous"; conservatives typically named the American Civil Liberties Union, the feminist movement, or prochoice groups, while liberals mentioned neo-Nazis, the Ku Klux Klan, or pro-lifers. And although activists in each group are more tolerant than the mass public, there are significant variations between conservatives and liberals. Half or fewer of the conservative groups' members scored in the top quarter of the tolerance scale, compared with two-thirds of the liberals. These results reflect both the higher education level among liberals—which encourages tolerance—and the impact of fundamentalism among conservatives—which has the opposite effect.[20]

Competing Agendas: Priorities and Issues

Although all five organizations are based in religious communities, their members have different perspectives on social reform and Christian politics. They also have very distinctive ideas about national priorities. We first asked respondents to list "the two or three most important problems confronting the United States" (table 5.3). Most CWA members, AFR contributors, and Focus members mentioned at least one spiritual or religious problem. The same pattern reappears on "moral"

TABLE 5.3
Political Agendas of Group Activists (in percent)

	CWA	AFR	FOCUS	JL	BFW
Percentage mentioning each category					
Most important problems					
Religious/spiritual	74	70	62	27	19
Morality problems	58	40	45	43	27
Public order	28	28	30	31	38
Political process	19	25	18	14	14
Defense, military spending	16	15	6	31	30
Economic issues	28	34	44	32	38
Environment	5	6	10	33	42
Social welfare	8	8	19	44	49
Priorities for government					
Raising moral standards	97	94	94	65	54
Maintaining public order	41	45	43	15	18
Maintaining free speech	32	35	28	36	39
Giving people more say	21	20	20	27	21
Promoting economic growth	5	6	9	7	7
Protecting the environment	6	12	15	59	65

Source: 1990 Religious Activist Survey conducted by authors.

issues, such as abortion, gay rights, and prayer in schools. Not surprisingly, BFW and JustLife members worry more about defense spending, social welfare, and the environment. Mentions of economic issues, public order problems, and the political process are fairly uniform, although Focus members have a special interest in economics and AFR contributors complain more about politics. These responses are validated by activists' reasons for entering politics: conservatives cite anger or concern over a moral issue, whereas liberals often want to alter social welfare or regulatory programs (data not shown).

We also tapped deep-seated views about the public agenda, using a modified version of political scientist Ronald Inglehart's "Postmaterial Values" battery to determine what activists thought were the most important government functions in the 1990s.[21] Table 5.3 is instructive: CWA, AFR, and Focus members all stress "raising moral standards," followed by the related goal of "maintaining public order." Surprisingly, JustLife and BFW members also give morality a fairly high ranking, although their responses to another set of questions (not shown) confirms that by morality they often mean something quite different than preserving traditional sexual and social mores. JustLife and BFW members emphasize "protecting the environment," which conservative activists put close to the bottom of their lists. Finally, conservatives and liberals differ little on "protecting freedom of speech" or "giving people more say in government." Nor does any group put a high priority on "maintaining a high rate of economic growth." Regardless of ideological stripe, religious activists are not motivated primarily by economic issues.

Quite clearly, activists of the Right and Left disagree over what government should do: shape personal and social morality, on the one hand, or address environmental and social justice issues, on the other. This helps us understand how evangelicals justify their departure from a traditional individualistic, antipolitical social theology: When government abandons traditional morality or, worse yet, protects "deviant" behavior, political action must be taken.[22] In contrast, Christian liberals see political involvement as intrinsic to the churches' role and have simply incorporated new issues and needs into an established social theology, stressing government action in pursuit of social justice.

Ideology, Issues, and Alliances

The interest group literature predicts that active members of purposive or expressive organizations such as these should share the policy preferences of group leaders.[23] Is this the case here? To locate activists politically, we asked about their attitudes on specific political issues, ideological and partisan self-identifications, and proximity to prominent political organizations and leaders. The findings in table 5.4 confirm that activists generally agree with the group's founders. CWA, AFR, and Focus members are very conservative on touchstones of the Christian Right agenda: pornography, teaching of evolution in public schools, capital punishment, abortion, gay rights, sex education, and support for traditional morality. On the other hand, JustLife and BFW members favor a modern-day social gospel: the Equal Rights Amendment, national health insurance, racial justice, and environmental protection, as well as tax hikes to address world hunger, aid the needy, and cut the budget deficit. Note, however, that JustLife members are less liberal on moral issues, such as abortion, reflecting Ron Sider's "seamless garment" ideology.

The ideological gaps between groups are also clear from members' political self-identifications and 1988 vote choices. Ideological self-identification encapsulates the activists' policy preferences, with CWA

TABLE 5.4
Political Attitudes and Identifications of Group Activists (in percent)

	CWA	AFR	FOCUS	JL	BFW
"Conservative" agenda issues					
Favor strong pornography laws	98	99	95	78	66
Teach creationism with evolution	97	96	95	41	34
Support capital punishment	93	90	80	27	18
Abortion: only mother's life	91	66	74	51	22
Not allow gay teachers	90	90	78	21	13
No birth control info in school	88	74	68	34	14
Highly traditional moral views	77	63	57	10	4
"Liberal" agenda issues					
Adopt Equal Rights Amendment	5	8	14	51	68
Raise taxes to help needy	12	16	27	84	87
Adopt national health insurance	13	20	31	72	75
Raise taxes for world hunger	14	20	25	83	90
Help minorities more	21	22	28	81	87
Save environment despite costs	27	39	41	89	93
Raise taxes to cut deficit	30	47	35	77	82
Ideological self-identification					
Conservative	97	93	83	18	10
Moderate	3	7	14	23	26
Liberal	0	0	3	59	64
Party identification					
Republican	93	85	78	18	16
Independent	5	11	15	24	20
Democrat	2	4	7	58	65
1988 presidential vote					
Bush	99	99	96	31	22
Dukakis	1	1	4	69	78

Source: 1990 Religious Activist Survey conducted by authors.

the most conservative group and BFW the most liberal. Partisanship is a little less polarized: CWA members are overwhelmingly Republican; AFR and Focus members slightly less so. JustLife and BFW are dominated by independents and Democrats. The liberals' Democratic propensities are weaker than the corresponding Republican bias among conservatives. Activists' current partisanship has often resulted from personal migrations. Many conservatives were raised as Democrats but have moved toward the GOP, whereas many JustLife and BFW members have abandoned a Republican family heritage for the Democratic party. Finally,

1988 presidential choices range from a Bush monopoly in CWA, AFR, and Focus to the strong preference of JustLife and BFW members for Dukakis. Observe once again the greater political consensus among the three conservative organizations.

A slightly different picture is provided by activists' reports of how close they feel to interest groups and political leaders. Table 5.5 shows "net proximities" of activists to certain groups, calculated by subtracting the percentage of respondents who felt "far" from the group from the percentage feeling "close." Positive numbers indicate more members of a group feel close to an organization or leader; negative ones indicate the reverse. As expected, conservatives feel very close to the National Right to Life Committee, but less close to the more militant Operation Rescue

TABLE 5.5
Ideology: Proximities and Ideological Clusters of Group Activists (in percent)

	CWA	AFR	FOCUS	JL	BFW
Net proximity to other groups and political leaders					
National Right to Life	+93	+83	+71	+30	(–23)
Operation Rescue	+62	+54	+26	(– 9)	(–36)
American Family Association	+61	+54	+21	(–18)	(–54)
George Bush	+76	+66	+60	+ 1	(–29)
Ronald Reagan	+67	+69	+29	(–73)	(–78)
Pat Robertson	+57	+93	+17	(–70)	(–78)
Jimmy Carter	(–69)	(–50)	(–25)	+74	+75
Jesse Jackson	(–86)	(–90)	(–73)	+15	+21
NAACP	(–71)	(–68)	(–63)	+41	+53
American Civil Liberties Union	(–97)	(–96)	(–86)	(–35)	(– 0)
People for the American Way	(–99)	(–79)	(–81)	(–45)	(–28)
National Organization for Women	(–98)	(–88)	(–84)	(–52)	+ 6
Gay Rights Movement	(–99)	(–99)	(–97)	(–38)	(– 9)
Political cluster					
Christian Right	73	51	39	2	0
Traditional conservatives	25	44	45	9	6
Christian moderates	2	6	15	33	25
Seamless garment liberals	0	0	1	48	34
Christian Left	0	0	1	7	36

Source: 1990 Religious Activist Survey conducted by authors.

Note: Proximities with (+) signs indicate net positive evaluation; those in brackets (–), net negative ones.

and the American Family Association, an anti-pornography group. Once again, however, some significant differences exist among the three conservative groups, and JustLife's moderation falls short of BFW's consistent liberalism. Similar patterns appear in ratings of liberal organizations. Conservatives reserve special ire for enemies of traditional values: the American Civil Liberties Union (ACLU), a foe on many church-state issues; People for the American Way (PAW), formed to oppose Christian Right politics; NOW, a venerable feminist and prochoice group; and the gay rights movement. The NAACP does poorly with the conservatives, and although liberal activists feel warmly toward this mainstream civil rights group, they are hardly admirers of the ACLU, PAW, NOW, or the gay rights movement. Thus, conservatives may be a better fit with potential conservative allies than liberals are with some possible coalition partners on the left.

Among recent presidents and presidential candidates, George Bush does well with the conservative groups, splits JustLife, and has negative ratings only from BFW, while disapproval of Ronald Reagan becomes a factor among Focus members and rises to overwhelming proportions among the liberals. Not surprisingly, Pat Robertson gets almost unanimous support from AFR members, warm ratings from CWA, but mixed assessments from Focus, and matches Reagan in unpopularity among the liberals. On the other hand, Jimmy Carter is disliked by CWA and AFR activists, gets better reviews from Focus members, and is warmly regarded by JustLife and BFW members. Jesse Jackson is even more unpopular than Carter with conservatives but has a comfortable positive margin among liberals.

To summarize the dominant ideological tendencies in each organization, we assigned activists to ideological "clusters," based on responses to all our questions on issues, political self-identifications, and proximities, including many not reported here.[24] The most satisfying solution apportioned activists into five groups, which we labeled "Christian Right," "traditional conservatives," "Christian moderates," "seamless garment liberals," and "Christian Left" (table 5.5).

Despite many commonalities, each group has its own ideological center of gravity, accurately embodying the political preferences of the organizations' entrepreneurs and other officials.

Political Activity

To this point, we have learned that our activists come from different religious communities, have distinctive orientations on religion's political role, and espouse divergent ideologies. What about their political activity? Do they learn about the political world from different sources? Do they specialize in different kinds of political activity? Are conservatives or liberals more active?

Mechanisms of Communication and Mobilization

Activists are mobilized politically by means as varied as the people themselves, but several sources of contact and information are especially relevant to religious activists: churches and clergy, religious publications and media, the intense personal networks common to church loyalists, and direct mail from special purpose groups (table 5.6).[25] Christian conservatives and Christian liberals nevertheless have distinct patterns of information acquisition. CWA, AFR, and Focus members regard religious TV or radio as their most important sources. Not surprisingly, AFR members, presumably fans of Pat Robertson's *700 Club*, see religious television as very important, while Focus members, probably recruited by James Dobson's program, favor religious radio over religious TV. CWA members rely on both. The conservatives use direct mail more

TABLE 5.6
Sources of Information for Group Activists (in percent)

	CWA	AFR	FOCUS	JL	BFW
Conservative sources					
Religious radio	76	49	67	10	6
Direct mail	62	41	28	24	22
Religious TV	44	73	28	3	3
Liberal sources					
Newspapers	59	57	70	86	89
TV news	50	61	68	66	72
News magazines	37	32	35	61	63
Radio news	35	27	47	50	54
Opinion journals	28	17	15	46	39
Coworkers/colleagues	13	11	16	29	31
Both use equally					
Religious magazines	74	56	55	60	51
Family/friends	39	29	41	39	37
Clergy/church	28	26	35	24	28

Source: 1990 Religious Activist Survey conducted by authors.

often than liberals, perhaps reflecting the American Right's pioneering use of this technique. Both ideological communities read religious magazines—though probably not the same ones.

Whereas conservatives prefer specialized religious sources not familiar to most Americans, liberals absorb the "public" media, using network TV, secular radio news, newspapers, news magazines, and opinion journals. If one sums the mentions of these secular sources, the liberal preference for secular news sources is even more noticeable. Thus, we see two disparate communities of political discourse. Conservatives rely on a few sources dominated by a clear ideological message, which surely fosters issue consistency, a certain militancy, and sense of political direction. Religious TV and radio, along with direct mail, mobilize conservatives directly for Christian Right causes and recruit them into specific organizations. Liberals, on the other hand, participate in a wider national community of discourse, encountering (and perhaps assimilating) a range of perspectives, especially liberal ones. These sources may produce more political sophistication and, ultimately, greater effectiveness, but they are not useful for direct mobilization and seldom produce the intense enthusiasm which makes the Christian Right a potent force.

The role of clergy as a source of information and mobilization is not altogether obvious. Local clergy do command substantial personal and institutional resources, but they encounter many constraints.[26] Table 5.6 shows that ministers and priests are not cited as a source of information by a majority in any group. Perhaps clergy abstain from preaching about political issues, or perhaps many activists want clergy to "stay out of politics" and therefore do not seek their views. We asked respondents if they approved of clergy addressing specific political issues, and whether their minister or priest actually did so. The results were straightforward: Religious activists endorse preaching on politics and say that their clergy often does so—but on different issues. Members of BFW and JustLife hear sermons addressing "social justice," but usually not abortion, prayer in schools, and sexual morality, while conservatives report the reverse pattern. Nevertheless, all the activists want more pulpit politics than they get—especially pronouncements on candidates for public office! Of course, their own ministers and less enthusiastic coparishioners might not concur—and survey data suggest they do not.[27] In any event, interest groups provide a political vehicle not matched by local churches, no matter how successfully they fulfill activists' spiritual needs.

Forms of Activism

Finally, we assessed the political activities of interest group members. We gave respondents a checklist for activities undertaken during "the past two years," a period including the 1988 elections. It was hardly a surprise to find them far more active than the average citizen (table 5.7).[28] Virtually all reported voting in the 1988 presidential primaries and the general election. Most signed petitions and large numbers reported participating in a boycott of a company or product, contacting public officials, making political donations, demonstrating, and writing letters to the editor. CWA and AFR members, however, excelled in electoral politics: attending rallies, campaigning door to door, and running for public or party office. Focus members were the least active, suggesting that many joined for James Dobson's pronouncements on child rearing, not on partisan politics.

Overall, the results are easily summarized. Religious activists invariably vote, engage at unusually high levels in unconventional activities such as boycotting and demonstrating, and frequently communicate with public officials. They are not as involved in other kinds of activity, such as partisan campaigns, but nevertheless represent potent resources for both parties if mobilized. Although our survey showed that CWA and AFR adherents performed the highest average number of acts of political participation, we should not make too much of the difference. The late 1980s were a period in which conservative elites were more effective in

TABLE 5.7
Political Activities Undertaken by Group Activists (in percent)

	CWA	AFR	FOCUS	JL	BFW
Voted in 1988 presidential election	98	97	92	86	88
Voted in 1988 presidential primaries	93	94	82	86	88
Signed or circulated petition	93	85	79	87	85
Contacted public official	74	44	37	53	52
Wrote letter to editor	47	23	19	36	29
Boycotted company or product	77	40	45	56	47
Participated in demonstration	53	20	23	38	30
Made financial contribution	59	84	26	49	51
Attended political rally	44	44	14	24	22
Door-to-door campaigning	25	18	7	11	10
Served as party official	12	14	1	3	1
Ran for public office	6	4	1	3	1
Average number of acts of political participation per activist	6.79	5.64	4.16	5.44	5.12

Source: 1990 Religious Activist Survey conducted by authors.

mobilization than their liberal counterparts and, in any event, a slightly varied list of activities might well have produced different totals.

Conclusions

Our examination of these five interest groups leads to some broader conclusions about religion's role in American politics. The first is the striking extent to which Christian conservatives and liberals meld into contemporary alignments. Although the former emphasize moral traditionalism and the latter social justice and environmental causes, their positions on most issues correspond to broader ideological and partisan patterns. In other words, these groups and similar ones are expressions of a new "two-party system" in American religion, in which theological conservatives are being absorbed by the political Right and theological liberals by the political Left.[29]

Both conservative and liberal activists represent potential sources of personnel, money, and talent for the Republican and Democratic alliances, but each presents a very different mix of assets and liabilities to its secular allies. The conservatives are far more numerous, have several organizations mobilizing varied religious constituencies, and possess greater enthusiasm for political combat. Some, however, may eventually be tempted back into the political quietism that is consistent with their social theology and typical of theological conservatives since the 1920s—especially if their political crusades are unsuccessful. Their political liabilities include espousal of some unpopular views, a certain political and intellectual rigidity, and the unwillingness of some to compromise— whether with political opponents or potential allies. The frequent tension between the Christian Right and other Republicans testifies to these characteristics.

Ironically, the strengths and weaknesses of Christian liberals are almost mirror images of the Right's. Although considerably less numerous—and drawn from a shrinking religious base—liberal activists share the same community of political discourse as their secular counterparts, appeal to powerful themes in the social theologies of mainline Protestant and Catholic traditions, and draw upon a history of successful activism. To the extent that they use religious language, however, they may find themselves outside the secularist intellectual frames of reference dominant among Democrats and activists in other liberal movements. Indeed, their coolness toward prominent organizations such as the ACLU and NOW reveals the tension that religious liberals feel when dealing with potential allies hostile to religious values.

What of the future? Will religious citizen groups grow in size and importance? In religion, like politics, prediction is hazardous, but the forces stimulating such groups are not likely to disappear and may intensify. The theological and political polarizations within religious traditions, the growing individualism of American religious expression, the declining efficacy of older organizational forms, the expanding social and economic resources of many religious citizens, the availability of organizing techniques and leaders willing to use them—all these combine with the heightened role of government in policies vital to religious people to ensure that this brand of citizen-group politics will have a future.

Notes

1. For essays on religious influence in American political history, see Mark A. Noll, ed., *Religion and American Politics* (Oxford: Oxford University Press, 1990).

2. James L. Guth, "The Politics of the Christian Right," in *Interest Group Politics*, ed. Allan J. Cigler and Burdett A. Loomis (Washington, D.C.: CQ Press, 1983), 60–83; Matthew C. Moen, *The Transformation of the Christian Right* (Tuscaloosa: University of Alabama Press, 1992).

3. Jeffrey Berry, *Lobbying for the People* (Princeton, N.J.: Princeton University Press, 1977); R. Kenneth Godwin, *One Billion Dollars of Influence* (Chatham, N.J.: Chatham House, 1988).

4. Lyman A. Kellstedt and Mark A. Noll, "Religion, Voting for President, and Party Identification," in *Religion and American Politics*, ed. Noll, 355–379.

5. Robert Wuthnow, *The Restructuring of American Religion* (Princeton, N.J.: Princeton University Press, 1988).

6. James F. Findlay, Jr., *Church People in the Struggle* (Oxford: Oxford University Press, 1993); Timothy A. Byrnes, *Catholic Bishops in American Politics* (Princeton, N.J.: Princeton University Press, 1991).

7. Wade Clark Roof and William McKinney, *American Mainline Religion* (New Brunswick, N.J.: Rutgers University Press, 1987); William R. Hutchison, ed., *Between the Times* (Cambridge: Cambridge University Press, 1989).

8. The evangelical community includes a variety of overlapping theological groups, including "fundamentalists," "pentecostals," "charismatics," and "evangelicals." Fundamentalists stress Biblical inerrancy, historic Christian orthodoxy, and separation from "the world." Pentecostals share many doctrinal views with fundamentalists but practice "gifts of the Spirit," such as speaking in tongues and faith healing. "Charismatic" usually refers to mainline Protestants and Catholics

who practice such gifts, without joining a pentecostal denomination. "Evangelical" can refer to any of these or, more specifically, to the moderate wing of the fundamentalist movement. The National Association of Evangelicals, founded in 1942, represents many (but by no means all) of these groups. For a good overview of the varied elements of the evangelical community, see Donald W. Dayton and Robert K. Johnson, eds., *The Variety of American Evangelicalism* (Downers Grove, Ill.: Intervarsity Press, 1991).

9. For the ideology of an earlier middle-class citizen group, see Andrew S. McFarland, *Common Cause* (Chatham, N.J.: Chatham House, 1984).

10. Moen, *Transformation of the Christian Right.*

11. For a widely read discussion (and critique) of the hostile reaction to religious group politics, see Stephen L. Carter, *The Culture of Disbelief* (New York: Basic Books, 1993).

12. A representative caution about political activism from a prominent evangelical is Charles Colson, *Kingdoms in Conflict* (New York: William Morrow, 1987).

13. For the political resources provided by church involvement, see Sidney Verba, Kay Lehman Schlozman, Henry Brady, and Norman H. Nie, "Race, Ethnicity and Political Resources: Participation in the United States," *British Journal of Political Science* 23 (October 1993): 453–497.

14. This study is based on a 1990–91 national survey of a stratified random sample of the membership of eight religious interest groups. Six of the organizations cooperated by making membership lists available; a subsample for Concerned Women for America was drawn from CWA's monthly magazine, and for Americans for Robertson, from the public records of the Federal Election Commission in Washington. We sent questionnaires to well over nine thousand group members and after four mailings, received 5,002 completed forms, a response rate of 56 percent. More details on the study and many of the measures used here can be found in James L. Guth, Corwin E. Smidt, Lyman A. Kellstedt, and John C. Green, "The Sources of Antiabortion Attitudes: The Case of Religious Political Activists," *American Politics Quarterly* 21 (January 1993): 65–80.

15. Steven J. Rosenstone and John Mark Hansen, *Mobilization, Participation, and Democracy in America* (New York: Macmillan, 1993); John C. Green and James L. Guth, "Big Bucks and Petty Cash: Party and Interest Group Activists in American Politics," in *Interest Group Politics,* 2d ed., ed. Allan J. Cigler and Burdett A. Loomis (Washington, D.C.: CQ Press, 1986).

16. For more on individualistic and communitarian perspectives, see David C. Leege and Lyman A. Kellstedt, "Religious Worldviews and Political Philosophies," in *Rediscovering the Religious Factor in American Politics,* ed. David C. Leege and Lyman A. Kellstedt (Armonk, N.Y.: M. E. Sharpe, 1993).

17. Timothy P. Weber, *Living in the Shadow of the Second Coming* (Chicago, Ill.: University of Chicago Press, 1987).

18. For data on public approval of clergy involvement, see Michael R. Welch, David C. Leege, Kenneth D. Wald, and Lyman A. Kellstedt, "Are the Sheep

Hearing the Shepherds?" in *Rediscovering the Religious Factor,* ed. Leege and Kellstedt, 235–254.

19. John L. Sullivan, James Piereson, and George E. Marcus, *Political Tolerance and American Democracy* (Chicago: University of Chicago Press, 1982).

20. For comparisons with the mass public and other political activists, see James L. Guth and John C. Green, "An Ideology of Rights: Support for Civil Liberties Among Political Activists," *Political Behavior* 13 (December 1991): 321–344.

21. Ronald Inglehart, *Culture Shift* (Princeton, N.J.: Princeton University Press, 1990).

22. Clyde Wilcox, *God's Warriors* (Baltimore: Johns Hopkins, 1992); Steve Bruce, *The Rise and Fall of the New Christian Right* (Oxford: Oxford University Press, 1988).

23. Terry M. Moe, *The Organization of Interests* (Chicago: University of Chicago Press, 1980).

24. For a brief description of cluster analysis, see Mark S. Aldenderfer and Roger K. Blashfield, *Cluster Analysis* (Newbury Park, Calif.: Sage, 1984).

25. Leege and Kellstedt, *Rediscovering the Religious Factor,* chaps. 6, 12, and 13.

26. Harold Quinley, *The Prophetic Clergy* (New York: Wiley, 1974); James L. Guth, John C. Green, Corwin E. Smidt, and Margaret M. Poloma, "Pulpits and Politics: Protestant Clergy in the 1988 Presidential Campaign," in *The Bible and the Ballot Box,* ed. James L. Guth and John C. Green (Boulder, Colo.: Westview, 1991).

27. Welch, Leege, Wald, and Kellstedt, "Are the Sheep Hearing the Shepherds?"

28. Rosenstone and Hansen, *Mobilization,* chap. 3.

29. Guth and Green, *The Bible and the Ballot Box,* chap. 12.

The Christian Right in the Republican Party: The Case of Pat Robertson's Supporters

John C. Green
James L. Guth

The candidacy of Rev. Marion "Pat" Robertson for the 1988 Republican presidential nomination poses important questions about the role of conservative Christians in the Republican party. Conventional wisdom claims the Robertson campaign is doomed to one or another kind of failure, either by fracturing the GOP or fading into obscurity (Edsall, 1987). Even the potential for realignment among conservative Christians is seen as unproductive, creating intense demands for unpopular issues or a quarrelsome new bloc in the Republican coalition. Indeed, to many observers the Christian Right represents the newest wave of Republican "purists": activists willing to risk electoral defeat rather than compromise on important issues or cooperate with the more pragmatic party "professionals."

Our study of Republican presidential activists offers a broader assessment: some remarkable similarities between Robertson's key supporters and more conventional Republicans suggests the eventual assimilation of Christian activists into the GOP. Whatever friction the Robertson campaign generates within the party, and it could be intense, may well preview sharper conflict between Republicans and Democrats over "traditional values."

The Politics of the Christian Right

The advent of the "New Christian Right" in the late 1970s produced a heated debate over its size, organization and political impact. To this point, scholarship suggests that Christian conservatives have neither the numbers nor the unity allies hoped for and foes feared (Sigelman, Wilcox and Buell, 1986; Guth and Green, 1987a). And despite impressive grass-roots activism, the Christian Right's political impact has been modest: while some observers credit Christian conservatives with adding to President Reagan's margin of victory in 1980 and 1984 (Smidt, 1985) and with influencing Congress on social issues (Johnson and Tamney, 1985), others dispute these claims, pointing to alliances with larger, more moderate groups as the basis for any success (Hertzke, 1986; Wald, 1987, ch. 6). The question of political impact aside, however, most analysts believe that Christian activists have become increasingly involved in the Republican party, where they are reminiscent of the Goldwater and Reagan insurgencies of the last two decades (Smidt, 1986; Baker, Steed and Moreland, 1986; Guth, 1985–86). Thus, Pat Robertson's presidential bid represents a new, and perhaps inevitable, stage of political activity. To be credible, the Christian Right must have some influence in Republican politics, and, beyond credibility, a major role within the GOP is a prerequisite for influencing public policy.

At the risk of oversimplification, several roles suggest themselves. Most obviously, the Christian Right might act as a pressure group in Republican politics, much as the Right to Life movement and other "single issue" groups have done in both parties (Hershey, 1984). Pat Robertson might well be a "charismatic" Ellen McCormick. In addition to pressure politics, the Robertson campaign might solidify conservative Christians as a distinctive Republican constituency. While the Democrats are better known for "ethnic" blocs, Northern evangelical Protestants were once such a Republican constituency (Kleppner, 1985).

Beyond constituency building, Christian activists might be assimilated into the ideological alignment in the GOP, complementing and bolstering the Republican right. Both major parties have recently experienced an influx of new kinds of ideologues via presidential politics, and "confessional" conservatism may be compatible with other strains of conservatism crystallized by recent Republican candidates (Blumenthal, 1986). Of course, these roles are not mutually exclusive: we will present some evidence for all three, though the latter is most clearly indicated.

Data and Methods

This essay is based on data drawn from a mail survey of contributors to state and national GOP committees and to multi-candidate PACs sponsored by prominent presidential hopefuls. The survey instrument was a 10-page, 426-item questionnaire designed to distinguish among varieties of Republicans (Guth and Green, 1987b). a stratified random sample of 3400 donors was drawn from the records of the Federal Election Commission in August 1986. The survey was conducted between September 1986 and June 1987, producing 1145 usable questionnaires, for a return rate of 37% (excluding 275 forms returned as undeliverable). There was no serious response bias by gender or region, but the Robertson donors responded at a slightly higher rate than other contributors (44%).

To explore the relationship of Christian Right activists to the GOP, we divide the sample into four categories: donors to Robertson's Committee for Freedom, the base of his pre-nomination campaign (n = 143); donors to a New Right PAC, Citizens for the Republic, founded by Ronald Reagan and the launching pad for his 1990 nomination drive (n = 132); donors to Republican party committees, such as the Republican National Committee, the House and Senate Campaign Committees and seventeen state party committees (n = 400); and lastly, donors to the PACs of other Republican presidential hopefuls, including Bush's Fund for America's Future, Baker's Republican Majority Fund, Dole's Campaign America, Kemp's Campaign for Prosperity and the Pete DuPont for President Committee (n = 451) (cf. Miller and Jennings, 1986).

In tables 6.1–6.5 we compare the Robertson donors to the other categories of Republican contributors. In each table the first column contains correlation coefficients associated with cross-tabulations of the four donor categories (Robertson followed by Reagan, Republican party and other candidate donors) and each of the independent variables. (Because of the skewed distribution of the marginals on the opinion questions, gamma was chosen for the correlation coefficient.) The second column on each table ("Robertson vs. Republicans") contains standardized structure coefficients of the principal multiple discriminant function using all four donor categories (in the same order as above) and the independent variables (Klecka, 1980). In the last column, multiple discriminant analysis is applied to the Robertson and Reagan donors only. All independent variables have been coded so that positive coefficients indicate higher scores for the Robertson donors; higher scores generally represent more conservative positions or attributes associated with conservatism (see appendix for coding).

Measures of salience, ideology, demography and partisanship usually vary systematically across our donor categories, as shown by the gammas in each table. And as the canonical correlations indicate, there are significant differences between the Robertson donors and other categories of Republicans when all variables are taken into account. Comparison with the Reagan donors indicate where the largest differences occur between Robertson and other right-wing Republicans.

Agenda and Opinion Cleavages

Many observers believe the Christian Right has brought a new agenda and ideological edge to the GOP (cf. Green and Guth, 1986). Social and foreign policy issues are seen as central to this agenda, contrasting sharply with the economic concerns of mainstream Republicans. Such differences in priorities are a prerequisite, and indeed the motivation, for pressure groups in party politics.

We approached the agenda question from two different angles. First, we asked donors to name the most important problem facing the country. As the gammas and discriminant coefficients in table 6.1 show, the Robertson donors do have a strikingly different agenda than even the Reagan loyalists. A majority of the Robertson donors name a social problem, as opposed to less than a fifth of the Reagan donors and even fewer GOP and candidate contributors. The other Republican activists clearly perceive economic problems as most salient, and surprisingly, are twice as likely to name a foreign policy problem as Robertson's supporters.

A slightly different perspective, however, is provided by respondents' assessment of how much specific issues influence their vote (table 6.1). Concern for social issues, especially pornography, school prayer and abortion, most clearly differentiate the Robertson donors. However, on economic issues, and to a lesser extent foreign policy, there are fewer and smaller differences. Indeed, only on inflation do the mainstream Republicans show markedly greater concern. Thus, Christian activists have an expanded—not a foreshortened—agenda.

Salience measures do not, of course, reveal activists' stances on the issues. If Robertson donors have a "compleat" conservative shopping list, do their attitudes conform to the conservative line? Much analysis of the Christian Right stresses the economic populism or even liberalism of the conservative religious community (Shafer, 1985). Does this caveat apply to the Robertson activists?

Apparently it does not. The ideological profile of Robertson donors is

TABLE 6.1
Issue Salience: Most Important Problem and Influence on Vote

	Robertson vs. Republicans (Gamma)	Robertson vs. Republicans (Discriminant)	Robertson vs. Reagan Only (Discriminant)
Most Important National Problem	.36*	.39	.32
Much Influence on Voting:			
Pornography	.41*	.32	.27
School Prayer	.38*	.35	.45
Abortion	.33*	.30	.48
Drug Enforcement	.29*	.21	.25
Nicaragua	.26*	.17	−.11
Defense Spending	.24*	.09	−.21
USSR Policy	.17*	.11	−.07
Affirmative Action	.10*	.13	.04
Arms Control	.06	.19	.07
Tax Rates	.02	.09	−.03
Budget Deficit	.02	.14	.23
Trade Restrictions	.01	.04	.05
Interest Rates	−.01	−.03	−.05
Unemployment	−.08	−.16	.05
Inflation	−.12*	−.35	−.32
Canonical Correlation	—	.68	.53

Positive signs indicate Robertson donors have higher scores.
*Chi square = p<.05 level. For all discriminant functions p<.05. See appendix for variable codings.

consistently conservative. As table 6.2 shows, there are few major differences between the Robertson donors and other Republicans on economic issues in either the bivariate or multivariate analysis. Indeed, where a gap exists, Robertson donors are often to the right. For example, they are more enthusiastic about the gold standard (even more than Kemp donors) and are far more concerned about the federal deficit (particularly compared to Reagan donors).

Large divisions do appear on social issues, where the Robertson donors are much more conservative than other Republicans. As the discriminant coefficients indicate, however, the most important differences are on school prayer and sexual issues: public provision of birth control, abortion and regulation of adult sexual behavior. Indeed, Reagan and party donors are markedly more moderate on these issues and candidate donors dramatically so; for example, a quarter of the Reagan activists and nearly

TABLE 6.2
Opinion Cleavages: Ideology and Issue Positions

	Robertson vs. Republicans (Gamma)	Robertson vs. Republicans (Discriminant)	Robertson vs. Reagan Only (Discriminant)
Anti Birth Control	.50*	.35	.24
Anti Abortion on Demand	.47*	.39	.39
Anti United Nations	.40*	.26	.19
Self-identified Ideology	.37*	.25	−.11
Regulate Adult Sex	.38*	.49	.41
Pro Drug Enforcement	.35*	.06	.06
Anti Pornography	.35*	.13	.11
Pro Gold Standard	.33*	.26	.22
Pro Star Wars Deployment	.31*	.06	.01
Anti Affirmative Action	.24*	.03	.01
Anti Arms Control	.22*	.24	.08
Pro School Prayer	.23*	.33	.22
Pro Contra Aid	.18*	.11	−.23
Pro Afghan Resistance	.16*	.05	−.04
Restrict Immigration	.13*	.01	.07
Anti S. Africa Sanctions	.13*	.17	−.26
Anti Federal Deficit	.08*	.13	.31
Anti Aid to Business	.06*	.09	.16
Pro Trade Restrictions	.07*	.07	.05
Pro Poland Sanctions	.03	.01	−.18
Pro Supply Side Tax	.04	.15	−.25
Pro Tight Money Policy	.05	.01	.02
Pro Flat Tax	.02	.06	−.14
Inflation over Jobs	−.02	−.18	−.14
Canonical Correlation	—	.57	.55

Positive signs indicate Robertson donors have higher scores.
*Chi square = p<.05 level. For all discriminant functions p<.05. See appendix for variable codings.

half of the candidate donors accept abortion on demand compared to 3% of the Robertson supporters. Robertson donors are also very conservative on foreign policy, from leaving the United Nations to deploying Star Wars, when compared to the party and candidate contributors, though Reagan's supporters are often the most conservative on such issues.

Thus, the Christian Right could well function as a pressure group in the GOP, but the pressure would be on a broad front. While social issues are far more salient to the Robertson elite, these priorities do not

preclude concern for economic and foreign policy issues equal to that of
more conventional Republicans. And social traditionalism is combined
with economic and foreign policy conservatism every bit as intense.
Indeed, there is a striking lack of symmetry in these cleavages: the
Christian Right is even more consistently conservative than the other
New Right activists, who display more moderation on, and less concern
for, social issues.

Religious and Social Cleavages

The agenda and ideological leanings of Robertson activists may well be
rooted in demographic traits, creating a distinctive "Christian" constituency in the GOP. The common assumption is that the Christian Right
threatens GOP unity by introducing social heterogeneity (Freeman,
1986). Some analysts, however, have found few social differences between
Christian Rightists and conventional Republican activists: a slight bias in
favor of rural and Southern origins, lower levels of education, and sharply
higher levels of religiosity (Hauss and Maisel, 1986).

Do "evangelical Christians" indeed confront a "three-martini, country
club set" in the Republican party? In one sense, yes: the Robertson
contingent displays an intense and distinctive religiosity. As the gammas
in table 6.3 indicate, they are more likely to accept a liberal interpretation
of the Bible, believe in an afterlife, consider religion important to their
lives and regularly attend church services in conservative denominations.
They are also more likely to have changed denominations in an unusual
way, moving "downward" from mainline to charismatic churches. In
addition, they exhibit greater support for "civil religion," believing that
God has blessed America above other nations and that religion should
play an important role in politics.

Other Republicans, including the Reagan donors, are progressively
less devout, with substantial minorities regarding the Bible as a collection
of fables, rejecting notions of an afterlife and rarely darkening a church
door—at least not of a Protestant church. Very few have changed
denominations, and when they have, it was in the more common "upward" direction, from sectarian to mainline churches. And even fewer
are willing to recognize a special role for religious beliefs or churches
in politics.

However, as the discriminant coefficients indicate, Republicans are
hardly a secular lot. When all religiosity measures are taken into account,
most differentiate poorly. Indeed, the Robertson donors are distin-

TABLE 6.3
Religiosity and Demography

	Robertson vs. Republicans (Gamma)	Robertson vs. Republicans (Discriminant)	Robertson vs. Reagan Only (Discriminant)
Religiosity			
Biblical Literalism	.50*	.13	.23
Life After Death	.40*	.11	.12
Religious Salience	.38*	.04	.16
Denomination	.35*	.13	.16
Church Attendance	.30*	.03	.08
Denomination Change	.28*	.18	.21
Religious Self-Identification			
Charismatic	.80*	.55	.52
Born Again	.77*	.35	.27
Evangelical	.75*	.04	.13
Fundamentalist	.53*	.04	.03
Other	−.42*	−.10	.02
Mainline	−.28*	−.23	−.11
Conservative	−.23*	−.08	−.09
Civil Religion			
God Blessed America	.40*	.15	.13
Religion Influences Vote	.40*	.24	.12
Churches in Politics	.31*	.19	.16
Demography			
Income	−.37*	−.16	−.14
Sex	−.32*	−.16	−.14
Education	−.22*	−.22	−.11
Size of Place	−.16*	−.09	−.08
Region	.13*	.08	.17
Age	−.11*	−.13	−.38
Occupation	−.06*	−.04	−.05
Canonical Correlation	—	.84	.84

Positive signs indicate Robertson donors have higher scores.
*Chi square = p<.05 level. For all discriminant functions p<.05. See appendix for variable codings.

guished best by their strong self-identification as "charismatic" Christians, paralleling Robertson's sectarian background. Even the impact of "civil religion" is reduced. Thus, the Robertson activists by and large represent one segment of conservative Protestantism while most other Republicans partake of more conventional, mainline Protestantism (Reichley, 1985).

The demography of Robertson activists differs modestly from other donors in ways consistent with their greater religiosity (cf. Conover, 1983). While their incomes are quite impressive, Robertson's donors are less affluent than other Republicans. They are less well educated and include twice as many women as the other groups. They are also somewhat more likely to come from rural areas and the South, and are somewhat younger, particularly compared to Reagan's supporters.

Of course, social differences may be muted by the nature of our sample, since campaign contributors are social elites by most definitions. Nevertheless, Robertson activists are clearly in the correct party: most would be greatly out of place among Democratic donors (Guth and Green, 1986). The Robertson supporters are not so much a distinctive constituency as the more traditional members of social groups long attracted to the GOP.

The Christian Right in the GOP

Given the limited, yet intense, ideological and religious distinctiveness of Robertson's supporters, how strong is their attachment to the GOP? In fact, they have looser ties than the Reagan or party donors—but, as it turns out, equal to those of other candidate donors. And Robertson donors are much less likely to be "Strong Republicans" at the state and local level, a trend which appears with less clarity among other Republicans (table 6.4). They are also far less positive in their evaluation of Republican leaders—with the exception of President Reagan—when compared to other Republicans. These findings hint that for many activists, national personages and issues rather than more parochial concerns influence attachment to party. Robertson's candidacy may represent just such a phenomenon for Christian Rightists.

In fact, the Robertson donors, like other Republicans, seem to have been drawn to the GOP by their special issues. We asked respondents how strongly they agreed with Republican policy on key issues, and their responses mirror our asymmetrical findings on agenda and ideology (table 6.4). The Robertson contributors are more satisfied with Republican policy on most social and foreign policy issues, but differ only modestly on GOP economic policies, even when partisanship is controlled. While not as satisfied as the Reagan donors, they often exceed the party and candidate donors by large margins. Thus, approval of party economic stands links the Christian Right and the GOP regulars, though the latter are less enthusiastic about the party's social and foreign policies.

TABLE 6.4
Partisan Attachments: Identification, Leaders and Issue Positions

	Robertson vs. Republicans (Gamma)	Robertson vs. Republicans (Discriminant)	Robertson vs. Reagan Only (Discriminant)
Partisanship			
Natl Self-Identification	−.15*	−.15	−.20
Local Self-Identification	−.07*	−.07	−.11
Party Leaders			
President Reagan	.31*	.50	−.18
Natl GOP Party Leaders	−.08*	−.19	−.45
State GOP Leaders	−.11*	−.33	−.13
Local GOP Party Leaders	−.08*	−.01	−.10
Senate GOP Leaders	−.03*	−.24	−.10
House GOP Leaders	−.01*	−.19	−.06
Support GOP Policy on:			
Abortion	.36*	.46	.94
School Prayer	.29*	.15	.22
Pornography	.29*	.13	.17
Affirmative Action	.22*	.09	.23
Nicaragua	.21*	.41	−.12
Arms Control	.20*	.26	−.10
Defense Spending	.18*	.08	−.02
Drug Enforcement	.18*	.01	−.22
USSR Policy	.16*	.13	−.46
Budget Deficits	.13*	.09	−.09
Trade Restrictions	.12*	.21	−.02
Unemployment	.10*	.13	−.37
Interest Rates	.09*	.04	−.02
Tax Rates	.06*	−.03	−.06
Inflation	.01*	−.18	−.07
Canonical Correlation	—	.48	.40

Positive signs indicate Robertson donors have higher scores.
*Chi square = p<.05 level. For all discriminant functions p<.05. See appendix for variable codings.

These findings raise two other questions: first, are Robertson's followers new to politics and, second, are they newcomers to the GOP? Both assertions are frequently made by journalists and scholars—and both are partially true. Almost 30% of the Robertson donors report becoming active in the last ten years compared to 7 to 12% of the other groups. A similar situation holds for partisanship. Although stand-pat Republicans are a plurality in each camp, Robertson's adherents are the most frequent party switchers: 19% are Democratic and 16% Independent converts for a total of 35%, compared with 30%, 27% and 26% for the Reagan, party and candidate donors, respectively. And the Robertson donors are no less likely to vote Republican in presidential elections, matching closely the 90% support level of other donors. The only exceptions are the 25% who voted for fellow evangelical Jimmy Carter in 1976, and for Lyndon Johnson in 1964—when comparable numbers of other Republicans defected as well. Thus, Robertson has mobilized activists who have always been at least "proto-Republicans."

Given their growing attachment to the GOP, do the Robertson people fit into the long-standing GOP factional divisions (Reichley, 1982)? Generally speaking, yes: as a group the Robertson donors are, and have been, strongly attracted to the Republican right. We asked contributors to specify their active preferences in Republican pre-convention struggles since 1952, and as table 6.5 indicates, Robertson activists were more supportive of conservative candidates as far back as 1964, even when other measures of factionalism are taken into account. Indeed, only the Reagan donors show greater consistency.

In the present, the Robertson donors are more fully aligned with right-wing politicians and groups than the Reagan donors (table 6.5). They report greater proximity to Jack Kemp, Jesse Helms and Pat Robertson himself. The other Republican contributors progressively prefer more moderate candidates, such as Bush, Baker and former President Ford. Much the same can be said for proximity to GOP interest group allies. The Robertson donors strongly prefer New Right groups: the Moral Majority, Eagle Forum and Right to Life movement. Other Republicans, including the Reagan donors, prefer business groups, such as the National Association of Manufacturers, Chamber of Commerce and American Bar Association.

Note, however, that Robertson is by far the most divisive leader and the Moral Majority, emblematic of the entire Christian Right, is the most divisive group. Large numbers of other Republicans, including the Reagan donors, hold negative evaluations of the Christian Right—a level of hostility the Robertson donors do not extend to more mainstream leaders and interests. This lack of symmetry, reminiscent of our findings on salience and attitudes, is also revealed in donor preferences for the 1988 GOP nomination. Robertson's donors overwhelmingly pick him as their first choice (84%), but he receives virtually no backing from the Reagan (6%), party or candidate donors (less than 1%). Nor does he pick up support from donors' second and third choices (about 2% across the board), though his supporters' subsequent choices include

TABLE 6.5
GOP Factionalism: Nominees, Politicians and Interest Groups

	Robertson vs. Republicans (Gamma)	Robertson vs. Republicans (Discriminant)	Robertson vs. Reagan Only (Discriminant)
Supported Right-Wing Candidate for:			
1980 GOP Nomination	.32 *	.18	−.17
1976 GOP Nomination	.34 *	.12	−.12
1968 GOP Nomination	.20 *	.01	−.05
1964 GOP Nomination	.33 *	.14	−.29
1952 GOP Nomination	.10 *	.11	−.19
Close to Politicians			
Robertson	.64 *	.83	.78
Helms	.39 *	.21	−.19
Kemp	.12 *	.26	−.33
Dole	−.11 *	−.05	−.18
Bush	−.14 *	−.14	−.27
Baker	−.15 *	−.19	.01
Ford	−.18 *	−.20	−.26
Close to Groups			
Moral Majority	.48 *	.25	.06
Eagle Forum	.45 *	.29	.07
Right to Life	.41 *	.23	.18
NCPAC	.19 *	.17	−.36
Natl Assn Manufacturers	−.06 *	−.08	−.18
Chamber of Commerce	−.06 *	−.06	−.23
American Bar Assn	−.16 *	−.19	−.11
Political "Purism"			
Compromise is Betrayal	.31 *	.05	.08
Controversial Platforms	.12 *	.06	.09
Pluralistic Parties	.11 *	.06	.06
Canonical Correlation	—	.82	.74

Positive signs indicate Robertson donors have higher scores.
*Chi square = p<.05 level. For all discriminant functions p<.05. See appendix for variable codings.

moderate (27%) and conservative (30%) candidates. Also, significant numbers of other Republicans claim they could not support Robertson on the GOP ticket under any circumstances. In contrast, 71% of the Robertson donors claim there is no Republican nominee they could not support.

Full participation of the Robertson donors in internal party politics may be hindered by their lesser commitment to the conventional rules of

coalition building, however. Past insurgent movements in the GOP have
been characterized by "purists" (Polsby and Wildavsky, 1968), activists
whose commitment to political principles over electoral success produced
conflict with the more pragmatic and instrumental party "professionals."
Classic purist traits include refusal to compromise on issues, willingness
to take controversial platform stands, and distaste for pluralism within
the GOP. Robertson donors show such tendencies to a greater extent
than do other Republicans (table 6.5), reinforcing factional alignments
with differences in political style.

However, as the discriminant coefficients indicate, once other measures
of factionalism are taken into account, Robertson donors are only
modestly more purist than other right-wing Republicans. Hence, Robertson's backers are likely to reinforce existing divisions between purists
and professionals within the GOP rather than create new ones. And
participation in party affairs may render the Robertson donors less
"pure." It is worth noting that representatives of the most recent GOP
insurgency, the Reagan donors, show somewhat greater professionalism
than Robertson's supporters, perhaps the result of their longer sojourn
in party politics.

Thus, Robertson's followers are by and large caught up with their
own candidate who represents their special priorities, attitudes and
background. Still, taking into account agenda, ideology and demography, Robertson's activists are enough like other Republicans to suggest
their eventual assimilation into the right wing of the GOP.

Conclusions

Our findings support the conventional wisdom on the Robertson candidacy on several points—and offer counterpoints as well. Clearly, Robertson is a divisive force in the GOP, even for New Right activists, having
yet to attract significant support beyond his own special following. The
Robertson campaign could well be a bitter one, pitting a small group of
intense, religious "purists" against a mass of equally hostile "professional" moderates. A general conflagration may be averted largely by the
limited appeal of the Christian Right's social agenda.

Thus, immediate accommodation with mainstream Republicans is unlikely, unless it comes from conservative Christians themselves. Even if
other GOP influentials could be pressured to accept further platform
concessions, electoral realities will militate against such a move. The
Christian Right differs from mainstream Republicans precisely where

GOP differs most from the Democrats and the public at large: sexual regulation and intervention abroad. And Christian Right activists are neither distinct enough demographically nor independent enough in partisan terms to be effective on the periphery of the GOP.

If short-run prospects for harmony are dim, the future appears brighter. Many characteristics of the Robertson donors suggest that assimilation into the GOP is possible and likely. On the economic issues the Robertson and regular Republicans are in agreement—the very issues on which the GOP has recently competed successfully with the Democrats for votes. Further, the cleavages between the Rightists and Republicans are not symmetrical: the latter are far more hostile to Robertson's candidacy, issue-positions and agenda than Robertson's followers are to mainstream Republicanism. In addition, Robertson donors show considerable attachment to the GOP and a willingness to support other candidates if his campaign fails. And political experience may enhance their willingness to compromise and cooperate. The Reagan donors are perhaps an example of this kind of political maturation: while they belong to a distinct faction in the GOP, their partisanship and "professionalism" rivals that of the party regulars, far exceeding that of the followers of other candidates.

Hence, the full impact of the Robertson campaign may not be felt for many years, as Christian conservatives become part of the Republican right, and perhaps the party establishment. Like Ronald Reagan and "movement" conservatism, the Christian Right may find the GOP a more effective vehicle for organization and a more efficacious channel for political activity. If so, Republicans will be further identified with "traditional values," and given the secular drift of Democrats, sharper partisan conflict will ensue.

Appendix: Variable Codings

Table 6.1

MOST IMPORTANT NATIONAL PROBLEM: dichotomous variable
1 = social issue, 0 = other issues
INFLUENCE ON VOTE: five point scales
5 = very important to vote, 1 = not important

Table 6.2

SELF-IDENTIFIED IDEOLOGY: seven point scale
7 = extremely conservative, 1 = extremely liberal

ALL ISSUE QUESTIONS: seven point scales
7 = most conservative position, 1 = most liberal position

Table 6.3

BIBLICAL LITERALISM: three point scale
3 = Bible literally true, 2 = Bible inspired,
1 = Bible a book of fables
LIFE AFTER DEATH: seven point scale
7 = believe in afterlife, 1 = do not believe in afterlife
RELIGIOUS SALIENCE: seven point scale
7 = religion very important, 1 = religion not important
DENOMINATION: nine point scale
9 = charismatic churches, 8 = fundamentalist, 7 = evangelical,
6 = Lutherans and Presbyterians, 5 = Methodists, 4 = Other mainline,
3 = Roman Catholics, 2 = Jews, 1 = None
CHURCH ATTENDANCE: seven point scale
7 = more than once a week, 1 = seldom or never
DENOMINATIONAL CHANGE: dichotomous variable
1 = move to more sectarian denomination, 0 = to mainline or no change
RELIGIOUS SELF-IDENTIFICATION: dichotomous variable
1 = checked identification, 0 = did not (multiple answers possible)
CIVIL RELIGION: seven point scale
7 = strongly agree, 1 = strongly disagree
INCOME: 1 = less than $15,000 a year, 7 = over $500,000 a year
SEX: 1 = male, 0 = female
EDUCATION: 1 = less than twelve years, 7 = postgraduate degree
SIZE OF PLACE: 1 = rural, 9 = suburb of city of 250,000 or more
REGION: 1 = South, 0 = non-South
AGE: 1 = under 35, 4 = over 65
OCCUPATION: 1 = blue-collar, clerical, farm, 2 = small business,
3 = corporate officials, 4 = professionals

Table 6.4

SELF-IDENTIFIED PARTISANSHIP: seven point scales
7 = strong Republican, 1 = strong Democrat
PARTY LEADER EVALUATIONS: seven point scales
7 = very good job, 1 = very poor job
SUPPORT FOR GOP POLICIES: five point scales
7 = strongly agree with policy, 1 = strongly disagree

Table 6.5

GOP NOMINATION PREFERENCES: dichotomous variables
1 = supported conservative candidate, 0 = supported other candidates
PROXIMITY TO POLITICIANS: five point scales
5 = feel very close, 1 = feel very far
PROXIMITY TO INTEREST GROUPS: seven point scales
7 = feel very close, 1 = feel very far
PURISM MEASURES: seven point scales
7 = strongly agree, 1 = strongly disagree

Note

An earlier version of this chapter was presented at the annual meeting of the Midwest Political Science Association in Chicago, April 9–11, 1987. We would like to thank the anonymous reviewers for their helpful comments and Sharon B. Smith, our Dana Research Fellow, for her invaluable assistance. Financial support for this project was provided by the American Political Science Research Grant Program and Furman University.

References

Baker, Tod A., Robert P. Steed, and Laurence W. Moreland. 1986. The Emergence of the Religious Right and the Development of the Two-Party System in the South. Presented at the annual meeting of the American Political Science Association, Washington, D.C.

Blumenthal, Sidney. 1986. *The Rise of the Counter-Establishment*. Times Books: New York.

Conover, Pamela Johnston. 1983. The Mobilization of the New Right: A Test of Various Explanations. *Western Political Quarterly*, 36: 632–49.

Edsall, Thomas. 1987. The Political Impasse. *New York Review of Books*, 34: 8–14.

Freeman, Jo. 1986. The Political Culture of Democrats and Republicans. *Political Science Quarterly*, 101: 327–44.

Green, John C., and James L. Guth. 1986. Big Bucks and Petty Cash: Party and Interest Group Activists in American Politics. In Allan Cigler and Burdett Loomis, eds., *Interest Group Politics*, 2d ed. Washington: CQ Press.

Guth, James L. 1985–86. Political Converts: Partisan Realignment Among Southern Baptist Ministers. *Election Politics*, 3: 2–6.

Guth, James L., and John C. Green. 1986. Faith and Politics: Religion and Ideology Among Political Contributors. *American Politics Quarterly*, 14: 186–99.

————. 1987a. The Moralizing Minority: Christian Right Support Among Political Contributors. *Social Science Quarterly*, 67: 598–610.

————1987b. Robertson's Republicans: Christian Activists in the GOP. *Election Politics*, 4: 9–14.

Hauss, Charles S., and L. Sandy Maisel. 1986. Extremist Delegates: Myth and Reality. In Ronald B. Rapoport et al., eds., *The Life of the Parties*. Lexington: University Press of Kentucky.

Hershey, Marjorie R. 1984. *Running for Office*. Chatham, NJ: Chatham House.

Hertzke, Allen D. 1986. Representing God in Washington: The Role of Religious Lobbies in the American Polity. Unpublished Ph.D. dissertation, University of Wisconsin-Madison.

Johnson, Stephen D., and Joseph B. Tamney. 1985. The Christian Right and the 1984 Presidential Election. *Review of Religious Research*, 27: 124–33.

Klecka, William. 1980. *Discriminant Analysis*. Beverly Hills: Sage.

Kleppner, Paul. 1985. *The Third Party System, 1853–1892*. Chapel Hill: University of North Carolina Press.

Miller, Warren E., and M. Kent Jennings. 1986. *Parties in Transition: A Longitudinal Study of Party Elites and Party Supporters*. New York: Russell Sage.

Polsby, Nelson, and Aaron Wildavsky. 1968. *Presidential Elections: Strategies of American Electoral Politics*. New York: Scribner's.

Reichley, James. 1982. The Reagan Coalition. *The Brookings Review*, 1: 6–9.

————1985. *Religion in American Public Life*. Washington: Brookings.

Shafer, Byron E. 1985. The New Cultural Politics. *PS*, 28: 221–31.

Sigelman, Lee, Clyde Wilcox, and Emmett Buell. 1986. An Unchanging Minority: Popular Support for the Moral Majority, 1980 and 1984. Presented at the annual meeting of the Society for the Scientific Study of Religion, Washington, D.C.

Smidt, Corwin. 1985. Evangelicals and the 1984 Elections: Continuity or Change? Presented at the annual meeting of the Society for the Scientific Study of Religion, Savannah.

————. 1986. The Partisanship of American Evangelicals: Changing Patterns Over the Past Decade. Presented at the annual meeting of the Society for the Scientific Study of Religion, Washington, D.C.

Stark, R., and C. Y. Glock. 1970. *American Piety: The Nature of Religious Commitment*. Berkeley: University of California Press.

Wald, Kenneth. 1987. *Religion and Politics in the United States*. New York: St. Martin's.

Faith and Election: The Christian Right in Congressional Campaigns 1978–1988

John C. Green
James L. Guth
Kevin Hill

The United States House of Representatives has long been a target of social movements: the "people's house" combines enticing proximity to the grassroots with infuriatingly slow responses to new agendas. And given the candidate-centered nature of American politics, movements have strong incentives to become involved in congressional campaigns. In this article, we assess the involvement in recent congressional campaigns by a social movement of some notoriety, the Christian Right. Overall, we find that the movement was most active, and apparently most successful, where the motivations, resources, and opportunities for political action converged. In politics, unlike religion, faith does not guarantee election, but neither do movements live by good works alone.

Theoretical Perspectives on the Christian Right

The advent of the Christian Right in the late 1970s produced an extensive literature on its origins, public support, and national activities, but little systematic evidence on its involvement in campaigns below the presidential level (Guth et al. 1988). In this literature, we can identify three important theoretical perspectives, those emphasizing, respectively: (1) the "demand" for Christian Right activism by discontented populations; (2) the "supply" of resources for such activism by religious organizations; and (3) "strategic choice" in the deployment of such resources by movement leaders.

Each of these perspectives identifies a different locale and type of Christian Right involvement in congressional campaigns, although they are not mutually exclusive and all three may be necessary for a full account of the movement (Oberschall 1973). The demand perspective suggests that activism should arise in areas with traditionalist demography and should be characterized by candidacies of movement members. The supply perspective suggests that activism should appear where religious institutions are strong and should be characterized by local movement organizations supporting the most congenial, mainstream candidates. Finally, the strategic choice perspective suggests that activism should occur in electorally competitive areas and should be characterized by national movement organizations supporting the most viable candidates.

1. The Demand for the Christian Right in Congressional Campaigns. The most common approach to the Christian Right stresses the reaction of social traditionalists to the processes of modernization. Students of "status politics" and "politics of life-style concern" view the Christian Right as the latest attempt by parochial populations to defend status threatened by social change and relieve accompanying anxieties (Lipset and Rabb 1978; Patel, Pilant, and Rose 1985). Christian Right activism should thus occur where discontented traditionalists "demand" political action, much as consumers demand goods in the marketplace.

Measuring such demand is not an easy task, however. Despite the pioneering efforts of Wald, Owen, and Hill (1989) to assess status threat directly, most researchers assume that remoteness from modernity is key to relevant discontent, and use demographic proxies instead, including older, rural, WASP, low-income, blue-collar, and poorly educated populations (Lipset and Rabb 1978). Other analysts locate such discontent at the point of contact between traditionalists and modern society, such as rapidly growing suburban areas in culturally conservative regions (Ammerman 1987).

While such demand could be met in many ways, the most direct responses are campaigns by "members" of the movement itself: self-starting amateur enthusiasts who embody the motivating discontents. Indeed, such protest candidacies occur frequently in American politics and are often connected with social movements. Thus, demand factors should be most closely associated with the candidacies of Christian Right members.

2. *The Supply of Christian Right Activism in Congressional Campaigns.* The major alternative perspective on the Christian Right stresses organization over discontent. While acknowledging the importance of demand factors, "resource mobilization" theorists see social movements as resulting from the redirection of preexisting organizations into politics by entrepreneurs (McCarthy and Zald 1977). Religious institutions have often been such an "institution constituency" for social movements (Salisbury 1989). Christian Right activism should thus occur where concentrations of religious organizations "supply" political action, much as firms supply goods in the marketplace.

There is some disagreement on the source of such supply, however. Some scholars emphasize the churches and membership of sectarian Protestant denominations, such as fundamentalists and charismatics, in mobilizing the Christian Right, while others point to the more moderate evangelical denominations (Liebman 1983; Wald, Owen, and Hill 1988). Still others argue that the movement relied heavily on preexisting political organizations, including secular conservative groups and, perhaps, the Republican party (Johnson and Bullock 1991).

While such resources may have many uses, the most direct use is their regular deployment in local politics: organizational imperatives to produce results and gain influence encourage local movement organizations to back the mainstream candidate most congenial to the movement's goals. Indeed, such grassroots constituencies are quite common in American politics and often appear in the wake of social movements. Thus, supply factors should be most closely associated with local Christian Right support for mainstream candidates.

3. *Strategic Choice by the Christian Right in Congressional Campaigns.* Although less often applied to the Christian Right, other scholars emphasize opportunity over discontent and organization. While mindful of demand and supply factors, students of "political opportunity structures" argue that social movements occur where there are good opportunities for political gain (McAdam 1982; Gamson 1975). Candidates with realistic but uncertain prospects of victory are central to such strategic considerations. Christian Right activism should thus occur where "strategic choice" has identified the best prospects for success, much as investors pursue the most profitable ventures in the marketplace.

Good electoral opportunities have been identified in different ways, however. Most scholars look to electoral competitiveness, both in general elections and primaries, as the best measure of opportunity, while others stress the chances of electing new personnel to office, such as open seat candidates and viable challengers (Jacobson and Kernell 1983; Welch

1979). Still others point to ideological mismatches between constituents and their representatives, such as districts with liberal incumbents that also voted for Ronald Reagan, the hero of the Christian Right (McAdams and Johannes 1987).

While strategic choice may have many manifestations, the most direct application is by national movement leaders, who have the knowledge to exploit good opportunities across the country. Indeed, movement leaders are frequently part of the political networks that handicap congressional races. Thus, strategic choice factors should be most closely associated with national Christian Right support of viable candidates in competitive races.

Despite their different predictions concerning Christian Right involvement in congressional campaigns, these perspectives are not mutually exclusive. For example, conservative Protestants could be a source of demand for the Christian Right, local organizations could engage in strategic calculation, and even the most pragmatic strategist could be influenced by deep-seated discontent. Indeed, all three perspectives may be necessary for a full account of Christian Right activism. Such an account would:

> firstly explain why there is a market for such a movement. Secondly, it should explain how potential supporters were sensitized, politicized, and mobilized . . . Thirdly, because neither leaders nor followers act in a vacuum, it will consider the social and political structure within which this mobilization took place (Bruce 1988, 24).

In fact, we find that such a convergence of motivations, resources, and opportunities best accounts for Christian Right involvement in congressional campaigns.

Data and Methods

Our study is based on evidence of Christian Right involvement in House campaigns from 1978 to 1988. The data were collected in an extensive search of published materials, ranging from standard news sources to a host of sectarian organs, internal documents from movement groups, and, in addition, 40 interviews with Christian Right activists, knowledgeable journalists, and officials of both major parties, conducted between 1987 and 1990. Only campaigns identified by two or more sources were included.

To test our theoretical expectations, all cases were assigned to three nominal categories. The first included candidates who were "members" of the Christian Right, defined as officers of movement groups, ministers in conservative Protestant churches, or self-advertised Christian rightists. The second category included candidates who received "local support" from grassroots Christian Right activists, but were themselves not directly associated with the movement. The final category included candidates who received "national support" from major Christian Right organizations but were neither tied to the movement directly nor supported by local activists. In the surprisingly few instances in which more than one kind of activism occurred in a particular campaign, we assigned cases to the "purer" category, e.g., a candidate who was a member and received national support was coded as a member. Alternative codings produced very similar results. All told, we found 443 instances of Christian Right activity in 171 House districts between 1978 and 1988, representing 39% of all districts and 8% of all campaigns. Of all the contests with Christian Right involvement, 23% were movement Right members, 26% drew local backing, and 51% gained national support.

We employed three sets of independent variables. First, we gathered demographic data from the 1980 census, expressed as a percentage of district population; region was coded for cultural conservatism. Second, we estimated church membership and church numbers in sectarian (fundamentalist and charismatic) and other evangelical Protestant denominations for each district, using the 1980 Glenmary Research Center study (Quinn et al. 1982).[1] And third, we used standard information on congressional elections: margin of victory in general and primary elections, candidate status (incumbent, challenger, open seat), challenger viability (measured by having at least 75% of the money available to incumbent foes), election outcome (won election, won nomination, no success), vote for Reagan in 1980 and 1984, and Christian Voice Moral Government scores for House members, 1977–1988.

These last two variables were used to calculate a crude measure of ideological mismatch between constituents and their representatives. For each district, the mean Christian Voice score was subtracted from the mean percentage vote for Reagan in 1980 and 1984. In this variable, large positive values indicate that a constituency's support for Reagan was much larger than its representative's support for the Christian Right agenda, while large negative values suggest the opposite, namely, that a representative was more conservative than his constituency. Values near zero reveal a close match between constituents' and their representatives' ideology.

Given our nominal dependent variables, we were limited to comparing districts with Christian Right activism (and the three forms of involvement) to those without such activism, and for this purpose we used logistic regression. Since year-by-year results were very similar, the data were pooled for the entire period.[2]

The Christian Right in Congressional Campaigns

What explains the locale and type of Christian Right activism in House campaigns? Table 7.1 tests the relative impact of the demand, supply, and strategic choice factors on the incidence of activism, first for all districts combined, and then for those with member candidacies, local backing, and national support.

The first and most important finding is negative: most of the demographic measures identified by the demand perspective do not perform as expected. Measures of blue-collar, rural, and WASP population are never statistically significant, while other variables including poorly educated, low-income, and older populations have negative signs, both overall and for districts with local and national Christian Right support. Only districts with member candidacies fit the expected patterns for lower social status and age.

On the other hand, all three types of involvement exhibit a more common demographic pattern: positive coefficients for population growth and suburban population. Together with positive signs for regional conservatism, these data paint a striking picture: Christian Right activism occurred predominantly in rapidly growing—and relatively prosperous—suburban areas in the South, Southwest, and Midwest. Interestingly, this pattern is strongest for districts with local and national Christian Right involvement.

Although we are aware of the limitations of aggregate data analysis, these findings suggest that Christian Right activism drew on higher-status traditionalists confronting modern society directly, rather than their lower-status brethren left behind in the hinterland. This conclusion comports well with surveys of Christian Right activists (Green and Guth 1988) and with many accounts of the movement's origin (Wald 1990). Although low-status and parochial voters may have been the ultimate targets, the "effective" demand for the Christian Right came from critics deeply enmeshed in modern life.

Our findings for religious variables identified by the supply perspective are consistent with expectations. Sectarian Protestants and their churches

TABLE 7.1
Christian Right (CR) Activism in Congressional Campaigns 1978–1988
Logistic Regression***

	Districts with CR Activism	Districts with CR Members	Districts with Local CR Support	Districts with Nat'l CR Support
Demographic Factors				
% Blue Collar	−.01	−.02	−.00	−.03
% Low Education	−.04*	.05*	−.08*	−.09**
% Low Income	−.05**	.06*	−.07*	−.10**
% Older	−.19**	.06*	−.08*	−.10**
% Rural	.02	.04	.02	−.01
% WASP Stock	.02	.04	.02	−.00
% Population Change	.03**	.01*	.02**	.05*
% Suburban	.13**	.05**	.12**	.14**
Region	.10**	.11**	.15**	.18**
Religious Factors				
Sectarian Protestants				
% Members	.17**	.15**	.18**	.14**
# Churches	.18**	.17*	.17**	.15*
Evangelical Protestants				
% Members	.13*	.12*	.13**	.11*
# Churches	.14*	.08*	.10**	.07*
% Unchurched	.15**	.01	.05*	.10**
Political Factors				
Margin of Victory:				
General Election	−.21**	−.10**	−.13**	−.20**
Primary Election	−.05*	−.03*	−.06*	−.09*
Open Seats	.14*	.12*	.07**	.17**
Viable Challengers	.10*	−.07*	.06*	.09*
Ideological Mismatch	.05*	−.20**	.01	.07**
Goodness-of-Fit	410**	316*	351**	444**
% Predicted				
All Cases	78%	89%	87%	81%
CR Cases	67%	66%	69%	70%

*Significant at .10 level; **significant at .05 level.

***In each column, the dependent variable measures the incidence of Christian Right activism (CR activism = 1; no activism = 0). In the first column, the dependent variable includes all districts with Christian Right activism, followed by districts with only Christian Right members, local support, and national support. For variable coding see note 2.

are positively associated with Christian Right activism, and a weaker relationship holds for evangelicals. Note, however, that the "unchurched" population is also positively associated with movement activism, both overall and for local and national support, as is non-Protestant population (data not shown). This evidence points to the religious diversity of the areas where the Christian Right was active. As the supply perspective suggests, this pattern is strongest for local Christian Right support.

Taken *alone*, however, conservative Protestantism does not predict activism particularly well. Even casual inspection of the data reveal why: the Christian Right was much less active in districts where conservative Protestants dominate—which are also largely rural, less affluent, and noncosmopolitan. Conservative Protestant dominance is positively associated with conservative voting in Congress, but not with Christian Right activism (Green and Guth 1991b). instead, activism occurs where conservative Protestants confront direct challenges to their values.

Rapidly growing suburbs, even in the Sunbelt, are not usually thought of as hotbeds of conservative Protestantism, and overall they may not be. But much of the recent growth of these churches has occurred in such places, responding to the combination of increased resources, social dislocations, and cultural diversity (Quinn et al. 1982). These findings make intuitive sense: traditionalist movements are less likely to occur where traditional values are commonplace and unchallenged.

Christian Right activism was also complemented by well-organized political allies. For example, activism was most common in states with strong New Right groups, such as North Carolina and Texas, and those with strong Republican Parties, such as Indiana and Ohio. The most telling fact, however, was the movement's overwhelming preference for the Republican party: 92% of Christian Right activity occurred *within* the GOP, and all primary or general election winners were Republicans.

The political factors identified by the strategic choice perspective were strongly associated with Christian Right involvement across the board. Mean electoral margins were negatively correlated with Christian Right activism, most strongly for general elections, but for primaries as well. To some extent this reflects the Christian Right's support for open seats candidates and viable challengers. For example, 82% of all challengers supported for the Christian Right met a minimum standard of financial viability (raising at least 75% of the money available to incumbent foes). But even when the Christian Right backed incumbents, which occurred with increasing frequency over the period (Wilcox 1988a), they tended to be in competitive districts. As expected, these patterns were strongest for national Christian Right support.

A similar pattern obtained for our crude measure of ideological mismatch between constituents and their representatives. Overall and for national support, Christian Right activism was more common in districts where constituents were more conservative than their representatives. And note the opposite pattern for Christian Right members, indicating that they were more common where representatives were more conservative than their constituents. These data point to the relative diversity of the districts where the Christian Right was most active.

The Christian Right was thus most active in competitive districts. Growing suburbs, particularly in the Sunbelt, were among the most competitive areas in the 1980s, offering good chances to influence electoral outcomes. And such areas were particularly attractive to the Christian Right: modern irritants and religious resources were concentrated in relatively conservative milieus, where the movement's agenda was at least plausible, if not universally popular (Himmelstein 1990).

In sum, Christian Right activism occurred most often in districts where the motivations, resources, and opportunities for political action converged. And each set of factors contributed to Christian Right activism in roughly the same proportion. For example, while all variables together accurately predict 78% of the districts with Christian Right involvement, demand factors alone predict only 48%, supply factors 44%, and strategic choice factors 52%. Similar results obtain for each type of involvement.

The same set of variables helps explain the frequency of Christian Right activity within districts.[3] Conservative Protestants and their churches, regional conservatism, and suburban population were also important predictors of repeated activity. However, margin of victory drops out when a measure of electoral success is included: activism persisted where the movement's favored candidates won, and this usually occurred in competitive districts (data not shown). Not surprisingly, national and local Christian Right activity were most associated with general election "winners" (61% and 50%, respectively), while Christian Right members did poorly (30%). Similar patterns obtain for prenomination contests. While assessing the independent impact of the movement on these victories is beyond the scope of this essay, the Christian Right activism was strongly associated with "success," however defined.

Discussion

Our findings may surprise some observers, influenced by the popularity of the demand perspective on social movements. In fact, the Christian Right would have been less active and influential in congressional campaigns if it had merely reflected the discontent of lower-status and parochial traditionalists. Indeed, the candidates who fit this perspective best, Christian Right members, were neither numerous nor effective. Further, our research hints that such candidates were no more common in the 1980s than in previous decades.

Clearly, Christian Right activism was not usually associated with lower-status or parochial populations. One element of the demand perspective was confirmed, however: Christian Right activism appeared in culturally conservative areas experiencing rapid modernization, particularly growing suburbs in the Sun Belt. Here tradition clashes with modernity on even terms, fed by the upward mobility of traditionalists and an influx of cosmopolitans. Surely these conditions produce discontented traditionalists, but higher-status ones who turn to political action because of their ideology rather than status threats or anxieties.

Our findings on the supply perspective fit this pattern as well. Conservative Protestants have flourished in growing suburbs where their close-knit communities and sophisticated parachurch networks represent potent political resources. The development of such grassroots constituencies may be the chief difference between the "New" Christian Right of the 1980s and the "Old" Christian Right of previous decades (Wilcox 1988b). And even greater grassroots mobilization would have produced more success in the 1980s, a fact not lost on movement leaders.

Indeed, some scholars have noted that the Christian Right "returned to the grassroots" as the Reagan era closed (Moen 1989, 173–75). Our data support this view: by the late 1980s the movement was concentrating on mobilizing local constituencies as opposed to national organizations and activities. This change reflects both the success of the former and the decline of the latter, along with the fortunes of the broader New Right (Himmelstein 1990). However, this shift does not represent a retreat from electoral politics, exclusive concern with local issues, or desire to nurture the movement in isolation. Rather, the Christian Right now seeks stronger grassroots organizations to influence federal elections, pursue national issues, and participate fully in a broader conservative alliance.

Thus, greater grassroots emphasis was the sort of strategic choice which, as we have seen, has often characterized the Christian Right. While the movement's instrumental rationality should not be overstated, it was clearly as capable of exploiting opportunities as more established groups. Indeed, the conjunction of motivations, resources, and opportunities reveals the political character of the Christian Right: much of its activity was a calculated response to real grievances by increasingly self-conscious and empowered traditionalists.

The Christian Right has also become progressively integrated into the Republican Party (Guth and Green 1989; Green and Guth 1991a). Such incorporation serves the movement in three ways. First, the GOP is a crucial forum for assembling a broader coalition of conservatives, including the disparate elements of the Christian Right itself. Second, although elected offices are few and difficult to obtain, party posts are more numerous and more accessible. And third, only through the Republican party can the Christian Right have any hope of influencing the composition of Congress. Indeed, the more entrenched and powerful the movement becomes within the GOP, the more likely it is to achieve some of its legislative goals.

Like other movements, the Christian Right has discovered that Congress is a tough nut to crack. And while the causes of congressional insulation are too well known to require comment here, it is clear that few social movements have the strength and staying power to overcome these factors on their own. They can, however, help build stronger organizations and broader coalitions to achieve these goals. Thus, the Christian Right's future lies within broader political alignments, which will require both faith and good works.

Notes

The authors would like to acknowledge the helpful comments of Kenneth Wald, Corwin Smidt, Lyman Kellstedt, Clyde Wilcox, Ted Jelen, and David Leege. This project was generously supported by Furman University and the Bliss Institute at the University of Akron.

1. To calculate these measures, county-level membership and number of churches in 111 denominations were aggregated into broad denominational families; these figures were then aggregated by congressional district. Denominational figures were further combined into politically relevant groupings for members and churches—Sectarian Protestants: all Pentecostal and charismatic churches, such as the Assemblies of God, Foursquare Gospel and Church of

God (Cleveland, TN); fundamentalist Baptists, such as the Baptist Missionary Association, Conservative Baptist Association, and the North American Baptist Conference; all other fundamentalist churches, such as the Church of Christ and Southern Methodist Church; and all fundamentalist split-offs from Mainline Protestant denominations (33 bodies in all). Evangelical Protestants: Southern and American Baptists, Christian and Missionary Alliance, Christian Reformed Church, Christian Church, Evangelical Free and Evangelical Covenant Churches, Free Methodists, all Holiness, Adventists, and Peace Churches, Missouri and Wisconsin Synod Lutherans, and evangelical split-offs from Mainline Protestant denominations, such as Evangelical Congregational Church, Cumberland Presbyterian Church, and Evangelical Lutheran Synod (45 bodies in all). These data also allow for estimates of the unchurched and non-Protestant population (cf. Green and Guth, 1991b for details).

2. The variables in the logistic regression were coded as follows. The dependent variables were dichotomous (1 = Christian Right activism or particular type of activism; 0 = no Christian Right activism). Demographic and church membership variables were measured as a percentage of the population; the number of churches was used directly. Demographic variables were defined as: low income (0% less than $15,000 annually), low education (% less than high school diploma), older (% 65 years of age or older), blue collar (% skilled and unskilled laborers), WASP stock (% British ancestry), and the percentage of rural and suburban population. Region was coded as an ordinal variable according to the degree of cultural conservatism (South = 4; Midwest = 3; West = 2; Northeast = 1) (cf. Schlitz and Rainey 1978). General election and primary margins were expressed as a percentage of the two-party vote and averaged over the period for each district. Open seats and viable challengers were measured by dummy variables. Ideological mismatch was calculated by subtracting the mean Christian Voice score from the mean vote for Reagan in 1980 and 1984.

3. These comments are based on multiple regression analysis where the dependent variable, the number of times the Christian Right was active, ranged from 0 to 6. The statistically significant beta weights were: sectarian Protestants (.29), sectarian churches (.46), region (.20), suburban population (.17), and degree of success (.38), coded on a three-point scale (1 = no success; 2 = major party nomination; 3 = general election victory). These coefficients were significant at the .05 level; $R^2 = .40$.

References

Ammerman, Nancy. 1987. *Bible Believers: Fundamentalists in the Modern World.* New Brunswick, NJ: Rutgers University Press.

Bruce, Steve. 1988. *The Rise and Fall of the New Christian Right.* Oxford: Clarendon Press.

Gamson, William A. 1975. *Strategy of Social Protest.* Homewood, IL: Dorsey Press.

Green, John C., and James L. Guth. 1988. "The Christian Right in the Republican Party: The Case of Pat Robertson's Supporters." *The Journal of Politics* 50:150–65.

Green, John C., and James L. Guth. 1991a. "Apostles and Apostates? Religion and Politics among Party Activists." In *The Bible and the Ballot Box: Religion and Politics in the 1988 Election,* ed. James L. Guth and John C. Green. Boulder, CO: Westview Press.

Green, John C., and James L. Guth 1991b. "Religion, Representatives, and Roll Calls: A Research Note." *Legislative Politics Quarterly* 16:571–84.

Guth, James L., and John C. Green. 1989. "God and the GOP: Varieties of Religiosity among Political Contributors." In *Religion and American Political Behavior,* ed. Ted G. Jelen. New York: Praeger.

Guth, James L., Ted G. Jelen, Lyman A. Kellstedt, Corwin E. Smidt, and Kenneth D. Wald. 1988. "The Politics of Religion in America: Issues for Investigation." *American Politics Quarterly* 116:118–59.

Himmelstein, Jerome L. 1990. *To the Right: The Transformation of America Conservatism.* Berkeley: University of California Press.

Jacobson, Gary C., and Samuel Kernell. 1983. *Strategy and Choice in Congressional Elections.* New Haven: Yale University Press.

Johnson, Loch, and Charles Bullock III. 1991. "The New Religious Right and the 1980 Congressional Elections." In *Do Elections Matter?,* ed. Benjamin Ginsberg and Alan Stone. 2d ed. Armonk, NY: M. E. Sharpe.

Liebman, Robert. 1983. "Mobilizing the Moral Majority." In *The New Christian Right,* ed. Robert Liebman and Robert Wuthnow. New York: Aldine.

Lipset, Seymour M., and Earl Rabb. 1978. *The Politics of Unreason.* 2d ed. New York: Harper & Row.

McAdam, Doug. 1982. *Political Process and the Development of Black Insurgency 1930–1970.* Chicago: University of Chicago Press.

McAdams, John C., and John R. Johannes. 1987. "Determinants of Spending by the House Challengers 1974–84." *American Journal of Political Science* 31:457–83.

McCarthy, J. D., and M. Zald. 1977. "Resource Mobilization and Social Movements: A Partial Theory." *American Journal of Sociology* 82:1,212–41.

Moen, Matthew C. 1989. *The Christian Right and Congress.* Tuscaloosa, AL: University of Alabama Press.

Oberschall, Anthony. 1973. *Social Conflict and Social Movements.* Englewood Cliffs, NJ: Prentice Hall.

Patel, Kant, Denny Pilant, and Gary L. Rose. 1985. "Christian Conservatism: A Study in Alienation and Life Style Concerns." *Journal of Political Science* 12:17–30.

Quinn, Bernard, Herman Anderson, Martin Bradley, Paul Goetting, and Peggy Shriver. 1982. *Churches and Church Membership in the United States 1980.* Atlanta: Glenmary Research Center.

Salisbury, Robert H. 1989. "Political Movements in American Politics: An Essay on Concept and Analysis." *National Journal of Political Science* 1: 15–30.

Schlitz, Timothy D., and R. Lee Rainey. 1978. "The Geographic Distribution of Elazar's Political Subcultures among the Mass Population: A Research Note." *Western Political Quarterly* 31:410–15.

Wald, Kenneth D., Dennis E. Owen, and Samuel S. Hill, Jr. 1988. "Churches as Political Communities." *American Political Science Review* 82: 531–48.

Wald, Kenneth D., Dennis E. Owen, and Samuel S. Hill, Jr. 1989. "Evangelical Politics and Status Issues." *Journal for the Scientific Study of Religion* 28:1–16.

Wald, Kenneth D. 1990. "The New Christian Right in American Politics: Mobilization Amid Mobilization." In *Religious Resurgence and Politics in the Contemporary World,* ed. Emile Sahliyeh. Albany, NY: SUNY Press.

Welch, W. P. 1979. "Patterns of Contributions: Economic Interest and Ideological Groups." In *Political Finance,* ed. Herbert Alexander. Beverly Hills, CA: Sage.

Wilcox, Clyde. 1988a. "Political Action Committees of the New Christian Right: A Longitudinal Analysis." *Journal for the Scientific Study of Religion* 27: 60–71.

Wilcox, Clyde. 1988b. "The Christian Right in Twentieth Century America: Continuity and Change." *The Review of Politics* 50:659–81.

8

Politics in a New Key: Religiosity and Participation among Political Activists

James L. Guth
John C. Green

Few events surprised observers of American politics as much as the recent increase in religiously based conflict in American politics (Wald 1987: 6–12). The decade-long rise of the Christian Right is a case in point: dominant theories of modern politics predicted the decline of religion in public life (Guth et al. 1988). Equally troubling, if less commented upon, was the surge of left-wing church activism in the 1960s and its revival in the Reagan era on such issues as disarmament, sanctuary and aid for the homeless. And secular activists, in organizations such as the ACLU and People for the American Way, entered politics with hostility toward religious values. Robert McAfee Brown's *Theology in a New Key* (1978) symbolizes well this religio-political foment. His demand that churches become more responsive to political concerns anticipated a "new key" in politics as well—though not entirely in tune with his expectations.

Explanations of the link between religion and politics frequently emphasize the role of elites in linking religious communities and commitments to political alignments (Ammerman 1987). Here we report on this connection for an increasingly important set of political activists: major financial donors to national party and political action committees. While donors may not fully represent all kinds of activists, campaign contributors are an active, influential and diverse set of political elites (Jones and Miller 1985) and one central to recent trends in national politics (Sorauf 1988).

Instead of a recent "revival" of religion in politics, we find that a "reformation" of the political spectrum has been taking place among activists, with the traditional ethnocultural connection of religion and politics shifting to a secular-versus-religious underpinning for political alignments. These changes are best accounted for by demographic factors rather than the mobilization of new activists or new methods of political organization.

Religion and Political Activists

Secularization theories lead most scholars to see religious elements in contemporary politics as largely anachronistic, short-term reactions to the process of modernization (Wilson 1982). This view is not without its critics (Hadden 1987) and consequently, there is disagreement over the variety, number, behavior and history of religious activists. Similarly, different explanations are advanced for increased religio-political conflict, including a new political agenda, new methods of political organization and demographic change.

Variety, Number, Behavior and History of Religio-Political Activism

The religious differences that underlie political alignments come in at least three varieties: between particular denominational traditions, such as ethnocultural disputes among Protestants, Catholics and Jews; within denominations, such as ideological conflict between theologically conservative and liberal factions; and between believers of all sorts and nonbelievers (Wuthnow 1988). Scholars impressed with the power of modernization see a steady movement away from these sources of political conflict, while their critics see more complex processes at work (Halebsky 1976; Hadden and Shupe 1986).

While not entirely a denominational phenomenon, the political differences between evangelical and non-evangelical denominations have received the most attention (Reichley 1985: 311–30). The common view is that clergy and lay activists in theologically conservative Protestant churches represent a large, hyperactive and newly mobilized cadre of traditionalists, reacting to the penetration of modernity into the hinterlands (Hadden and Shupe 1988). Given the large reservoir of Protestant orthodoxy in the United States, many observers see in this movement great potential for conservatives and Republicans, but little staying power, since the forces which aroused it will eventually erode its base (Lipset 1981).

Other scholars, however, see evangelical activists as less numerous, less active and less mercurial (Guth 1983). Some point to the small following of the Moral Majority and related organizations (Buell and Sigelman 1985), the political diversity of religious traditionalists (Rothenberg and Newport 1984), and the fact that many Christian Rightists have long been politically active (Wilcox 1987). Still others find evangelicals to differ little from other kinds of right-wing and Republican activists, suggesting their political impact will be less divisive and longer lasting (Green and Guth 1988).

Beyond evangelical churches most observers note the decline of denominational differences, and hence pay less attention to clergy and lay activists in mainline Protestant and Catholic churches (Quinley 1974; Hallum 1988). Many scholars see the numbers, participation and political distinctiveness of mainline Protestants and Catholics waning because of encroaching secularization (Wald 1987: 248). Others note political diversity: a large liberal contingent serving in the vanguard of reform movements and a growing conservative element active in counter-movements (Chittister and Marty 1983). Similar strains may exist in denominations attached to the political left, such as black and liberal Protestants, and Jews. While little is known about these kinds of activists, their numbers are probably small and participation high, though perhaps less focused than in the past (Hatch 1988; De Leon 1988; Lekachman 1987).

There is more agreement on secular activists, the expected end product of modernization (Glock and Wuthnow 1979). Most scholars believe their numbers and participation have expanded dramatically in recent times, and their politics to be liberal and Democratic (Williamsburg Charter Foundation 1988). However, some surveys show the secular to be far less active than their social status would predict (Ornstein, Kohut, and McCarthy 1988) and the presence of "adversarial culture" since the 1950s suggests that some secular activists have long been involved in politics (Trilling 1954). Other observers point to diversity as well, identifying "social democratic" and "libertarian" groups among the secular (Phillips 1983: 225–27).

Explanations of Religio-Political Activism

These controversies aside, scholars offer different explanations for increased religio-political conflict, including a new political agenda, new methods of political organization, and demographic change (Wald 1987:

206). While these explanations are rarely seen as mutually exclusive, few scholars give them equal weight.

1. *Agenda Change.* Many analysts see a new set of issues arising from secularization as the catalyst for religio-political activism (Lipset and Raab 1981). Intense disputes between reformers and traditionalists over social issues, such as ERA, abortion, and school prayer, are given particular stress (Simpson 1983), although some scholars include economic and foreign policy as well (Smidt 1988). A related argument points to the alienation common in modern societies, particularly discontent with political parties and other institutions growing out of the Vietnam War, Watergate, and the relative decline of American power, as a source of political mobilization (Patel, Pilant, and Rose 1985).

2. *New Methods of Political Organizations.* Other scholars emphasize the role of modern technology in mobilizing religious activists (Latus 1984). The Christian Right's well-known reliance on both the electronic church and direct mail needs no elaboration here (Hadden and Swann 1981) nor does the role of parachurch networks in organizing evangelical interest groups (Liebman 1983). Of course, liberal reformers employed similar tactics earlier, though less extensively, than their right-wing counterparts (Godwin 1988). And the greater use by traditionalists of new organizational techniques is balanced perhaps by greater access to the news media and other modern institutions enjoyed by reform-oriented activists (Rothman and Lichter 1982b).

3. *Demographic Factors.* Still other scholars look to new social groups for the origins of religiously based political activism (Roof and McKinney 1987). As suggested by theories of modernization, right-wing religious activists are seen as part of the "old upper class" composed of owners and managers of property. This "Old Class" is characterized by "materialist" values that are found most strongly among older, non-cosmopolitan and less educated activists (Berger 1981; Pollock et al. 1981). Some writers see the recent upward mobility of rural and blue-collar groups as reinforcing the Old Class with a new cadre of affluent, but provincial activists (Roof 1979). Others add to this pattern short-term decline or stasis in personal fortunes (Burnham 1981).

Left-wing activists have also experienced upward mobility and short-term disappointments, but here scholars emphasize the role of modernization, particularly education and affluence, in producing "post-materialist" values (Abramson and Inglehart 1987) that are found most strongly among younger, cosmopolitan, and better educated citizens (Bruce-Briggs 1979). These values are especially common in the "new upper class" of professional knowledge experts. Secular activists are seen as the quintessential members of this "New Class," whose world views and lifestyles directly challenge traditional values (Rothman and Lichter 1982a).

Our principal task below is to assess the variety, number, behavior and history of religio-political activists among campaign contributors in light of the literature, and then consider the utility of a new agenda, new methods of political organization and demographic factors in accounting for increased religio-political conflict.

Data and Methods

Our data are from a mail survey of a stratified random sample of 5650 contributors to 60 party, ideological and interest group PACs, conducted during 1982–83.[1] We received 2827 usable returns for a return rate of 52.3 percent (excluding mail returned as undeliverable), a rate superior to other studies of contributors (Brown et al. 1980b).[2] Due to the over-representation of smaller PACs in the sample, the data were weighted according to the amount of money each committee raised in the 1981–82 election cycle.[3]

We used a ten-page, 350-item questionnaire tapping political activity, attitudes, affiliations and demography. Our principal measure of political activity was the respondent's recall of thirteen forms of participation for the 1980 election and all presidential elections back to 1960. Our attitudinal measures included an open-ended query on the "three most important problems facing the country today"; five-point Likert items on twenty-four issues covering economic, social and foreign policy; five-point Likert items assessing the respondent's agreement with major party positions on sixteen of these issues; standard seven-point Likert items on partisanship and ideology; and self-assessments of partisan and ideological change.

In addition, we had three-point Likert items concerning trust in leaders of twenty-two social and political institutions; the respondent's use of twelve common sources of political information; the relative importance of fourteen values to the respondent; and five-point Likert items gauging the respondents' proximity to sixteen prominent political groups and leaders. We also asked the respondents whether they considered themselves to be members or active members of fourteen kinds of social and political organizations.

Our demographic questions were extensive, including closed-ended questions on gender, place of residence, religious denomination, years of education, income, recent changes in economic well-being, geographic mobility, occupational change, and marital status; and open-ended questions on ethnicity, their own occupation and that of their spouses and parents, age, region of residence now and during their childhood. If they received collegiate or post-collegiate training, we asked for their major field and the name of the school(s) attended.

Four common measures of religiosity were culled from this extensive data set. First, as a proxy for theological orientation, we collapsed our list of denominational preferences (with over fifty categories) into an eight-point ordinal scale of traditional religiosity, ranging from the most orthodox denominations through the more modernist churches to those with no preference.[4] This kind of scale has been found to be a valid proxy for the acceptance of traditional religious values, such as belief in God and an afterlife, and the intensity with which such values are held (cf. Stark and Glock 1970: 57–80). While this kind of measure is most successful for the denominational families in American Protestantism (Beatty and Walter 1984), other scholars have found that American Roman Catholics and Jews constitute denominational families matching the diversity and intensity of belief of mainline and liberal Protestants, respectively (Roof and McKinney 1987: 94–97; Harrison and Lazerwitz 1982). The use of such a scale does not imply that any denomination is conceptually more or less religious than any other, but only that as a matter of fact their members are more or less likely to hold and hold with intensity values that have been central to the major religious traditions in America. Our other religious measures support such a pattern in these data.

Second and third, we use two three-point Likert items on the importance of "following God's will" and "following a strict moral code" to assess the salience of religion and moralism (Gallup 1982).[5] Fourth, as a measure of involvement in religious institutions, we used the respondents' assessment of whether they considered themselves "not to be a member," "a member," or "an active member" of a church or religious organization. As with our other variables, this one must be considered ordinal in nature.

Although we would have preferred better measures of religiosity, a subsequent survey of campaign contributors showed these variables to be highly correlated with more sophisticated measures of theological orientation, religious salience and church attendance (Guth and Green, 1986). All four of our measures are correlated with one another in the present data,[6] and factor analysis shows them to represent a single dimension of "traditional religiosity."[7] This finding differs from the common finding that religion is multidimensional (Hilty, Morgan, and Burns 1984) and may illustrate greater religious constraint among activists. Indeed, a more detailed study of religiosity among political donors produced similar results (Guth and Green 1989) as have other studies (Tamney and Johnson 1987).

To make analysis more manageable, we used factor analysis to produce a single measure of religiosity, a factor score ranging from the most secular donors to the most orthodox and active contributors. We then partitioned the range of the factor score into thirds to produce an ordinal measure of traditional religiosity (the least, intermediate and most religious donors). To connect this measure to political orientations, we further divided the sample by self-identified political ideology[8] ("liberal," "moderate" and "conservative") to produce a three-by-three tabulation. For ease of presentation, we report on the four "corners" of this tabulation, which together account for 52 percent of the sample: the "Secular Left," "Religious Left," "Secular Right" and "Religious Right." With rare exceptions, the five "middle" categories fall between the four "corner" groups in behavior, attitudes, and demography.

While lacking in fine distinctions, these four "corner" categories capture important religious and political differences.[9] Extensive experimentation failed to produce categories that were more intuitively satisfying or more strongly associated with our independent variables. All findings presented below were confirmed by means of multiple discriminant analysis.[10] However, our findings are presented in a simpler form in tables 8.1–8.7 to preserve their nuance.

Variety, Extent, Behavior and History of Political Activism

Denominational profiles of our categories help sort out the variety, number and alignment of religious activists—at least insofar as they have penetrated the national activist corps. Our evidence supports a more complex view of secularization: conservative Protestants do not have the prominence many assign them, mainline and Liberal Protestants play a major role on the right and left, and all groups show residual ethnocultural political attachments (McCormick 1974).

The Religious Right fits the popular image somewhat, drawing 29 percent of its members from charismatic, fundamentalist, evangelical and other conservative Protestant churches, but twice as many, 55 percent, from mainline and liberal Protestant bodies. And the historical Protestant hegemony of the right is unbroken: only 14 percent are Catholic, 1

Chapter Eight

percent Jewish and 1 percent from other groups. By contrast, the Religious Left is far more diverse, containing many groups long associated with Democratic politics. Mainline and Liberal Protestants account for 43 percent of this group. Conservative Protestants 19 percent (many of them black), Catholics 28 percent, Jews and other liberal groups 8 percent. The secular categories are nearly as diverse: some three-fifths are unaffiliated and the next largest categories are Jews (many of whom claimed to be "culturally Jewish") and Others (mostly Unitarians, "humanists" and "New Age" religions), followed by a smattering of other denominations.

As table 8.1 shows, these categories vary greatly in size. The Religious Right is the largest group, accounting for 35 percent of the weighted

TABLE 8.1
Political Participation, 1980 Election: Secular and Religious Donors

	Secular Left	Religious Left	Secular Right	Religious Right	Entire Sample
Weighted N	(259)	(155)	(94)	(977)	(2827)
% of Total Sample	9%	5%	3%	35%	100%**
In 1980:					
Voted for President	94%	96%	100%	97/	96%
Talked Politics	59	77*	60	71	63
Attended Rally	46	62	33	45	41
Distributed Literature	36	52	36	58	35
Joined Political Club	34	43	35	40	34
Gave Donation to:					
Candidate	78*	71	80*	73	72
PAC	53	45	46	56	50
Party	49	60	82*	56	64
Served as Fund-raiser	40*	63*	39*	45	47
Attended Demonstration	23*	16*	7	3	8
Wrote Letter to Editor	15	22*	14	19	15
Served as Delegate	15	13	14	12	12
Ran for Public Office	2	10	1	3	3
Supported Third Party	40*	28*	23*	3*	17
Usually:					
Contact Officials	35	46*	40	35	34
Help with Problems	27	42*	35*	24	28
Active Local Politics	24	36*	20	26	26
Mean # of Acts in 1980	4.5	5.5*	4.1	4.7	4.4
% 7 + Acts in 1980	25%	44%*	22%	35%*	16%

*Chi-square p < .05 or better.
**Row does not add to 100% because of categories not reported on; see text for explanation.

sample, nearly twice as numerous as the Secular Right (3 percent), Religious Left (5 percent) and Secular Left (9 percent) put together. The Religious Right accounts for more than half of all self-identified conservatives and outnumbers the Secular Right ten to one. Among liberals, the balance is more even, with the Religious Left accounting for a fifth and the Secular Left a third.

These data fit the common sense association of religiosity with conservatism as well: conservatives account for three-quarters of the most religious activists and liberals make up three-fifths of the most secular group (Guth and Green 1986). And divisions within the mainline churches are clearly visible in these data: more traditional donors tend towards the Republican right while the less traditional tend towards the Democratic left (Wuthnow 1988: ch. 7).

Our Religious Right category includes more than just donors associated with the Moral Majority, Christian Voice or other Christian Right organizations: only 3 percent of this category donated to Christian Right PACs and another 35 percent claim to feel "close" to the Moral Majority or related organizations (Guth and Green 1987). Thus, religious traditionalists explicitly associated with the "new" Christian Right are vastly outnumbered by equally religious conservatives who are not explicitly linked to such organizations. Relevant differences between Christian Right donors and the broader group of Religious Right donors will be noted below (Guth and Green 1989).

Religious donors are indeed more active in politics than the secular, but liberals are more so than conservatives (table 8.1). In 1980, religious donors were more involved in conventional campaign activities, such as distributing campaign literature and attending rallies, and in local politics. Participation levels were more uniform for less common activities, such as running for office or contacting public officials, and varieties of financial support, in which donors specialize (Brown et al. 1980a). Secular activists outperform the religious only on unconventional participation, such as attending demonstrations and supporting third parties, and donating to individual candidates.

The Religious Left was the most active on average by a wide margin, followed by the Religious Right, which was modestly ahead of the secular groups. This pattern can be seen more dramatically in the proportion of donors who were very active (performing seven or more acts). Furthermore, the participatory advantage of the religious over their secular counterparts is long standing—at least among donors still active in 1982. As figures 8.1 and 8.2 indicate, their participatory advantage dates back to 1964 on the left and 1960 on the right. The Religious Right began to

FIGURE 8.1
Average Participation Rates, 1960–1980: Secular and Religious Donors

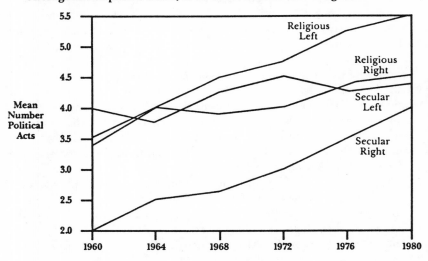

FIGURE 8.2
High Participation Rates, 1960–1980: Secular and Religious Donors

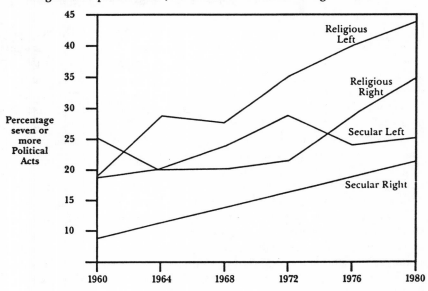

exceed the Secular Left in the early 1970s, as might be expected (Wuthnow 1988: 198–200). But even in this case, the evidence does not suggest large-scale mobilization of new activists.

These patterns must be interpreted with caution since they are based on recall data and apply only to donors still active in 1982. (For purposes of figures 8.1 and 8.2, donors were excluded if they were too young to vote in a particular election or if they claimed not to be active in politics at that time.) Recall error is minimized, however, by the high levels of education and knowledge which characterize such activists (Nesbit 1988: 324).

In addition, independent evidence lends credence to these patterns. First, increased participation from 1960 to 1980 reflects in part aging (Jennings and Marcus 1988) and in part increasing opportunities for elite participation (Brody 1978). Second, these patterns fit well the flux of national politics (Beck and Jennings 1984). For example, the largest reported gains in activism *and* new recruits by the Religious Left were in 1964 and 1976 during the Johnson and Carter campaigns (Wuthnow 1988: 236), while the Secular Left claims to have increased their activity most in 1968 and 1972, paralleling the McCarthy and McGovern insurgencies (Kirkpatrick 1976: 360). The biggest reported expansion of the Secular and Religious Right occurred in the Goldwater and Reagan years, 1964 and 1980 (Phillips 1983: 180). Third, the beginning of our time series is supported by evidence amassed by Wuthnow (1988: 198) and the end by more recent surveys of campaign contributors (Guth and Green 1989).

Donors to Christian Right PACs provide only a mild exception to these patterns. In 1980 such activists were only slightly more active than the broader Religious Right (mean acts = 4.9, very active = 40 percent), though more of them entered politics for the first time (14 percent to 3 percent). The largest influx of Christian Right activists was reported for 1964 (28 percent), however, and their participation rose in step with other Religious Rightists through the seventies.

Table 8.2 summarizes our findings thus far. More than half of each category was involved in politics prior to 1980, but nearly twice as many religious donors were very active. The religious groups include only slightly more new and newly active participants than the secular. Thus, there is some support for conventional views on the bulk and aggressiveness of religious conservatism. While its activist corps is very large, they are neither particularly new, growing, sectarian nor lacking in competitors, even among the religious. Religious activism, right and left, is "far from a flaming meteor" and "more like a fixed star in our heavens" (Lienesch 1982: 425).

TABLE 8.2
Political Activism in the 1980 Election: Secular and Religious Donors

	Secular Left	Religious Left	Secular Right	Religious Right	Entire Sample
Old Activists, Low Participation	75%	56%*	78%	65%*	74%
Old Activists, High Participation	16	32*	15	25*	16
Old Activists, New High Participation	7	9	5	7	7
New Activists	2	3	2	3	3
	100%	100%	100%	100%	100%

Low Participation: Six or fewer political acts in 1980
High Participation: Seven or more political acts in 1980
Old Activists: Active prior to 1980
New Activists: First active in 1980
*Chi-square p < .05 or better

Explanations of Religio-Political Activism

If neither new nor existing activists were mobilized in large numbers in 1980, the upsurge in religio-political conflict needs to be accounted for in other ways. Although the explanations mentioned above (i.e. a new political agenda, new methods of political organization and demographic factors), usually address the recruitment of activists, they can also help account for heightened sensitivity to religious concerns among existing activists.

1. Agenda Change

None of our categories is characterized by an agenda of salient noneconomic issues, and discontents associated with agenda change, such as extreme opinions and cynicism, are more common for secular activists (table 8.3).

To measure salient opinion, we asked respondents to name the "three most important issues facing the country today" (coded with Center for Political Studies categories). These data show social issue priorities to be remarkably constant across the spectrum, with economic issues dominating every group by a two-to-one margin. Foreign policy concerns do vary, but are the special province of liberal donors, particularly the Secular Left, who interestingly, are the least likely to mention economic issues.

It may be that social and foreign policy issues are more salient now

TABLE 8.3

Issue Salience, Extreme Opinion and Partisan Evaluation: Secular and
Religious Donors

	Secular Left	Religious Left	Secular Right	Religious Right	Entire Sample
Salience					
Most Important National Problems:					
Economic Issues	46%*	50%	58%	56%	56%
Social Issues	23	23	22	23	21
Foreign Policy	26*	20	16	14	18
Government Process	5	7	4	7	6
Opinion Intensity					
Mean # of Extreme Issue Positions (24 issues)	11.0*	9.0*	9.4*	8.6	8.4
Partisan Evaluation					
Mean # of Party Position Approvals (16 issues)	6.8	7.8*	6.4	8.0*	7.2
Cynicism					
Mean # of Institutions Distrusted (22 institutions)	6.3	5.5	7.8*	5.6	6.0

*Chi-square p < .05 or better

than in the past (Dawson 1973). And we can certainly find subsets of donors who give priority to such issues: morality for Christian Rightists, arms control for peace activists, and so forth for a host of "single-issue" groups (Green and Guth 1986). Activists who report changes in partisan affiliation are also more concerned with non-economic issues. But religiosity itself does not seem to be associated with large agenda differences.

Of course, religiously based conflict may required an "agreement to disagree" among opponents. Our categories do hold predictably liberal and conservative views on specific issues. As we have shown previously, however, religious donors are consistently more conservative than their secular counterparts (Guth and Green 1986). On school prayer, for instance, the Religious Left is less than half as likely to give a liberal response as the Secular Left, and a similar relationship holds on the right (Green and Guth 1989). This pattern extends to many foreign policy and economic questions as well, although ideology has a stronger direct influence than religiosity on most issues.

Religious donors do not have more extreme opinions than their secular counterparts, measured by the mean number of "strongly agree" and "strongly disagree" positions taken on twenty-four issue questions (table

8.3). In fact, secular donors have on average more extreme issue positions than do the religious. The extreme views of Christian Right leaders (and some donors to Christian Right PACs) do not extend to our Religious Right category as a whole—while much more of this kind of "contagion" has taken place among the secular, particularly on the left.

Much the same obtains for the evaluation of the major parties, institutions often seen as indifferent to new agendas. Religious donors approve more strongly of party issue stances than do the secular, measured by the mean number of "strongly agree" positions taken on major party stands on sixteen issues (table 8.3). This pattern of support extends to other institutions as well: religious donors express on average more confidence in a broad range of social and political authorities (Lipset and Schneider 1987: 105).

As one might expect, sharply different patterns of party evaluation underlie these data, with liberals preferring the Democratic party and distrusting Republican leaders, and conservatives having opposite assessments. These activists also distrust different institutions. Religious donors, left and right, are more skeptical of the news media and public interest groups, and secular donors dislike religious organizations, state and local governments. But in general, cynicism follows extreme opinion.

These findings are complemented by reported changes in self-identified partisanship. Religious donors are the most stable partisans: 35 percent of the Religious Left are standpat, strong Democrats and 40 percent of the Religious Right are standpat, strong Republicans. By comparison, only 25 and 28 percent of the secular groups are strong, unchanged partisans. There is some religious pull toward the Republicans, however: 17 percent of Religious Leftists and 35 percent of Religious Rightists report having moved toward the GOP since their youth. The secular donors show shifts of similar magnitude toward weak Democratic and Republican identifications, respectively.

Thus, the less active secular donors are more likely to display discontents associated with agenda change than their more active religious counterparts, who, by contrast, represent bulwarks of moderation, party loyalty and confidence. However, there is considerable agreement on the political agenda, with no group giving social or foreign policy issues top priority.

2. New Methods of Political Organization

If agenda change and its discontents apply only, and modestly, to the mobilization of secular activists, perhaps new methods of political organization, such as televangelism or religious interest groups, apply to the religious. Table 8.4 suggests this may be the case, but not in accordance with expectations.

When asked to evaluate their use of political information sources, religious donors were indeed more likely to report religious broadcasting, clergy and direct mail as important. But they also consulted commercial TV and radio news more often, despite their distrust of the news media. Although their numbers do not differ significantly from the sample as a whole, the religious donors, left and right, actually use more sources of political information than the secular. Personal contacts show the most dramatic differences: the religious were far more likely to consult their family, friends and co-workers on political matters. For example, 40 percent of the religious donors claimed their immediate family was an important source of political information, compared to 21 and 22 percent of the Secular Left and Right, respectively.

These data suggest a lesser degree of social integration among secular donors, which is reinforced by their lack of organizational memberships: the secular belonged to fewer groups on average than their religious counterparts. The religious were indeed more likely to claim membership in agents of recent political movements, such as PACs and public interest groups, but also to belong to traditional vehicles of community power, such as civic and fraternal organizations. The most telling point, however, is that the religious are nearly twice as likely to be active in the organizations to which they belong. For example, more religious liberals

TABLE 8.4
Information, Organizations and Movements: Secular and Religious Donors

	Secular Left	Religious Left	Secular Right	Religious Right	Entire Sample
Sources of Information Mean # of "Important" Information Sources (12 sources)	2.5	3.0	2.1*	2.9	2.8
Group Memberships Mean # of Memberships in Organizations (12 kinds of groups)	3.5	5.0*	2.9	4.3*	3.0
Proximity to Movements Mean # of Groups/Leaders Felt "Close to" (16 political groups)	4.8*	5.0*	3.6	4.0	4.0

*Chi-square p < .05 or better

were active members of civic associations than secular liberals (23 to 12 percent) and the same pattern holds for conservatives (15 to 8 percent).

We also asked our donors to assess their proximity to organizations and leaders representative of recent political movements, from the Moral Majority to the ACLU. In line with the foregoing evidence, religious donors on average reported feeling "close" to more groups and leaders than their secular counterparts, although liberals outscored conservatives in this regard.

One kind of organization not available to secular activists are churches and religious organizations themselves (Wald 1988). Our evidence shows the religiosity to be significantly more active in their churches than the Religious Right. But as might be expected, the subset of donors to Christian Right PACs shows the highest rate of church-related activity (Liebman 1983).

Thus, religious donors, left and right, are indeed more involved with new methods of political organization, but also more active with conventional methods as well. Religious activists are better integrated into social and political life than the secular, a pattern consistent with their greater moderation, confidence, and participation (Lekachman 1987:254).

3. Demographic Factors

If agenda change applies modestly to secular donors, and new methods of political organizations apply somewhat to the religious, perhaps a fuller explanation for increased religio-political activism lies with new kinds of people. Indeed, the demography of our categories parallel important social changes of the recent past. Despite greater social traditionalism among religious donors, liberal activists show the traits of the "New class" of knowledge experts while conservatives exhibit the characteristics of "Old Class" property owners. The patterns in tables 8.5–8.7 are quite remarkable given the generally high status of campaign contributors.

Region and place of residence show secular donors to be concentrated in the most cosmopolitan parts of the country: major metropolitan areas of the Northeast and West coast, with liberals in the former and conservatives the latter. By contrast, the Religious Left is found most heavily in smaller cities and rural areas of the Northeast and Midwest, and the Religious Right favors the non-metropolitan South and Midwest.

Secular donors are roughly twice as mobile as the religious (based on the number of states lived in as adults) and all groups show net migration

TABLE 8.5
Region, Residence, Age and Ethnicity: Secular and Religious Donors

	Secular Left	Religious Left	Secular Right	Religious Right	Entire Sample
Region					
Northeast	50%*	38%*	37%*	13%*	30%
West	23	11*	45*	24	23
Midwest	19	28	7	25	22
South	8*	22	11	38*	25
Place of Residence					
Major Metropolitan	69%*	42%	57%*	32%	46%
Small Cities	28	46*	40	48*	40
Small Town, Rural	3*	12	3*	21*	14
Net Migration					
Northeast	-7%	4%	-5%	-4%	-3%
West	13	3*	23*	5	11
Midwest	-9	-9	-22*	-15	-13
South	3	2	4	14*	5
Age					
Over 65 years old	19%*	26%*	10%*	42%*	31%
50 to 65 years old	31	31	36	37	36
Under 50 years old	49*	44*	54*	21*	32
Ethnicity					
British, "American"	39%	34%	38%	50%*	42%
Northern, Central Europe	13*	20	19	28	24
Irish	8	23*	6	6	9
Southern, Eastern Europe	35*	11*	37*	15	20
Non-European	5	12*	0	1	5

*Chi-square p < .05 or better

from the Frostbelt to the Sunbelt (measured by comparing state of birth to state of current residence). Migration among the secular is associated with career changes (they are twice as likely to report changing jobs in the previous decade) while migration among the religious reflects retirement. It is not surprising then, that secular donors are younger— about half are less than 50 years old—while two-fifths of religious conservatives and one-quarter of religious liberals are retirement age or older.

Another striking difference is self-reported ethnicity (coded with Census Bureau categories), which closely parallels the denominational profiles described above and reveals the vestiges of the ethnocultural patterns that once defined American political alignments (McCormick 1974). For example, three-quarters of the Religious Right is of British, Northern or Central European descent. The Religious Left is much more diverse, including one-quarter of Irish extraction and the largest contingent with

TABLE 8.6
Education
Secular and Religious Donors

	Secular Left	Religious Left	Secular Right	Religious Right	Entire Sample
Education					
Post Graduate Study	63%*	44%*	55%*	31%*	43%
College Graduate	25	32	28	29	28
No College Degree	12*	25	14*	40*	29
Prestige of College					
Prestige Private	41%*	30%	26%	22%*	28%
Other Private Schools	17	28*	8*	9*	19
State Schools	39*	40*	65*	53*	48
Technical and Trade	2	3	2	17*	5
Selectivity of College					
Most Selective	28%*	19%	23%	16%	20%
Highly Selective	30*	21	23	15	18
Selective	24	28	29	34	30
Non-selective	18*	32	25*	35	32
College Major					
Social Sciences	42%*	33%	26%	20%	29%
Humanities	33*	32	25	14	23
Sciences	13	9	10	11	10
Business	9	16	19	24*	15
Applied Subjects	3	10	20	34*	23

*Chi-square p < .05 or better

non-European backgrounds. And the secular donors, right and left, have the largest proportions of Southern and Eastern European descent.

It is education, however, that discriminates best among these activists, being as Hunter (1983: 60) suggests, "the veritable classroom for the inculcation of the world view of modernity." Secular activists are the best educated, with almost two-thirds of the left and more than half of the right having some post-graduate training, and less than one-sixth lacking a college degree. And religious donors are less educated: slightly more than two-fifths of liberals and less than one-third of conservatives have post-graduate work; one-quarter and two-fifths of these donors, respectively, did not attend or complete college (table 8.6).

The quality and kind of higher education reported are equally revealing (Lipset and Ladd 1975). While the Secular Left and Right spent nearly as many years in school, they studied at different kinds of institutions and majored in different subjects (table 8.6). Secular liberals attended more prestigious and secular private colleges and majored in the social sciences

TABLE 8.7
Occupation, Income and Gender: Secular and Religious Donors

	Secular Left	Religious Left	Secular Right	Religious Right	Entire Sample
Occupation					
Professionals	62%*	66%*	21%*	10%*	31%
Technical Professionals	11	5	14	10	11
Business, Management	18*	17*	57*	58*	43
Other	8*	13	7*	21	16
Occupational Mobility					
Higher than father's	49%*	38%*	19%*	20%*	31%
Comparable to father's	45*	38*	76*	70*	61
Lower than father's	6	14	5	10	8
Personal Fortunes					
Improved last decade	66%*	66%*	83%*	74%	73%
Stayed about the same	24*	15	11	10	16
Declined last decade	9	20*	6	16	11
Income					
Over $100,000	24%*	23%*	56%*	46%*	39%
$40,00 to $100,000	37	34	30	28	33
Under $40,000	28	43*	11*	24	26
Gender					
Female	41%*	25%*	3%*	13%*	19%

*Chi-square p < .05 or better

or humanities. In contrast, secular conservatives attended less prestigious and selective public institutions and pursued more business and applied degrees. The Religious Left also attended less prestigious and selective schools, many of them denominationally based, but like the Secular Left, they majored in the liberal arts. Lastly, those members of the Religious Right with college degrees were most likely to have studied business and applied subjects at the least prestigious and selective colleges. Post-college education shows a very similar pattern. (The prestige and selectivity of colleges were derived from Cass and Birnbaum 1983; college majors were coded using National Science Foundation codes.)

Ideological rather than religious distinctions are more prominent in other measures of social status: occupation, income and gender (table 8.7). For example, some two-thirds of liberal donors hold New Class occupations, non-technical professional jobs such as lawyers, doctors, teachers, and journalists; adding technical professions (engineers, computer programmers) raises the proportion of knowledge specialists to nearly three-quarters of each group. By contrast, more than half of the conservative activists are business owners or managers, the cornerstone of the Old Class. Religious donors are distinguished by larger numbers of farm, clerical, and blue-collar occupations.

Liberals are roughly half as affluent as conservatives, and religious liberals are the least well-off, with two-thirds earning less than $100,000 annually (table 8.7). The Secular Right is the wealthiest group, with more than half earning over $100,000 a year, followed closely by the Religious Right. And it is the Left, not the Right, that shows the greatest long-term gains in occupational status (measured by higher occupational status than their father's, using the Duncan SES scale). The Secular Left shows the most upward mobility and the Religious Right shows the least. Indeed, conservatives are roughly twice as likely to have the same occupational status as their parents. Short-term assessments of personal fortunes show a similar pattern. The Secular Left is most likely to report declines in the 1970s and the Religious Left is the most likely to claim no gain. By contrast, far fewer conservative donors give these assessments and Secular Rightists report the most personal gains (table 8.7).

There is also a pronounced "gender gap": female donors are much more common on the left, accounting for two-fifths of the secular and one-quarter of the religious (table 8.7). There are few women in the Secular Right, and only marginally more among the Religious (most of whom are widows). Much the same pattern obtains for measures of family status (Sapiro 1983). Only 15 percent of the Secular Left have four or five of the traits often associated with "traditional" families (married, never divorced, female spouse and/or mother as housewife, and more than one child). The Religious Left is more than twice as traditional by this measure, with 33 percent having four or five of these traits, and the Right is even more so: 43 percent of the Secular and 57 percent of the Religious have these traits.

Cultural differences often associated with these demographic patterns (Inglehart 1981) are found in donor reports of non-religious values. For example, the secular donors are the most likely to rate personal freedom as "very important" in their lives. However, the Secular Left and Right differ sharply on materialism: liberals value personal income and material possessions the least while conservatives value them the most, particularly income. In contrast, religious donors place the most value on personal relationships and "working to better America." But religious leftists care most about "living up to their potential" while their rightist counterparts are most concerned with personal security.

Thus, demography, and the demographic changes implied, account for the largest differences among our categories. The numerous and active

Religious Right undergirds strong support for political and social institutions with Old Class social traits. The less numerous and more active Religious Left shows a similar pattern, but among social groups traditionally hostile to the WASP-dominated Old Class. Secular donors, across the political spectrum, combine weaker support for, and participation in, political institutions with New Class demography.

Discussion

"Our political and social quarrels," writes Patrick Buchanan (1988: 337), "now partake of the savagery of religious wars because, at bottom, they are religious wars." Hyperbole aside, our findings support such a conclusion: alignments among political activists have a strong religious component. However, the link between religion and politics is increasingly defined by the fact of traditional religiosity rather than particular religious traditions. Although the remnants of ethnocultural alignments are evident, traditionally-religious activists are moving towards the political right and less traditional activists are moving left. Rather than a "revival" of religious activism, a "reformation" of the political spectrum is taking place.

Our data suggest that the premise of uniform secularization of American politics is inadequate: religious elements in contemporary politics cannot be dismissed *simply* as anachronistic or reactionary in character. The processes of modernization have indeed secularized large segments of the national activist corps, but they have also made politically relevant the traditional religiosity of many influential elites. The emerging division between the religious and secular—a pattern common in modern European politics—may represent the more lasting effects of modernization (Martin 1978).

In the post-war period, secular activists were both the products and agents of this restructuring process. Produced by unprecedented access to higher education and economic growth, these New Class activists were drawn disproportionately from social groups traditionally hostile to the Old Class. Further "alienated" from the social and political "establishment" and characterized by post-material values, they populated the liberal reform movements of the 1960s and 1970s (Wuthnow 1988), supporting the "social democratic" image of secular activists. The "new politics" of reform stressed the characteristics and resources of the New Class: an expanded political agenda, accompanied by intense opinion and distrust of institutions, and new methods of political organization emphasizing knowledge, leisure and mobility. However, the very social trends that produced secular liberals, education and upward mobility, seem to have stripped them of the social and political connections crucial to sustaining high levels of participation (Verba and Nie 1978).

Secular reformers had a profound impact on religious activists, particularly those attached to Democratic and liberal politics (Quinley 1974). Many made common cause with the Secular Left, sharing with them many New Class social traits, if not all the same values. Indeed, great efforts were made to "reform" religious traditions and institutions and make them relevant to secular society (Wald 1987: 245). But other religious activists became disenchanted with reform politics and its advocates, even to the point of deserting to the GOP and more conservative venues. These strains are critical to reform politics because religious liberals represent an important source of political activism. Their higher rate of participation results from a combination of New Class resources and Old Class connections.

If social integration supports political activism, then the eventual arousal of the Religious Right should have come as no surprise, being a key element in the "silent majority." Made up largely of conventional businessmen, these Old Class activists have used their considerable resources and social connections to defend "order and tradition" against reform politics. Religion is simply one way in which these sophisticated and established activists can be accessed politically. By contrast, the less numerous members of Christian Right organizations are purer traditionalists to whom religious concerns are salient (Guth and Green 1987).

Indeed, recognition of the broader Religious Right helps explain the failures and successes of Christian Right organizations. On the one hand, much of the Religious Right is already mobilized politically, with far better connections and a far greater stake in the social order, and thus likely to resist extreme and disorderly politics. On the other hand, the followers of Jerry Falwell and Pat Robertson find a sympathetic, if not always supportive audience in Republican and conservative circles (Bruce 1988).

The same cannot be said of the Secular Right, New Class activists with strong materialist values. When compared to the other categories, these activists seem to seek "order without tradition" and may represent the archetype of post-industrial conservatism, the "libertarian" right (Green and Guth 1987). However, neither their numbers, resources nor political location suggest they will be an important force in the near future—though perhaps more so in the long run.

Thus, religious communities and commitments underlie basic alignments among political activists, and through them, perhaps, the mass
public. While secularization is indeed an important trend in American
politics, it transforms rather than negates the political significance of
religion. Contemporary politics is indeed played in a new key, but
hymns are still part of the repertory.

Notes

1. The sample was drawn primarily from ideological and party committees,
chosen on the basis of three criteria: (1) the top ten nonconnected PACs in the
1981–82 election cycle; (2) the largest and most visible "single issue" PACs,
minor party and candidate movements; (3) the three national Republican and
Democratic party committees and the largest business and labor peak associations. Because federal law requires reporting only contributors of $200 or more
per election cycle, the sample consists largely of major donors (Green and
Guth 1986).

2. We employed a version of the Dilman (1978) survey technique: maximum
personalization and repeated contacts. Analysis of the response rates by type of
PAC, region of residence and size of contribution revealed no significant response
bias, although Republican party and conservative PAC donors responded at a
slightly higher rate.

3. Extensive experimentation revealed that the total funds raised by each PAC
in the 1981–82 election cycle approximates well the number of donors to each
PAC, thus approximating the probability of selection of each sub-sample from
the universe of donors (Kish 1965; Guth and Green 1986). However, Republican
and conservative donors gave on average smaller donations than other kinds
of donors.

4. Our denominational scale had the following eight categories: CHARIS-
MATIC AND FUNDAMENTALIST (Assemblies of God, all Pentecostal and
independent charismatic churches, Bible and independent Baptists, Bible and
independent fundamentalist churches, Church of Christ. Church of God, and
split-offs from mainline Protestant churches); CONSERVATIVE PROTES-
TANTS (Southern, American and Black Baptists, Christian and Missionary
Alliance, Christian Church, Christian Reformed Church, Evangelical Free and
Evangelical Covenant Churches, Free Methodists, Nazarene, Holiness, Adventist
and Peace churches, Missouri and Wisconsin Synod Lutherans, and independent
evangelical churches); MAINLINE PROTESTANTS (the major Lutheran,
Methodist, Presbyterian and Reformed bodies, Disciples of Christ); CATHO-
LICS (Roman Catholics and all Eastern Orthodox groups); LIBERAL PROTES-
TANTS (Episcopalians, Congregationalists, Christian Scientists, Quakers);
JEWS (all Jewish bodies); OTHERS (Unitarian/Universalists, Humanists, Metro-
politan Community Church, all new religious groups and non-Western religions);

NONE (respondent claimed to have no denominational affiliation). This categorization is based on Stark and Glock (1970) and Roof and McKinney (1987), supplemented by Piepkorn (1978).

5. The wording of the Gallup items was as follows: "How important are each of these things to you personally? . . . Following God's Will . . . Following a strict moral code"; response categories were: "very important, fairly important, not important."

6. The intercorrelations among our four variables are as follows: denominational scale and God's Will r = .45; denominational scale and strict moral code r = .20; denominational scale and church membership r = .25; God's Will and strict moral code r = .48; God's Will and church membership r = .30; Moralism and church membership r = .20.

7. Factor analysis of our religious variables produced one factor with an eigenvalue greater than one (2.05), accounting for 52 percent of the variance. The factor loadings were as follows: following God's will .85, denomination .73, church membership and activity .67, and following a strict moral code .64.

8. We used the standard seven-point scale for self-identified ideology: "We hear a lot these days about liberals and conservatives. Where would you place yourself on the following scale?"; response categories were: "extremely liberal, very liberal, liberal, moderate, conservative, very conservative, extremely conservative." Our "liberal category combines all three liberal self-identifications and our "conservative" category all three conservative self-identifications.

9. Despite their limitations, our categories fit common sense notions of secular and religious individuals to a large degree, as the following table illustrates.

	Secular Left	Religious Left	Secular Right	Religious Right	Entire Sample
Following God's Will "Very Important"	0%	85%	0%	93%	51%
Belong to a Church or Religious Institution	5%	93%	1%	86%	56%
Following Strict Moral Code "Very Important"	15%	66%	24%	86%	51%
Denomination					
Charismatic/ Fundamentalist	0	7	0	12	4
Conservative Protestant	0	12	0	17	10
Mainline Protestant	3	32	8	49	30
Roman Catholic	3	28	4	14	14
Liberal Protestant	5	13	2	6	15
Jewish	21	6	13	1	7
Others	11	2	13	1	7
None	57	—	60	—	13
	100%	100%	100%	100%	100%

10. A series of multiple discriminant analyses were performed "round robin" for each pair of our categories and for the sample as a whole. All discriminant

functions were significant at the .05 level or better, and confirmed the findings presented in Tables 8.3–8.7. Demographic variables outperformed agenda and organizational variables by a large margin in every case. Measures of education and discriminated best, followed by occupation, age, gender, geography and income. Further information is available from the authors.

References

Abramson, Paul R., and Ronald Inglehart. 1987. "Generational Replacement and the Future of Post-Materialist Values." *Journal of Politics* 49: 231–41.

Ammerman, Nancy. 1987. *Bible Believers: Fundamentalists in the Modern World.* New Brunswick, NJ: Rutgers University Press.

Beatty, Kathleen, and Oliver Walter. 1984. "Religious Preferences and Practice: Reevaluating Their Impact on Political Tolerance." *Public Opinion Quarterly* 48: 312–24.

Beck, Paul Allen, and M. Kent Jennings. 1984. "Updating Political Periods and Political Participation." *American Political Science Review* 78: 198–201.

Berger, Peter. 1981. "The Class Struggle in American Religion." *Christian Century.* February: 194–99.

Brody, Richard A. 1978. "The Puzzle of Political Participation in America." In Anthony King, ed., *The New American Political System,* pp. 287–324. Washington, D.C.: American Enterprise Institute.

Brown, Clifford Jr., Roman Hedges, and Lynda Powell. 1980a. "Modes of Elite Political Participation: Contributors to the 1972 Presidential Candidates." *American Journal of Political Science* 23: 259–90.

———. 1980b. "Belief Structure in a Political Elite: Contributors to the 1972 Presidential Candidates." *Polity* 13: 134–46.

Brown, Robert McAfee. 1978. *Theology in a New Key: Response to Liberation Themes.* Philadelphia: Westminster.

Bruce, Steve. 1988. *The Rise and Fall of the New Christian Right.* Oxford: Clarendon Press.

Bruce-Briggs, B. 1979. *The New Class?* New Brunswick, NJ: Transaction Books.

Buchanan, Patrick J. 1988. *Right from the Beginning.* Boston: Little, Brown.

Buell, Emmett, and Lee Sigelman. 1985. "An Army that Meets Every Sunday? Popular Support for the Moral Majority in 1980." *Social Science Quarterly* 66: 427–34.

Burnham, Walter Dean. 1981. "The 1980 Earthquake: Realignment, Reaction, or What?" In Thomas Ferguson and Joel Rogers, eds., *The Hidden Election,* pp. 89–141. New York: Pantheon.

Cass, James, and Max Birnbaum. 1983. *Comparative Guide to American Colleges.* New York: Harper and Row.

Chittister, Joan, and Martin Marty. 1983. *Faith and Ferment: An Interdisciplinary*

Study of Christian Beliefs and Practices. Minneapolis: Augsburg Publishing House.

Dawson, Richard E. 1973. *Public Opinion and Contemporary Disarray.* New York: Harper and Row.

De Leon, David. 1988. *Everything is Changing: Contemporary U.S. Movements in Historical Perspective.* New York: Praeger.

Dilman, Don. 1978. *Mail and Telephone Surveys: The Total Design Method.* New York: Wiley.

Gallup, George Jr. 1982. *Religion in America.* Princeton, NJ: Princeton Religious Research Center.

Glock, Charles Y., and Robert Wuthnow. 1979. "Departures from Conventional Religion: The Nominally Religious, the Nonreligious and the Alternatively Religious." In Robert Wuthnow, ed., *The Religious Dimension: New Directions in Quantitative Research*, pp. 47–68. New York: Academic Press.

Godwin, Kenneth. 1988. *The Direct Marketing of Politics.* Chatham, NJ: Chatham House.

Green, John C., and James L. Guth. 1986. "Big Bucks and Petty Cash: Party and Interest Group Activists in American Politics." In Allan Cigler and Burdett Loomis, eds., *Interest Group Politics*, 2nd ed., pp. 91–113. Washington, D.C.: CQ Press.

———. 1987. "The Sociology of Libertarians." *Liberty* 1: 5–12.

———. 1988. "The Christian Right in the Republican Party: The Case of Pat Robertson's Supporters." *Journal of Politics* 50: 150–65.

———. 1989. "The Missing Link: Political Activists and Support for School Prayer." *Public Opinion Quarterly* 53: 41–57.

Guth, James L. 1983. "The Politics of the Christian Right." In Allan Cigler and Burdett Loomis, eds., *Interest Group Politics*, pp. 60–83. Washington, D.C.: CQ Press.

Guth, James L., and John C. Green. 1986. "Faith and Politics: Religiosity and Ideology among Campaign Contributors." *American Politics Quarterly*, 14: 186–200.

———. 1987. "The Moralizing Minority: Christian Right Support Among Political Contributors." *Social Science Quarterly* 63: 598–610.

———. 1989. "God and the GOP: Varieties of Religiosity among Political Contributors." In Ted G. Jelen, ed., *Religion and American Political Behavior*, pp. 223–41. New York: Praeger.

Guth, James L., Ted Jelen, Lyman Kellstedt, Corwin Smidt, and Kenneth Wald. 1988. "The Politics of Religion in America: Issues for Investigation." *American Politics Quarterly* 116: 118–59.

Hadden, Jeffrey. 1987. "Towards Desacralizing Theory." *Social Forces* 65: 587–611.

Hadden, Jeffrey, and Anson Shupe. 1986. "Introduction." In Jeffrey Hadden and Anson Shupe, eds., *Prophetic Religions and Politics*, pp. xi–xxix. New York: Paragon House.

————. 1988. *Televangelism: Power and Politics on God's Frontier.* New York: Holt.

Hadden, Jeffrey, and Charles E. Swann. 1981. *The Prime Time Preachers.* Reading, MA: Addison-Wesley.

Halebsky, Sandor. 1976. *Mass Society and Political Conflict.* New York: Cambridge University Press.

Hallum, Anne Motley. 1988. "Presbyterians as Political Amateurs." In Charles W. Dunn, ed., *Religion in American Politics*, pp. 63–74. Washington, D.C.: CQ Press.

Harrison, M. I., and B. Lazerwitz. 1982. "Do Denominations Matter?" *American Journal of Sociology* 88: 356–77.

Hatch, Roger D. 1988. "Jesse Jackson in Two Worlds." In Charles W. Dunn, ed., *Religion in American Politics*, pp. 87–102. Washington, D.C.: CQ Press.

Hilty, Dale M., Rick L. Morgan, and Joan E. Burns. 1984. "Dimensions of Religious Involvement." *Journal for the Scientific Study of Religion* 23: 252–63.

Hunter, James D. 1983. *American Evangelism.* New Brunswick, NJ: Rutgers University Press.

Inglehart, Ronald. 1981. "Post-Materialism in an Environment of Insecurity." *American Political Science Review* 75: 880–900.

Jennings, M. Kent, and Gregory B. Marcus. 1988. "Political Involvement in the Later Years: A Longitudinal Survey." *American Journal of Political Science* 32: 302–16.

Jones, Ruth, and Warren Miller. 1985. "Financing Campaigns: Macro Level Innovation and Micro Level Response." *Western Political Quarterly* 38: 187–210.

Kirkpatrick, Jane J. 1976. *The New Presidential Elite.* New York: Russell Sage and Twentieth Century Fund.

Kish, Leslie. 1965. *Survey Sampling.* New York: Wiley.

Latus, Margaret. 1984. "Mobilizing Christians for Political Action: Campaigning with God on Your Side." In David Bromley and Anson Shupe, eds., *New Christian Politics*, pp. 251–68. Macon, GA: Mercer University Press.

Lekachman, Robert. 1987. *Visions and Nightmares.* New York: Macmillan.

Liebman, Robert. 1983. "Mobilizing the Moral Majority." In Robert Liebman and Robert Wuthnow, eds., *The New Christian Right*, pp. 50–74. New York: Aldine.

Lienesch, Michael. 1982. "Right-wing Religion: Christian Conservatism as a Political Movement." *Political Science Quarterly*, 97: 403–25.

Lipset, Seymour M. 1981. "The Revolt Against Modernity." In Seymour M. Lipset, ed., *Consensus and Conflict.* New Brunswick, NJ: Transaction Books.

Lipset, Seymour M., and Everett C. Ladd. 1975. *The Divided Academy: Professors and Politics.* New York: Norton.

Lipset, Seymour M., and Earl Rabb. 1981. "The Election and the Evangelicals." *Commentary* 71: 25–31.

Lipset, Seymour M., and William Schneider. 1987. *The Confidence Gap.* Baltimore: Johns Hopkins University Press.

Martin, David. 1978. *A General Theory of Secularization.* New York: Harper and Row.

McCormik, Richard L. 1974. "Ethnocultural Interpretations of Nineteenth-Century American Voting Behavior." *Political Science Quarterly* 89: 351–77.

Nesbit, Dorothy D. 1988. "Changing Partisanship among Southern Party Activists." *Journal of Politics* 50: 322–34.

Ornstein, Norman, A. Kohut, and L. McCarthy. 1988. *The People, the Press and Politics.* Reading, MA: Addison-Wesley.

Patel, Kant, Denny Pilant, and Gary L. Rose. 1985. "Christian Conservatism: A Study in Alienation and Life Style Concerns." *Journal of Political Studies* 12: 17–30.

Phillips, Kevin P. 1983. *Post-Conservative America.* New York: Random House.

Piepkorn, Arthur C. 1978. *Religious Bodies of the United States and Canada. Vol. II: Protestant Denominations.* New York: Harper and Row.

Pollock, John C. 1981. *The Commercial Mutual Life Report on American Values in the 80's: The Impact of Belief.* Hartford, CT: Connecticut Mutual Life Insurance Co.

Quinley, Harold. 1974. *The Prophetic Clergy.* New York: Wiley.

Reichley, A. James. 1985. *Religion in American Public Life.* Washington, D.C.: Brookings Institution.

Roof, Wade Clark. 1979. "Socioeconomic Differentials among White Socioreligious Groups in the United States." *Social Forces* 58: 280–89.

Roof, Wade Clark, and William McKinney. 1987. *American Mainline Religion.* New Brunswick, NJ: Rutgers University Press.

Rothenberg, Stuart, and Frank Newport. 1984. *The Evangelical Voter: Religion and Politics in America.* Washington, D.C.: Free Congress Research and Education Foundation.

Rothman, Stanley, and S. Robert Lichter. 1982a. *Roots of Radicalism: Jews, Christians and the New Left.* New York: Oxford University Press.

———. 1982b. "Media and Business Elites: Two Classes in Conflict?" *The Public Interest* 69: 117–25.

Sapiro, Virginia. 1983. *The Political Integration of Women.* Urbana, IL: University of Illinois Press.

Simpson, John. 1983. "Moral Issues and Status Politics." In Robert Liebman and Robert Wuthnow, eds., *The New Christian Right,* pp. 188–207. New York: Aldine.

Smidt, Corwin. 1988. "The Mobilization of Evangelical Voters in 1980: An Initial Test of Several Hypotheses." *Southeastern Political Review* 16 (2): 3–33.

Sorauf, Frank J. 1988. *Money in American Elections.* Glenview, IL: Scott, Foresman/Little, Brown.

Stark, Rodney, and Charles Y. Glock. 1970. *American Piety: The Nature of Religious Commitment.* Berkeley, University of California Press.

Tamney, Joseph B., and Stephen B. Johnson. 1987. "Church-State Relations in the Eighties." *Sociological Analysis* 48: 1–16.

Trilling, Lionel. 1954. *The Liberal Imagination*. Garden City, NY: Doubleday.

Verba, Sidney, and Norman Nie. 1978. *Participation in America*. New York: Harper and Row.

Wald, Kenneth D. 1987. *Religion and Politics in the United States*. New York: St. Martin's Press.

————. 1988. "Churches as Political Communities." *American Political Science Review* 82: 531–48.

Wilcox, Clyde. 1987. "America's Radical Right Revisited: A Comparison of Activists of the Christian Right in Two Decades." *Sociological Analysis* 48: 46–57.

Williamsburg Charter Foundation. 1988. *The Williamsburg Charter Survey of Religion and Public Life*. Washington, D.C.: Williamsburg Charter Foundation.

Wilson, Bryan. 1982. *Religion in Sociological Perspective*. Oxford: Oxford University Press.

Wuthnow, Robert. 1988. *The Restructuring of American Religion*. Princeton, NJ: Princeton University Press.

9

The Bully Pulpit: Southern Baptist Clergy and Political Activism 1980–92

James L. Guth

When Christian Right leaders made their initial foray into politics during the 1980 elections, they had great plans for clergy, who would be critical to the mobilization of evangelical Christians. Reverend Jerry Falwell, head of the controversial Moral Majority, implored pastors to "urge people to vote, register them, tell them how to vote—right there in the pulpit." The Religious Roundtable, led by prominent evangelical clergy, invited thousands of ministers to gigantic rallies for Ronald Reagan, where they were given instruction in the fine art of electioneering. Indeed, the real muscle of the Moral Majority, the Roundtable, and other early Christian Right groups was provided by fundamentalist pastors (Liebman and Wuthnow 1983).

After this initial effort to mobilize clergy, the movement shifted its attention to evangelical laity. Second-generation Christian Right organizations, such as Focus on the Family and the Christian Coalition, often made no special effort to activate clergy and sometimes even consciously circumvented local ministers. Although many evangelical pastors found their way into Christian Right groups, their centrality to the movement was certainly lost. Indeed, the conventional wisdom among both scholars and many practitioners is that the Christian Right became a major force only when it moved beyond pastor-centered strategies of mobilization.

Why this pessimistic perspective on the role of clergy? Organizers and scholars alike identify several limits to pastoral leadership in the political kingdom. Some barriers are theological: unlike the "prophetic" mainline Protestant activists of the 1960s, who saw social reform as a prime responsibility of the church, evangelicals still put top priority on "soul winning" and not on the "things of this world" (Zwier 1982; Jelen 1993). In addition, many evangelicals are premillennialists, who stress the inevitable decline of society and the imminent Second Coming of Jesus, views that discourage political engagement (Wilcox, Linzey, and Jelen 1991). Many pastors fear congregational resistance or think that political activity might prove divisive in institutions in which good fellowship and consensus are highly valued. Others fear that activism may harm their reception in the larger community (Hayes 1995). Thus, the argument runs, evangelical clergy are an unlikely base for a conservative Christian political movement (cf. Olson 1994).

Most such scholarly assessments are based on anecdotal evidence, local case studies, or ethnographic analyses of individual congregations. On the other hand, the daily news offers many counterexamples of clerical leadership in Christian Right activities, suggesting a more optimistic evaluation. Of course, to determine definitively which perspective is closer to reality would require a systematic review of the political interests, attitudes, and participation of evangelical clergy over time.

Unfortunately, we have no comprehensive study of the full spectrum of evangelical clergy. We do have, however, data on ministers in the nation's largest evangelical (and biggest Protestant) denomination, the Southern Baptist Convention (SBC). The SBC has almost forty thousand churches and over fifteen million members, concentrated in the South (where it is sometimes characterized as "The Established Church") but found in every region. The SBC's eighty thousand ordained clergy outnumber Roman Catholic parish clergy or the combined ministerial corps of all mainline American Protestant churches. Historically committed to vigorous evangelism and the strict separation of church and state, in recent years the SBC and state Baptist conventions have often been drawn into the Christian Right movement, contributing, as many observers see it, to growing Republican strength in the South. Thus, because of their number, organization, and strategic location, SBC ministers provide a critical case study of pastoral politics in the heyday of the Christian Right.

In each presidential election year since 1980, we have polled a random sample of Southern Baptist pastors, using a mail questionnaire that has evolved over time but maintains a large body of core items. Responses to these four surveys form the basis for analysis.[1] In this essay, we address the following questions: First, what do Southern Baptist clergy think about their own role in the political process? How interested are they in politics and government? Do they want to be involved? What kinds of political activities do they deem appropriate for pastors? Have these assessments changed over time? Next, how involved are Baptist ministers? In what sort of activities? Have they become more active in politics since the 1980 emergence of the Christian Right? Which clergy factions are most involved? Finally, what factors explain the rise of activism among Southern Baptist clergy? Is participation tied more closely to personal, ideological, or mobilization factors? What should we expect for the future?

Changing Attitudes About Political Involvement

Harold Quinley's (1974) classic work *The Prophetic Clergy* argued that the future of clerical politics lay with theologically liberal mainline Protestants, who not only vested the church with crucial social and political functions but also favored sustained political engagement by ministers. Quinley found that the evangelicals in his California sample, including Southern Baptists, were much less positive about either a political role for the church or activity by clergy. Of course, the contemporary Christian Right emerged after Quinley's study, so we must consider whether evangelical attitudes have changed in the twenty-five years since his survey.

Even a quick perusal of our data shows that Southern Baptist clergy hardly fit the old stereotype of otherworldly evangelicals, concerned only to rescue souls for heaven. In both 1988 and 1992, about 75 percent claimed more than a "mild interest" in politics (above the mid-point on a seven-point scale), comparing favorably with responses of mainline Protestants (see Guth et al. forthcoming). In 1992, over three-fourths also rejected the notion that "clergy and churches should not try to influence or lobby public officials." In every survey after 1980, at least two-thirds also thought that "clergy have great potential to influence the social and political attitudes of their congregations." Finally, Baptist clergy became more willing to jettison theological separatism to join politically with clergy of other persuasions, with "cooperators" multiplying from 55 percent in 1984 to 63 percent in 1992.

Thus, Baptist clergy exhibit strong political interest, openness to political influence activities, a strong sense of leadership efficacy, and great willingness to cooperate with those who may differ theologically. But they also hold some attitudes that may counsel political restraint, at least for some. In each year, a solid majority (ranging from 54 to 64 percent) found that "it is difficult for ministers to know the proper political channels to use to accomplish some goal." In 1988, 49 percent also believed that "political activism usually hurts churches," while another 32 percent were "not sure." In 1992, 49 percent concurred that "some Southern Baptist leaders have gone too far in mixing religion and politics," but another 36 percent disagreed. Despite such cautionary notes, however, Baptist clergy seem eager to join the political fray. The number who would "like to be more involved in social and political activities" rose throughout the period, from 25 percent in 1980, to 31 percent in 1984, 41 percent in 1988, and 48 percent in 1992. In parallel fashion, ministers who thought that the SBC should "be more involved in vital social and political issues" grew from 40 percent in 1988 to 52 percent in 1992. Thus, for the most part, the SBC clergy's attitude toward political life appears quite positive.

Of course, these affirming views do not provide detailed guidance on which specific activities ministers deem proper. As Quinley showed, orthodox clergy not only were less supportive of ministerial activism but were especially critical of militant tactics, such as civil disobedience and protest marches. Indeed, Quinley's focus on just such unconventional acts probably led him to understate conservatives' willingness to endorse "normal" forms of political leadership, often neglected in his analysis. In any event, we can trace the evolution of Baptist attitudes toward individual political acts. Most items in table 9.1 were drawn originally from Quinley's pathbreaking work and, whatever their limitations, have been repeated in the quadrennial Baptist surveys. Respondents were asked whether they approved or disapproved of ministers engaging in each action, and how strongly, with scores ranging from 1 ("strongly approve") to 5 ("strongly disapprove"). We report the mean approval for the individual acts. Thus, means below 3.0 represent net approval, while scores over 3.0 indicate disapproval. We have also reported an eta statistic; the larger the eta, the greater the mean change over time.

Two important conclusions can be drawn from table 9.1. First, ministers have quite different attitudes toward various forms of involvement. Nearly all support urging their congregation to vote and taking public stands on issues (but not from the pulpit). They also express net approval for (in declining order of support): preaching a whole sermon on an issue, taking pulpit stands on issues, forming a church group to study a social or political issue, endorsing candidates (not from the pulpit), and forming a political or social action group in the church. Stronger opposition appears to more militant or direct political activities: committing civil disobedience, endorsing candidates from the pulpit, participating in a protest march, joining national political organizations, or running for

TABLE 9.1
Approval of Types of Political Activities by Southern Baptist Clergy,
1980–1992

Approve of Ministers Who:	1980	1984	1988	1992	Eta
Urge Congregation to Vote	1.20	1.25	1.19	1.15	.07*
Take Public Stand on Political Issue	1.86	1.81	1.89	1.84	.03
Preach a Whole Sermon on Issue	2.39	2.22	2.15	1.81	.17**
Take Pulpit Stand on Political Issue	2.47	2.45	2.55	2.23	.08**
Organize Political Study Group	2.54	2.42	2.42	2.20	.10**
Publicly Endorse Candidate (not Pulpit)	2.55	2.44	2.38	2.43	.05
Organize Political Action Group	2.91	2.87	2.98	2.68	.09**
Run for Public Office	3.06	3.14	2.98	3.02	.05
Join National Political Organization	3.26	3.00	2.88	2.98	.11**
Participate in Protest March	3.73	3.50	3.06	2.77	.27**
Endorse Candidate from Pulpit	—	4.07	4.14	4.13	.04
Commit Civil Disobedience	4.31	4.20	3.46	3.60	.31**
Summary Score					
All SBC Clergy	2.91	2.81	2.68	2.55	.18**
Fundamentalists	2.99	2.79	2.57	2.50	
Conservatives	2.95	2.82	2.73	2.53	
Moderate or Liberal	2.70	2.76	2.56	2.62	

Entries are mean scores (1="Strongly Approve" and 5="Strongly Disapprove").
* $p < .05$
** $p < .001$

public office. Clearly, certain activities are sanctioned by clergy, but others are far more controversial.

Second, ministerial opinion has evolved considerably over the past fifteen years, as signified by the etas. Pastors have become much more open to civil disobedience and protest activity—the latter actually receives a net approval rating by 1992. Perhaps antiabortion protests, picketing of adult bookstores and nightclubs, and similar campaigns by conservative groups have created a more positive perspective among evangelical clergy. Or it may be, as Verba, Schlozman, and Brady (1995:47) have argued, that protest is now a "relatively mainstream activity" in America. By 1992, SBC clergy had also warmed somewhat more to preaching sermons on political issues, taking pulpit stands on such issues, and forming study and action groups within the church; in addition, they were more adamant than ever about urging parishioners to vote. On the other hand, opinion had not changed significantly in a few areas, such as taking public stands on issues and candidates (both perennially approved) or running for office and endorsing candidates from the pulpit (which found less favor throughout the period).

To summarize changes in clerical opinion, we calculated an approval index from the ten items available in all four surveys.[2] Even more than the individual items, the mean index scores show mounting support for the "typical" act, moving from 2.91 in 1980 to 2.55 in 1992. Thus, Southern Baptist clergy have clearly become more accepting of political involvement. The theological "home" of participatory attitudes has also moved. As a rough guide to theological orientation, we asked ministers to choose a factional label from those often used by Southern Baptists: "fundamentalist," "conservative," "moderate," and "liberal" (Ammerman 1990). Despite the much discussed "fundamentalist takeover" of the SBC during the 1980s, the "market share" of each group remained fairly stable (see note 4), but vital changes had transpired in factional attitudes. Quinley's pattern still held in 1980: moderates and liberals were most friendly toward political activism, with conservatives next, and fundamentalists least favorably inclined. After 1980, however, fundamentalists and conservatives steadily increased their approval, while moderates and liberals showed only modest fluctuations. By 1992, in fact, fundamentalists endorsed activism most strongly, followed closely by conservatives and, at a little more distance, by moderates and liberals. Thus, theology still influences approval, but in a way quite different than it did in 1980.

What factors other than theology shape ministers' attitudes? Although the pattern is complex and varies over time, we can note the major correlates of approval. Throughout the period, younger ministers are more positive than older ones; thus, generational replacement explains much of the growing approval. During the earlier years, urban upbringing, middle-class origins, and extended secular and seminary education also produced greater approval (see Guth 1989), but by 1992 ministers with these social class advantages were not statistically more likely to approve activism. Republicans have always been somewhat more supportive than Democrats, an advantage that peaked in 1992. And although political liberals approved activism more in 1980, by 1992 conservatives had a substantial edge.

To recapitulate: participatory attitudes have grown among Southern

Baptist clergy, who exhibit strong political interest, want to be more active, and think that their denomination should be engaged as well. In addition, they are more willing today to consider many political acts, including (for some pastors) even militant ones. This transformation is most visible among younger clergy, who have shed their elders' hostility to politics. And, in a portentous change, the SBC's proactivism contingent shifted away from moderates and liberals to the newly dominant theological and political conservatives. These changes have also seemingly nullified the old demographic correlates of approval of political activism, such as middle-class origins and educational achievement.

The Rise of Activism among Southern Baptist Clergy

These new attitudes obviously create the potential for greater participation. As our earlier studies have shown, not all ministers practice each activity they accept in theory, but few commit acts they reject in principle (Guth 1983, 1984). Has the attitudinal transformation been reflected in greater actual involvement?

To answer this question, we will look first at "career political participation," the extent to which SBC ministers have at some time undertaken political activities. We will track the accumulation of political activity in the clerical corps from 1980 to 1992. Not all pastors are active continuously; like other citizens, they are pushed or drawn into participation at some times and refrain from engagement at others (Rosenstone and Hansen 1993). Once having undertaken specific acts, however, we suspect that ministers may well have a lower threshold for future activation—and perhaps can draw on a greater fund of expertise. Thus, in some sense, career political participation may identify the "potential" clerical activists at any one time.

What do we find? First, Southern Baptist clergy as a group have accumulated much political experience since 1980. As table 9.2 shows, in virtually every case the number of ministers reporting that they had at some time undertaken each action has grown, often dramatically. Taking public stands on political issues, touching on issues in sermons, leading petition drives, and contacting public officials are now almost universal in the repertoire of SBC clergy. Public endorsement of candidates outside the pulpit has rapidly approached the same status.

Other activities have migrated from "rarely done" status to "much more common." Good examples are writing letters to the editor, organizing political study and action groups, joining national political organi-

TABLE 9.2
Career Political Activities of Southern Baptist Clergy, 1980–1992

Approve of Ministers Who:	1980	1984	1988	1992
Taken Public Stand on Political Issue	84.7	90.6	91.5	95.1
Touched on Issue in Sermon	85.6	90.8	93.9	94.8
Circulated a Petition	69.6	87.7	91.4	90.6
Contacted Public Official	68.9	76.4	79.3	87.0
Publicly Endorsed Candidate	52.7	64.5	68.5	80.7
Preached Whole Sermon on Issue	—	—	—	79.2
Participated in Issue Boycott	—	—	—	72.9
Taken Pulpit Stand on Issue	59.0	70.1	—	—
Written Letter to Editor	34.1	44.8	50.6	57.0
Given Money to PAC, Party, etc.	—	45.2	45.3	43.7
Organized Political Action Group	13.9	22.7	22.6	28.4
Organized Political Study Group	13.1	19.9	24.3	27.8
Joined National Political Organization	11.1	20.2	20.7	24.8
Protested by March	3.5	7.4	12.6	21.5
Endorsed Candidate from Pulpit	3.9	11.9	10.6	11.8
Ran for Public Office	5.2	5.0	3.6	5.9
Committed Civil Disobedience	1.8	3.2	3.1	3.2

zations, and engaging in protest marches. Endorsing candidates from the pulpit has also become more common but is distinctly a minority enterprise even in 1992. In addition, there are other activities for which we lack longitudinal data but in which ministers have frequently engaged: contributing money to parties, PACs, or candidates (almost half have done this); preaching whole sermons on issues; participating in issue-based boycotts; and taking pulpit stands on political issues. Of course, running for office and committing civil disobedience are still uncommon acts for Baptist clergy, as for most Americans.

Thus, the kinds of public pronouncement and "citizen" involvement long favored by Southern Baptist ministers have become ever more common over time, while some clergy have also experimented with the more aggressive or militant activities once thought the special purview of the 1960s "New Breed" liberals. A comparison of tables 9.1 and 9.2 shows a nice correspondence between growth in approval for such activities and involvement itself. Of course, whether attitude shifts preceded or followed engagement is an open question (probably some of both occurred). But it is clear, to borrow an ancient Baptist aphorism, that in politics many SBC clergy have "left preaching and gone to meddling."

Career participation data tell us little about frequent or habitual activities of SBC clergy, however. Growth in career participation might conceivably reflect a stronger propensity for occasional incursions into politics, ventures that are not repeated. Any sustained political impact by clergy, however, depends on regular involvement. On this point, we have data from presidential election years from 1984 through 1992, when we asked whether ministers had engaged in each activity "during the past year." As we expect and table 9.3 confirms, many fewer clergy report involvement in each activity in a year than have at some time committed that act, but by any comparison with the American public their participation rates are quite impressive. And despite a few fluctuations, involvement has generally risen.

Ministers report notable increases in the issue content of sermons, taking public stands on issues, making public endorsements of political candidates, contacting public officials, and circulating petitions. More have also engaged in some less common activities: writing letters to the editor, endorsing candidates from the pulpit, joining national political organizations, participating in protest marches, and organizing study and action groups in the church. All told, the mean number of acts per year from among the fourteen common to all surveys rose steadily from 3.04 in 1984 to 3.38 in 1988, to 3.78 in 1992. This general pattern is buttressed by the large numbers reporting activities we asked about for the first time in 1992: preaching whole sermons on issues (55 percent), taking pulpit stands on issues (49 percent), and participating in boycotts (46 percent).

Although Baptist ministers are more and more active, the governmental focus of their efforts is not clear. According to conventional wisdom, Christian Right leaders initially concentrated on presidential and congressional elections; but after disappointment with the Reagan administration's lukewarm commitment to their agenda and the failure of Pat Robertson's 1988 campaign for the GOP nomination, they shifted attention to local politics (Moen 1992). As we have demonstrated earlier, however, Southern Baptist clergy were certainly not enthusiastic participants in the 1988 Robertson campaign but rather were solid Bush supporters, in both the primary and general election (Guth et al. 1991). So the strategies of leading movement organizations might not be imitated by other groups of Christian conservatives.

As we did not ask ministers about the specific governmental "targets" of their activities, we cannot apportion these to the appropriate level. In

TABLE 9.3
Election Year Activities of Southern Baptist Clergy, 1984–1992

Percentage having engaged in activity in past year:	1984	1988	1992
Touched on Issue in Sermon	68.5	74.9	75.9
Public Stand on Political Issue	62.9	62.8	75.6
Publicly Endorsed Candidate	41.7	46.5	63.6
Contacted Public Official	35.0	38.2	51.2
Circulated a Petition	37.6	58.7	44.7
Letter to Editor	12.7	14.2	18.4
Gave Money to PAC, Party etc.	20.3	18.5	18.4
Endorsed Candidate from Pulpit	6.7	10.6	11.8
Joined National Political Org	8.7	8.5	10.5
Protested by March	2.2	3.9	9.6
Organized Action Group	7.2	7.3	9.5
Organized Study Group	4.9	5.7	6.6
Ran for Public Office	0.7	0.5	0.7
Committed Civil Disobedience	0.7	0.6	0.5
General Activism Summary:			
Mean Acts:			
All Clergy	3.04	3.38	3.78
Fundamentalists	3.36	3.93	4.68
Conservatives	3.02	3.26	3.72
Moderates/Liberals	2.74	3.35	3.33
Presidential Campaign:			
Active in Primaries			
All Clergy	—	17.3	27.2
Fundamentalists	—	20.4	47.0
Conservatives	—	17.3	25.7
Moderates/Liberals	—	14.4	21.4
Active in General Election			
All Clergy	—	37.3	59.0
Fundamentals	—	50.0	81.8
Conservatives	—	38.3	58.1
Moderates/Liberals	—	22.5	44.9

1988 and 1992, however, we did ask directly about participation in presidential politics. After ascertaining their choices for the Republican and Democratic nominations and their vote in the general election, we asked pastors these question(s):

> Besides voting, many people also work for a candidate, by wearing campaign buttons, putting a sign in front of their house, attending speeches and rallies, etc. Beyond voting, did you ACTIVELY SUPPORT a candidate during the presidential primaries and caucuses (in the presidential election)? If yes, how actively? VERY, SOMEWHAT, SLIGHTLY?

Table 9.3 contains the results for primaries and general elections in both years. Southern Baptist clergy report remarkable amounts of presidential campaign involvement, with 17 percent engaged during the 1988 primaries, rising to 27 percent in 1992. General election activism mounted even more dramatically, from 37 percent in 1988 to 59 percent in 1992.

As we found in the case of approval of activism, the summary measures for both general activity and presidential activism show a major transition in theological location. All theological factions have shared in the rising general activism, but fundamentalists have witnessed the most marked growth. Their advantage is even more impressive in presidential elections, in which 47 percent report involvement in the 1992 primaries and an incredible 82 percent say they were active in the 1992 general election contest among Episcopalian George Bush, Southern Baptist Bill Clinton, and Presbyterian Ross Perot. As the theological pattern suggests, the overwhelming amount of clerical activism was on behalf of Republican Bush, who won about 80 percent of Baptist ministers' votes in both years but was the beneficiary of about 85 percent of their activity.

Explaining Political Participation

What accounts for the extent to which Southern Baptist ministers engage in political life? To explore this issue, we conclude our longitudinal analysis and move to a cross-sectional look at the 1992 data set, which has the most extensive participation battery and a wide array of independent variables for testing several theoretical propositions. The dependent variable in our remaining analysis is a participation index for 1992, constructed by adding the number of activities in which each minister engaged. These include seventeen general activity items plus activism in the presidential primaries and general election. (Note that primary and general election voting is *not* included.[3]) Thus, the index's potential range is from zero to nineteen; some clergy, in fact, did nothing at all, while a few actually performed eighteen acts!

Scholarly analysis of political participation has traditionally focused on the mass public, with little attention to professional or elite groups, except those that are themselves regular political activists, such as campaign contributors (Green and Guth 1986). As we have seen, however, many studies have surveyed ministers' political involvement. In the following analysis, we draw on converging perspectives from the literature on mass participation and clerical politics. Together, these offer three partially competing perspectives stressing: (1) personal and organizational resources available to the potential activist, (2) ideological sources of mobilization, and (3) effects of organizational networks.

1. Personal Resources. Classic works on political participation use what is often called the "socioeconomic status (SES) model." From this perspective, the primary facilitators of participation are high social class origins and current status, wealth, and higher education—all of which provide citizens with the means for effective involvement (Verba and Nie 1972:148). Most studies also find that older citizens, who have more life experience, know more about politics, and are more settled in their communities, are also more active (Rosenstone and Hansen 1993:136–41). Metropolitan residence appears in some studies as a facilitator of participation, but others find life in smaller communities to encourage involvement (cf. Verba and Nie 1972: 229–47).

The literature on clergy suggests some variations on these themes, however. At first glance, ministers might seem somewhat less diverse than the mass public on SES measures, as professionals with extended education and middle-class incomes. The SBC clergy, however, have still not experienced full professionalization; they come from a wide range of social class backgrounds, have differing educational experiences, and enjoy rather varied incomes. Their personal status is reflected in the congregations they serve: those with larger, middle-class congregations not only are wealthier personally but have at their disposal additional resources (and perhaps incentives) for political involvement (Sapp 1975:164).

Age may also have a different impact among clergy than in the mass public. Quinley's studies found that younger clergy—not older ones—were more politically engaged, perhaps because of more extensive education or because of cohort effects influencing young ministers during the civil rights and Vietnam War eras. Similar cohort effects might well have shaped the young, conservative clergy of the 1980s and 1990s, who grew up in the years of abortion battles, gay rights controversies, and fights over values in the public schools. Some evidence also suggests that ministers with long tenure with a particular congregation—like longtime residents in a community—are more likely to have the social networks and congregational support to engage in activism (Sapp 1975:161). We will test these hypotheses as well.

Other analysts argue that the most important personal characteristics for participation are attitudinal, not demographic. Psychological predispositions such as political interest, sense of political efficacy, and strong ties to parties and ideologies lead to greater political activity (Verba and Nie 1972; Rosenstone and Hansen 1993). Studies of ministerial activism have stressed other attitudinal characteristics, but ones that may well entail high levels of interest, efficacy, and ideological commitment: theological beliefs that highlight the importance of this-worldly social and political involvement, approval of the Church's political role, and the belief that political involvement is appropriate for ministers (Hadden 1969; Quinley 1974). Indeed, we expect that such professional role orientations will be extremely powerful.

What do we find? On the whole, psychological orientations are indeed far more potent than socioeconomic factors. As table 9.4 shows, correlations between ministers' "social status resources" and political involvement are modest, at best. Younger clergy and those with less experience are indeed more active, as Quinley discovered a generation earlier. So are those who live in larger urban areas, where political stimuli may be stronger and opportunities for involvement more extensive. Most surprisingly, social class background, urban upbringing, advanced secular and seminary education, and financial status have virtually no bivariate relationship with participation. Size of church, social class of the congregation, and length of tenure at the church bear no statistically significant relationship to activism, either, and only the size coefficient is in the expected direction. Ministers in working-class congregations and those with relatively brief tenures are actually slightly more likely to be engaged than those in middle-class congregations and with long tenure. These findings are something of a reversal of the situation among Southern Baptist pastors in the 1970s and early 1980s when "advantaged" clergy dominated activism (Sapp 1975; Guth 1989).

Psychological engagement with politics is much more powerful: interest, efficacy, strength of partisanship, and ideology all have solid bivariate relationships with activism and as Verba, Schlozman, and Brady (1995:348) discovered, are positively related to each other as well. Not surprisingly, the approval index is the strongest correlate of involvement.

TABLE 9.4
Personal Resources and Activism, Baptist Clergy, 1992

Social Resources	Pearson's r	b
Age	-.26**	-.08
Years in the Ministry	-.19**	.10
Social Class Origins	-.01	.07
Urban Origins	.07	.03
Urban Residence	.11*	.10*
Secular Education	-.03	-.04
Seminary Education	-.00	.01
Financial Status	.01	-.06
Size of Church	.05	.04
Social Class of Church	-.07	-.03
Years at Church	-.06	-.05
Psychological Resources		
Political Interest	.39**	.18**
Political Efficacy	.23**	.11*
Strength of Partisanship	.25**	.09*
Strength of Ideology	.33**	.24**
Political Role Approval	.60**	.46**

$$R = .71 \qquad \text{Adj. } R^2 = .48$$

* $p < .05$
** $p < .001$

And the lessons of the bivariate correlations are borne out by multiple regression. Of the SES variables, only urban residence persists. Although age and years in ministry come close to statistical significance, most of their impact is absorbed by the psychological engagement variables: younger clergy have higher levels of interest and efficacy and are most likely to approve involvement. Social class background also comes close to statistical significance, but the sign is in the wrong direction: ministers from working-class origins tend to be more active, once other factors are controlled. On the other hand, the psychological orientations survive the regression, with political role approval having the largest impact (cf. Verba, Schlozman, and Brady 1995:351). All in all, the personal resources model is quite powerful, accounting for almost half the variance in 1992 activity scores, with almost all of that power derived from attitudinal, not socioeconomic, variables.

2. *Ideological Mobilization.* Many analysts of participation have stressed ideological mobilization: the way in which ideas prompt people to become involved. Recent social resource mobilization theorists, for example, have emphasized development of "insurgency" consciousness in social movements (cf. Smith 1991). Similarly, political scientists have long noted the role of ideological conviction in creating "asymmetrical activism" in the party system (Nexon 1971; Verba and Nie 1972). More recently, Verba, Schlozman, and Brady (1995:391–415) have argued for the importance of "issue mobilization," by which citizens with strong sentiments on issues such as abortion or the environment become active by virtue of those feelings. Others have argued that consciousness of political conflict generates activism among those who fear mobilization by their opponents (Verba and Nie 1972:83–84).

The literature on clerical politics has parallel concerns. Hadden (1969) and Quinley (1974) argued that liberal Protestants developed a theology of politics that stressed religion's role in accomplishing social reform, responding to issues such as civil rights, the Vietnam War, and the arms race, while their more orthodox peers stuck to soul winning. But the Christian Right's emergence suggests that ideological mobilization can work for a conservative clergy as well; the rise of issues such as abortion, gay rights, and family values, often couched in a rhetoric of "culture wars" (Hunter 1991, 1994), has presumably stimulated conservative clergy. Indeed, many orthodox ministers are abandoning their former apolitical stance, adopting instead what we have elsewhere called a "civic gospel" as a rationale for involvement. This social theology argues that the United States was founded as a Christian nation but has fallen from that status, and that Christian citizens need to take aggressive political action to protect their own rights, buttress private and public morality, and restore the American constitutional system (Guth et al. forthcoming).

To test the power of ideological mobilization, we used a number of theological, agenda, and ideological measures[4] (table 9.5). First, the correlations show that the old relationship between liberal theology and political involvement has been reversed, at least among Southern Baptists. Whether measured by theological self-identification, adherence to traditional Christian orthodoxy, or belief in premillennialist tenets, the more *conservative* a minister is, the more active. Even stronger is the positive

TABLE 9.5
Ideological Influences on Activism, Baptist Clergy, 1992

Ideological Mobilization	Pearson's r	b
Theological Mobilization		
Theological Self-Identification	.24**	.03
Christian Orthodoxy	.20**	.13
Premillennialism	.23**	-.02
Civic Gospel	.30**	.19*
Agenda Mobilization		
Abortion Top National Problem	.19**	.15*
Spiritual Problems	.15*	.14*
Moral Problems	.11*	.08
Economic Problems	-.08	.06
Gays Politically Dangerous	.18**	.14*
Christian Right Politically Dangerous	-.10*	.12*
Partisan and Issue Mobilization		
Conservative Issue Positions	.33**	.14
Republican Identification	.32**	.20**
	R = .45 Adj. R² = .18	

* p<.05
** p<.001

correlation between adherence to the social theology of the new "civic gospel" and political involvement.

We also used two questions to tap "agenda" or "issue" mobilization. First, we asked ministers to list the "most important problem confronting the country" and second, to name the "most dangerous" political group in the United States. As table 9.5 shows, ministers who volunteered abortion as the top problem are considerably more active than average, as are those who mentioned spiritual issues or moral problems. On the other hand, pastors offering an economic issue (the centerpiece of the 1992 presidential campaign) were slightly less active, although not by a statistically significant margin. Among ministers who perceived that gays and gay rights organizations were the most dangerous political groups, activism was greater, but ministers fearing the Christian Right participated less than the clergy as a whole. Not surprisingly, then, the political agenda fostered by the conservative Christian movement demonstrates some mobilizing power.

We have already seen that strength of partisan and ideological attachments fosters activism, but we have not considered the direction of those attachments. To tap the impact of conservative ideology, we tested issue items, such as attitudes on gay rights, abortion, prayer in school, sex education, and others, but found that a single composite measure of "issue conservatism" outperformed any individual item or combination of such items.[5] This composite measure also performs considerably better than ideological self-identification, although the two measures are highly correlated (r = .77). Whatever measure is used, however, the outcome is basically the same: the more politically conservative the minister, the more active in 1992. And as we should expect by now, activism is also strongly correlated with Republican identification.

Of course, all these ideological measures—theological orthodoxy, adherence to the civic gospel, social issue priorities, conservative political attitudes, and Republican attachments—are closely interrelated. To sort out the proximate influences over activism, we used multiple regression. As the second column of Table 9.5 shows, the most potent direct influences on involvement are Republican identification, belief in the civic gospel, and concerns over abortion, gays, and spiritual problems. Conservative ideology and Christian orthodoxy retain fairly large coefficients but just miss statistical significance. (Note that concern over the Christian Right retains a respectable coefficient but becomes a force *for* activism once other ideological variables are controlled.) Thus, ideological mobilization is certainly a force among Southern Baptist clergy, embodied in a complex of attitudes including conservative theology, social issue agendas, conservative policy attitudes, and Republican allegiance. Note, however, that these variables in combination explain only about half the amount of variance accounted for by the psychological measures in table 9.4.

3. Organizational Mobilization. Finally, many analysts argue that activism is at least in part the product of organizational mobilization. Whether it is the effort of party organizations, unions, churches, or other institutions to turn out the vote (Teixeira 1992) or the actions of partisan and organizational elites who seek to elicit citizen involvement (Rosenstone and Hansen 1993; Verba, Schlozman, and Brady 1995), activists often respond to stimuli from the outside.

Clergy, of course, are organizational creatures. They are employed (in the Southern Baptist case) by individual congregations and work with other ministers in local Baptist associations, state conventions, and a national organization, the SBC itself. They join organizations designed to mobilize clergy for special causes, either outside or inside the denomination. They become involved in denominational networks by holding office and official responsibility. And they have to satisfy congregations that, according to SBC surveys, have become increasingly hard to please.

We asked ministers in 1992 whether they belonged to a wide variety of organizations, both outside and inside the SBC. And although a full discussion of these networks is far beyond the scope of this essay, some results are revealing. First, Baptist ministers join groups that seek to influence politics in fairly large numbers. The most popular is James Dobson's Focus on the Family, to which 19 percent of SBC ministers belong, followed by Donald Wildmon's American Family Association (AFA; 11 percent) and the Christian Coalition (5 percent). Altogether, one-fourth of SBC ministers report membership in at least one conservative organization, while 12 percent belong to two or more. Many others do not belong but "feel close" to these groups (e.g., 84 percent to Focus, 50 percent to AFA, and 33 percent to the Christian Coalition). Only a scattering of ministers join liberal groups, such as Bread for the World and Americans United for Separation of Church and State, despite the prominent role Southern Baptist clergy have played in both over the years, but a significant additional number feel close to their activities.

For many Baptist clergy, however, internal denominational and congregational networks may be more influential, especially given the SBC's long history of organizational separatism and self-sufficiency. Within the SBC itself are several groups combining theological and political positions that compete for influence. Christian Right political interests within the SBC have been led by Christian Life Commission head Richard Land, who has established a Washington lobbying office and led the move for greater denominational involvement. On the other side of the religious and political divide is the Alliance of Baptists, whose original founding entailed a rejection of SBC-Christian Right dalliances and which still provides lonely SBC liberals with a voice. The Cooperative Baptist Fellowship (CBF) is a much larger dissident group of conservative and moderate SBC leaders seeking alternative organizational vehicles for mission projects, theological education, and other SBC functions, without fully withdrawing from the denomination. And although the CBF leadership is obviously more moderate politically than the current SBC elite, they often reject what many see as the "politicization" of the denomination.

Activism within the denomination itself is a traditional outlet for clerical ambitions and energies. Traditionally, Southern Baptist ministers have been enmeshed in strong local association, state convention, and national convention networks. In the 1992 sample, 52 percent report holding or having held local office, 25 percent, a state office, and 6 percent, a national post. Our expectations on the political effects of such responsibilities are not clear. On the one side, participation in internal politics may well divert time and energies from activities "outside" church and denomination. Thus, denominational activists should be less involved in politics. On the other hand, skills developed in internal tasks, the networks and connections maintained, and exposure to larger issues might serve to politicize or activate. Of course, any such influences probably vary by organizational level. Although the national SBC has clearly become a "fellow traveler" in the Christian Right movement, until fairly recently most state conventions tended to represent traditional Baptist separatism and were minimally "political." Local associations have, perhaps, been least affected by Christian Right mobilization.

What about the ministers' congregations? Clergy and laity are tightly linked within the Baptist congregational polity, making their relationship potentially important for ministerial activism. Indeed, the literature on clergy politics has argued that the "New Breed" liberals of the 1960s were ultimately frustrated by hostile parishioners, who not only rejected ministerial involvement but favored much more conservative stances on policy (Hadden 1969; Quinley 1974; Balmer 1996). Although most surveys show that evangelical clergy are more in tune with their laity on both counts, some observers have suggested a new "gathering storm" in these churches, as conservative clerical activists confront and antagonize a more moderate laity (Campolo 1995).

Unfortunately, we had no direct measures of congregational attitudes toward ministerial activism or of congregational ideology, so we had to rely on ministers' own assessments. As successful Baptist clergy survive by being able to "read" their people, we anticipate that their judgments are not far out of line. In any event, pastors' actions are likely to be governed by their perceptions, rather than "reality" (cf. Zeigler 1966). We found that ministers' assessment of their congregations' reactions to potential activism corresponded closely to their own approval of activism, so we separated statistically the common element and used the residual in our analysis. We also calculated a score summarizing ministers' assessment of the differences between their own views and their congregations' on a total of twenty-one political issues. Experimentation showed that the mere extent of political differences between pastor and congregation had little relationship to activism, so here we use scores tapping both the magnitude and the direction (more liberal, more conservative) of differences.[6]

What do we find? Organizational factors clearly do have an impact on political activity. As table 9.6 shows, membership in Focus on the Family, the Christian Coalition, American Family Association, and Bread for the World is positively correlated with political activism. Of course, this relationship may simply represent a tendency for politically motivated ministers to join politically active religious groups, but it is fascinating to note that members are heavily engaged in the very activities in which each organization specializes. Members of Focus and the Christian Coalition, for example, participate in voter registration drives at very high rates; AFA members favor petition campaigns and issue boycotts; and members of Bread for the World unanimously report contacting public officials directly. If organizational affiliation does not stimulate activism, at least it channels that activism.

TABLE 9.6
Organizational Influences on Activism, Baptist Clergy, 1992

	Pearson's r	b
External Mobilization		
Focus on Family	.32**	.22**
Christian Coalition	.27**	.22**
American Family Association	.24**	.04
Bread for the World	.11*	.09
Denominational Mobilization		
Christian Life Commission	.18**	.16**
Alliance of Baptists	.08	.09
Cooperative Baptist Fellowship	-.07	-.17**
State Office Held	-.10*	-.05
SBC National Office Held	.07	.03
Congregational Context		
Church Approval of Activism	.08*	.06
More Liberal Than Church	-.15**	.05
More Conservative Than Church	.20**	.17**
	R = .49	Adj. R^2 = .22

* p < .05
** p < .001

Denominational allegiances and involvement also have some impact. Clergy tied to the Christian Life Commission (CLC) are more active politically than those without such connections, while Alliance members are slightly more active than average, although the coefficient barely misses statistical significance. CBF membership, on the other hand, is negatively associated with political activism, although, again, the coefficient skims the significance level. Denominational office holding has remarkably little impact in either direction. Local office holding has no impact whatever on political activity (and is omitted from table 9.6). State convention office-holding has a small (and barely significant) negative correlation with activism, while responsibilities in the more politically conscious national organization have a slight positive effect (which barely misses statistical significance). Nevertheless, on the whole, internal denominational involvement has only a minor impact on ministerial activism.

Perhaps more surprisingly, congregational influences also play only a minor role. Those who perceive their congregation as supportive of activism are slightly more engaged. Ministers who see themselves as much more liberal than their congregation participate less, but those who regarded themselves as more conservative are actually *more* active. Clearly, simple differences in political ideology between pastor and congregation do not restrain involvement, or many conservative pastors would be much less active than in fact they are.

The multivariate analysis in the second column of table 9.6 does not alter much the conclusions from the bivariate data. Membership in Focus on the Family or the Christian Coalition encourages activism, but AFA membership drops out and Bread for the World membership falls just below statistical significance. Attachment to the CLC remains a powerful influence, but Alliance membership still barely misses significance. On the other side, CBF affiliation, when all else is considered, becomes a powerful *negative* influence on activism. Interviews with CBF officials suggest that many members are preoccupied with creating their new quasi-denominational structures and have little time for politics, while others maintain a strict traditional Baptist separationism. Neither national nor state office holding is significant, while pastors more conservative than their congregations retain their participatory edge, even with other factors accounted for. When all is considered, pastors more liberal than their church actually become slightly more active, but the coefficient does not reach statistical significance. All the organizational factors combined explain somewhat less than a quarter of the variance in activism.

A Combined Model of Clerical Activism. To summarize our findings, we present in table 9.7 a combined model of political activism among SBC pastors in 1992. To simplify the analysis and conserve cases (given missing data), we ran a series of multiple regressions, starting with those variables that demonstrated influence in the three partial models, then eliminating those that contributed little to the analysis.

Psychological dispositions and organizational mobilization clearly dominate the final results. The most important factor, not surprisingly, is a minister's approval of political activity, and political interest, strength of ideological conviction, and sense of efficacy are also major factors. In

TABLE 9.7
Combined Model: Influences on Activism, Baptist Clergy, 1992

	Full Model b	Without Approval b
Social Resources		
Social Class	-.06*	-.08*
Urban Residence	.10*	.10*
Psychological Resources		
Interest	.16**	.30**
Efficacy	.08*	.15**
Strength of Partisanship	.07*	.13**
Strength of Ideology	.14**	.15**
Political Role Approval	.43**	—
Ideological Mobilization		
Civic Gospel	.12*	.13*
Gays Politically Dangerous	.07*	.08*
Organizational Mobilization		
Focus on Family	.15**	.20**
Christian Coalition	.12**	.15**
Alliance of Baptists	.12*	.13**
Cooperative Baptist Fellowship	-.11**	-.14**
Adj. R^2 =	.56	.42

* p < .05
** p < .001

addition, several organizational influences persist: members of Focus on the Family and the Christian Coalition are significantly more involved, even when all other factors are taken into account, as are the liberals in the Alliance of Baptists. On the other hand, ministers engaged with the CBF are markedly less politically active. Among demographic traits, only residence in urban areas and, when all else is accounted for, working-class origins produce somewhat higher levels of engagement. Among ideological factors, only adherence to the new civic gospel and a conviction that gays are politically dangerous produce higher involvement; the effects of orthodox theology, conservative ideology, and Republican preferences are absorbed by other variables.

To preclude charges that our robust results reflect primarily the powerful effects of the activism approval score, which some might think is excessively close to activism itself, we reran the analysis without that variable. As the second column in table 9.7 shows, when the approval index is omitted, its effects are in large part absorbed by political interest, efficacy, and strength of partisanship and ideology, with organizational mobilization also playing a larger role. And although the reduced equation does not match the explanatory power of the full model, it still performs quite respectably, explaining 42 percent of the variance compared to 56 percent in the full model. Thus, although approval of activism makes a unique contribution to the analysis, it is clearly not the only factor influencing participation.

Summary and Conclusions

After initial preoccupation with clerical leadership in the Christian Right, scholars joined many movement leaders in neglecting the role that ministers may play in the movement. Our longitudinal study of Southern Baptist ministers suggests that not only do they provide a numerous corps of potential activists for conservative and Republican causes but that their opinion leadership in Baptist congregations may have a long-term, if subtle, effect on public attitudes, especially in the South. As we have seen, Southern Baptist clergy have grown steadily more interested and psychologically engaged in political life, have become more active in a variety of ways, and have adapted themselves to a permanent role in the political world.

In the midst of this transformation, some old scholarly truisms have been negated. Pastoral politics among Southern Baptists is rooted in theological attitudes long thought inimical to activism: otherworldly orthodoxy, often buttressed by premillennial beliefs. Adherents to these "conservative" theological perspectives have reoriented themselves to contemporary politics by the adoption of a new social theology, what we have called the "civic gospel," which connects historic Baptist theology with the state of the contemporary world in a way that suggests the necessity for activism. Closely tied to this new perspective is the mobilizing impact of abortion, gay rights, sex education, and other "culture war" issues, which have had a disproportionate impact on a new generation of young, theologically orthodox, and politically conservative ministers. Indeed, their concern with such questions is intense enough to overcome even some SES disadvantages, aided perhaps by the external stimulation of Christian Right organizations (and perhaps Republican party organizations).

What should we expect in the future? First, it is likely that most SBC clergy will remained aligned with the conservative party, the Republicans. Even fellow Southern Baptist Bill Clinton failed to pull them back to their ancient Democratic home in 1992. And, no doubt, participation in the political lives of their communities will remain at a higher level than that of a generation ago and perhaps even increase. The clergy's high level of political interest, efficacy, and approval of participation ensures that much. Having said this, we must stress that the actual level of participation at any time is likely to reflect a variety of forces external to the clergy itself: the nature of the issues on the federal, state, and local political agendas; the attractiveness of Republican candidates, especially their commitment to conservative social values; the activities of Christian Right organizations, which have served to mobilize at least some Southern Baptists during the past few election cycles; and, perhaps, the encouragement provided by denominational leaders and agencies at all levels of Southern Baptist life. As most of these factors are variables, not constants, we anticipate some fluctuations in participation, in both the amount and the targets of activity. Whatever the variations, however, Southern Baptist clergy have become one building block in an increasingly Solid (Republican) South.

At the same time, we must not assume that the politicization of the clergy in one conservative Protestant denomination, however prominent, is typical of all parts of the evangelical community. Ministers in other evangelical Protestant churches may well be less active in partisan politics than Southern Baptists (Guth et al. forthcoming). On the other hand, religious leaders in many of the burgeoning new nondenominational megachurches often seem especially prominent in both local political activities and the Christian Right. A great deal more work needs to be done on the ways in which theology, denominational traditions and structures (or the lack of them), regional context, lay attitudes, and leadership strategies influence the politics of preachers in "the new American Mainline," evangelical Protestantism.

Notes

1. The surveys were conducted in a very similar manner in each year. In 1980, 1984, and 1992, the author drew a random sample from among "pastors" in the most recent SBC *Convention Annual*; in 1988 a random sample was provided by the SBC Sunday School Board Research Office. Ministers were mailed cover letters explaining the project and questionnaires just after each presidential election. At least three follow-ups were sent to those who did not respond to the initial survey. The final N and response rate for each year were as follows: 1980, 460 and 63 percent; 1984, 902 and 56 percent, 1988, 653 and 48 percent; and 1992, 458 and 47 percent. Comparison of demographic data from the surveys with information from SBC publications suggests that the respondents are quite representative of the SBC clerical corps, although they are slightly better educated in some years. Analysis of changes in major variables in responses to each successive mailing suggests no major biases by time of response.

2. We omitted the urging to vote item, as it is almost universally approved and shows no significant variation by other important variables. Inclusion in the present analysis would increase the total approval scores somewhat but would not modify any conclusions. Although a principal components analysis reveals three subdimensions in approval of activism, the overall index accounts for most of the explained variation and has an alpha reliability of .81. We therefore use it in the rest of the analysis.

3. The mean of the 1992 participation index is 5.86, with a standard deviation of 3.51. The alpha reliability coefficient is a robust .80. Although further analysis reveals that activism has three subdimensions worthy of analysis, we shall focus here on this powerful measure of general involvement.

4. Theological self-identification is the four-category measure described in the text. Over the period, the percentage of self-identified fundamentalists declined from 24 percent to 15 percent, while conservatives grew slightly from 60 to 66 percent of the clergy. Moderates fluctuated around 16 percent, while only 1 or 2 percent of the SBC clergy in each year admitted to being theological liberals. Christian orthodoxy is a factor score derived from a principal components analysis of six items on the inerrancy of Scripture, the historicity of Adam and Eve, the Virgin Birth of Jesus, the literal existence of Hell and the Devil, and the physical Second Coming of Jesus. The score has a theta reliability of .85. The premillennialism variable is a similarly derived combination of four items on dispensationalist belief, premillennial views, the Rapture of the Church, and the special role of Israel in God's future plans for humanity. The score has a theta

reliability of .82. The civic gospel score was also produced by a principal components analysis from six items on the Christian origins of the United States, the preferred status of free enterprise as a Christian economic system, the incompatibility of political liberalism with true Christian faith, the existence of a single correct Christian view on most political issues, the conviction that religious people face real threats to their freedom today, and sentiment that the United States needs a Christian political party. The theta reliability for this variable is .81.

5. We experimented extensively with the best way to measure conservatism and liberalism. Using the twenty-one policy items in the 1992 survey, we discovered three ideological dimensions, focusing respectively on social, economic, and foreign policy issues. Conservative social and foreign policy views correlated most strongly with participation. We also discovered, however, that the unrotated first principal component from the initial analysis, on which virtually all the variables loaded strongly, was the best measure of ideology, representing a kind of "general conservatism" factor. We therefore use it in the rest of the analysis; it has a theta reliability of .92.

6. To determine the degree of difference between pastor and congregation on political activism, we simply calculated and summed the differences between the pastor's own assessment of each activity and the pastor's perception of the congregation's. We then regressed the pastor's score on the congregation's to remove the common element and used the residual. On policy issues, we similarly constructed a score for the differences, as seen by the pastor, and then broke the scale at the zero point i.e., where differences were nonexistent. The scale scores in the conservative direction became the "more conservative" variable, while those in the liberal direction became the "more liberal" variable.

References

Ammerman, Nancy Tatom. 1990. *Baptist Battles*. New Brunswick, N.J.: Rutgers University Press.

Balmer, Randall. 1996. *Grant Us Courage*. New York: Oxford University Press.

Campolo, Tony. 1995. *Can Mainline Denominations Make a Comeback?* Valley Forge, Penn.: Judson Press.

Green, John, and James Guth. 1986. "Big Bucks and Petty Cash: Party and Interest Group Activists in American Politics." In *Interest Group Politics*, 2d ed., ed. Allan Cigler and Burdett Loomis. Washington D.C.: Congressional Quarterly Press.

Guth, James. 1983. "Preachers and Politics: Varieties of Activism among Southern Baptist Ministers." In *Religion and Politics in the South: Mass and Elites Perspectives*, ed. Tod A. Baker, Robert P. Steed, and Laurence W. Moreland. New York: Praeger.

———. 1984. "The Politics of Preachers: Southern Baptist Ministers and Christian Right Activism." In *New Christian Politics,* ed. David Bromley and Anson Shupe. Macon, Ga.: Mercer University Press.

———. 1989. "Southern Baptists and the New Right." In *Religion in American Politics,* ed. Charles W. Dunn. Washington D.C.: Congressional Quarterly Press.

Guth, James, John Green, Corwin Smidt, Lyman Kellstedt, and Margaret Poloma. n.d. *The Bully Pulpit: The Politics of Protestant Preachers.* Lawrence: University of Kansas Press. Forthcoming.

Guth, James, John Green, Corwin Smidt, and Margaret Poloma. 1991. "Pulpits and Politics: The Protestant Clergy in the 1988 Election." In *The Bible and the Ballot Box,* ed. James Guth and John Green. Boulder, Colo.: Westview.

Hadden, Jeffrey K. 1969. *The Gathering Storm in the Churches.* Garden City, N.Y.: Doubleday.

Hayes, Jeffrey. 1995. "Pre-existing Social Networks and the Christian Right." Paper presented at the annual meeting of the Midwest Political Science Association, Chicago.

Hunter, James D. 1991. *Culture Wars.* New York: Basic.

———. 1994. *Before the Shooting Starts.* New York: Free Press.

Jelen, Ted G. 1993. *The Political World of the Clergy.* New York: Praeger.

Liebman, Robert, and Robert Wuthnow. 1983. *The New Christian Right.* New York: Aldine.

Moen, Matthew. 1992. *The Transformation of the Christian Right.* Tuscaloosa: University of Alabama Press.

Nexon, David. 1971. "Asymmetry in the Political System: Occasional Activists in the Republican and Democratic Parties, 1956–1964." *American Political Science Review* 65:716–30.

Olson, Laura R. 1994. "The Implications of Issue Definition among Protestant Clergy." Paper presented at the annual meeting of the Social Science History Association, Atlanta.

Quinley, Harold E. 1974. *The Prophetic Clergy: Social Activism among Protestant Ministers.* New York: Wiley.

Rosenstone, Steven J., and John Mark Hansen. 1993. *Mobilization, Participation, and Democracy in America.* New York: Macmillan.

Sapp, William D. 1975. "Factors in the Involvement of Southern Baptist Pastors in Governmental Decision-Making." Ph.D. dissertation, Southern Baptist Theological Seminary, Louisville, Ky.

Smith, Christian. 1991. *The Emergence of Liberation Theology.* Chicago: University of Chicago Press.

Teixeira, Ruy A. 1992. *The Disappearing American Voter.* Washington, D.C.: Brookings.

Verba, Sidney, and Norman H. Nie. 1972. *Participation in America.* Chicago: University of Chicago Press.

Verba, Sidney, Kay Lehman Schlozman, and Henry E. Brady. 1995. *Voice and Equality: Civic Voluntarism in American Society.* Cambridge, Mass.: Harvard University Press.

Wilcox, Clyde, Sharon Linzey, and Ted G. Jelen. 1991. "Reluctant Warriors: Premillennialism and Politics in the Moral Majority." *Journal for the Scientific Study of Religion* 30:245–58.

Zeigler, Harmon. 1966. "Attitude Consensus and Conflict in an Interest Group." *American Political Science Review* 60:655–65.

Zwier, Robert. 1982. *Born-Again Politics*. Downers Grove, Ill.: Intervarsity Press.

10

Grasping the Essentials:
The Social Embodiment of Religion
and Political Behavior

Lyman A. Kellstedt
John C. Green
James L. Guth
Corwin E. Smidt

The advent of the "new" Christian Right in the late 1970s had a broad, sweeping impact on the study of religion and politics. At first scholars scrambled to understand the source of this religious force in national politics, finding the available survey data inadequate to the task and the conceptual apparatus for studying the topic rusty and out-of-date. For example, the measures of religious affiliation in the premier survey of political behavior, the National Election Studies, dated from the early 1950s. A decade of careful scholarship and innovations in survey questions have now produced more accurate and useful survey data (Leege and Kellstedt 1993), which allows for an assessment of the mass constituency of the Christian Right (Kellstedt, Smidt, and Kellstedt 1991).

Of greater importance, however, was the reintroduction of religion to political science after some sixty years of often purposeful neglect (Swierenga 1990:145–49). From political philosophy to comparative politics, a new interest has emerged in the political implications of religion. One result of this foment has been the careful reconsideration of what might be called the "social embodiment of religion." Simply put, scholars want to know as precisely as possible the religious context of individual

174

attitudes and behaviors, both the kind of religious communities to which citizens belong and the extent of that belonging.

The purpose of this chapter is to demonstrate that the social embodiment of religion matters politically in the mass public. We begin with a discussion of two concepts, religious tradition and religious commitment, each of which minimally taps the belonging aspects of religion and, when combined, locate the religious context of individual citizens. Then we will operationalize and test these measures with survey data. Our conclusions are straightforward: grasping the essentials of religion is a potent first step in understanding its connection to politics.

The Social Embodiment of Religious Beliefs

At its core, religion is a set of beliefs about the divine, humankind's relationship to it, and the consequences of that relationship (Stark and Bainbridge 1985). For such beliefs to be more than abstractions, however, they must be learned, applied, and practiced by individual believers in their daily lives. The principal mechanisms for the worldly realization of beliefs are religious communities. To use a metaphor from Christianity, such communities are quite literally "the Word made flesh," and the resulting collection of believers is a "body" of faith in this world. These communities are the critical social context of individuals' political attitudes and behaviors. Although the most basic link between religion and politics is surely a direct connection of beliefs to issues, the social context highlights, solidifies, and can even substitute for such a direct linkage. Indeed, the relationship between religious beliefs and communities is analogous to the connection between beliefs derived from education and an individual's educational background. Specifying "educationally relevant beliefs" is difficult, but a first step is measuring the extent and type of education.

The social embodiment of belief thus represents the "belonging" aspect of religion, and it has two basic features. The first is *affiliation*, the individual's attachment to a particular religious community. The second is *involvement*, the extent of an individual's attachment to their affiliation. Because there are numerous religious beliefs, there are many religious communities with which individuals can affiliate. Similarly, there are many ways individuals can become involved with such communities. Taken together, measures of affiliation and involvement can provide the basic rubric for identifying the religious context of individual citizens. Thus, developing at least minimum measures of affiliation and involvement is a first step toward understanding the connection between religion and politics.

Minimum Affiliation: Religious Tradition. Scholars have long been interested in religious affiliation, and have searched diligently for conceptually sound and analytically useful categories of attachment to religious communities. The most popular approach relies on the historical origins of such communities, combining denominations with similar roots (and usually similar names) into "denominational families" (Melton 1991). The problem with this approach is that the categories are insensitive to change, amalgamating groups that have grown apart since their origins and now hold quite different beliefs. With this problem in mind, scholars sometimes use another approach that incorporates religious change into categories of affiliation. Typically (and often implicitly), these categories are based on the "fundamentalist-modernist" debate of the early twentieth century. So, for instance, churches are placed in "fundamentalist," "moderate," or "liberal" categories (Smith 1990) or similar groupings (Roof and McKinney 1987). This strategy assumes, often incorrectly, that the underlying religious beliefs can be arrayed along a single continuum. Finally, affiliations are often classified by religious tradition, such as "Protestant," "Catholic," and "Jew" (Herberg 1960). The problem here is that the categories are usually too broad, including diverse sets of believers under the same heading.

As we have argued elsewhere (Kellstedt and Green 1993:57–58), religious tradition can be a useful way of classifying affiliations if it is defined with care and measured with precision. By *religious tradition,* we mean a group of religious communities that share a set of beliefs that generates a distinctive worldview. At any point in time, the beliefs that define such a tradition are rooted in a common past and yet modified by present-day factors.

The building blocks of religious traditions are the specific communities to which individuals typically belong. Certainly the most common of these are denominations (Greeley 1972), which are religious institutions (Kellstedt and Green 1993:53–54). Of course, not all religious people belong to denominations, an important fact given the recent growth of nondenominational or independent churches. Many of these churches reflect sect and church movements across denominations, such as fundamentalism and ecumenism, respectively (Finke and Stark 1992:40–46). Other individuals have more generic affiliations, linking directly with beliefs, experiences, or religious traditions. Still others have highly personal affiliations, only nominal attachments, or no attachments at all (Wuthnow 1993). In principle, these varied affiliations can be aggregated into religious traditions, some perhaps quite small, including a secular or nonreligious category.

Thus defined, religious tradition is a minimal, general, and flexible measure of affiliation. The number and content of the categories are largely empirical questions, influenced by the specific purposes for which the categories are defined. Scholars have long noted the connections of religious traditions to political attitudes and behaviors (Kellstedt and Noll 1990). As the embodiment of religious beliefs, practices and personal identity, such traditions are one of the staples of electoral competition and party coalitions in the United States (Kellstedt et al. 1994).

Minimum Involvement: Religious Commitment. Scholars have also had a long standing interest in religious involvement and have sought conceptually sound and analytically useful ways of assessing the extend of an individual's attachment to a religious community. Typically, various aspects or "dimensions" of involvement have been identified, which are regularly discussed under the general label of "religious commitment" (Roof 1979:18). Five dimensions are especially popular: two forms of religious behavior (ritual observance or participation in public religious activities; devotional observance or participation in private religious activities); a psychological attachment, the subjective salience of religion; a belief dimension; and, interestingly enough, affiliation (Verbit 1970). Less popular dimensions are religious knowledge, experience, and moral behavior (cf. Stark and Glock 1968).

None of these dimensions perfectly tap the extend of belonging to a religious community. Behavioral measures, such as church attendance, overemphasize institutional connections and neglect old, infirmed, and mobile populations. In contrast, subjective measures, such as salience, deemphasize institutional connections and disadvantage religious behavior. Beliefs and affiliation are afflicted by the low levels of opinion consistency, constraint, and knowledge that characterize the mass public. All of these measures routinely suffer from social desirability effects, and some may be biased toward a particular denomination or religious tradition.

Largely for these reasons, the standard practice in the sociology of religion is to treat each of the dimensions as an equally valid measure of religious involvement. If, however, each form of involvement is equally valid, then it stands to reason that an individual who scores high on all the dimensions would have a stronger level of religious commitment than an individual who scores high on fewer dimensions. As we have argued elsewhere (Kellstedt 1993:293–98; cf. Hammond 1992 for a similar measure), a powerful measure of minimum commitment can be calculated by summing the *lack of commitment* on the various dimensions of involvement, measuring, in effect, the *absence of belonging*. Individuals who show a lack of commitment on all the dimensions of involvement are likely to be much less involved than those who show at least some commitment on all the dimensions. This approach solves a number of problems associated with single dimensions of involvement. First, it does not favor a particular type of involvement over any other. Second, because it weights all dimensions equally, the multi-dimensional character of involvement is recognized. Third, it lessens the impact of social desirability effects. Fourth, it mitigates against favoring one religious tradition over another. Finally, it lessens measurement error associated with any single measure.

Thus defined, religious commitment is a minimal, general, and flexible concept of involvement. The number and scope of commitment are also empirical questions, and, once again, the researcher's purposes are an important factor. Scholars have long noted the connection of religious involvement to political attitudes and behavior (Kellstedt and Noll 1990). Individuals with higher levels of commitment are most likely to partake of the beliefs, practices, and identifications that may make their affiliation distinctive in politics (Kellstedt, Smidt, and Kellstedt 1991) and receive matching political cues (Shaefer 1991:43). Furthermore, participation in religious communities teaches political skills (Verba, Schlozman, and Brady 1995).

Data and Methods

In the following pages, we will operationalize religious tradition and religious commitment, and then test their impact on politics. The analyses are based on the results of a large random sample of adult Americans conducted in the spring of 1992 by the Survey Research Center at the University of Akron. Both the large sample size (4,001 cases) and the questionnaire were designed to measure religious affiliation and involvement precisely. An extensive series of screens and probes was used to ascertain religious affiliation in more detail than previous surveys, and extensive batteries of religious items covered the major dimensions of religious involvement (Wald and Smidt 1993). These data were weighted to match the 1990 U.S. Census in terms of basic demography (race, gender, education, income and region). (Analysis with unweighted data produced very similar results.)

Operationalizing Religious Tradition

We began to operationalize religious tradition by recognizing distinctive sets of beliefs embodied in the present-day affiliations. Even at a conceptual level, such distinctions were difficult to make among Protestants. After extensively researching denominations and beliefs, we identified three large traditions and a host of smaller ones. The two largest of these were "evangelical" and "mainline" Protestants. The division between these historically white denominations was complicated by the relationship between them: many evangelical denominations resulted from sectarian revolts against mainline churches, while many mainline churches derive from the accommodation of evangelical sects (Finke and Stark 1992). Not surprisingly, some denominations have a mixed character. Overall, we identified evangelical denominations as those that subscribed to four beliefs: (1) a high view of Scripture, (2) a belief that "Jesus was the only way to salvation," (3) emphasis on a conversion experience, and (4) a strong emphasis on evangelism and missions, all within the general rubric of Christian orthodoxy (see Dayton and Johnston 1991). In contrast, the mainline churches held modernist variants on these beliefs but also within the general rubric of Christian orthodoxy.

Although the historic black Protestant churches share many religious beliefs with the evangelical tradition, they constituted a separate religious tradition, reflecting the special experiences of African Americans (Sernett 1991).[1] In addition, we found several smaller Protestant traditions that we aggregated into "conservative nontraditional" and "liberal nontraditional" categories because of their small numbers. The former category includes groups that add a special revelation to Christian orthodoxy, such as the Church of Jesus Christ of the Latter-Day Saints (Mormons); the latter category includes groups that have explicitly abandoned key elements of Christian orthodoxy, such as the Unitarian-Universalists. (See the appendix for a list of denominations in each category.)

Traditions outside of Protestantism were much easier to define, including the Roman Catholic, Eastern Orthodox, and Jewish communities. Non-Judeo-Christian groups were also easy to define, but because of small numbers, these were combined into an "other non-Christians" category. Finally, we recognized a "secular" category, made up of atheists, agnostics, and respondents with no religious preference (Kellstedt and Green 1993).

These distinctions produced ten categories of religious tradition. We then set about assigning specific affiliations to these categories, a process as complex as defining the traditions themselves. The basic problem reflects the nominal character of religious affiliation: even a detailed measurement of affiliation yield an extraordinary variety of "names" from the respondents. Table 10.1 summarizes these responses using two dimensions: (1) the degree of institutional focus, ranging from "denomination" through "nondenominational" to "no denomination" responses; and (2) the degree of specificity, including "specific," "generic," and "nominal" responses. When combined, these dimensions generate nine types of response; examples of each are listed in table 10.1, along with the relative size of each category (in brackets).

By far the most common kind of response was a *specific denomination* (cell 1), such as "Southern Baptist" (69.2 percent). Such responses were the easiest to assign to a tradition. Nearly as easy were *specific nondenominational* affiliations (cell 4)—an example being proto-denominations like the Calvary Chapel (0.8 percent).[2] The *specific no denomination* (cell 7; e.g., "atheists or agnostics," 2.5 percent) and *nominal no denomination*

TABLE 10.1
A Classification of Affiliation Responses
(Examples in "quotes")

INSTITUTIONAL FOCUS OF RESPONSE	SPECIFICITY OF RESPONSE		
	Specific Preference	**Generic Preference**	**Nominal Preference**
Denomination	(1) *"Southern Baptist"* [69.2%]	(2) *"independent Baptist"* [3.8%]	(3) *"just a Baptist"* [5.9%]
Non-Denominational	(4) *"Calvary Chapel"* [.8%]	(5) *"independent evangelical"* [3.0%]	(6) *"just a Christian"* [2.8%]
No Denomination	(7) *"Atheist or Agnostic"* [2.5%]	(8) *"a spiritual person"* [1.5%]	(9) *"no preference; none"* [10.5%]

(cell 9; "no preference," 10.4 percent) responses were placed in the secular category.

The remaining cells were more difficult to assign and presented an important problem because they made up more than one-sixth of the sample. These included *generic denominational* (cell 2; "independent Baptist," 3.8 percent), *nominal denomination* (cell 3; "just a Baptist," 5.9 percent), *generic nondenominational* (cell 5; "independent evangelical," 3.0), *nominal nondenominational* (cell 6; "just a Christian," 2.8 percent), and *generic no denomination* (cell 8; "a spiritual person," 1.5 percent). These responses have in common an ambiguous or incomplete naming of the affiliation. This ambiguity could come from several sources, including a lack of institutional connection, a lack of knowledge or recall of affiliation, or a lack of affiliation.

To sort out these possibilities, we attempted to fill out the respondents' affiliation using other religious variables, assigning those that qualified to the appropriate religious tradition. For example, we assigned a respondent who said they were "just a Baptist" but who also claimed to be a fundamentalist to the evangelical tradition. But we placed someone claiming to be "just a Baptist" who showed no other evidence of religiosity at all in the secular category.[3] This procedure starkly reveals the minimal nature of religious tradition: it captures only the most basic attachment to a kind of religious community.

The result of these efforts is reported in table 10.2 for the seven largest traditions. The first point of interest is their relative size. The evangelical Protestant tradition is the largest group, making up just over one-quarter of the adult population, whereas the mainline and black Protestant traditions are much smaller, at less than one-fifth and one-tenth respectively. The relative sizes of the evangelical and mainline traditions may surprise some readers expecting the Protestant mainline to be much larger. The "shrinking" of the mainline reflects in part the well-documented and continued historical decline of these churches (Kelly 1972; Finke and Stark 1992) but mostly the careful defining, measuring and sorting of affiliation, which put some respondents typically assigned to the mainline in other categories. Roman Catholics are the second largest tradition also at about one-quarter of the sample, and Jews are, as expected, a small group. Finally, the seculars category is quite large, actually exceeding the size of the Protestant mainline at just under one-fifth of the population. Four small groupings were left out of the table because of their small size: conservative nontraditional, 1.9 percent; liberal nontraditional, 0.9 percent; Eastern Orthodox churches, 0.4 percent; and other non-Christians, 1.1 percent.[4]

Do these categories matter politically? Table 10.2 reports on four attitudes (abortion, gay rights, ideology, and partisanship) and two behaviors (vote for Bush and turnout in the 1988 election). In all cases, these figures have been adjusted to control for the effects of social-demographic factors.[5] These large religious traditions are quite different on a number of these variables. Note, for instance, the patterns on abortion, where evangelicals—and black Protestants—hold the most pro-life positions, Jews and seculars are the most pro-choice, and mainline Protestants and Catholics fall in between. A similar, if more muted, pattern obtains for opposition to gay rights. Evangelicals are also the most conservative in self-reported ideology, but here their mainline cousins comes in second, followed closely by Catholics. The same lineup occurs for party identification, with white Protestants most solidly in the Republican camp. Black Protestants and Jews were the least conservative and Republican, followed by the seculars. These patterns also appear in political behavior, with support for Bush in the 1988 presidential election paralleling partisanship. The mainline and Catholics had the highest turnout in 1988, followed by Evangelicals, with seculars going to the polls the least often.[6]

These are strong findings for the mass public, particularly since they involve a single, minimum measure of religious tradition, control for other powerful social factors such as income and race, and make no reference to other religious factors, such as religious commitment. It is to religious commitment that we now turn.

TABLE 10.2
Religious Tradition and Political Behavior
(Controlling for Social Demographic Factors)

Religious Tradition	% Pop.	Abortion ProLife	OppGay Rights	Ideo Cons	Party GOP	Bush '88	Vote '88
Protestants:							
Evangelical	25.9	52%	45%	57%	50%	78%	71%
Mainline	18.0	30	27	47	48	72	74
Black	7.8	49	32	36	16	36	68
Catholic	23.4	40	25	45	38	66	71
Jewish	2.0	12	17	15	17	33	66
Secular	18.5	21	24	40	30	58	62
Beta	—	.27	.19	.18	.23	.27	.11

Operationalizing Religious Commitment

Operationalizing and measuring minimum religious commitment are much easier that doing the same for religious tradition. For one thing, the dimensions of religious involvement and responses to them were less complex than affiliation. We developed a seven-point scale that, in effect, measures the lack of religious commitment by summing low commitment across five crucial dimensions of involvement (Kellstedt 1993). The components were are follows:

1. Low affiliation—reports no religious affiliation of any kind
2. Low belief—reports uncertainty about or lack of belief that God exists
3. Low salience—reports religion is not important
4. Low ritual observance—reports attending religious services a few times a year or less
5. Low private devotionalism—reports praying privately once per week or less

We are persuaded that each of these dimensions captures an essential facet of religious involvement. Affiliation and belief anchor the respondent in crucial elements of substantive religiosity (Kellstedt 1993). Salience taps the psychological dimension of commitment; attendance and prayer capture important religious behaviors (Guth and Green 1993). We are firmly convinced that the levels of commitment listed here are so low that they truly represent a lack of commitment. Indeed, it strains credulity to argue that anyone who fails to pass these low hurdles displays any religious involvement in that regard. Extensive experimentation with additional dimensions produced very similar results.[7]

Our religious commitment scale was constructed as follows. Each time a respondent failed to meet a criterion, one was added to the scale; when the process was completed, the scale ranged from 0 (scored low on all five dimensions) to 5 (scored low on none of the five). We then extracted respondents with scores of 5 who also had the highest level of commitment on these dimensions (prayed daily, attended weekly, were certain God exists, reported a specific denominational affiliation, and claimed their religion provided "a great deal of guidance" in their daily lives). The order of the scale was then reversed so that the lowest level of commitment was 1 (low on all dimensions) and the highest was 7 (low on no dimensions, high on all).

The results of this exercise are reported in table 10.3. Clearly, the

TABLE 10.3
Religious Commitment and Political Behavior
(Controlling for Social Demographic Factors)

Religious Commitmen	% Pop.	Abortion ProLife	OppGay Rights	Ideo Cons	Party GOP	Bush '88	Vote '88
7. Highest	11.3	68%	46%	59%	49%	72%	74%
6. Very High	27.9	47	34	49	42	70	72
5. High	24.7	40	36	48	39	68	69
4. Moderate	11.1	27	28	36	37	63	68
3. Low	6.8	21	23	43	37	64	67
2. Very Low	10.4	19	23	37	31	55	64
1. Lowest	7.9	15	22	38	27	53	61
Beta	—	.32	.15	.15	.12	.12	.08

American population tends to cluster at the high end of the scale, with almost two-fifths of the population in the "highest" (7) and "very high" (6) categories of commitment, and another one-quarter in the "high" group. We must remember, however, that these respondents passed minimal hurdles, so that entering the "high" and "very high" categories was not difficult. By the same token, the bottom categories represent very low levels of commitment, containing respondents who had only the most modest involvement. Just about one-quarter of the population fell into the three bottom categories of commitment. These finding support two apparently contradictory claims often made about American society. On the one hand, a very large portion of the adult population has more than a minimal commitment to their religion, making the United States a highly "religious" society, particularly compared to Europe. On the other hand, many of these same people do not have especially high levels of commitment, and a large portion of the population scores very low, making the United States a "secular" society, particularly compared to some points in the past.

Do levels of religious commitment matter politically? Table 10.3 reports on the same political variables as table 10.2, also controlling for social demographic factors. Abortion attitudes again set the basic pattern: the Highest level of commitment is the most pro-life, a position that declines in a monotonic fashion to the Lowest category, which is the least pro-life. Opposition to gay rights, conservatism, and partisanship show the same tendency, with just a few modest departures from the overall trend. Religious commitment affects political behavior as well: the higher the level of commitment, the more support for Bush and the greater voter turnout in 1988. Once again, these are strong findings for the mass public, given that we are using a single, minimal measure of religious commitment, controlling for other potent social forces and making no reference to other religious factors, such as religious tradition, which, as we have seen above, has a similar relationship to politics.

Combining Religious Tradition and Commitment

This last point begs the question: What is the relationship between religious tradition and commitment? Table 10.4 provides an answer by cross-tabulating these measures. Among the major traditions, evangelical and black Protestants show the highest levels of religious commitment: over one-half of each group scores in the top two categories. Mainline Protestants and Catholics show lower levels of commitment, with just over two-fifths in the top two categories and corresponding numbers toward the middle of the scale. Jews have a bimodal distribution, with almost two-fifths above the moderate category and about one-half below. Not surprisingly, seculars are concentrated at the lower levels of the scale, but note that a few still pass some of the minimum hurdles of religious commitment.

TABLE 10.4
Religious Tradition and Religious Commitment
(Row Percentages)

Religious Tradition	Religious Commitment						
	Highest	6	5	Moderate	3	2	Lowest
Protestants:							
Evangelical	20	34	28	11	5	3	0
Mainline	9	32	27	18	8	7	0
Black	21	44	24	8	2	2	0
Catholic	9	34	29	12	6	10	0
Jewish	1	27	9	13	24	26	0
Secular	0	0	15	5	10	27	43

Eta = .67

How does the combination of religious tradition and commitment relate to politics? In table 10.5, we look at the same set of political variables, controlling for social demographic effects, dividing each tradition into three groups in terms of commitment: "most" (categories 7 and 6), "moderately" (categories 5 and 4), and "least" (categories 3, 2, and 1) committed. The first column of table 10.5 reproduces the results of table 10.4 as a percentage of the total population. Note that most

TABLE 10.5
Religious Tradition, Religious Commitment, and Political Behavior
(Controlling for Social Demographic Factors)

Religious Commitment	% Pop.	Abortion ProLife	OppGay Rights	Ideo Cons	Party GOP	Bush '88	Vote '88
Protestants:							
Evangelical:							
Most Committed	13.9	65	53	64	56	82	74
Modr Committed	10.1	42	37	49	44	74	67
Least Committed	1.9	23	34	49	35	67	65
Mainline:							
Most Committed	7.3	39	31	53	51	74	78
Modr Committed	8.1	26	26	45	48	72	71
Least Committed	2.6	19	18	40	38	67	69
Black:							
Most Committed	5.1	50	36	38	18	38	64
Modr Committed	2.5	47	25	31	11	35	73
Least Committed	0.3	37	0	48	21	21	61
Catholic:							
Most Committed	10.1	51	25	45	39	68	74
Modr Committed	9.7	36	26	46	36	66	70
Least Committed	3.6	20	23	38	37	58	64
Jewish:							
Most Committed	0.6	23	28	23	20	31	61
Modr Committed	0.5	10	15	16	5	25	77
Least Committed	1.0	9	12	9	21	38	63
Secular:							
Modr Committed	3.7	34	30	43	33	61	58
Least Committed	14.8	17	23	39	29	57	62
Beta	—	.33	.22	.22	.27	.26	.12

committed Evangelicals and least committed seculars are about equally numerous. These groups anchor the social issue disputes that are often referred to as the "culture wars" in contemporary politics (Hunter 1991). But also note that the combinations of religious tradition and commitment create a welter of religious groupings, the source of complex, variegated, and subtle battle lines in cultural disputes.

Once again, abortion attitudes illustrate the patterns best. Within each major tradition, the most committed category is the most pro-life and the least committed, the least. And, as before, religious tradition matters as well: Evangelicals are the most pro-life, followed by a virtual tie between black Protestants and Catholics, with mainline Protestants, Jews, and seculars showing the least opposition to abortion. Note, however, the very small differences obtain between the least committed groups in each tradition; among the religiously uncommitted, tradition has little effect.

Much the same situation holds for the other variables, particularly for evangelical and mainline Protestants. The most committed Evangelicals oppose gay rights and tend to be conservative Republicans who turned out in large numbers to vote for Bush in 1988. The most committed mainliners show a similar pattern but, with the exception of turnout, scored below Evangelicals. Note that some modest exceptions to these patterns occur outside of white Protestantism. For example, the least committed black Protestants and Jews show higher levels of Republicanism than might otherwise be expected. No doubt these anomalies reflect the complexities of ethnic assimilation. Overall, however, table 10.5 shows the power of religious context in shaping individual attitudes and behaviors.

Grasping the Essentials

Our basic conclusion is straightforward: the social embodiment of religion matters politically. Even minimal measures of religious affiliation and involvement show impressive relationships with political attitudes and behaviors, quite apart from other social and demographic characteristics. The combination of tradition and commitment is particularly powerful. To many readers this finding may seem commonplace, but not so long ago religion was routinely dismissed as a proxy for underlying economic interests or resulting anxieties (Lipset 1964), a position still advocated today, albeit less frequently (Jorstad 1990:63–64).

We must stress again that the measures of religious tradition and religious commitment employed here are minimal: a fuller elaboration of affiliation and involvement may well produce even more powerful results. For instance, our measurement of affiliation is mostly nominal in character, bolstered modestly by other religious variables to fill incomplete affiliation data. Taking into account other elements of affiliation, such as strength of affiliation, identification with religious movements and local church connections, may allow for the development of a more complete measure of affiliation. Much the same can be said for religious commitment. Additional dimensions of involvement and a commitment scale differentiated at the high end could allow for a measure of maximal commitment. Finally, getting back to basics, as it were, a fuller understanding of the social embodiment of religion can allow scholars to focus productively on religious beliefs, and thus assessing more precisely the direct links between religious values and political issues. For now, grasping the essentials of the social embodiment of religion is a powerful first step in understanding the connections between religion and politics.

Appendix
Religious Affiliations and Religious Traditions: Specific Assignments for Protestants

1. *Evangelical Protestant:* Nondenominational (fundamentalist, charismatic, neo-evangelical); all Adventists; all Baptists; all Brethren; Christian Church; Church of Christ; Conservative Congregationalists; Evangelical Congregationalists; Reformed Episcopal; Evangelical Covenant; Evangelical Church in North America; Evangelical Free Church; Moravians; Evangelical Friends; Independent Fundamentalists; Plymouth Brethren; Christian and Missionary Alliance; Church of God-Anderson, Indiana; Church of God-Holiness; Free Methodist; Salvation Army; Wesleyan; generic Holiness; Free Lutheran; Lutheran Brethren; Missouri Synod Lutheran; Wisconsin Synod Lutheran; sectarian Lutheran; sectarian Methodists; Mennonites; Assemblies of God; Church of God-Cleveland, Tennessee; Church of God-Huntsville, Alabama; Church of God of Prophecy; Church of God-Apostolic; Four Square Gospel; Pentecostal Church of God; Pentecostal Holiness; generic Pentecostal; Cumberland Presbyterian; Orthodox Presbyterian; Presbyterian Church in America; Reformed Presbyterian; sectarian Presbyterian; Christian Reformed Church

2. *Mainline Protestant:* Nondenomination mainline; ecumenical or community church; Disciples of Christ; United Church of Christ; ge-

neric Congregational; Episcopal; Society of Friends; Evangelical Lutheran Church in America; generic Lutheran; United Methodist Church; generic Methodist; Presbyterian Church U.S.A.; generic Presbyterian; Reformed Church in America

3. *Black Protestant:* Black non-denominational; National Baptist Convention; Progressive Baptist Convention; other black Baptists; black Holiness; African Methodist Episcopal Church; African Methodist Episcopal Zion; Christian Methodist Church; Church of God in Christ; other black Pentecostals

4. *Conservative Nontraditional:* Jehovah's Witnesses; all Latter-Day Saints (Mormons); Worldwide Church of God; Christian Science

5. *Liberal Nontraditional:* Unitarian-Universalists; Unity; Humanists; Spiritualists; Divine Science; New Age

Notes

1. Many black Protestants are often hard to identify precisely because they give responses easily confused with historically white denominations. When we found large numbers of African Americans in historically white denominations, such as the Southern Baptist Convention, we assigned the black respondents in the South to a special code. This situation occurred for Baptists, Holiness, and Pentecostal families. Careful analysis suggested these cases belonged with other black Protestants.

2. Calvary Chapel in Cosa Mesa, California, was founded one-quarter century ago, arising from the "Jesus People Movement." As this local church grew, some of its leaders moved to other locations in California and across the country, founding other "Calvary Chapels." Calvary Chapel is thus a series of loosely affiliated local churches moving toward denominational status. In table 10.1, we count in this category any specific name of a nondenominational church given by the respondent.

3. This process occurred as follows. Respondents with ambiguous answers were checked for religious identification (fundamentalist to mainline), religious beliefs (such as views of the Bible, born-again status), practices (speaking in tongues, church attendance), and religious salience, in that order. On the basis of these responses, individual cases were assigned to the Evangelical (labeled "sectarian"), mainline (labeled "generic"), or secular categories.

4. Because of the small number of cases, these four smaller categories are excluded from the rest of the analysis. In political terms, conservative nontraditionals resembled evangelical Protestants, the liberal nontraditionals looked like the Protestant mainline, the Eastern Orthodox matched the Catholics, and the other non-christians resembled Black protestants.

5. All the percentages in tables 10.2, 10.3, and 10.5 control for social-

demographic characteristics including age, education, gender, income, marital status, race, region, and occupation. This approach assures that the relationships between religious tradition and the dependent variables in the table are not impacted by these social-demographic traits. We accomplished these controls by using multiple classification analysis with the social demographic variables used as covariates.

6. The data on vote choice and turnout suffer from the typical overstatement in the mass public.

7. Including measures of religious experience did not alter the results, and we suspect religious knowledge would have little impact. Moral behavior and other measures of the "consequential" dimension of religious commitment are probably not properly part of religious commitment any more than positions on abortion or other attitudes that may flow from religious beliefs.

References

Dayton, Donald W., and Robert K. Johnston, eds. 1991. *The Variety of American Evangelicalism.* Knoxville: University of Tennessee.

Finke, Roger, and Rodney Stark. 1992. *The Churching of America 1776–1990.* New Brunswick, N.J.: Rutgers University Press.

Greeley, Andrew M. 1972. *The Denominational Society.* Glenview, Ill.: Scott, Foresman.

Guth, James L., and John C. Green. 1993. "Salience? The Core Concept?" In *Rediscovering the Religious Factor in American Politics,* ed. David C. Leege and Lyman A. Kellstedt. Armonk, N.Y.: Sharpe.

Hammond, Philip E. 1992. *Religion and Personal Autonomy.* Columbia: University of South Carolina.

Herberg, Will. 1960. *Protestant-Catholic-Jew.* Garden City, N.Y.: Doubleday.

Hunter, James D. 1991. *Culture Wars.* New York: Basic Books.

Jorstad, Erling. 1990. *Holding Fast/Pressing On: Religion in America in the 1980s.* New York: Praeger.

Leege, David, and Lyman A. Kellstedt, eds. 1993. *Rediscovering the Religious Factor in American Politics.* Armonk, N.Y.: Sharpe.

Lipset, Seymour Martin. 1964. "Religion and Politics in the American Past and Present." In *Religion and Social Conflict,* ed. Robert Lee and Martin E. Marty. New York: Oxford University Press.

Kelley, Dean. 1972. *Why Conservative Churches are Growing.* New York: Harper & Row.

Kellstedt, Lyman A. 1993. "Religion, the Neglected Variable: An Agenda for Future Research on Religion and Political Behavior." In *Rediscovering the Religious Factor in American Politics,* ed. David C. Leege and Lyman A. Kellstedt. Armonk, N.Y.: Sharpe.

Kellstedt, Lyman A., and John C. Green. 1993. "Knowing God's Many People:

Denominational Preference and Political Behavior." In *Rediscovering the Religious Factor in American Politics*, ed. David C. Leege and Lyman A. Kellstedt. Armonk, N.Y.: Sharpe.

Kellstedt, Lyman A., John C. Green, James L. Guth, and Corwin E. Smidt. 1994. "Religious Voting Blocs in the 1992 Election: The Year of the Evangelical?" *Sociology of Religion* 55:307–26.

Kellstedt, Lyman A., and Mark A. Noll. 1990. "Religion, Voting for President, and Party Identification, 1948–1984." In *Religion and American Politics*, ed. Mark A. Noll. New York: Oxford University Press.

Kellstedt, Lyman A., Corwin E. Smidt, and Paul M. Kellstedt. 1991. "Religious Tradition, Denomination, and Commitment: White Protestants and the 1988 Election." In *The Bible and the Ballot Box*, ed. James L. Guth and John C. Green. Boulder, Colo.: Westview Press.

Melton, J. Gordon. 1991. *American Religions*. 3 vols. Tarrytown, N.Y.: Triumph Books.

Roof, Wade Clark. 1979. "Concepts and Indicators of Religious Commitment: A Critical Review." In *The Religious Dimension*, ed. Robert Wuthnow. New York: Academic Press.

Roof, Wade Clark, and William McKinney. 1987. *American Mainline Religion*. New Brunswick, N.J.: Rutgers University Press.

Sernett, Milton G. 1991. "Black Religion and the Question of Evangelical Identity." In *The Variety of American Evangelicalism*, ed. Donald W. Dayton and Robert K. Johnston. Knoxville: University of Tennessee.

Shafer, Byron E., ed. 1991. *The End of Realignment: Interpreting American Electoral Eras*. Madison: University of Wisconsin Press.

Smith, Tom W. 1990. "Classifying Protestant Denominations." *Review of Religious Research* 31:225–45.

Swierenga, Robert P. 1990. "Ethnoreligious Political Behavior in the Mid-Nineteenth Century: Voting, Values, Cultures." In *Religion and American Politics*, ed. Mark A. Noll. New York: Oxford University Press.

Stark, Rodney, and William Bainbridge. 1985. *The Future of Religion*. Berkeley: University of California Press.

Stark, Rodney, and Charles Glock. 1968. *American Piety: The Nature of Religious Commitment*. Berkeley: University of California Press.

Verba, Sidney, Kay Schlozman, and Henry Brady. 1995. *Voice and Equality*. Cambridge: Harvard University Press.

Verbit, Mervin. 1970. "The Components and Dimensions of Religious Behavior: Toward a Reconceptualization of Religiosity." In *The American Mosaic: Social Patterns of Religion in the United States*, ed. Philip Hammond and Benton Johnson. New York: Random House.

Wald, Kenneth D., Lyman A. Kellestedt, and David C. Leege. 1993. "Church Involvement and Political Behavior." In *Rediscovering the Religious Factor in American Politics*, ed. David C. Leege and Lyman A. Kellstedt. Armonk, N.Y.: Sharpe.

Wald, Kenneth, and Corwin Smidt. 1993. "Measurement Strategies in the Study of Religion and Politics." In *Rediscovering the Religious Factor in American Politics*, ed. David C. Leege and Lyman A. Kellstedt. Armonk: N.Y.: Sharpe.

Wuthnow, Robert. 1993. *Christianity in the 21st Century*. New York: Oxford University Press.

11

Measuring Fundamentalism: An Analysis of Different Operational Strategies

Lyman Kellstedt
Corwin Smidt

The resurgence of fundamentalism over the past decade, and particularly the activity of the New Christian Right, have prompted a great deal of media and scholarly interest. In fact, Roof (1986: 18) has stated: "Not since the Scopes trial in 1925 has there been so much public attention focused on religious fundamentalism in the United States." The media have been the source of much of this attention, but often in a manner that has confused more than enlightened. Terms like fundamentalist, evangelical, born-again, and conservative Christian have been used indiscriminately without much consideration given to their different meanings. Fortunately, the scholarly community has begun to analyze fundamentalism in greater depth. Historians have been particularly active, attempting to explore the roots of fundamentalism (Sandeen 1970a, 1970b; Marsden 1980; Carpenter 1980; and Ellis 1981). Other scholars have explored contemporary fundamentalism from the perspective of the participant observer (Peshkin 1986; Ammerman 1987), while still others have examined fundamentalism in terms of its conceptual meaning or empirical import (Ethridge and Feagin 1979; Hood 1983; Rothenberg and Newport 1984; Hood and Morris 1985; Lechner 1985; Burton et al. 1989).

Despite these recent efforts, however, the concept of fundamentalism does not have a widely shared meaning among journalists, scholars, or the general public. This creates problems for social scientists who wish to study fundamentalism by means of survey research. The lack of definitional consensus has led to a variety of measurement strategies for identifying fundamentalist respondents. While it is well known that *how* concepts are measured has important consequences for substantive findings, relatively little attention has been paid to assessing the effects of adopting different measurement approaches in the study of fundamentalism. Consequently, the purpose of this paper is to begin such an analysis by examining how different measurement strategies in identifying fundamentalist respondents influence substantive findings concerning fundamentalism.

Fundamentalism

The contemporary fundamentalist movement in the United States constitutes a sub-group within American evangelicalism. All fundamentalists are evangelicals, but not all evangelicals are fundamentalists. Despite scholarly debate about the conceptualization of evangelicalism,[1] there is general agreement that evangelicals share a commitment to the authority of the Bible, adherence to salvation through faith in Jesus Christ, and a passion for evangelism and missions (Johnston 1991; Askew 1987; Smith 1987; Marsden 1991). However, evangelicalism is something more than shared beliefs; it is also rooted in religious group affiliations. Hunter (1983:6), for example, has suggested that there are four major "religious and theological traditions" found in contemporary evangelicalism: Baptist, Holiness-Pentecostal, Anabaptist, and Reformed-Confessional. To these, however, should be added a fifth: the Independent-Fundamentalist tradition with its non-denominational ecclesiology and its dispensational, premillennialist eschatology.[2] Finally, it should be noted that individuals may well accept evangelical beliefs and/or be members of a denomination within one of the above religious or theological traditions, yet still not identify as evangelicals. However, those who do identify as evangelicals are more likely to exhibit the attitudes and behaviors associated with contemporary evangelicalism: e.g., to read their Bibles regularly, to oppose abortion on demand, and to have voted for Republican candidates for president in recent elections.

As a sub-group within evangelicalism, fundamentalists accept biblical authority, salvation through Christ, and a commitment to spreading the faith. They defend these beliefs militantly. Yet, in comparison to other evangelicals, fundamentalists are more likely to interpret the Bible literally and to accept a dispensational, premillennialist eschatology.[3] In addition, fundamentalists are more likely to be separatists in lifestyle and in their relationships with the culture than are other evangelicals. While fundamentalists also form religious group affiliations, they do not tend to do so in large denominations. Although a "fundamentalist" segment (defined in terms of the above beliefs) has captured positions of authority within the Southern Baptist Convention, it would be a mistake to label this largest of Protestant denominations as entirely fundamentalist in nature. Fundamentalists are concentrated in smaller denominations (like the Plymouth Brethren), in certain Baptist churches, or within non-denominational Bible churches. Finally, there is a self-identification component to fundamentalism. As Jerry Falwell used to put it: "I'm a fundamentalist and proud of it."

These sketches of evangelicals and fundamentalism, however, are relative to time and place. They do not constitute stable, permanent categories. Rather, they suggest tendencies which are rooted in history and are subject to change. After all, there were no self-identified fundamentalists in American society until the early twentieth century.

Will modern American fundamentalism persist? Scholars have given two diametrically opposed answers to this question. One perspective among historians (c.f., Ellis 1981) views fundamentalism largely as an agonized defense of a dying way of life, socially located outside the mainstream of American life. Its assumption is that fundamentalism is being undermined by modern culture and will eventually disappear, or at least be significantly diminished in its influence (e.g., Hofstadter 1963). A second perspective views fundamentalism as "an authentic conservative tradition" within the framework of American pluralism. It assumes that the movement will persist and should be examined on its own merits (Sandeen 1970a, 1970b; Marsden 1980; Carpenter 1980). While we share the latter perspective, a final answer to the question of the persistence of American fundamentalism will have to be left to future historians.

Nonetheless, several strands of social science theory can be brought to bear on the likely survival of the movement. In particular, the debate over secularization provides a useful perspective. Some scholars (Wallace 1966; Wallis 1975; Wilson 1975; Martin 1978) have argued for the coming demise of religion in the face of the secularizing tendencies in modern society. Religion is reduced in influence because it supposedly no longer permeates other societal institutions (the state, education) but is simply relegated to its own sphere; particular attention has also been given to science and its role in undermining religious belief. Other scholars, in particular Stark and Bainbridge (1980, 1985), have argued that religion will persist because it serves basic human needs. Despite segmentation and the influence of science, religions survive because they are "human organizations primarily engaged in providing general compensators based on supernatural assumptions" (1985:8). Secularizing tendencies are always threats to the vitality, if not the survival, of religious organizations. Religious organizations that survive, and even grow, in the face of secularizing trends continue to emphasize the supernatural, and religions that live in tension with societal norms are more likely to emphasize the supernatural than are those which are not in such tension. It is not that religions are immune from secularization and modernization. Some become so much like the surrounding culture that they eventually lose adherents or die out. Those that do so either lose members to, or are replaced by, newer sects or cults more in touch with the supernatural. Older sects and cults that retain their emphasis on the supernatural survive and even thrive as they maintain some distance or separation from society, particularly if they develop social networks that help them overcome their decentralization. Among those social conditions which help to develop such networks are the development of seminaries, colleges, publishing houses, radio and television programs and stations, and the like.

Fundamentalism is not a sect, a cult, or a church; it is a religious movement made up of numerous sects and independent or local church bodies. Its persistence (its roots can be traced to the early nineteenth century) can be explained by its commitment to supernatural assumptions. As two participant observers of contemporary fundamentalism have noted, God is at the center of the movement (Ammerman 1987; Peshkin 1986). Heaven and hell are real places, and the Devil is a very real person. The resurrection and the Second Coming of Jesus are universally accepted. The Bible is read literally and studied assiduously. Seeking to bring others to faith in Christ is a way of life.

Following the theoretical insights of Stark and Bainbridge (1985:435), we maintain that fundamentalism is one example of the numerous classic "revival" movements that "arise to restore the potency of the conventional religious traditions." Although revival movements seem "vulnerable to secularization and to lack long-term staying power," fundamentalism has already demonstrated its staying power and is also less likely to fall prey to secularizing tendencies. This is due, in part, to the loosely structured nature of the movement, which from another perspective might be deemed a weakness. Since fundamentalism is made up of numerous smaller sects and thousands of local churches, when secularization does strike these bodies and cause some churches to weaken or die, they are likely to be replaced by other smaller sects and independent churches. Thus, the movement's decentralization is an asset in meeting the challenges of secularization. As long as fundamentalism retains colleges and universities, seminaries for training pastors, publishing houses, radio and television stations and programs, and loose organizational networks (e.g., the American Council of Christian Churches), it will retain vitality. Fundamentalism's commitment to separated lifestyles for its adherents (c.f., Ammerman 1987; Peshkin 1986) is also a strength in terms of its persistence as a movement. This separation makes clear to these adherents that they are different from the rest of society, particularly in their emphasis on the supernatural (the formation of identity), and that these differences are a virtue and a sign of faithfulness to God (the ascription of meaning).

Measurement Strategies

Regardless of the theoretical perspective employed by scholars, three different measurement strategies are generally used to identify fundamentalists. One strategy employs the denominational affiliation of the respondent. Individuals affiliated with certain denominations, such as Southern Baptists, are classified as fundamentalists (Grupp and Newman 1973; Petersen and Mauss 1976; Ethridge and Feagin 1979; Jelen 1984; Beatty and Walter 1984). At times, this approach is justified simply as a "necessary evil" when theological beliefs, the preferred measures of classification, are absent from the survey instruments. At other times, however, the use of denominational affiliation is justified on sociological grounds (e.g., Petersen and Mauss 1976:246), with fundamentalist denominations placed at the sect end of a church-sect continuum. Finally, other efforts within this measurement tradition classify denominations into broader religious categories such as fundamentalist, moderate, or liberal (c.f., Smith 1986). These efforts assume that different denominations can be grouped together on the basis of sharing certain theological beliefs, religious practices, historical roots, and ongoing institutional relationships. Even if individuals who are affiliated with a denomination labeled as fundamentalist do not subscribe to every doctrinal tenet associated with fundamentalism, they still may be labeled as fundamentalists because of their social group "membership." It is social group membership, rather than doctrinal beliefs, which is presumed to affect attitudes and behaviors.

A second measurement strategy uses theological beliefs as the basis for classifying respondents into fundamentalist and non-fundamentalist camps. In this case, analysts frequently emphasize belief in biblical inerrancy, with its tendency toward biblical literalism, as a central characteristic of fundamentalism (Ford 1960; DeJong and Ford 1965; Orum 1970; Marsden 1980; Stackhouse 1982; Miller and Wattenberg 1984). As Ford (1960:41) has argued, "the core of fundamentalism is Biblicism, or belief in the inerrancy of the literally interpreted Scriptures." George Dollar (1973:xv), a self-identified fundamentalist, has made a similar point: "Historic Fundamentalism is the literal exposition of all the affirmations and attitudes of the Bible and the militant exposure of all non-Biblical affirmations and attitudes." Finally, participant observation has confirmed that biblical literalism is central to fundamentalism (Ammerman 1987). Thus, the survey analyst with a theological perspective on fundamentalism looks for questions probing respondents' attitudes toward the Bible, particularly ones which include a literal response category.

A third measurement strategy uses self-identification procedures to identify fundamentalist respondents, simply asking respondents whether or not they consider themselves to be fundamentalists (Moberg 1969; Berg 1971; Balswick et al. 1975; Steed et al. 1983; Rothenberg and Newport 1984; Wilcox 1986, 1989; Smidt 1988). This approach assumes that fundamentalists represent more than a categorical group of respondents who can be classified together on the basis of doctrinal beliefs or religious practices. Rather, it assumes that fundamentalists constitute an "organic" entity, in which members have forged a common identity, communicate with each other disproportionately, and share certain values and norms not shared by those outside their group.

Thus, survey analysts have employed a variety of measurement strategies for operationally identifying fundamentalist respondents. As yet, however, little is known about the relative effects of one's choice of measurement strategy in the study of fundamentalism. For example, to what extent do the different measures overlap? Will respondents classified as fundamentalists by one approach be similarly classified by other approaches? Also, if relatively large numbers of respondents are uniquely labeled as fundamentalists through different operational measures, then what effects may the adoption of a particular measurement approach have upon one's findings? Finally, are some measurement approaches better suited for testing certain theoretical concerns than are others? In the next section, we turn to these questions.

Data and Methods

To answer such questions, operational measures reflecting all three strategies are needed within a single survey. Fortunately, such a study is available: a 1983 national survey of evangelicals which served as the basis for Rothenberg and Newport's (1984) book, *The Evangelical Voter*.[4] This survey provided, first of all, a detailed categorization of the respondents' denominational affiliations. Although the diversity within denominations makes assignments into broader categories difficult, the various denominational affiliations reported by the respondents were grouped into three broad categories: fundamentalist, evangelical, and "other Protestant."[5]

Second, the survey contained a question concerning biblical literalism. Respondents were asked whether the story of creation in Genesis (a) "is literally true, exactly as we find it in the Bible—that is, it took six 24-hour periods for God to create the world," (b) "is a true account of how God created the world," or (c) "reflects man's feelings about how the world may have been created." Having *both* a "literally true" and a "true" option is important, for as Ammerman (1982:171) has suggested, adherence to "an historical, six-day creation may be the most accurate indicator available for a truly 'literal' belief in scripture and membership in the fundamentalist party of evangelicals."

Finally, the study contained a direct measure of fundamentalist identification. It asked: "When you describe your religious views to someone, do you generally call yourself a fundamentalist, or not?"

To ascertain how these three fundamentalism measures relate to external criteria, four criterion variables were chosen for analysis: (1) religiosity, (2) separatist orientation, (3) ideological self-identification, and (4) attitudes toward abortion. The observations of both Ammerman (1987) and Peshkin (1986) have documented the extraordinary levels of religiosity on the part of fundamentalists: They attend church on a regular basis, often going to religious services more than once a week. As befits such regular attenders, fundamentalists attach a great deal of importance to their faith. Consequently, our first criterion, religiosity, combined a church attendance item with a measure of the salience of religion: "How important is your religion to you in your daily life—extremely important, very important, somewhat important, or not important?"[6]

As both Ammerman and Peshkin have suggested, separatism tends to be part of the fundamentalist lifestyle. While the authors of *The Evangel-*

ical Voter (Rothenberg and Newport 1984:22) have also made it clear that fundamentalists "do not drink, smoke, go to the movies or mix with non-fundamentalists," they expressed some uncertainty about how best to measure such separatist inclinations. In the end, they opted for an item which tapped attitudes toward the militant fundamentalist publication *Sword of the Lord.* However, given the particular problems associated with this measure, we chose a different path.[7] Since separatists must learn from whom they are to keep apart, they must develop very clear notions of who their friends and adversaries are (i.e., who are the "good guys" and who are the "bad guys"). Consequently, our second criterion measure was a "separatist orientation" variable which combined responses to three items: attitudes toward Jerry Falwell, toward the Moral Majority, and toward the Roman Catholic Church. We expected the fundamentalism measures to relate positively toward the first two objects and negatively toward the Roman Catholic Church.[8]

While the links between political conservatism and fundamentalism have been found somewhat elusive (Wuthnow 1973), recent research has again emphasized the connection. For example, Ammerman (1987) and Peshkin (1986) in their observation of fundamentalist churches have reported that significant attention is given to conservative causes and candidates. In addition, leaders for the New Christian Right have made the linkages between fundamentalism and conservative political ideology loudly and clearly. Consequently, we expected the fundamentalism measures to relate positively with political conservatism.

Finally, we chose a major, contemporary political issue with strong religious ties, i.e., abortion, as our fourth criterion measure. Previous studies have shown that both membership in fundamentalist denominations and religiosity are associated with abortion attitudes (Petersen and Mauss 1976; McIntosh et al. 1979; Jelen 1984, 1988; Hertel and Hughes 1987) and that the relationship between fundamentalism and abortion attitudes persists even after a control for religiosity (Petersen and Mauss 1976; McIntosh et al. 1979; Hertel and Hughes 1987). Therefore, we expected the fundamentalism measures to be related to anti-abortion attitudes even after controls for religiosity.

The order of analysis of these criterion variables began with basic religious orientations, turned to attitudes towards religious groups and individuals, then examined general political orientations, and, finally, looked at a specific issue which has strong religious overtones. The analysis that follows was restricted to white Protestants only.[9] While the increased homogeneity among the sample's remaining 618 white

Protestant respondents may have restricted some of the variance associated with the criterion variables, this strategy provided a more stringent test of the discriminating power of the particular fundamentalism measures. The use of any religious measure, when we are comparing religious with non-religious people, might make any such religious person appear to be a "fundamentalist."[10] Consequently, if distinct differences remain in comparisons of fundamentalist and non-fundamentalist Protestant respondents, such differences are likely to reflect "real" differences; confidence in the particular measure is thereby enhanced.

Data Analysis

If fundamentalism has a number of components conceptually, then are these components and their attendant measures closely interrelated? This question was examined via correlations among the fundamentalism measures. Given that the analysis was based upon white Protestants only, the correlation between the denominational and the literalism measure was .22; that between the denominational and self-identification measure was relatively strong and roughly equivalent (.24); but the correlation between the literalism and the self-identification measure was a somewhat more modest .12 (all significant at the .001 level). Thus, while the three measures of fundamentalism are interrelated, the strength of the relationships varies.

Overall, such differences in the magnitude of the correlation coefficients among this relatively homogeneous sample lead one to suspect that either some of these measures of fundamentalism are inadequate or that which has been conventionally labeled "fundamentalism" is multidimensional rather than unidimensional in nature. However, while these three measures may not be "perfect" measures of fundamentalism, they would seem on the basis of face validity to be adequate. The denominational categories are relatively precise when compared to other denominational measures. The doctrinal measure directly taps biblical literalism and not simply biblical inerrancy or biblical infallibility, while the self-classification measure also appears to be valid on its face. It is thus more likely that the concept of fundamentalism taps a multidimensional rather than a unidimensional phenomenon. For example, these measures suggest that theological (doctrinal beliefs), sociological (patterns of affiliation), and psychological (self-identification) factors may tap different facets, rather than a single dimension, of the phenomenon of fundamentalism. If this is the case, then the use of a single operational indicator or the use of a composite index to measure the concept may be misleading. In addition, alternative measures of fundamentalism may have different social correlates and may relate to dependent variables in different ways. The remaining analysis seeks to ascertain whether or not such differences are evident across different measures of fundamentalism.

Social Correlates

Do the social characteristics of fundamentalists vary by the particular measure adopted? Fundamentalists are generally viewed as less well educated, older, and more southern in composition than are non-fundamentalists. Table 11.1, therefore, examines the relationships between the three measures of fundamentalism and education, age, and region. It is evident in table 11.1 that the denominational and literalism measures are strongly related to level of education, but the self-identification measure is not. A similar pattern is found for region. In contrast, the literalism and self-identification measures are significantly related to the age variable (though at relatively low levels of significance), while the denominational measure is not. Note, however, that there are greater differences

TABLE 11.1
Measures of Fundamentalism and Sociodemographic Characteristics

	Denominational Affiliation			Doctrine			Self-Identification	
	Fund. (N = 70)	Evan. (N = 275)	Other Prot. (N = 273)	Literal (N = 275)	True (N = 257)	Man's Feelings (N = 86)	Fund. (N = 97)	Non-Fund. (N = 521)
Education								
% High Sch. or Less	64.3	55.3	40.3	62.5	40.9	34.9	48.5	49.9
% College Graduates	10.0	18.2	26.3	12.8	24.9	34.9	22.6	20.5
		Tau = .14 p ≤ .001			Tau = .21 p ≤ .001			Tau = .04 n.s.	
Region								
% South	57.1	61.5	33.8	56.9	42.4	41.9	51.5	48.3
		Tau = .26 p ≤ .001			Tau = .15 p ≤ .001			Tau = .02 n.s.	
Age								
% Under 30	25.7	21.1	17.9	18.5	21.4	22.1	19.6	20.3
% Over 60	30.0	24.7	32.6	34.5	26.1	18.6	21.6	30.1
		Tau = .07 n.s.			Tau = .10 p ≤ .03			Tau = .06 p ≤ .04	

Note: The data analyzed in this table, as well as in all subsequent tables, are based upon white Protestants only.

between age and the literalism and self-identification measures than may be evident at first glance. While both measures are significantly related to age, the patterns of the relationships move in opposite directions. Fundamentalists, when defined by biblical literalism, tend to be significantly older than non-fundamentalists, but when defined by self-identification, they tend to be significantly younger than non-fundamentalists.

Thus, the social correlates of fundamentalism vary with the particular measure employed. Once again, it appears that fundamentalism is far from a unidimensional phenomenon and that the choice of one's measure of fundamentalism is likely to have important consequences.

Criterion Variables

Perhaps such differences associated with the three measures of fundamentalism are less evident with the four criterion variables. Table 11.2 examines the 12 bivariate relationships obtained through crosstabulations. At first glance, it appears that the use of different measures of fundamentalism may be less problematic than might be inferred from table 11.1. All of the relationships are in the expected direction, and all meet minimal levels of statistical significance (.05), except one—the relationship between fundamentalist self-identification and attitudes toward abortion. Note, however, that the *magnitude* of the relationship between fundamentalism and a criterion variable varies depending upon the particular measure of fundamentalism employed. It is not clear if this variation reflects real differences in the discriminating ability of the particular measure of fundamentalism or if such variation is simply a reflection of the different social correlates of each measure.

In order to test the relationships between the fundamentalism measures and the criterion variables, and yet control for other variables, Multiple Classification Analysis (MCA) was employed. MCA enables one to make comparisons of the deviations from the mean score on the dependent variable for each category of the independent variable. The procedure yields a bivariate measure of association (*eta*) between the independent and the dependent variable. In addition, MCA provides deviations from the mean score on the dependent variable for each category of the independent variable *after* controls for each of the other independent measures have been entered into the analysis, with the statistic *beta* being the multivariate equivalent of *eta*. Because MCA presents mean scores for each category of the independent variable, one can ascertain the relative importance of different "cutting points" or responses given to the independent variable via the criterion variable. Finally, in addition to

TABLE 11.2
Crosstabulations Between Measures of Fundamentalism and Criterion Variables

	Denominational Affiliation			Doctrine			Self-Identification	
	Fund. (N = 70)	Evan. (N = 275)	Other Prot. (N = 273)	Literal (N = 275)	True (N = 257)	Man's Feelings (N = 86)	Fund. (N = 97)	Non-Fund. (N = 521)
High Religiosity*	58.5%	49.5% Tau = .25 p ≤ .001	24.5%	46.9%	40.5% Tau = .18 p ≤ .001	12.8%	59.8% Tau = .19 p ≤ .001	35.7%
Separatist Orientation+	51.4%	42.2% Tau = .23 p ≤ .001	24.2%	37.8%	36.6% Tau = .10 p ≤ .05	23.2%	58.7% Tau = .20 p ≤ .001	30.9%
Very Conservative Self-Id.	25.7%	12.0% Tau = .07 p ≤ .02	12.1%	13.8%	16.0% Tau = .05 p ≤ .01	5.8%	28.9% Tau = .16 p ≤ .001	10.7%
Abortion/ Pro Life@	38.6%	26.5% Tau = .15 p ≤ .001	20.9%	34.9%	21.0% Tau = .22 p ≤ .001	8.1%	34.0% Tau = .06 n.s.	23.8%

* Respondents were placed in a "high religiosity" category if they attended church weekly and stated that religion is "extremely important" in their lives.

+ Combines attitudes toward Falwell, the Moral Majority, and the Roman Catholic Church. Percents are those who "favor" Falwell and the Moral Majority and "oppose" the Roman Catholic Church.

@ Those who favor abortions under *no* circumstances.

the ease of interpretation, the MCA procedure is able to handle the problem of interaction effects among independent variables, easing a difficulty plaguing standard regression techniques (Andrews et al. 1969:12).

Religiosity. The relationships between fundamentalism and religiosity are examined in table 11.3. The first column presents the deviations from the religiosity mean for each category of the three fundamentalism measures, as well as the resultant *eta* coefficient. It is evident that there is a relatively strong covariation between religiosity and each of the three measures of fundamentalism. For each measure, the deviations from the mean move in the expected direction. For example, those who are affiliated with fundamentalist denominations exhibit greater religiosity

TABLE 11.3
A Comparison of the Relationships Between Various Measures of
Fundamentalism and Religiosity

Fundamentalism Measure	Deviations from Religiosity Mean	Same Deviations with Controls for Other Fund. Measures	Same Deviations with Controls for Other Fund. Measures and Demographics
Denominational Affiliation			
Fundamentalist	.77*	.38	.44
Evangelical	.20	.21	.22
Other Protestant	−.40	−.30	−.23
Eta or Beta	.26	.18	.20
Statistical significance of differences among denominational categories: $p \leq .001$			
Creation Story:			
Literal	.23	.13	.13
True	.08	.13	.13
Man's Feelings	−.99	−.81	−.82
Eta or Beta	.26	.21	.22
Statistical significance of differences among doctrinal categories: $p \leq .001$			
Fundamentalist Self-ID:			
Yes	.76	.50	.47
No/Unsure	−.14	−.09	−.09
Eta or Beta	.21	.14	.13
Statistical significance of differences between self-identification categories: $p \leq .002$			

*Positive scores indicate higher religiosity, while negative scores indicate lower religiosity.

than do those who are affiliated with evangelical denominations, who, in turn, exhibit greater religiosity than do those affiliated with other Protestant denominations. Likewise, biblical literalists on the doctrinal measure exhibit greater religiosity than do non-literalists, while self-identified fundamentalists have higher religiosity scores than do non-fundamentalists. Finally, it is evident from the first column that the *eta* coefficients are moderately strong and roughly equivalent for all three measures.

The second column presents the deviations from the religiosity mean and the resultant *beta* coefficient for each measure of fundamentalism, after controls for the other two measures of fundamentalism. The introduction of such controls reduces the strength of the relationships between each measure of fundamentalism and religiosity and alters the findings in other ways as well. For example, differences in religiosity between fundamentalist and evangelical denominations remain but are greatly reduced when controls for the other independent variables are introduced. Second, there are no differences in religiosity between biblical literalists and those who accept the creation story in Genesis as a true but not literal account. However, major differences in religiosity continue to persist between those who view the creation story as "authoritative" and those who understand it as a reflection of man's feelings about how it occurred. Nevertheless, despite the introduction of such controls, the relationship between each measure of fundamentalism and religiosity remains relatively strong, as is evident from the sizes of the resultant *beta* coefficients.

Finally, the third column of table 11.3 presents the relationship between each measure of fundamentalism and religiosity, with controls for the other two fundamentalism measures, as well as for age, education, and region.[11] The addition of socio-demographic controls has only marginal effects upon the relationships between each of the three measures of fundamentalism and religiosity. The *betas* for all three fundamentalism measures remain strong and statistically significant. In terms of denominational affiliation, fundamentalists, as expected, exhibit the highest levels of religiosity. Doctrinally, no differences in religiosity are evident between those who expressed "literal" versus "true" answers to the creation item, but great differences exist between these two categories and the "man's feelings" category. Finally, significant differences in religiosity also existed between those white Protestants who do and those who do not classify themselves as fundamentalists.

In summary, all three fundamentalism measures are significantly related to religiosity, even after the introduction of controls. However, the denominational and the doctrinal measures are more strongly related to religiosity than is the self-identification measure. Finally, while the doctrinal measure is significantly related to religiosity, it did not discriminate between fundamentalists ("literalists") and non-fundamentalists ("non-literalists") as it did between authoritative ("literal" and "true" responses) and non-authoritative ("man's feelings") responses.

Separatist Orientations. The relationships between the three measures of fundamentalism and our second criterion measure, separatist orientations, are presented in table 11.4. While all three fundamentalism measures are significantly related to religiosity, only two of the three measures are significantly related to the "separatist orientation" after the introduction of controls. As evident in the third column of table 11.4, the *betas* associated with the denominational measure (.23) and the self-identification measure of fundamentalism (.20) are roughly equivalent

TABLE 11.4
A Comparison of the Relationship Between Various Measures of Fundamentalism and Separatist Orientation

Fundamentalism Measure	Deviations from Separatism Mean	Same Deviations with Controls for Other Fund. Measures	Same Deviations with Controls for Other Fund. Measures and Demographics
Denominational Affiliation			
Fundamentalist	1.91*	1.04	.95
Evangelical	.56	.61	.58
Other Protestant	−1.05	−.88	−.83
Eta or *Beta*	.31	.24	.23
Statistical significance of differences among denominational categories: $p \leq .001$			
Creation Story:			
Literal	.47	.19	.10
True	−.26	−.12	−.06
Man's Feelings	−.73	−.24	−.12
Eta or *Beta*	.14	.05	.03
Statistical significance of differences among doctrinal categories: n.s.			
Fundamentalist Self-ID:			
Yes	1.91	1.37	1.50
No/Unsure	−.36	−.26	−.28
Eta or *Beta*	.25	.18	.20
Statistical significance of differences between self-identification categories: $p \leq .001$			

*Positive scores indicate a stronger separatist orientation, while negative scores indicate a weaker separatist orientation.

and statistically significant at the .001 level, while the *beta* associated with the doctrinal measure is very small and statistically insignificant.

In terms of denominational affiliation, fundamentalists have, as expected, a higher separatist orientation score than do evangelicals, who, in turn, have a higher score than do other Protestants. Likewise, self-identified fundamentalists express a significantly higher separatist orientation than do those Protestants who do not classify themselves as fundamentalists. On the other hand, while the adjusted mean scores for the doctrinal measure reflect differences in separatist orientation in the expected direction, such differences are two small to be statistically significant. Thus, as one shifts the criterion measure from one which is more directly religious to one which is more social in nature, those measures of fundamentalism which tap social group affiliation or social group identification are more strongly related to the group criterion variable than is the measure which taps religious doctrine, i.e., the biblical literalism measure.

Political Conservatism. The association between the three measures of fundamentalism and a self-reported political ideology variable are presented in table 11.5. Once again, only two of the three fundamentalism measures are significantly related to the ideology variable, in this instance, the self-identification and doctrinal measures. The former is far more significantly related than the latter. In addition, the doctrinal measure does not act in a monotonic fashion. Those who view creation as a "true" account are more likely to label themselves as conservatives than are those who view the creation story literally, even after the introduction of controls.

In the final analysis, then, it is the self-identification item which holds

TABLE 11.5

A Comparison of the Relationship Between Various Measures of Fundamentalism and Ideological Self-Classification

Fundamentalism Measure	Deviations from Ideology Mean	Same Deviations with Controls for Other Fund. Measures	Same Deviations with Controls for Other Fund. Measures and Demographics
Denominational Affiliation			
Fundamentalist	.31*	.05	.09
Evangelical	−.03	−.01	.00
Other Protestant	−.05	.00	−.02
Eta or *Beta*	.10	.02	.03
Statistical significance of differences among denominational categories: n.s.			
Creation Story:			
Literal	.03	.01	.00
True	.07	.08	.09
Man's Feelings	−.33	−.27	−.27
Eta or *Beta*	.18	.11	.11
Statistical significance of differences among doctrinal categories: $p \le .03$			
Fundamentalist Self-ID:			
Yes	.46	.41	.41
No/Unsure	−.09	−.08	−.08
Eta or *Beta*	.18	.17	.17
Statistical significance of differences between self-identification categories: $p \le .001$			

*Positive scores indicate a more conservative ideological orientation. negative scores indicate a less conservative ideological orientation.

up as a significant predictor of ideological conservatism when the selected socio-demographic variables and the other two measures of fundamentalism are added to the analysis. These findings are consistent with previous research that has shown that ideological self-placement tends to be determined more by group evaluations than by issue stances (Conover and Feldman 1981), and that group identities tend to have a greater political impact than do political values (Conover and Feldman 1984). Given the pattern of our findings, it would appear that self-classification as a fundamentalist reflects an identity which has political, as well as religious, overtones. Consequently, studies on the relationship between fundamentalism and political orientations are likely to find stronger relationships between the two if the self-identification measure is employed rather than a doctrinal or denominational measure.

Attitudes toward Abortion. While abortion can be viewed as a political issue, it is an issue which, for many, constitutes a moral and religious issue rather than simply a political issue. Consequently, it is unclear whether the more "religious," "social," or "political" measures of fundamentalism should have the strongest relationship to abortion attitudes. Table 11.6 presents the association between the three measures of fundamentalism and attitudes toward abortions. All three measures of fundamentalism are related to abortion attitudes in the expected direction: Fundamentalists are pro-life. However, once again, only two of the three fundamentalism measures are significantly related to abortion attitudes. Yet, in this instance, it is the doctrinal and denominational measures which are significantly related to the criterion variable, with the former more closely related than the latter. In data not presented here, a further control for religiosity was introduced, since both fundamentalism and religiosity have been found to be associated with abortion attitudes. The introduction of this control slightly reduces the relationship between literalism and abortion attitudes, while eliminating the relationship with denomination. Thus, it is the biblical literalism item which most strongly taps attitudes toward abortion.

Conclusions

This analysis has supported various hypotheses linking fundamentalism with religiosity, separatist orientations, conservative political ideology, and attitudes toward abortion. Despite the employment of a relatively homogeneous sample of white Protestants, all three of the fundamental-

TABLE 11.6

A Comparison of the Relationship Between Various Measures of
Fundamentalism and Attitudes toward Abortion

Fundamentalism Measure	Deviations from Abortion Mean	Same Deviations with Controls for Other Fund. Measures	Same Deviations with Controls for Other Fund. Measures and Demographics
Denominational Affiliation			
Fundamentalist	.23*	.12	.11
Evangelical	.07	.05	.06
Other Protestant	−.12	−.09	−.08
Eta or *Beta*	.16	.10	.10
Statistical significance of differences among denominational categories: $p \leq .05$			
Creation Story:			
Literal	.17	.15	.12
True	−.06	−.04	−.03
Man's Feelings	−.38	−.35	−.31
Eta or *Beta*	.25	.22	.19
Statistical significance of differences among doctrinal categories: $p \leq .001$			
Fundamentalist Self-ID:			
Yes	.14	.03	.06
No/Unsure	−.03	.00	−.01
Eta or *Beta*	.08	.02	.03
Statistical significance of differences between self-identification categories: n.s.			

*Positive scores indicate a stronger anti-abortion stance, while negative scores indicate a stronger pro-abortion stance.

ism measures were significantly related to at least one of the criterion variables. However, the measure of fundamentalism which had the strongest relationship with the four dependent variables differed from one criterion variable to another. All three measures of fundamentalism were significantly related to religiosity, even after the introduction of controls. However, biblical literalism had the strongest association with attitudes toward abortion, fundamentalist identification with political conservatism, and denominational affiliation with separatist orientations.

Such findings point to the need in future studies for multiple measures of fundamentalism. While some measures of fundamentalism may be related to certain criterion variables, they may not be related to others. For example, the linkages between fundamentalism and political conservatism hold only when the former is measured by fundamentalist self-identification. If denominational affiliation had been the only measure of fundamentalism employed, no relationship would have been found between fundamentalism and conservatism. Thus, some of the difficulties that previous studies have had in finding a link between fundamentalism and conservatism (Wuthnow 1973) may have been due to an inadequate set of fundamentalism measures employed in those studies. While cursory observation, and much prior research, suggests an association between fundamentalism and political conservatism, it does not point to how the concept of fundamentalism should be measured.

Table 11.7 summarizes the relationships among the three measures of fundamentalism and each of the four criterion measures. It appears that the doctrinal measure of fundamentalism, a direct measure of religious belief, is most closely tied to those criterion variables which are more "religious" in nature, i.e., religiosity and abortion attitudes. Note, however, that the creation story item is not always a successful predictor, suggesting the need to qualify somewhat the contention made by Ammerman (1982) that such a measure may be the best indicator of fundamentalist membership. Sometimes it seems to be; at other times it does not. The denominational measure of fundamentalism which taps social group affiliation is most clearly related to religiosity and to separatist orientations. Despite the difficulty of locating fundamentalists through denominational categorization, the analysis demonstrates that it can be done and that differences among fundamentalists, evangelicals, and the remaining Protestant groups are significant for certain dependent variables. Finally, the self-identification measure of fundamentalism, which taps a politicized identity, is most closely related to the political and separatist orientations of the respondents and somewhat moderately tied to religiosity. The self-identification measure works just as well as the other two measures and likely should be used increasingly in future research efforts, particularly when political dependent variables are employed. Thus, in conclusion, it appears from table 11.7 that the nature of the dependent variable under consideration (i.e., whether the dependent variable is religious, social, or political in nature) affects which measure of fundamentalism is most strongly related to the dependent variable.

Fundamentalism deserves continued study for several reasons. As a religious phenomenon, it is surviving, if not growing, with the passage of time. As Wuthnow (1988:484) has noted: "Implicitly, fundamentalism is generally assumed to be a short-term phenomenon unlikely to survive in the modern milieu. But . . . fundamentalism has surprised many observers by its persistence and, in some cases, growth." The movement will likely persist, given its emphasis upon the supernatural—the very real presence of God and His protagonist, Satan, and the certainty about

TABLE 11.7

Overview of the Relationships Between Each of the Fundamentalism Measures
and the Four Criterion Variables

	Denominational Affiliation	Doctrine	Self-Identification
Religiosity	strong	strong	moderate
Separatist Orientations	strong	x	strong
Political Conservatism	x	x	strong
Abortion Attitudes	x	strong	x

life after death, either in heaven or in hell. The very tensions between fundamentalism and American culture which lead the movement to emphasize separation from the world also enhance its survival. Moreover, in scholarship on American religion, fundamentalism deserves study on its own merits as a religious "tradition" within American culture.

However, future research on the topic must work toward greater conceptual and measurement precision. Findings based upon "crude" measures of fundamentalism, with little attention given to the dimension of fundamentalism under investigation, are more likely to detract from than to add to our understanding of the phenomenon. The measures of fundamentalism available for this analysis were themselves limited. Questions on dispensational premillennialism, separatist attitudes and behaviors, and religious practices associated with fundamentalism (e.g., Bible reading and witnessing) were not available. Measures of such variables need to be developed in the future. As the analysis presented here has shown, when one engages in the study of fundamentalism, explicit attention must be given both to the particular facet of fundamentalism under investigation and to the particular operational measures employed.

Notes

1. As one scholar has put it, "There is [an evangelical] whole, even if sometimes it is difficult to define precisely" (Johnston 1991:257).

2. We separate the Independent-Fundamentalist tradition from its closest allies among the four traditions noted by Hunter, i.e., the Baptist and Reformed-Confessional, because its origins are different (John Nelson Darby and the

Plymouth Brethren), and it has a non-denominational character and an emphasis upon eschatology.

3. Although Wheaton College, the academic home of one of the authors, holds a premillennial position with regard to the Second Coming of Christ in its "Statement of Faith," students from non-fundamentalist backgrounds often express uncertainty as to the meaning of this doctrine. It has not been emphasized in their recent religious socialization.

4. This survey, which was conducted in 1983, employed random digit-dialing techniques to select one thousand registered voters who met certain religious criteria (see Rothenberg and Newport 1984:17–20).

5. Denominational fundamentalists included members of Independent, Hard Shell, Missionary, and Fundamental Baptists, Evangelical Methodists, Bible Church, Full Bible Church, and Congregational Evangelical churches. In addition, those members of denominations who, as individuals, met all of the following criteria were also classified as denominational fundamentalists: those who claimed to be "born again," held a literal view of the creation story, and classified themselves as fundamentalists. This latter category included respondents who met the specified criteria from the following denominations: "Baptists," Southern Baptists, Northern Baptists, "First" Baptists, Conservative Baptists, Baptist/"Other" and Full Gospel Church. This procedure was justified on the grounds that, because of the congregational form of government found within some denominations, it is possible that particular individuals and congregations could be classified as fundamentalist, although one could not classify the whole denomination as fundamentalist (e.g., the Southern Baptists). Evangelicals included respondents in these latter denominations (e.g., Southern Baptists) who did not meet all of the specified criteria for inclusion as fundamentalists. In addition, evangelical denominations included United Baptists, Free Methodist, Wesleyan Methodist, Covenant Presbyterian, Church of Christ, Church of God, Nazarene, Seventh Day Adventist, Salvation Army, Dutch Christian Reformed, Christian, Christian Reformed, Holiness, and Church of the Brethren, as well as those respondents who claimed membership in a non-denominational church. Responses of the latter showed that they belonged in the evangelical category. Pentecostals included United Pentecostal, "Pentecostal," Pentecostal Holiness, Pentecostal Church of God, Pentecostal Church of God in Christ, and Assemblies of God. All other denominations were included in the "Other Protestant" grouping. A variety of recent research has demonstrated that fundamentalist and non-fundamentalist evangelicals can be differentiated both analytically and empirically (see, for example, Wilcox 1986 and Smidt 1988).

6. The two items were normalized using a z score transformation and then added together. The coefficient alpha was .62.

7. We worked with this item at some length before discarding it. Its major problem is that few of the evangelical respondents had heard of *Sword of the Lord*.

8. In data not presented here, the three fundamentalism measures (denominational affiliation, doctrine, and self-identification) were crosstabulated with each

of the three "separatist orientation" items. The relationships were in every instance what had been hypothesized, and in seven of the nine cases were statistically significant by the chi square test. In addition, there were no major regional biases when links to the three component items were examined, other than the slight tendency of southerners to identify with one of their own, Jerry Falwell. Those who favored Falwell and the Moral Majority but opposed the Roman Catholic Church tended to be older and less educated than were those who opposed the first two objects and favored the last. The coefficient alpha for these three items was a relatively low, yet acceptable, .47. As a result, we feel that this separatist orientation measure was adequate, though not necessarily ideal. While questions might be raised about the choice of the Roman Catholic Church item, George Dollar (1973:252), a self-identified fundamentalist and an historian of the movement, has suggested that opposition to the Catholic Church is part and parcel of the movement.

9. The sample was originally composed of 1000 respondents. The exclusion of non-whites and Roman Catholics dropped the number of respondents in the sample to 645. However, in addition, a small group of white Pentecostals were excluded from the analysis because their numbers (27) were too few for extensive evaluation and because their presence confounded efforts to compare fundamentalist and non-fundamentalist evangelicals. As a result, 618 white Protestants remained in the study.

10. For example, the "fundamentalism scale" created by Miller and Wattenberg (1984) is largely composed of religiosity items.

11. The analysis presented in table 11.1 revealed that the social correlates of each measure of fundamentalism varied somewhat. Consequently, these sociodemographic variables were also entered into the analysis in order to control their differential effects.

References

Ammerman, Nancy
  1982   Operationalizing evangelicalism: An amendment. *Sociological Analysis* 43(2): 170–72.
  1987   *Bible believers: Fundamentalists in the modern world.* New Brunswick: Rutgers University Press.
Andrews, Frank, James Morgan, and John Sonquist
  1969   *Multiple classification analysis.* Ann Arbor, MI: Institute for Social Research.
Askew, Thomas
  1987   A response to David Wells. In *A time to speak out: The evangelical-Jewish encounter,* edited by A. James Rudin and Marvin R. Wilson, 41–43. Grand Rapids, MI: Eerdmans.

Balswick, Jack, Dawn McWard, and David Carlson
1975 Theological and socio-political belief change among religiously conservative students. *Review of Religious Research* 17 (Fall):61–67.
Berg, Philip
1971 Self-identified fundamentalism among protestant seminarians: A study of persistence and change in value orientations. *Review of Religious Research* 12 (Winter):88–94.
Beatty, Kathleen Murphy, and Oliver Walter
1984 Religious preference and practice: Reevaluating their impact on political tolerance. *Public Opinion Quarterly* 48 (Spring):318–329.
Burton, Ronald, Stephen Johnson, and Joseph Tamney
1989 Education and fundamentalism. *Review of Religious Research* 30(4):344–359.
Carpenter, Joel
1980 Fundamentalist institutions and the rise of evangelical Protestantism, 1929–1942. *Church History* 49(March):62–75.
Conover, Pamela, and Stanley Feldman
1981 The origins and meaning of liberal/conservative self-identifications. *American Journal of Political Science* 25(4):617–645.
1984 Group identification, values, and the nature of political beliefs. *American Politics Quarterly* 12(2):151–175.
DeJong, Gordon, and Thomas Ford
1965 Religious fundamentalism and denominational preference in the southern Appalachian region. *Journal for the Scientific Study of Religion* 5(October):24–43.
Dollar, George
1973 *A history of fundamentalism in America.* Greenville, SC: Bob Jones University Press.
Ellis, William
1981 Evolution, fundamentalism, and the historians: An historiographical review. *The Historian* 14(November):15–35.
Ethridge, F. M., and J. R. Feagin
1979 Varieties of "fundamentalism": A conceptual and empirical analysis of two Protestant denominations. *Sociological Quarterly* 20(1):37–48.
Ford, Thomas
1960 Status, residence, and fundamentalist religious beliefs in the southern Appalachians. *Social Forces* 39(October):41–49.
Grupp, Jr., Fred, and William Newman
1973 Political ideology and religious preference: The John Birch Society and Americans for Democratic Action. *Journal for the Scientific Study of Religion* 12(December):401–412.
Hertel, Bradley, and Michael Hughes
1987 Religious affiliation, attendance, and support for "pro-family" issues in the United States. *Social Forces* 65(3):858–882.

Hood, Ralph W. Jr.
1983   Social psychology and religious fundamentalism. In *Rural psychology*, edited by A. W. Childs and G. Melton, 169–198. New York: Plenum Press.

Hood, Ralph W. Jr., and Ronald J. Morris
1985   Boundary maintenance, social-political views, and presidential preference among high and low fundamentalists. *Review of Religious Research* 27(Winter):134–145.

Hofstadter, Richard
1963   *Anti-intellectualism in American life.* New York: Knopf.

Hunter, James
1983   *American evangelism: Conservative religion and the quandary of modernity.* New Brunswick: Rutgers University Press.

Jelen, Ted
1984   Respect for life, sexual morality, and opposition to abortion. *Review of Religious Research* 25(March):220–231.

1988   Changes in the attitudinal correlations of opposition to abortion. 1977–1985. *Journal for the Scientific Study of Religion* 27(2):211–228.

Johnston, Robert
1991   American evangelicalism: An extended family. In *The variety of American evangelicalism*, edited by Donald Dayton and Robert Johnston, 252–272. Downers Grove, IL: Inter-Varsity Press.

Lechner, Frank J.
1985   Fundamentalism and sociocultural revitalization in America: A sociological interpretation. *Sociological Analysis* 46(3):243–260.

Marsden, George
1980   *Fundamentalism and American culture: The shaping of twentieth century evangelicalism.* New York: Oxford University Press.

1991   Fundamentalism and American evangelicalism. In *The variety of American evangelicalism*, 22–35. See Johnston 1991.

Martin, David
1978   *A general theory of secularization.* New York: Harper & Row.

McIntosh, William Alex, Letitia Alston, and Jon Alston
1979   The differential impact of religious preference and church attendance on attitudes toward abortion. *Review of Religious Research* 20(2):195–213.

Miller, Arthur, and Martin Wattenberg
1984   Politics from the pulpit: Religiosity and the 1980 election. *Public Opinion Quarterly* 48(Spring)301–317.

Moberg, David
1969   Theological self-classification and a view of students. *Review of Religious Research* 10(Winter):100–107.

Orum, A. M.
1970   Religion and the rise of the radical right: The case of southern Wallace support in 1968. *Social Science Quarterly* 30(September):411–417.

Peshkin, Alan
   1986   *God's choice: The total world of a fundamentalist Christian school.* Chicago: University of Chicago Press.
Petersen, Larry, and Armand Mauss
   1976   Religion and the "right to life": Correlates of opposition to abortion. *Sociological Analysis* 37(3):243–254.
Roof, Clark
   1986   The new fundamentalism: Rebirth of political religion in America. In *Prophetic religions and politics*, edited by Jeffrey Hadden and Anson Shupe, 18–34. New York: Paragon House.
Rothenberg, Stuart, and Frank Newport
   1984   *The evangelical voter: Religion and politics in America.* Washington, D.C.: Free Congress.
Sandeen, Ernest
   1970a   *The roots of fundamentalism.* Chicago: University of Chicago Press.
   1970b   Fundamentalism and American identity. *The Annals* 387(January):56–65.
Smidt, Corwin
   1988   Evangelicals within contemporary American politics: Differentiating between fundamentalist and non-fundamentalist evangelicals. *Western Political Quarterly* 40(September):601–620.
Smith, Timothy
   1987   Evangelical Christianity and American culture. In *A time to speak out*, 58–75. *See* Askew 1987.
Smith, Tom
   1986   Classifying Protestant denominations. GSS Technical Report No. 67. Chicago: National Opinion Research Center.
Stackhouse, Max
   1982   Religious right: New? Right? *Commonweal* 109(January):52–56.
Stark, Rodney, and William Bainbridge
   1980   Towards a theory of religious commitment. *Journal for the Scientific Study of Religion* 19(2):114–128.
   1985   *The future of religion.* Berkeley: University of California Press.
Steed, Robert, Laurence Moreland, and Tod Baker
   1983   Religion and party activists: Fundamentalism and politics in regional perspective. In *Religion and politics in the South*, edited by Tod Baker, Robert Steed, and Laurence Moreland, 105–132. New York: Praeger.
Wallace, Anthony
   1966   *Religion: An anthropological view.* New York: Random House.
Wallis, Roy
   1975   *Sectarianism.* New York: Wiley.
Wilcox, Clyde
   1966   Evangelicals and fundamentalists in the new Christian right: Religious differences in the Ohio Moral Majority. *Journal for the Scientific Study of Religion* 25(3):355–363.

1989 The fundamentalist voter: Politicized religious identity and political attitudes and behavior. *Review of Religious Research* 31(September):54–67.

Wilson, Bryan
1975 The secularization debate. *Encounter* 45(October):77–83.

Wuthnow, Robert
1973 Religious commitment and conservatism: In search of an elusive relationship. In *Religion in sociological perspective*, edited by Charles Glock, 117–132. Belmont, California: Wadsworth.
1988 Sociology of religion. In *Handbook of sociology*, edited by Neil J. Smelser, 473–509. Newbury Park, CA: Sage.

12

The Spirit-Filled Movements and American Politics

Corwin E. Smidt
John C. Green
Lyman A. Kellstedt
James L. Guth

Over the past few decades, political analysts have noted the new prominence of evangelical Protestants in American public life. They have been less cognizant of the parallel activation of Pentecostal and charismatic Christians, groups that overlap with the evangelical community but extend into other religious traditions. American Pentecostalism began in a series of revivals during the early 1900s, and the charismatic movement is a recent extension of that impulse. For the most part, scholars have given little attention to the political characteristics of these religious groups.[1] It is fitting, then, as the twentieth century comes to a close, that we give some systematic effort to assessing the political significance of the "spirit-filled movements."[2]

This chapter seeks to remedy the current inattention by answering certain basic questions about the politics of the spirit-filled movements. Consequently, we examine their (1) composite size, (2) religious location, (3) political cohesion, (4) partisanship, and (5) degree of politicization. As we shall see, not only do the spirit-filled comprise a significant portion of the American electorate, but they permeate several religious traditions. As a result, they possess great political potential, in both size and ability to forge alliances that cut across traditional political cleavages. Yet, this ability to penetrate different religious traditions also poses important challenges for the spirit-filled, which currently mitigate against achievement of their full political potential.

The Spirit-Filled Movements

Pentecostalism takes its name from the day of Pentecost in the Book of Acts in the New Testament, when an outpouring of the Holy Spirit enabled the apostles to "speak in tongues." Although some early Christians continued to speak in tongues, as attested in Paul's letters, the practice largely disappeared from the early church. Then, after centuries of absence,[3] the gift of tongues emerged again in the early 1900s. Like the original Pentecost, this outpouring of tongues occurred rather suddenly, unexpectedly, and in different parts of the country (e.g., Topeka, Kansas, and Los Angeles, California) at roughly the same time. These particular revivals gave birth to a movement emphasizing the "second baptism of the Holy Spirit,"[4] with the gift of speaking in tongues as its defining mark. Early Pentecostals understood their special religious experience as a clear sign that the "latter days" preceding the Second Coming of Christ had begun; thus, there was a special urgency to convert nonbelievers; and speaking in tongues was a mark of such conversion. For many Pentecostals as well as other religious people, this last point implied that non-Pentecostals were either "second-class" believers or, worse yet, not part of Christ's church. As a result, early relationships between Pentecostals and other Christians were often turbulent, marked by great disdain, skepticism, and mistrust.

The new spirit-filled Christians were at first defined by distinctive religious practices, such as speaking in tongues, and related theological perspectives, such as the need for the second baptism of the Holy Spirit. At first Pentecostals remained within existing Protestant denominations, but the tensions caused by their distinctiveness soon led to withdrawal into new religious organizations. Thus, a series of Pentecostal denominations formed during a few short years following the revivals. Not surprisingly, their adherents tended to be isolated from other Protestants as well as from the broader society. Such isolation reinforced the otherworldly focus of Pentecostal beliefs and rendered the movement apolitical. Unlike contemporary movements such as fundamentalism, Pentecostalism did not seek to reclaim American institutions; with rare exception, Pentecostals directed their energies to private life. Thus, for most of this century, these distinctive people eagerly awaited Christ's imminent return, living apart from the world that cared little for them and for which they cared little in return.

After World War II, however, significant changes occurred. At the institutional level, the movement rejoined American life, as Pentecostal denominations joined the National Association of Evangelicals and other religious organizations. Of even greater importance was the emergence of a new spirit-filled movement outside the historic Pentecostal denominations, including the charismatic renewal movement within mainline Protestant and Roman Catholic churches, and the "third wave" movement in evangelical denominations and non-denominational churches.[5] These new groups can be traced in large part to April 1960, when California Episcopal priest Dennis Bennett announced that he had been baptized by the Holy Spirit. Soon such experiences quickly spread into Lutheran, Methodist, Presbyterian, and after 1967, into Roman Catholic congregations (Marty 1976:107). Thus, whereas the early Pentecostal movement was strongest among the small-town and urban poor, the charismatic movement was more middle-class and suburban in social composition (Quebedeaux 1983:11–12; Flowers 1984:71).

Important changes occurred at the individual level as well. Social distance between spirit-filled and other Christians eroded both physically and psychologically; as a result, the early animosities between Pentecostals and non-Pentecostals declined as well (Wacker 1988:208; Anderson 1979:236). Moreover, with the general social mobility and educational advancement of American society after World War II, the earlier images of Pentecostals as uneducated and poor required amendment, though Pentecostals were still somewhat less advantaged economically than the newer charismatic elements or third-wave movements (Smidt et al. 1994).

These changes eventually moved the spirit-filled toward greater political involvement. For example, these groups were a critical element in the Christian Voice, an early Christian Right group contemporaneous with the Moral Majority (Jorstad 1990). In addition, charismatics and their Pentecostal allies formed the core of Pat Robertson's 1988 presidential bid (see Smidt and Penning 1990). In recent years, considerable efforts have been made to further mobilize the spirit-filled, and they remain central elements in the Christian Coalition and other second-generation Christian Right groups.

Despite the social emergence of spirit-filled movements and efforts to mobilize their members politically, little is known about the basic characteristics of these believers, traits that affect their political potential. For example, just how large are the movements? To what extent have they permeated non-Pentecostal denominations? Do spirit-filled Christians express similar positions on political issues regardless of their religious tradition, or does their religious location (e.g., mainline Protestantism, Roman Catholicism) color the issue stands and political evaluations they express? Have members of the spirit-filled movements been activated politically, or is activism characteristic of only certain segments? We now turn to these questions.

Measurement and Data

To make these assessments, we must first identify members of spirit-filled movements, which is not an easy task. No single definition fully captures these movements; instead, we employ three separate measures: (1) affiliation with denominations spawned by the original movement; (2) distinctive religious practices tied to the movements, such as speaking in tongues;[6] and (3) psychological identification with the movements themselves. These three measures allow us to explore the general contours of the movements as well as the extent to which respondents are fully embedded within them.

One approach is to include respondents who belong to denominations and local churches that affirm the doctrinal essentials, specifically the second baptism of the Holy Spirit. This approach gets at the association of spirit-filled Christians with each other on a regular basis. Thus, some analysts have examined the spirit-filled through the institutions that have emerged in the wake of the original revivals (e.g., Nichol 1966). Although this technique identifies most Pentecostals, it fails to locate charismatics—those spirit-filled Christians outside of traditional Pentecostal churches. Thus, this approach is only a start in identifying certain segments of the spirit-filled community; it is insufficient as a total strategy.

Others identify the spirit-filled by focusing on their most distinctive religious practice: the gift of speaking in tongues, or *glossolalia*. In fact, many scholars argue that speaking in tongues is the defining characteristic of membership (e.g., Marty 1976:106–25). Several scholars have contended, however, that glossolalia is not an adequate defining trait. Many charismatics hold that though speaking in tongues is important, it is not the only authenticating gift of the Holy Spirit (Farah 1987), and growing numbers of Pentecostals report that they do not possess the gift.[7] Not surprisingly, some scholars (e.g., Dayton 1991:37) argue that speaking in tongues should not serve as the defining characteristic of membership.

Finally, to overcome these difficulties, some analysts have used self-identification: those who willingly label themselves as Pentecostals or charismatics constitute the spirit-filled movements. Religious movements are composed of individuals dedicated to reforming and revitalizing existing religious institutions, and they serve as crucial "change agents" in religion. From this perspective, it is self-conscious association with a movement that matters rather than practices, beliefs, or institutional connections (Poloma 1986:330). Although this approach possesses certain advantages, individuals may use the same self-identification but understand very different things by that label.

We will employ data from a national survey of 4,001 Americans conducted in the spring of 1992 to assess the spirit-filled movements. This survey had an unusually large sample and, most importantly, included many religious questions relevant for our purpose, such as detailed measures of denominational affiliation, religious identification, and frequency of speaking in tongues. These questions permit us to employ each measurement strategy. First, we analyze Pentecostalism by examining the characteristics of members of white and black Pentecostal denominations and churches. Second, we consider these movements defined behaviorally, on the basis of glossolalia. Finally, we analyze the movements as delineated by psychological measures: whether respondents identify as Pentecostals or charismatics. Each approach has strengths and weaknesses; as a result, we will combine all three in a single, encompassing measure.[8]

The Size of the Spirit-Filled Movements

How large are the spirit-filled movements? We begin our analysis with the distribution(s) of Pentecostal and charismatic Christians, shown in table 12.1, using each measurement approach: denominational affiliation, speaking in tongues, and self-identification. Denominational affiliation is collapsed into nine categories: (1) four groups of evangelical Protestants: white Pentecostal, black Pentecostal, nondenominational charismatics;[9] and other Evangelicals; (2) mainline Protestants; (3) other black Protestants; (4) Roman Catholics; (5) other traditions; and (6) seculars.[10]

The proportion of Americans who belong to classic Pentecostal denominations is relatively small, accounting for only 3.6 percent of the adult population. Those affiliated with white Pentecostal churches (2.5 percent) are twice as numerous as members of black Pentecostalism (1.1 percent). When nondenominational charismatics are added to this mix, the numbers expand to 5 percent of the population. Although this latter figure may seem relatively small, we should note that the only Protestant denominational families to exceed this size are Baptists, Methodists, and Lutherans, with Lutherans only a fraction larger (data not shown). Table 12.1 also reports the percentage of Americans who claim the gift of tongues. When the spirit-filled movements are measured this way, their

TABLE 12.1
The Distribution of Spirit-Filled Christians
(N = 4001)

Pentecostal-Charismatic Measure	Percentage	N
Denomination		
Evangelical Protestants		
White Pentecostal	2.5	100
Black Pentecostal	1.1	42
Nondenominational Charismatics	1.4	56
Other Evangelicals	21.7	868
Mainline Protestants	16.7	670
Black Protestant	6.8	273
Roman Catholic	23.2	948
Other Traditions	6.8	274
Seculars	19.7	790
Total	100.0	4001
Speaking in Tongues		
Daily or Weekly	3.3	133
Monthly or less	5.4	218
Never	91.3	3650
Total	100.0	4001
Self-Identification		
Pentecostal only*	4.7	187
Charismatic only*	6.6	266
Both Pentecostal and Charismatic	0.8	34
Neither*	87.9	3514
Total	100.0	4001

* May include some cases which combine other identifications such as evangelical and fundamentalist.

size grows considerably—doubling to 8.7 percent. Obviously, many more people exercise the gift of tongues than belong to Pentecostal denominations.

Finally, people may identify with spirit-filled movements without belonging to a Pentecostal denomination or speaking in tongues. Studies employing self-identification measures have often combined both identities in a single question, tapping identification "as a charismatic or Pentecostal Christian." Since many "classical Pentecostals balk at being identified with charismatics" (Farah 1987:25), however, our respondents were asked which of a battery of religious labels they would use to describe themselves (e.g., Pentecostal, charismatic, evangelical, fundamentalist, mainline). This approach enables us not only to assess the percentage of Pentecostals separately from that of charismatics but also to assess how many Americans claim both labels.

Some 4.7 percent of Americans label themselves simply as Pentecostal, while a slightly higher 6.6 percent choose only charismatic. Less than 1 percent (0.8 percent) employ both labels. Thus, when all three categories are combined, 12.1 percent can be classified as charismatic or Pentecostal Christians. This distribution of religious self-identifications reveals three important patterns: (1) the term *charismatic* is more widely adopted by Americans than *Pentecostal*, (2) few Americans employ both terms together, and (3) self-identification provides a more encompassing measure than either denominational affiliation or glossolalia.

What are the relationships among these measures of the spirit-filled? Table 12.2 reveals that slightly more that one-half of the members of white Pentecostal churches report speaking in tongues, compared to only one-third of black Pentecostals. Although the gift of tongues may still be visible within Pentecostal denominations, it is far from universal.[11] On the other hand, speaking in tongues is hardly confined to Pentecostalism. Tongues-speakers comprise nearly three-fourths of those in nondenominational charismatic churches and about one-fifth of those in black non-Pentecostal churches. While the gift of tongues is also diffused throughout the remaining religious categories, it is less common there: Catholics have the highest percentage (9.0 percent), followed by evangelical Protestants (6.6 percent) and mainline Protestants (5.9 percent).

Second, the religious bases for adopting the Pentecostal and charismatic labels are different. First, outside the historic Pentecostal denominations, the label "charismatic" is much more common than "Pentecostal." The only exception is among non-Pentecostal black churches where approximately equal numbers chose the two identities. Probably more surprising, relatively few respondents reported both identities. Of those claiming either identification, only 7 percent chose both. Thus, a high wall of separation exists between Pentecostal and charismatic identifiers. Whether this disjunction results from different religious discourse or reflects social and psychological distance is not clear. Nevertheless, three decades after the emergence of the charismatic renewal movement, psychological linkages between the two groups still have not been deeply forged. Few charismatics and Pentecostals identify with their religious "cousins." Comparing these responses to the first measures in table 12.2, we find that self-identification is more widespread among white and

TABLE 12.2
Religious Affiliation and Measures of Spirit-Filled Movements: Denomination,
Tongues, Self-Identification, and Proximities
(In percentages; N = 4001)

Denominational Affiliation

(N)	Wh Pent (100)	Blk Pent (42)	Non Demn (56)	Other Evng (868)	Main Prot (670)	Blk Prot (273)	Rom Cath (948)
Speak in Tongues							
Yes	55.6	33.1	74.6	6.6	5.9	19.0	9.0
No	44.4	66.9	25.4	93.4	94.1	81.0	91.0
Self-Identification							
Pentecostal	66.9	50.9	15.3	3.0	3.0	9.5	1.7
Charismatic	12.0	7.1	54.7	6.3	5.7	9.6	7.4
Both Pent/Char	8.3	0.0	10.7	0.6	0.5	2.0	0.6
Neither	12.8	42.1	19.3	90.2	90.8	78.9	87.9
Proximity:							
Close to							
Pentecostals	38.0	47.0	20.1	8.5	4.0	9.5	3.8
Charismatics	3.6	0.0	11.9	3.7	1.7	2.8	4.6
Both Pent/Char	38.7	12.7	42.0	7.3	2.0	11.6	1.4
Far from							
Pentecostals	2.1	3.6	6.6	8.9	11.9	10.4	16.8
Charismatics	27.0	25.4	8.4	10.9	7.9	8.7	6.1
Both Pent/Char	3.0	3.2	3.0	29.3	35.0	26.8	38.7

The column headers above also show the grouping: **Wh Pent**, **Blk Pent**, **Non Demn**, and **Other Evng** fall under **Evangelical Protestants**; while **Main Prot**, **Blk Prot**, and **Rom Cath** are separate.

black Pentecostals and nondenominational charismatics than is speaking
in tongues. Likewise, given their membership in Pentecostal denominations, the percentage of self-identification among these groups is significantly higher than the 12 percent figure for the nation as a whole (see
table 12.1).

The bottom portion of table 12.2 reveals how the different denominational families and religious traditions feel about Pentecostals and charismatics. Feelings of proximity cannot be taken as measures of membership (e.g., feeling close to Catholics does not make one a Roman Catholic). But membership is usually associated with feelings of proximity; thus, Catholics are likely to feel close to other Catholics. Not surprisingly, therefore, members of Pentecostal denominations and nondenominational charismatic churches most often feel close to Pentecostals and charismatics. Probably more revealing, however, are the substantial numbers of white and black Pentecostals who felt far from charismatics (approximately one-quarter). In addition, sizable percentages of those outside Pentecostal churches felt distant from the spirit-filled. Even one-third of evangelical Protestants expressed psychological distance from both Pentecostals and charismatics; the same is true for mainline and black Protestants, as well as for Roman Catholics. When these percentages are coupled with the percentages for the "Far from Pentecostals Only" and "Far from Charismatics Only" categories, it is clear that sizable segments (nearly a majority or more) of all four major Christian traditions express considerable distance from either or both spirit-filled groups.

Nevertheless, table 12.2 also reveals that these movements have made some important inroads among religious people not historically tied to Pentecostalism. Although identification as a Pentecostal/charismatic and speaking in tongues are evident within all religious traditions, the potential for further growth appears most favorable among Evangelicals, in whom expressions of proximity are far more common than among mainline Protestants or Roman Catholics.

Finally, table 12.2 reveals the limitations of employing only one measure, whether denominational affiliation, speaking in tongues, or self-identification. Different measures tap different facets of the movement, but these can be combined to classify respondents who, to some degree, at least, fall within the movement. As the three component measures do not overlap perfectly, this approach broadens the movement's base by incorporating anyone who exhibits only one of the three measures. When this is done, the spirit-filled movements constitute 13.4 percent of the American electorate (data not shown). Obviously, this approach does not expand the size of these spirit-filled movements much beyond that obtained by the self-identification measures (12.1 percent), which suggests that those who are affiliated with a Pentecostal denomination and/or who speak in tongues, for the most part, also identify as Pentecostal or charismatic.

The Religious Location of the Spirit-Filled Movements

Where do we find members of the spirit-filled movements? Table 12.3 uses our composite measure to locate the movements within the four large Christian traditions: evangelical, mainline, and black Protestantism, along with Roman Catholicism. Several conclusions can be drawn from table 12.3. First, the spirit-filled movement has broken out of its historic Pentecostal context; indeed, spirit-filled believers are found within all four major Christian traditions. Politically, the fact that the spirit-filled are so widespread is significant; by including white Pentecostals, charismatic mainliners, spirit-filled black Protestants, and charismatic Roman Catholics, these movements might create new political alliances and bridge old cleavages.

Nevertheless, those affiliated with spirit-filled movements are a distinct minority in each tradition. For example, charismatics comprise less than 10 percent of all mainliners, while charismatic Catholics make up

TABLE 12.3
Distribution of the Spirit-Filled by Religious Tradition

Religious Tradition	N	Percent of Trad.	Percent of All Spirit-Filled
Evangelical Protestant			
Non-member	780	77.2	
Spirit-Filled	231	22.8	43.9
Mainline Protestant			
Non-member	710	91.1	
Spirit-Filled	69	8.9	13.1
Black Protestant			
Non-member	172	64.2	
Spirit-Filled	96	35.8	18.3
Roman Catholic			
Non-member	848	86.7	
Spirit-Filled	130	13.3	24.7

approximately 13 percent of their tradition. Only within the evangelical and black Protestant camps do Pentecostals and charismatics constitute a substantial percentage; but even among Evangelicals, less than one in four are members, while slightly more than one in three can be counted among Black Protestants. Thus, although these spirit-filled movements have permeated all of the religious traditions, they are "outsiders" within each.

Third, no one group dominates the contemporary spirit-filled movements. Those found within evangelical denominations constitute a plurality of all spirit-filled believers (43.9 percent), with charismatic Catholics trailing (24.7 percent). Thus, table 12.3 suggests that the movements are arranged in a bipolar fashion, with Pentecostals and charismatics within the evangelical tradition at one pole and charismatics within the Catholic church at the other, and each contributing significantly to the movements' size.

The Political Cohesion of the Spirit-Filled Movements

The spirit-filled constitute a sizable group, widely distributed across the religious landscape, but whether they are a cohesive political bloc in unclear. Their location in different religious traditions constitutes a double-edged sword. Although such diffusion creates important political opportunities and strategic advantages, it also dilutes unity in political attitudes and behavior. In other words, their separate religious traditions may well shape the way movement members view the political world and act therein. Table 12.4 addresses this question by examining political attitudes of respondents from the four largest Christian traditions (evangelical Protestantism, black Protestantism, mainline Protestantism, and Roman Catholicism). Within each, respondents are classified as spirit-filled or not. The table reports mean scores on twelve political issues. With the exception of the abortion item (a four-point item), we employed a five-point Likert scale format, ranging from strongly agree to strongly disagree; in all cases, the data are coded so that higher scores indicate more conservative positions.

Several important patterns are evident in table 12.4. First, evangelical Protestants, whether spirit-filled or not, generally express the most conservative views, but among Evangelicals, the spirit-filled take more conservative stances than other Evangelicals. The differences are largest

TABLE 12.4
Issue Positions and Cohesion Levels of Members of the Spirit-Filled
Movements by Religious Tradition

Issue	Evan Prot	Main Prot	Black Prot	Roman Cath
Abortion				
Not Spirit-Filled	2.22*	1.71	1.99	1.99
Spirit-Filled	2.47	1.93	2.44	2.19
Affirmative Action				
Not Spirit-Filled	3.05	2.93	2.16	2.93
Spirit-Filled	3.09	2.74	2.06	2.44
Balanced Budget				
Not Spirit-Filled	3.05	3.02	3.01	3.14
Spirit-Filled	3.08	2.76	2.90	3.31
Defense Spending				
Not Spirit-Filled	2.81	2.71	2.50	2.62
Spirit-Filled	2.87	2.68	2.44	2.32
Environment				
Not Spirit-Filled	2.48	2.35	2.97	2.40
Spirit-Filled	2.61	2.52	2.83	2.57
Equal Rights Amendment				
Not Spirit-Filled	2.53	2.24	1.83	2.18
Spirit-Filled	2.62	2.29	2.00	2.12
Health Care				
Not Spirit-Filled	2.59	2.45	2.34	2.34
Spirit-Filled	2.43	2.39	2.32	2.32
Homosexual Rights				
Not Spirit-Filled	3.19	2.50	2.47	2.40
Spirit-Filled	3.39	2.64	2.96	2.48
Israel				
Not Spirit-Filled	3.08	2.76	2.44	2.70
Spirit-Filled	3.48	2.73	2.86	2.76
Job Protection				
Not Spirit-Filled	3.58	3.39	3.64	3.58
Spirit-Filled	3.55	3.68	3.55	3.75
School Choice				
Not Spirit-Filled	3.35	2.94	3.49	3.37
Spirit-Filled	3.57	3.14	3.31	3.67
Women Job Preference				
Not Spirit-Filled	3.78	3.69	3.31	3.63
Spirit-Filled	3.68	3.72	3.33	3.39

* The higher the mean score, the more conservative the position.

on social issues, and the primary exceptions occur on standard-of-living questions, such as health care and job protection. These exceptions relate in large part to the sizable presence of black Pentecostals within the evangelical Protestant tradition, where such standard-of-living questions move many poorer black Pentecostals away from the more conservative positions of their white Pentecostal counterparts (data not shown). This greater conservatism of spirit-filled believers generally holds for mainline Protestants and Roman Catholics as well, although exceptions extend to topics such as affirmative action and defense spending. But, among those affiliated with black Protestant denominations, the spirit-filled, if anything, move in a more liberal direction politically.

Second, religious tradition has an important impact on spirit-filled movements. The differences in mean scores between those who are spirit-filled and those who are not within each tradition are usually smaller than the differences among the spirit-filled across such traditions. In other words, there is greater similarity in issue stands within each tradition, regardless of whether the respondents are spirit-filled, than among the spirit-filled across traditions. Charismatic Catholics, for example, tend to take political positions closer to those of other Catholics than to those taken by charismatic mainline Protestants. Thus, although these spirit-filled movements have some potential to bridge long-standing divides in American religious and political life, they still have a long way to go to forge a united political bloc of voters across these major religious traditions.

Third, members of the spirit-filled movements are no more cohesive in their issue preferences than are other believers. The standard deviation for each issue item among the spirit-filled is generally no smaller in magnitude (which would reveal greater overall cohesion) than the standard deviation on the same item among those outside the movements (data not shown). Thus, though the spirit-filled may generally express more conservative positions, they are far from unified and may, in fact, be less unified than the non-spirit-filled.

Other factors also militate against the political unity of the spirit-filled movements. Pentecostals and other Evangelicals have historically exhibited strong anti-Catholicism, for theological, liturgical, and possibly nativist reasons.[12] At a minimum, such hostility contributes to potential misunderstandings between different segments of the spirit-filled movements and to the creation of distinct social and religious structures within different religious traditions. Ironically, then, the diffusion of the spirit-filled across religious traditions may produce obstacles to cooperation—at least in any organized religious or political sense. Similar barriers exist in trying to forge any political alliance between white and black Pentecostals.

The Partisanship of the Spirit-Filled Movements

Uniformity in political thinking may not be as crucial as cohesion in political behavior. After all, different people may use different issues as a basis for supporting the same party or candidate. Moreover, issues can be quite complex, but the American two-party system channels such complexity into simple choices at the ballot box. Do the spirit-filled behave alike, whatever their differences in policy perspectives? Table 12.5 examines the partisanship of spirit-filled believers, once again within and

TABLE 12.5
Partisanship of the Spirit-Filled Controlling for Religious Tradition

	Evan Non	Prot SF	Main Non	Prot SF	Black Non	Prot SF	Rom Non	Cath SF
Partisan Id.								
Democrat	34%	28%	34%	38%	82%	74%	45%	51%
Republican	48	55	50	45	10	13	38	30
Vote 1988								
Bush	79%	90%	75%	78%	39%	39%	71%	58%
Dukakis	21	10	25	22	61	61	29	42
Vote 1992								
Clinton	34%	26%	40%	28%	91%	84%	43%	50%
Bush	50	59	42	40	9	14	36	39
Perot	16	15	18	33	0	3	41	39
Vote 1990 Cong								
Democrat	46%	35%	44%	49%	92%	91%	59%	61%
Republican	54	65	56	51	8	9	41	39
Vote 1992 Cong								
Democrat	39%	42%	46%	39%	92%	89%	48%	57%
Republican	61	59	54	61	8	11	52	43

across religious traditions. Traditions clearly shape the political behavior of the spirit-filled. Overall, among evangelical Protestants, the spirit-filled are much more Republican than those Evangelicals who are not spirit-filled. Not only do nearly twice as many spirit-filled evangelical Protestants label themselves as Republicans (55 percent) than as Democrats (28 percent), but this difference in partisan identification is greater than that for Evangelicals who are not spirit-filled. Likewise, more spirit-filled Evangelicals reported voting for Bush in the three-way race in 1992 than their non-filled counterparts (59 to 50 percent). Similar patterns appear for each voting decision in table 12.5. The only exception is in the congressional elections of 1992—in which spirit-filled Evangelicals cast modestly fewer GOP ballots than their non-spirit-filled counterparts (59 to 61 percent).

In contrast, spirit-filled mainline Protestants differ politically from their spirit-filled Evangelical cousins. Despite some exceptions, spirit-filled mainliners tend to move away from the historic ties that exist between mainline Protestantism and the Republican Party. For example, spirit-filled mainliners were more likely to identify as Democrats. Similarly, they were less likely than non-charismatic mainliners in 1992 to have voted for Bush and more likely to have supported Perot. Finally, spirit-filled mainline Protestants were more likely to have voted for Democratic congressional candidates in 1990, even though they were more Republican in their 1988 presidential and 1992 congressional votes.

Not surprisingly, members of black Protestant churches, whether spirit-filled or not, are overwhelmingly Democratic, though the spirit-filled are somewhat less so. Thus, for example, "only" 74 percent of spirit-filled black Protestants classified themselves as Democrats, while 82 percent of other black Protestants did so; likewise, spirit-filled black Protestants were more supportive of Bush in 1992 than other Black Protestants. Nevertheless, no differences were evident between spirit-filled and non-spirit-filled black Protestants in their vote choices in the 1988 presidential race or the 1990 and 1992 congressional races. Spirit-filled Catholics, however, tend to be more Democratic than other Catholics. For example, non-spirit-filled Catholics were more likely to report a Bush vote in 1988 (71 percent) than were the spirit-filled (58 percent). Moreover, these differences are consistent for each variable in table 12.5. Thus, whereas being spirit-filled moves Evangelicals in a more Republican direction, being spirit-filled moves Catholics toward the Democrats.

Thus, religious tradition is an important factor shaping the way in which membership in these spirit-filled movements works itself out politically. For evangelical Protestants who, as a group, have become more Republican in partisanship over the past several decades (Kellstedt et al. 1994), falling within the ranks of the spirit-filled contributes to an even greater Republicanism. The opposite, however, is true for Roman Catholics, where being spirit-filled contributes to even greater Democratic allegiance. Obviously, such divergence in partisanship contributes, other things being equal, to a diminution of political influence.

The Politicization of the Spirit-Filled Movements

One final factor remains to be considered—namely, the level of politicization of the spirit-filled movements. Obviously, if only 10 percent of all spirit-filled Catholics are mobilized to vote compared to 90 percent of all spirit-filled evangelical Protestants, the partisan differences between spirit-filled Evangelicals and Catholics become less significant. Consequently, we conclude our analysis by examining the political participation of all these groups (table 12.6). Pentecostals have in the past usually been apolitical, and this historic pattern still obtains today. Overall, the spirit-filled participate less in politics than those who are not spirit-filled, particularly for turnout in presidential and congressional elections.

This participation gap declines, however, when we consider more difficult acts of participation—perhaps because the overall level of involvement declines. Only with regard to easier acts do differences emerge between the spirit-filled and those who are not, as a somewhat smaller percentage of the spirit-filled report having contacted a public official or having signed a petition than do those outside their ranks. No differences are evident in working for a political candidate within the last five years (about one-tenth of each category), attending a political meeting (about one-quarter each), or contributing money to a campaign (about one-third each). On occasion, spirit-filled mainline Protestants are more likely to vote than other mainliners. However, this is the exception to the pattern. Generally speaking, the spirit-filled participate less than others within their religious tradition. This pattern generally holds across all four religious traditions. Consequently, when one combines all eight participatory acts into an eight-item index, the mean number of participatory acts reported by the spirit-filled trails the scores of the non-spirit-filled across all four traditions. Still, as Table 12.6 reveals, these gaps are not always particularly large. Perhaps the spirit-filled have increased their level of politicization over the past several decades.

TABLE 12.6
The Relative Level of Politicization Evident Among the Spirit-Filled Movement Controlling for Religious Tradition

	Evan Prot Non	SF	Main Prot Non	SF	Black Prot Non	SF	Rom Cath Non	SF
Voted 1988	74%	65%	80%	87%	66%	58%	73%	64%
Voted 1990	48%	36%	57%	52%	41%	38%	46%	40%
Voted 1992	86%	76%	90%	93%	88%	73%	85%	81%
Signed Petition	56%	49%	63%	58%	41%	38%	57%	54%
Contacted Official	43%	39%	45%	39%	23%	31%	39%	32%
Gave Political Contribution	31%	33%	40%	42%	28%	32%	32%	35%
Attended Pol. Meeting	22%	20%	31%	26%	27%	33%	21%	20%
Worked for Candidate	10%	8%	13%	13%	13%	15%	10%	12%
Mean Score on Index of Pol. Particiaption	3.9	3.3	4.4	4.3	3.6	3.2	3.8	3.6

Although the participation gap does not disappear when one controls for religious tradition, some important differences emerge. First, spirit-filled evangelicals generally rank toward the bottom end in comparison to their spirit-filled mainline and Catholic counterparts. And, of course, almost half of the spirit-filled are in the evangelical tradition. In contrast, spirit-filled mainliners tend to be the most participatory and spirit-filled black Protestants, the least participatory, with charismatic Catholics falling between charismatic mainliners and spirit-filled Evangelicals. This "depressed" participation among spirit-filled Evangelicals may well stem from the numerical predominance of Pentecostals in the spirit-filled contingent of the evangelical tradition. Pentecostals continue to trail their charismatic cousins in possession of important political resources such as educational and monetary resources. Lack of resources is an important contributing factor, of course, to the lower turnout rates among spirit-filled black Protestants as well. Thus, higher rates of participation among spirit-filled mainliners and Catholics, coupled with their lower Republicanism and greater moderation on issues, offset the opposite tendencies among Evangelicals.

Conclusions

We can draw several conclusions from our analysis. First, determining the size of the spirit-filled movements is not easy. Any estimate depends on the measure employed. Substantially different conclusions result from using denominational affiliation, speaking in tongues, doctrinal stands, and/or religious self-identifications—because of the relatively low overlap of these variables. Speaking in tongues is not confined to particular denominations: many who identify as a Pentecostal/charismatic do not speak in tongues, and all who speak in tongues do not necessarily identify as a Pentecostal or charismatic.

Second, the penetration of these movements across such a diversity of religious traditions is a double-edged sword. On the one hand, it provides the potential for fostering a broader political coalition of religionists located in different, and historically antagonistic, religious traditions. On the other hand, this penetration has, at the same time, militated against a high level of cohesion. The political meaning of being spirit-filled varies considerably by denominational affiliation.

Third, important barriers exist to the movements' attempt to make further inroads within American religious and public life. In particular, many more Americans feel distant from Pentecostals and charismatics than feel close to them. Just how strong a barrier this attitude constitutes is less clear; it is hard to tell whether distance reflects "distaste for" or "little contact with." Nonetheless, many Americans frequently express feelings of distance from Pentecostals and charismatics.

Fourth, while differences between spirit-filled evangelical Protestants and those who are spirit-filled in other traditions presently serve to weaken the overall political significance of the movement, such differences also enhance that significance if viewed as potential opportunities for further growth in political influence rather than simply as factors limiting its current impact. If members of these spirit-filled movements were already fully participating and casting their ballots in a uniform fashion, less opportunity would exist for growth in political significance. But, to the extent that historic gaps in participation can be narrowed, and to the extent that greater unity in electoral choices can be developed, the political importance of spirit-filled Christians will be enhanced.

Finally, because these spirit-filled movements can be absorbed by varying theological traditions and permeate vastly different segments of society, the movements' future is not likely to be confined to particular segments of American society or to particular religious traditions. Thus, the potential for further growth is much greater than it would be if the movements were confined to a much narrower theological or social base. This important "strength," however, is also a great weakness. Although the riverbed within which the spirit-filled currents flow is very wide, it is rather shallow. Consequently, unity within the movement is not likely to be easily achieved.

Notes

1. Some exceptions, however, should be noted. See, for example, Poloma (1989), Smidt (1989), Jelen (1993), and Hertzke (1993).

2. For purposes of this essay, we reserve "Pentecostal" for those who are either members of Pentecostal denominations or who willingly label themselves as Pentecostals, while we use "charismatic" to refer to non-Pentecostals who exhibit particular spiritual gifts (primarily speaking in tongues), subscribe to certain doctrines related to the workings of the Holy Spirit, or who identify themselves as charismatics. Collectively, these believers are members of movements that emphasize the gifts of the Holy Spirit, or, for stylistic purposes, members of spirit-filled movements.

3. Some debate prevails over whether the practice actually vanished from the church during the centuries in which it was virtually unknown. Some, generally charismatics, see a certain continuity, while others, generally Pentecostals, see a radical discontinuity in which the gift of tongues once again bursts forth within the church after centuries of absence.

4. Historically, all Christian traditions have emphasized that every believer receives the baptism of the Holy Spirit. However, pentecostals came to emphasize a second experience of the Spirit beyond the "regeneration" associated with the initial baptism. This second baptism served as "initial physical evidence" of the baptism in the Holy Spirit.

5. How to view this third wave is a matter of some dispute. Here, the term will simply be used to designate the presence of the charismatic movement, whatever its form (e.g., tongues, worship style, or theology), within evangelical Protestant denominations and within nondenominational churches.

6. Membership could also be tapped by adherence to distinctive religious beliefs (e.g., belief in the need for the second baptism of the Holy Spirit). However, as our survey did not include doctrinal items tapping distinctive spirit-filled doctrinal beliefs, such an approach is not employed here.

7. The Reverend Thomas Trask, the newly elected leader of the Assemblies of God, cited a report at a meeting of the Assemblies of God General Council that states that nearly 50 percent of the church's laity may not have received the infilling of the Holy Spirit. "We may be Pentecostal in doctrine, but not in experience," he stated. See the *National & International Religion Report* 7(18) (August 23, 1993).

8. As a result, anyone who meets one of the following criteria is categorized as falling within the spirit-filled category: (1) being affiliated with a Pentecostal denomination, (2) having the gift of speaking in tongues, or (3) identifying as either a Pentecostal or charismatic Christian.

9. One of the more important, and least documented, religious changes taking place in the United States is the growth of nondenominational churches. Although such independent local church entities have been evident in American religious life for some time, many of the larger, megachurch bodies are nondenominational organizationally. The overwhelming proportion of these nondenominational bodies are evangelical in their theological orientation and emphasis.

10. See the appendix to Chapter 10 in this volume for denominational coding. White Pentecostals include Assemblies of God; Church of God-Cleveland, Tennessee; Church of God-Huntsville, Alabama; Church of God of Prophecy; Church of God-Apostolic; Four Square Gospel; Pentecostal Church of God; Pentecostal Holiness; and generic Pentecostals. Black Pentecostals include Church of God in Christ, and generic black Pentecostals; nondenominational charismatics make up the final category.

11. In analysis not presented in the tables, we found that the higher the level of religious commitment within these Pentecostal denominations (measured in terms of religious practice, belief, and salience), the greater the likelihood of the presence of the gift of tongues.

12. Analysis of proximity scores toward Roman Catholics on the part of members of white Pentecostal denominations and other evangelical Protestant denominations reveal that these feelings of distance continue to be evident today. Among white Pentecostals as a whole, only 7 percent reported feeling close to Catholics, while 62 percent reported feeling far from Catholics. The comparable percentages among evangelical respondents were 11 percent and 46 percent, respectively. For further analysis of anti-Catholicism evident among Evangelicals, see Kellstedt (1989).

References

Anderson, Robert Mapes. 1979. *Visions of the Disinherited: The Making of American Pentecostalism.* New York: Oxford University Press.

Dayton, Donald W. 1991. "The Limits of Evangelicalism: The Pentecostal Tradition." In *The Variety of American Evangelicalism*, ed. Donald W. Dayton and Robert K. Johnston. Knoxville: University of Tennessee Press.

Farah, Charles. 1987. "Differences Within the Family." *Christianity Today* 31(15):25.

Flowers, Ronald. 1984. *Religion in Strange Times*. Macon, Ga.: Mercer University Press.

Hertzke, Allen. 1993. *Echoes of Discontent: Jesse Jackson, Pat Robertson, and the Resurgence of Populism*. Washington, D.C.: CQ Press.

Jelen, Ted. 1993. "The Political Consequences of Religious Group Attitudes." *Journal of Politics* 55:178–190.

Jorstad, Erling. 1990. *Holding Fast/Pressing On: Religion in America in the 1980s*. New York: Greenwood.

Kellstedt, Lyman. 1989. "The Falwell Issue Core." In *Research in the Social Scientific Study of Religion*, vol. 1, ed. Monty Lynn and David Moberg. Greenwich, Conn.: JAI Press.

Kellstedt, Lyman A., John C. Green, James L. Guth, and Corwin E. Smidt. 1994. "Religious Voting Blocs in the 1992 Election: The Year of the Evangelical? *Sociology of Religion* 55:307-326.

Marty, Martin E. 1976. *A Nation of Behavers*. Chicago: University of Chicago Press.

Nichol, John Thomas. 1966. *Pentecostalism*. New York: Harper & Row.

Poloma, Margaret M. 1986. "Pentecostals and Politics in North and Central America." In *Prophetic Religions and Politics: Religion and the Political Order*, vol. 1, ed. Jeffrey K. Hadden and Anson Shupe. New York: Paragon House.

———. 1989. *The Assemblies of God at the Crossroads*. Knoxville: University of Tennessee Press.

Quebedeaux, Richard. 1983. *The New Charismatics II*. New York: Harper & Row.

Smidt, Corwin. 1989. " 'Praise the Lord' Politics: A Comparative Analysis of the Social Characteristics and Political Views of Evangelical and Charismatic Christians." *Sociological Analysis* 30:53–72.

Smidt, Corwin E., Lyman A. Kellstedt, John C. Green, and James L. Guth. 1994. "The Spirit-Filled Movements in Contemporary America: A Survey Perspective." Paper presented for the Conference on Mainstream Protestantism and Pentecostal and Charismatic Movements, Fuller Seminary, Pasadena, Calif., March 10–12.

Smidt, Corwin, and James Penning. 1990. "A Party Divided? A Comparison of Robertson and Bush Delegates to the 1988 Michigan Republican State Convention." *Polity* 23:129–38.

Wacker, Grant. 1988. "Playing for Keeps: The Primitive Impulse in Early Pentecostalism." In *The American Quest for the Primitive Church*, ed. Richard Hughes. Urbana: University of Illinois Press.

13

The Puzzle of Evangelical Protestantism: Core, Periphery, and Political Behavior

Lyman A. Kellstedt
John C. Green
Corwin E. Smidt
James L. Guth

In recent years, observers of American politics have confronted a puzzle: What is an "Evangelical"? How many are there and what are they like? Scholars and journalists have sought a solution so as to understand this increasingly prominent religious group (Himmelstein 1990:chap. 4; Jorstad 1993; Warner 1993). Terms such as *fundamentalist, born-again Christian, conservative Protestant,* or *religious right* are routinely but confusedly used to describe all or part of Evangelicalism. Those who adopt the label themselves have been of little help: the word *evangelical* is a "disputed concept" even among insiders (Abraham 1984), and one evangelical scholar goes so far as to recommend abandoning the term (Dayton 1991).

This is just the sort of puzzle social scientists can help solve. Drawing on a decade of research (Hunter 1983; Leege and Kellstedt 1993), we will offer a tentative resolution. First, we will discuss the variant meanings of "Evangelical" and thus of the different ways Evangelicalism can be measured. Then we will present evidence on the empirical utility of these measures in capturing political attitudes and behaviors. Finally, we will conclude with a description of the "core" and "periphery" of

Evangelicalism. The core consists of self-conscious adherents of religious movements holding a set of key beliefs and belonging to denominations linked historically to such movements and beliefs. This group is very conservative politically, particularly on social issues, and accounts for about one-twentieth of the adult population. More peripheral elements can be defined by various departures from these core characteristics. By including more peripheral adherents, the boundaries of Evangelicalism could be reasonably extended to include more than one-quarter of the American population, without eliminating the politically distinctiveness of the community.

Clarifying the Concept

The word *evangelical* originates in the Greek word, *euangelion*, used in the New Testament to describe the "good news" of salvation through Jesus Christ, often translated in English as the *"evangel"* (Hill 1989:253).[1] Of course, in the broadest sense, this term applies to all Christians, and in the adjectival form, *evangelical* can describe anything pertaining to the evangel. The term is still widely used in this way, as in the verb *to evangelize* (to proselytize on behalf of the evangel), and the noun *evangelist* (one who so proselytizes). Hence, even groups often thought of as outside of Evangelicalism proper, such as Mormons, comfortably engage in evangelism when they publicize their interpretation of the evangel.

Evangelical took on more specific meanings with the Protestant Reformation, when Martin Luther used the word to describe his alternative to the Roman Catholic Church. Although Luther and the other reformers did not intend to establish new churches, once the break with Rome occurred, they moved quickly to create institutions remarkably like their predecessors but with new priorities focused on an "evangelical" understanding of the faith, stressing the authority of Scripture (the source of the evangel) and salvation by grace through faith (the core content of the evangel) (Ellingsen 1991).

It is in this sense that many Lutherans still use *evangelical* today, meaning in the most basic sense "Protestant." Indeed, the major Lutheran denomination in the United States includes the word in its name, the "Evangelical Lutheran Church in America," even though few observers—including most Lutherans—regard it as evangelical in any other sense. In fact, contemporary Germans have developed a new word to distinguish the original meaning from more recent ones *(evangelisch* versus *evangelikal;* Dayton 1991:47–48).

Thus, with the Reformation the term *evangelical* expanded from a description of Christianity writ large (believing and proclaiming the evangel) to a description of certain kinds of Christians (those who emphasized the source and core content of the evangel). This shift began a pattern that would repeat itself many times: the rise of a sectarian movement charging that an established church had diluted the evangel by accommodation to the "world." This "church-sect cycle" is well known to sociologists of religion (Finke and Stark 1992; Stark and Bainbridge 1985) and has been especially common in the United States, where Protestants have been culturally dominant in the context of great social diversity. Its iterations have produced new meanings of *evangelical* without abandoning its pre- or post-Reformation connotations.

Two such shifts are important for our purposes here. On the one hand, *evangelical* was applied to narrow and particularistic interpretations of the evangel's core content by sectarian movements that arose against Protestant churches, much like the original Protestant reformers, but over a host of new disputes. Typically, these disputes focused on what might be called the "mechanism" of the evangel: the exact nature of God's offer of salvation. Such disputes generated a bewildering array of distinctive beliefs, practices, and affiliations, but what all such movements had in common was an attempt to maintain the purity of the evangel—at least as the movement understood it—against accommodation with the broader society.

A good example of this process is provided by pietistic movements of the late eighteenth and early nineteenth centuries, which put great stress on the mechanics of conversion. Another is the fundamentalist movement of the twentieth century, which offered, among other things, a militant defense of the mechanism of salvation, the substitutionary atonement. Thus, one can use *evangelical* to describe religious movements that aggressively espouse variations of the evangel's mechanism. In fact, several movements, including a contemporary one ("neo-evangelicalism"), actually used the term *evangelical* to describe themselves. Over time, the self-conscious distinctiveness of sectarian movements has been the principal source of the varieties of Evangelicals, as exemplified by Baptists and Pentecostals, and differences among them. Some movements went beyond reinterpretations of the evangel to add genuinely new beliefs, thereby founding new religious traditions. (Mormons and Jehovah's Witnesses are good examples.)

On the other hand, *evangelical* has also been applied to broad and generalized interpretations of the evangel as sectarian movements became institutionalized into churches—also replicating the trajectory of the Reformation. Typically, such adaptations focused on what might be called the "mechanics" of the evangel: the nature of individual response to the offer of salvation. Such adaptations served to institutionalize the beliefs, practices, and affiliation arising from sectarian movements, and they have in common the application of a reinvigorated faith to the social realities of the day.

A good example of this second process is the "soteriological reductionism" of mid-nineteenth-century Protestant churches, culminating in highly institutionalized proselytizing; it is in this sense that nearly all late nineteenth-century American Protestants were "evangelical." An equally good contemporary example is the convergence of many evangelical churches to the doctrine of biblical inerrancy: it is in this sense that many evangelicals have "fundamentalist" tendencies. Thus, one can use the term *evangelical* to describe denominations, churches, and parachurch organizations that have sought to routinize the distinctive beliefs, practices, and affiliations of sectarian movements. Indeed, some such denominations actually use the term *evangelical* in their name, such as the Evangelical Free Church and the Evangelical Congregational Church, as do many nondenominational churches and parachurch agencies (e.g. Evangelical Community Church, the Billy Graham Evangelistic Association). It is in this sense that both Baptist and Pentecostal denominations can be considered "evangelical," despite sharp doctrinal differences. Of course, in this process some churches so adapted to the world that they moved away from a sectarian interpretation of the core of the evangel and, in effect, became part of another religious tradition. Perhaps the classic example is the United Methodist Church, whose roots lay in John and Charles Wesley's sectarian enthusiasm but eventually became another "churchly" organization, although not without repeated revolts by many sectarian members.

This brief review uncovers the primary source of the puzzle of Evangelicalism: originally descriptive of a crucial aspect of Christianity, the evangel, the adjective *evangelical* has been repeatedly associated with different aspects of the evangel by sectarian movements and church institutions. Thus, it is hardly surprising that even careful scholars and astute observers would arrive at different definitions of Evangelicalism, depending upon the specific meaning emphasized (cf. Sweet 1984). This pattern has prompted scholars to describe Evangelicalism as a "conglomerate" (Stransky 1988), "kaleidoscope" (Smith 1980), "mosaic" (Askew 1987), "umbrella" (Webber 1976), "tent" (Murphy 1981), and "extended family" (Johnston 1991:252). Observers have identified twelve to fourteen different varieties of Evangelicals among Protestants, which are often combined into three or four basic types according to their common origins and doctrines. And because of the influence of evangelical movements beyond evangelical denominations, some scholars have discovered "Evangelicals" among mainline and black Protestants, Catholics, and even non-Christian groups, such as Jews, generating an even more complex picture (Hunter 1983). Noll and Kellstedt (1995:146) capture this reality cogently:

> Evangelicalism is not, and never has been, an "ism" like other Christian "isms". . . . Rather, "evangelicalism" has always been made up of shifting movements, temporary alliances, various factions in denominations, and the lengthened shadows of individuals. All discussions of "evangelicalism," therefore, are always both descriptions of the way things really are as well as efforts within our own minds to provide some order to a multifaceted, complex set of impulses, movements, and organizations.

We now turn to the challenge of such a description.

Operationalizing the Concept

One way to operationalize this complex concept is to focus on beliefs, specifically the core or distinctive elements of the evangel that underlie the church-sect disputes, an approach favored by Evangelical scholars (cf. Wells 1987; Bebbington 1989:2–19; Warner 1979). Four beliefs emerge consistently in their writings: (1) the importance of witness and mission (spreading the evangel's message), (2) a high view of biblical authority (the source of the evangel), (3) the belief that salvation comes only from faith in Jesus Christ (the mechanism of the evangel), and (4) an emphasis on personal acceptance of salvation (the mechanics of the evangel) (Johnston 1991:260–63). Although there is some disagreement over the exact meaning of such beliefs, most writers would minimally require adherence to all four to qualify as an "Evangelical."

Alone or in combination, core beliefs have been used to identify Evangelicals in the mass public with some success, despite often poor measurement techniques (Gallup 1978, 1980; Hunter 1982, 1983; Rothenberg and Newport 1984; Kellstedt 1988, 1989; Smidt and Kellstedt 1987; Smidt 1989, 1993). Sometimes, however, researchers include beliefs not distinctive to Evangelicalism. Hunter (1982), for example, regards belief in the divinity of Christ as a key criterion, and Barna (1992) includes belief in Satan, the omnipotence of God, and high religious salience. What all these items actually tap is Christian orthodoxy, and while Evangelicals certainly tend to be orthodox, not all orthodox Christians are Evangelicals (Stellway 1973). Similar confusion occurs over *fundamentalism* which, unlike orthodoxy, is a much narrower term best applied to a movement within Evangelicalism (Smidt and Kellstedt 1991). Although all fundamentalists are Evangelicals, not all Evangelicals are fundamentalists (Carpenter 1984:260).

Core beliefs are useful in defining Evangelicalism to the extent that they contribute directly to individual attitudes and behaviors. But two problems immediately arise: the inconsistent nature of mass opinion and the impact of social context (Wald and Smidt 1993; Wald, Owen, and Hill 1988). On the first count, beliefs matter more when individuals take them seriously; on the second count, they are likely to have impact when embodied in religious communities and practices.

These points lead us to the related issues of religious commitment and then religious affiliation. Many scholars add some minimal participation in religious activities to the definition of Evangelicalism, including high levels of church attendance, private devotionalism, or abstention from "immoral" activities, such as drinking and smoking (Johnston 1991:260– 63). In reality, however, few such behavioral standards are distinctively evangelical. After all, many people who are religiously observant or avoid temptations of the flesh on religious grounds would not be considered Evangelicals; conversely, not all Evangelicals would accept such standards (cf. Hunter 1982:366).

As suggested earlier, two kinds of social contexts have been important to Evangelicalism: sectarian movements and church institutions. Although scholars have catalogued numerous "evangelical" movements in the United States, only four of these are of major importance today: fundamentalism; neo-evangelicalism (usually abbreviated as "evangelicalism" to the great confusion of observers); and the "spirit-filled" movements, charismatics and Pentecostals. Relatively little effort has been made to measure movement affiliation in surveys. The few attempts commonly confuse movement affiliation with adherence to the distinctive movement beliefs. Typically, researchers have asked respondents to select their religious "identity" from among a list that includes movement affiliation (e.g., fundamentalist, charismatic), religious belief (born again, conservative), or organizational tendency (mainline, ethnic Catholic) terms, sometimes forcing a single choice and sometimes allowing multiple responses (see Wilcox, Jelen, and Leege 1993). Given this conceptual confusion, it is hardly surprising that such data have proven to be highly problematic (Kellstedt 1993:279–80).

This confusion is somewhat surprising since students of contemporary religion routinely distinguish between individuals who hold a movement's beliefs but do not identify with it and those who hold the beliefs and also consciously identify. The latter are often referred to as "card-carrying" movement members (Marsden 1984:vii–xix) or movement adherents "capitalized" (e.g., "big F fundamentalists") (Ammerman 1987). Unfortunately, only sporadic survey efforts have been made to distinguish self-conscious adherents from nominal identifiers. In this respect, perhaps, measures of group affect, such as proximity or "thermometer" items, used in reference group research offer a promising approach (Conover 1988; Miller, Wlezein, and Hildreth 1991). Thus, combining movement identity and affect measures might substitute for a direct measure of movement affiliation.

Recent improvements in the measurement of religious affiliation reveal that movement and denominational affiliation are separate but overlapping phenomena: only a few respondents give one kind of answer when asked for the other, and many people can report both kinds of affiliation when asked to do so.[2] This raises an important point: since sectarian movements arise and spread in reaction to developments in churches, the denominational context of movements is crucial. As with beliefs, abstract or disembodied measures of movement affiliations are less useful (Hunter 1982:367–68).

Of course, the most pervasive form of religious affiliation is identification with denominations (Greeley 1972). Evangelicalism can be defined as including those denominations characterized by core evangelical beliefs and influence by sectarian movements, forming an "evangelical tradition" (Kellstedt and Green 1993). Membership in such a tradition can thus be differentiated from other kinds of Protestantism, particularly the mainline and black traditions, as well as from other kinds of Christianity, such as the Catholic tradition. Although such differentiation is often subtle in practice, it has produced good results in explaining political attitudes and behaviors (Kellstedt, Smidt, and Kellstedt 1991; Kellstedt et al. 1994).

Although scholars have long recognized the importance of denominations (Stark and Glock 1968), until recently denominational affiliation was measured very poorly in survey research (Kellstedt and Green 1993). As a result, perhaps, few scholars have identified an evangelical tradition, preferring instead to work categories based on denominational families (Roof and McKinney 1987), degrees of Christian orthodoxy (Ethridge and Feagin 1979), or religious movements (Smith 1990). Other scholars have followed similar paths in defining groups of denominations that are larger and smaller than an evangelical tradition, including "ascetic Protestants" (Johnson 1964) and "fundamentalists" (DeJong and Ford 1965). Although such classifications have their uses, they are not much help in identifying Evangelicals because denominations with evangelical and non-evangelical beliefs and origins are combined together, such as "mainline" and "evangelical" Presbyterians, or Southern Baptists and Mormons. Hunter comes closest to defining an evangelical tradition with his four "subtraditions" (Hunter 1982; 1983; the "Baptist," "Pentecostal-Holiness," "Reformed-Confessional," and "Anabaptist" subtraditions). Scholars have tended to ignore the most dynamic and rapidly growing portion of Evangelicalism, nondenominational churches, partly because it is so difficult to measure.

In sum, then, Evangelicalism can be measured in at least three ways: acceptance of evangelical core beliefs, affiliation with evangelical movements, and affiliation with evangelical denominations. In standard practice (Stark and Glock 1968), such traits should be treated as equally valid measures of evangelical religious expression. However, if each measure is equally valid, then it stands to reason that individuals who exhibit more evangelical traits should be closer to the center of the phenomenon than individuals who exhibit fewer. Thus, one can think of the core of Evangelicalism as the conjunction of evangelical beliefs, movement, and denominational affiliations. Departures from this conjunction would define tiers moving away from the core toward the periphery of the concept (cf. Hunter 1982; 1983).

Data and Methods

The data analysis in this essay is based on a telephone survey of a random sample of the American adult population (eighteen years and older) conducted by the University of Akron Survey Research Center in the spring of 1992. The survey's large sample (N = 4,001) and its questions were specifically designed to assess the size and characteristics of American Evangelicalism. A number of the original questions were supplemented when the sample was reinterviewed in the fall of 1993 (N = 2,347). To preserve the number of cases for analysis, we used the recall survey items to fill in missing data for comparable questions in the original survey. In addition, the combined data set was weighted to match the 1990 U.S. Census in basic demography (race, gender, education, income, and region). (Analysis without the missing data replacement and unweighted data produced very similar results.)

Four items were designed to tap the core evangelical beliefs identified earlier. First, respondents were asked a five-point Likert scale item on how often they "shared their faith with others," ranging from daily to never. Mindful of the limitations of behavioral measures, in the recall survey we asked a question on the importance of witnessing, using a five-point scale, ranging from "very important" to "not at all important." The measures were strongly correlated ($r = .54$), with the bulk of discrepancies occurring at the low ends of each scale (rarely witnessing and believing it was less important). Moreover, the second question yielded similar results in statistical analysis, which suggests that reports of high levels of witnessing were consistent with belief in the importance of the activity. Accordingly, the first two points of the behavioral item (once a week or more) were used to measure support for witnessing, a position generally consistent with previous research (Gallup 1980).

Second, we employed a two-part question to tap views of the Bible. The first part asked whether the Bible was "the inspired word of God," "a great book of wisdom and history," or "a book of myths and legends." Respondents choosing the first option were then asked whether the Bible was "true, to be taken word for word," "true but not to be taken word for word," or "true for religion, but with some errors." These items were used to construct a five-point Bible item, the first two points of which (literal truth and nonliteral but error free) were used to measure a high view of biblical authority, which produced a measure consistent with previous research (Kellstedt and Smidt 1993).

Third, a single three-point item was asked in both surveys concerning life after death, the third option of which was "life after death is gained only through personal faith in Jesus Christ." As in previous research, this response was used to measure the Evangelical view of salvation (Gallup 1980). Finally, in the initial survey respondents were asked whether they considered themselves to be a "born-again Christian." The recall survey contained a dichotomous item asking whether the respondent believed a "life changing experience" was necessary for faith and another similar item asking whether the respondent had ever made a commitment to Christ. Taken together, these items reveal a great deal of complexity on the question of conversion, but nearly all those claiming to be born again either believed such an experience was necessary or if not, had made a personal commitment to Christ. Thus, being born again appears to be consistent with the evangelical position on personal conversion, and we employed the item this way, as have other researchers (Jelen, Smidt, and Wilcox 1993).

Two kinds of items were used to measure affiliation with sectarian movements. First, respondents were asked whether they identified as an "evangelical, fundamentalist, charismatic or Pentecostal." (Multiple answers were allowed but were not very numerous, and cases were assigned to one or another category on the basis of belief measures.) In addition, respondents were asked five-point proximity items ranging from "very close" to "very far" for evangelicals, fundamentalists, charismatics, and Pentecostals. These proximity items were combined in a fashion analogous to the multiple identities to produce a single measure of affect toward these movements. Although both the identity and proximity measures will be presented later, it is the combined measure, assessing movement identification and affect, that produces the best results, correcting for much of the measurement error endemic to religious self-identification (Kellstedt 1993:282–83). The use of the proximity items is analogous to the filter questions commonly used to ascertain accurate denominational affiliation.

The original survey employed an extensive set of screens and probes to assess denominational affiliation precisely; these items were more extensive than any currently used in academic surveys. This highly detailed information was then used to identify denominations in the evangelical, mainline, and black Protestant traditions as well as Catholics, Jews, other less numerous traditions (which are combined here), and secular respondents. The method and coding scheme is based on extensive research on the origins and current official beliefs of denominations as well as empirical work with their adherents in major surveys. (See the appendix in Chapter 10 for denomination codings.) In designating these traditions, we noted that the key differences between the two major wings of American Protestantism were sectarian origins and adherence to the core evangelical beliefs identified earlier (Kellstedt and Green 1993; Green and Guth 1993). As part of this process, we became persuaded that historically black Protestant churches constituted a separate religious tradition (cf. Sernett 1991), and they are treated as such. In the following analyses, we will use multiple classification analysis to control for social demographic factors.

Evangelical Traits: A First Cut

We thus have three kinds of measures of Evangelicalism drawn from the literature: four measures of belief (witnessing, high view of the Bible,

Christ as the only source of salvation, and born again), three measures of movement affiliation (identity, proximity, and a combination of the two), and denominational affiliation (expressed in terms of religious tradition). Table 13.1 reports on the proportion of the population with each of these traits.

A good place to begin is with the size of the population with each trait (first column of table 13.1). The Christ-Only and Bible items are the most popular, each with over two-fifths of the adult population affirming them. Witnessing follows at just under two-fifths and born again with just under one-third. Links to any of the major evangelical movements are less common than adherence to the core beliefs, with both the proximity and identity measures capturing just under three-of-ten respondents. The combined movement measure is smaller still, at just one-sixth. Affiliation with the evangelical tradition (denomination) is comparable in size to movement proximity or identity measures, with one-quarter of the sample. The mainline and black Protestant traditions are smaller, less than one-fifth and less than one-tenth, respectively. These two Protestant traditions sum to about one-quarter of the population, where they match first Catholics and then the other traditions and seculars combined.[3]

The distribution of evangelical traits in table 13.1 suggests two things. First, as many scholars have reported, evangelical beliefs extend beyond the confines of evangelical movements and denominations; even the least popular belief, born again, is larger than any of the religious traditions. Second, even the smallest trait, the combined movement measure, is substantial, almost matching the number of mainline Protestants. Thus, the core of evangelicalism could well be substantial, with various combinations of traits extending out to the periphery, which could include well over one-half of the population.

How do these individual traits relate to political matters? Table 13.1 reports on four political attitudes (partisan and ideological self-identification, opinion in abortion and welfare spending) and two behaviors (presidential vote choice and turnout in 1988) of interest to observers of American politics. The coefficients in this and subsequent tables reflect controls for sociodemographic characteristics arrived at by multiple classification analysis.[4] So, for instance, the very top coefficient under partisanship tells us that 48 percent of respondents who believe that "Christ is the only means to salvation" claim to be Republicans, taking into account the independent effects of social factors, such as income and race, on partisanship. For purposes of comparison, the last row reports figures for the entire sample.

TABLE 13.1
Evangelical Traits and Political Variables: American Adults (in percentages)

	Population	GOP	Conservative	ProLife	Oppose Social $	Vote Bush '88	Total Vote '88
Core Beliefs							
Christ Only	45	48*	57	50	24	71	72
Bible	45	49	59	52	24	72	70
Witness	37	47	55	54	24	67	71
Born Again	31	48	58	55	26	71	72
Movement							
Proximity	29	51	58	53	26	75	72
Self-Id	27	51	60	56	27	76	72
Combined	17	55	62	62	22	74	72
Tradition							
Protestants:							
Evangelical	26	53	60	50	25	75	69
Mainline	18	48	50	29	23	69	71
Black	8	29	52	40	21	45	70
Catholic	24	43	44	43	21	66	69
All Others	6	28	28	28	16	43	59
Secular	18	38	38	17	25	58	59
Entire Sample	—	39	47	39	25	65	65

* Coefficients represent percentage of cases in each category with the opinion or behavior, controlling for social demographic factors

The patterns in table 13.1 can be summarized succinctly: the individual belief, movement, and denominations measures show Evangelicals to be markedly more Republican and conservative than the population. As we expected, this tendency is quite strong on social issues, such as abortion. Note that the four belief measures generate comparable results, followed by the proximity and identity movement measures. The combined movement measure, however, always shows the strongest results, followed closely by evangelical tradition. Also note how different evangelical denominations are from mainline and black Protestants, Catholics, and particularly the other traditions and secular categories (cf. Kellstedt et al. 1994). Such conservatism does not extend to all issues, however, as illustrated by the lack of opposition to increasing government social spending to reduce hunger and poverty (cf. Hart 1992:chap. 7).

The same patterns appear on voting behavior, revealing a greater vote for George Bush and higher turnout in the 1988 election among Evangelicals. As with most surveys, the exact figures on vote choice and turnout must be viewed with some skepticism: respondents routinely overstate their support for election winners and level of turnout after the election.[5] However, these patterns are substantially similar to other studies with more accurate voting data. Overall, then, each measure tells essentially the same story, with the combined movement variable performing best, followed by religious tradition, and then beliefs.[6]

Combining Traits: A Second Cut

What happens when all these traits are combined? Table 13.2 reports on the results of such a combination. Following the strength of the findings in table 13.1, respondents were first divided by movement affiliation (using the combined measure), then by religious tradition (evangelical, mainline, and black Protestants, Catholics, other traditions, and seculars), and, finally, by the number of evangelical beliefs (four to none). This effort produced twenty-one usable categories, seven in the evangelical tradition, four among mainline Protestants, three for black Protestants and Catholics, and two each in the remaining categories.

Within the evangelical tradition, this strategy produced clear-cut categories for movement affiliation and all four or any three-of-four core beliefs, and a residual category with no traits at all. As the number of core beliefs declined, many of the possible categories contained only a few cases, often similar to one another. Accordingly, they were aggregated into categories with any two or one evangelical traits. This problem was much more severe outside of the evangelical tradition; consequently, a similar aggregation produced fewer categories. Although the aggrega-

TABLE 13.2
Combined Evangelical Traits and Political Variables: Adult Americans (in percentages)

	Entire Population	GOP	Conservative	ProLife	Oppose Social $	Vote Bush '88	Total Vote '88
Evangelical Protestants							
Movment/4 beliefs	4.8	63*	73	81	22	83	70
Movement/3 beliefs	3.8	62	72	69	28	80	77
All 4 beliefs only	3.4	47	67	58	24	75	75
Any 3 beliefs only	4.0	43	53	47	24	68	61
Any Two Traits	4.7	49	48	30	21	70	70
Any One Trait	3.1	53	52	21	17	76	58
No Traits	2.0	34	38	15	20	65	64
Mainline Protestants							
Movement/3 beliefs	1.5	47	54	45	30	71	75
Any 3 beliefs only	3.4	44	56	40	19	64	80
Any Trait	8.6	52	52	27	27	74	69
No Traits	4.5	45	37	14	18	61	66

TABLE 13.2 (continued)

Black Protestants							
Movement/3 beliefs	4.5	31	65	53	25	53	79
Any Trait	2.9	23	37	28	16	34	74
No Traits	.4	42	42	16	24	44	92
Catholics							
Movement/3 beliefs	3.6	46	49	59	20	71	71
Any Trait	12.6	44	44	46	19	66	70
No Traits	7.2	41	39	27	26	63	65
All Others							
Any Trait	3.5	38	39	49	24	57	57
No Trait	2.9	18	17	8	9	31	62
Seculars							
Any Trait	3.1	51	63	40	31	74	52
No Trait	15.4	37	33	12	23	55	59
Entire Sample	100.0%	39	47	39	25	65	65

* Coefficients represent percentage of cases in each category with the opinion or behavior, controlling for social demographic factors

tion was done primarily because of the lack of cases, it reveals an important regularity: combinations of more than two traits are rare outside the evangelical tradition.

As the first column of table 13.2 reveals, combining these traits generates many small categories. We will postpone a discussion of their size and focus instead on the political consequences of the combinations. Overall, the groups with the most evangelical traits are the most Republican, conservative, and pro-life, and those with the fewest are the least so. For example, respondents in the evangelical tradition with movement affiliation and all four core beliefs (the top row in table 13.2), exhibit these tendencies most fully, followed closely by a related category, respondents with movement affiliation and any three-of-four core beliefs. But note the sharp change with the next two groups, which have no movement affiliation and all four or any three of the core beliefs, respectively: these respondents are markedly less Republican, conservative, and pro-life than their counterparts with movement affiliation.

Thus, within the evangelical tradition, movement adherence has a powerful conservatizing effect on politics apart from beliefs, which suggests the importance of both measures. The number of core beliefs matter as well, but beliefs alone can actually shift political attitudes in a liberal direction. Indeed, on party and ideology, the next two groups with fewer traits (any two or one) actually show modestly higher numbers, reflecting the fact that there are other bases for partisanship and ideology than religion. On abortion, however, a monotonic decline occurs from the category with all the traits to the category with none.

This monotonic pattern holds for abortion in all the remaining religious traditions as well: the groups with the most evangelical traits are the most pro-life, and those with no traits, the least. But the situation is more confused on partisanship and ideology, particularly among mainline and black Protestants, revealing their historic political attachments, the former Republican and latter Democratic. These data sharply reveal the importance of religious tradition. For example, the mainline Protestant category with the most traits (movement, any three beliefs) is substantially less Republican and conservative than their counterparts in the evangelical tradition. These data reinforce the findings in table 13.1: movement affiliation is the most distinctive evangelical trait, followed by religious traditions, and then the number of core beliefs.

Varieties of American Evangelicalism

The explanatory power of movement affiliation is worth exploring in more detail, and table 13.3 breaks down the previous categories by major

TABLE 13.3

Varieties of Evangelicalism and Political Variables: Adult Americans (in percentages)

	Entire Population	GOP	Conservative	ProLife	Oppose Social $	Vote Bush '88	Total Vote '88
Evangelical Protestants							
Movement:							
Full Belief:							
Neo-evangelical	1.0	82*	77	85	28	92	76
Fundamentalist	1.6	64	74	75	30	78	65
Pentecostal	1.2	61	78	93	13	83	59
Charismatic	1.1	59	74	72	37	95	77
High Belief:							
Neo-evangelical	1.1	70	72	71	26	80	78
Fundamentalist	1.1	54	68	68	47	74	82
Charismatic	1.9	50	62	53	36	82	72
Non-Movement:							
Full Belief	3.2	47	68	58	24	72	74
High Belief	3.8	42	54	47	24	68	61
Low Traits	7.9	50	50	27	18	72	63
No Traits	2.0	38	15	20	65	64	10
Mainline Protestants							
Movement/Hi Belief	1.5	47	54	45	30	71	75
High Belief	3.4	44	56	40	19	64	80
Low Trait	8.6	52	52	27	27	74	69

Black Protestants

High Belief	4.5	31	65	53	25	53	79
Low Trait	2.9	23	37	28	16	34	74
Catholics							
High Belief	3.6	46	49	59	20	71	71
Low Trait	12.6	44	44	46	19	66	70
All Others							
Low Trait	3.5	38	39	49	24	57	57
Seculars							
Low Trait	3.1	51	63	40	31	74	52
Entire Sample	—**	39	47	39	25	65	65

* Coefficients represent percentage of cases in each category with the opinion or behavior, controlling for social demographic factors

** Sub-groups with no evangelical traits have been excluded, so first column does not add up to 100%

movements where possible. This further division produced seven new "movement" groupings in the evangelical tradition: "full-belief" (all four beliefs) neo-evangelicals, charismatics, Pentecostals, and fundamentalists; followed by "high-belief" (any three-of-four core beliefs) neo-Evangelicals, charismatics, and fundamentalists. Related and modest changes also led to the creation of a "low-belief" category (combining any one or two traits).[7] For purposes of presentation, the same nomenclature was adopted throughout table 13.3. This process produced no significant changes in any of the other religious groups, so that the figures for them in table 13.3 are the same as in table 13.2.

It is worth beginning with the size of the categories in table 13.3. First, the seven movement categories are each quite small, ranging from 1 percent (full-belief neo-evangelicals) to almost 2 percent (high-belief charismatics). Such small groups are hardly insignificant in American politics, however. For example, high-belief charismatics are about as numerous as Episcopalians, and full- and high-belief fundamentalists together are larger than the Jewish population. When combined, these seven movement groupings make up a substantial 9 percent of the sample, larger than all denominations except Roman Catholics, Southern Baptists, and United Methodists. On the basis of these numbers, we can conclude that "hard-core" Evangelicals (full-belief movement groupings) make up almost one-twentieth of the American population.

Second, the nonmovement portions of the evangelical tradition are small but still substantial: the full- and high-belief grouping account for some 7 percent of the sample, about the size of their movement counterparts, followed by a substantial group of low-trait respondents, at almost 8 percent. Interestingly, the no-trait group is more numerous than any one of the movement categories (2 percent).

What about the categories outside the evangelical tradition? Among mainline Protestants, all the movements were combined with full- and high-belief respondents,[8] and even so, the category is just 1.5 percent of the public—about the size of full-belief fundamentalists within the evangelical tradition. In addition, nonmovement high-belief mainliners are just about as numerous as their counterparts in the evangelical tradition and among Catholics, while high-belief black Protestants are slightly more numerous. These categories among black Protestants and Catholics contain the handful of movement adherents found in these traditions.[9] All told, these high-belief groups are three times more numerous outside as inside the evangelical tradition (11.5 percent to 3.8 percent). As one might expect, the low-trait groups are even larger in the mainline and Catholic traditions, but much smaller among black

Protestants, other traditions, and seculars. Not surprisingly, low-trait Evangelicals are almost four times as numerous outside the evangelical tradition (30.7 percent to 7.9 percent).

What about politics? The seven movement groupings in the evangelical tradition show some important political differences, within an overall conservative tendency. Contrary to some expectations, neo-evangelicals tend to be the most Republican and conservative, followed by fundamentalists and charismatics, a pattern that holds for both full- and high-beliefs. Note that some of these categories even show significantly greater opposition to increased social spending. The Pentecostals present a mixed political pattern: they are the most conservative and pro-life on abortion but also the least conservative on social spending and report the lowest voter turnout. Since these coefficients already reflect controls for the low socioeconomic status of Pentecostals, such a pattern may well reflect their distinctive religious views. The rest of the political data in table 13.3 are the same as in table 13.2, and just a few of these other categories reach the level of political conservatism of the seven movement groupings.

Interestingly, we found no strong warrant for a separate category of "progressive" Evangelicals: doctrinal traditionalists with liberal politics (Weber 1991:13). This negative finding may result from poor measures of "church" movements in our survey (the accommodationist counterparts of sectarian movements; cf. Stark and Bainbridge 1985). However, a small number of political liberals appear in all movement groupings, and a larger number are in the nonmovement categories. Together, these liberals account for about 3 percent of the adult population, or about one-eighth of the evangelical tradition. Better religious measures may well locate "progressives" in the mass public.[10]

Thus, specific movement affiliation matters politically, although not nearly as much as the initial combination of evangelical traits. For example, the original combined movement measure contained 62 percent conservatives (table 13.1), which expands to 73 percent conservative when full-beliefs and evangelical tradition are added (table 13.2), but grows to only 77 percent conservative when full-belief neo-evangelicals are identified (table 13.3). These findings are tangible evidence of the great diversity of Evangelicalism—as well as the value of measuring religious traits accurately.

Core and Periphery

We can now draw some conclusions regarding the puzzle of Evangelicalism. First, much of the confusion surrounding the topic is understandable: Evangelicalism includes a diverse set of religious groups, which by their very nature are difficult to define and identify in the mass public. Second, all the evangelical traits have some validity: the four core beliefs, movement, and denominational affiliation all tap important elements of evangelicalism. The combination of traits, however, is what produces the most distinctive description of the central tendencies and variations of Evangelicalism. Finally, we can quantify the core and five peripheral tiers of American Evangelicalism. If the core is taken as representing a good description of Evangelicalism, then it is a small but potentially significant group; if, however, the periphery is taken to represent Evangelicalism, the Evangelicalism accounts for more than one-half of the population.

1. *The Core.* The hard core of Evangelicalism (4.7 percent of the population) is made up of self-conscious adherents of movements who hold all four core beliefs and belong to the evangelical tradition. The hard core is more or less equally divided among neo-Evangelicals, fundamentalists, charismatics, and Pentecostals. Although very Republican and conservative, some political diversity is evident nevertheless in these groups.

2. *The Second Tier.* A second tier (8.8 percent of the population) is a step more diverse in all respects. It certainly includes the counterparts of the core movements groups with any three core beliefs. The nonmovement full-belief Evangelicals and mainline movement category probably belong here as well. This aggregation is very largely Republican and conservative, but not as strongly as the core. The core and second tier are similar enough to be treated as a single group for many religious and political purposes, and together make up almost one-seventh of the adult population.

3. *The Third Tier.* A third tier (7.2 percent of the population) includes the nonmovement, high-belief categories in the evangelical and mainline traditions. These groups are similar in religious terms but quite diverse politically. Thus, a wide gap stretches between the second and third tiers, but it is bridgeable on a number of issues. Adding in this tier raises the number of evangelicals to more than one-fifth of the population.

4. *The Fourth Tier.* A fourth tier (8.1 percent of the population) moves beyond the evangelical tradition to high-belief black Protestants and Catholics. These groups operate in a different denominational context, and differ from the previous tiers on a host of political issues. Indeed, except for social issues, this fourth tier can be combined with the previous tiers only with great difficulty. Adding these categories brings the Evangelical total to more than one-quarter of the population. Interestingly, this amalgamation is only slightly larger than the evangeli-

cal tradition by itself but never outperforms the tradition on political variables

5. *The Periphery.* A final tier (38.6 percent of the population) includes the low-trait members in all religious traditions, extending Evangelicalism to its farthest limit. Together these groups make up almost two-fifths of the population and raise the running total of Evangelicals to almost two-thirds. It is unclear, however, whether this final amalgamation has any meaning politically. Indeed, except for organizational connection through particular denominations (such as the low- and no-trait categories in the evangelical tradition), most members of this final tier are beyond any meaningful definition of Evangelicalism.

Notes

1. This discussion draws heavily on work of Hill (1981, 1989), Dayton (1991), Marsden (1984:vii–xvi; 1991), Weber (1991), and Stackhouse (1982). The four changes that we identify in the meaning of the word *evangelical* roughly match the three strains of Evangelicalism identified by each of these scholars. For purposes of parsimony, we have simplified this complex history.

2. In our detailed denomination questions, 2.8 percent of the respondents used a movement term to describe their affiliation (e.g., "charismatic"). However, most of these also used a denominational term (e.g., "charismatic Episcopalian"). Many individuals who described their affiliation with denominational terms exclusively could nevertheless choose a movement identity in a separate question.

3. It is worth commenting briefly on the content of the movement and denomination categories. The major evangelical movements vary somewhat in size. The best known of these, fundamentalism, is the smallest, with 7.0 percent of the population in terms of proximity, 9.9 percent in terms of identity, but only 4 percent when the two measures are combined. Neo-evangelicalism is somewhat larger at 7.9 percent, 10.3 percent, and 5 percent, respectively, while the spirit-filled movements, charismatic/Pentecostals are the largest, with analogous numbers of 12.0 percent, 9.0 percent, and 8.0 percent. Denominational affiliation is more diverse. The evangelical tradition is dominated by Baptists at 44 percent, led by the giant Southern Baptist Convention. Various kinds of nondenominational churches are the next largest at 17 percent, followed by a collection of churches from the Reformed and Confessional denominations at 14 percent (including the Missouri Synod Lutherans and the Presbyterian Church in America), Pentecostals (9 percent), Restorationists and Adventists (8 percent), Holiness and Pietists (6 percent), and Anabaptists (2 percent) complete the picture. Black Protestants are also mostly Baptists (61 percent), Pentecostals (16 percent), nondenominational (9 percent), and Holiness (9 percent). And the Protestant Mainline is dominated by the large United Methodist Church (43

percent), followed by Lutherans (17 percent), Presbyterians and the Reformed churches (10 percent), Episcopalians (10 percent) and Congregationalists (5 percent).

4. We used multiple classification analysis to control for social demographic factors, including gender, age, marital status, occupation, income, race, and region. For a fuller discussion of this technique, see Kellstedt, Smidt, and Kellstedt (1991). Controls for religious commitment have very little effect once beliefs are taken into account. We did make some very modest adjustments on the basis of very low levels of religious commitment in the last analysis.

5. Subtracting 11 percent from the Bush vote and 15 percent from the turnout column in each case offers a rough-and-ready correction for the exaggeration of voter choice and turnout.

6. In multivariate analysis, the born-again item outperforms the other belief measures. However, the combined movement item performs the best.

7. We carefully investigated the evangelical subtraditions identified by other scholars (Hunter 1982). Although we found some interesting patterns, only Pentecostals with all four beliefs were distinctive enough to warrant a separate category (Pentecostals with three-of-four beliefs were kept with the charismatics). Second, we moved respondents without movement affiliation but who frequently spoke in tongues to the appropriate charismatic and belief categories because glossolalia is often a form of identification with the spirit-filled movements. Finally, we shifted respondents with very low levels of religious commitment out of the high-trait movement categories into the corresponding nonmovement ones to correct for measurement error; this last modification was also applied to the other traditions. These changes involved very few cases and improved the distinctiveness of the categorization without altering the underlying relationships with independent variables.

8. The movement mainline contains respondents from all three major movements; just under one-half are neo-evangelicals, roughly one-quarter has charismatics, and the rest are fundamentalists.

9. Black Protestants and Catholics have many fewer movement identifiers, and nearly all of these are charismatics.

10. A survey of religious activists uncovered a significant number of "progressive" Evangelicals. Liberal movement identification and a scale of religious communitarianism distinguished them from other evangelicals (Smidt et al. 1994).

References

Abraham, William J. 1984. *The Coming Great Revival: Recovering the Full Evangelical Tradition.* San Francisco: Harper & Row.

Ammerman, Nancy. 1982. *Bible Believers: Fundamentalists in the Modern World.* New Brunswick, N.J.: Rutgers University Press.

Askew, Thomas A. 1987. "A Response to David F. Wells." In *A Time to Speak:*

The Evangelical-Jewish Encounter, ed. A. James Rudin and Marvin E. Wilson. Grand Rapids, Mich.: Eerdmans.

Barna, George. 1992. *Virtual America.* New York: Regal Books.

Bebbington, David. 1989. *Evangelicalism in Modern Britain.* London: Unwin Hyman.

Carpenter, Joel. 1984. "The Fundamentalist Leaven and the Rise of an Evangelical United Front." In *The Evangelical Tradition in America,* ed. Leonard I. Sweet Macon, Ga.: Mercer University Press.

Conover, Pamela J. 1988. "The Role of Social Groups in Political Thinking." *British Journal of Political Science* 18:51–76.

Dayton, Donald W. 1991. "The Limits of Evangelicalism: The Pentecostal." In *The Variety of American Evangelicalism,* ed. Donald W. Dayton and Robert K. Johnston. Knoxville: University of Tennessee Press.

DeJong, G. F., and T. R. Ford. 1965. "Religious Fundamentalism and Denominationalism in the Southern Appalachian Region." *Journal for the Scientific Study of Religion* 4:3–13.

Ellingsen, Mark. 1991. "Lutheranism." In *The Variety of American Evangelicalism,* ed. Donald W. Dayton and Robert K. Johnston. Knoxville: University of Tennessee Press.

Ethridge, F. M. and J. R. Feagin. 1979. "Varieties of 'Fundamentalism': A Conceptual and Empirical Analysis of Two Protestant Denominations." *Sociological Quarterly* 20:37–48.

Finke, Roger, and Rodney Stark. 1992. *The Churching of America 1776–1990.* New Brunswick, N.J.: Rutgers University Press.

Gallup, George. 1978. *The Unchurched Americans.* Princeton, N.J.: Princeton Religious Research Center.

———. 1980. "Research Report on American Evangelicalism for Christianity Today." Princeton, N.J.: Princeton Religious Research Center.

Greeley, Andrew M. 1972. *The Denominational Society.* Glenview, Ill.: Scott Foresman.

Green, John C., and James L. Guth. 1993. "From Lambs to Sheep: Denominational Change and Political Behavior." In *Rediscovering the Religious Factor in American Politics,* ed. David C. Leege and Lyman A. Kellstedt. Armonk, N.Y.: Sharpe.

Hart, Stephen. 1992. *What Does the Lord Require? How American Christians Think About Economic Justice.* New York: Oxford University Press.

Hill, Samuel S. 1981. "The Shape and Shapes of Popular Southern Piety." In *Varieties of Southern Evangelicalism,* ed. David E. Harrell, Jr. Macon, Ga.: Mercer University Press.

———. 1989. "What's in a Name?" In *Handbook of Denominations in the United States,* ed. Frank S. Mead and Samuel S. Hill, 9th ed. Nashville: Abingdon.

Himmelstein, Jerome L. 1990. *To the Right: The Transformation of American Conservatism.* Berkeley: University of California Press.

Hunter, James Davidson. 1982. "Operationalizing Evangelicalism: A Review, Critique, and Proposal." *Sociological Analysis* 42:363–72.

———. 1983. *American Evangelicalism.* New Brunswick, N.J.: Rutgers University Press.

Jelen, Ted G., Corwin E. Smidt, and Clyde Wilcox. 1993. "The Political Effects of the Born-Again Phenomenon." In *Rediscovering the Religious Factor in American Politics*, ed. David C. Leege and Lyman A. Kellstedt. Armonk, N.Y.: Sharpe.

Johnson, Benton. 1964. "Ascetic Protestantism and Political Preferences in the Deep South." *American Journal of Sociology* 69:356–66.

Johnston, Robert K. 1991. "American Evangelicalism: An Extended Family." In *The Variety of American Evangelicalism*, ed. Donald W. Dayton and Robert K. Johnston. Knoxville: University of Tennessee Press.

Jorstad, Erling. 1993. *Popular Religion in America: The Evangelical Voice.* Westport, Conn: Greenwood Press.

Kellstedt, Lyman A. 1988. "The Falwell Issue Agenda: Sources of Support Among White Protestant Evangelicals." In *Research in the Social Science Study of Religion*, ed. Monty Lynn and David Moberg. Greenwich, Conn.: JAI Press.

———. 1989. "The Meaning and Measurement of Evangelicalism: Problems and Prospects." In *Religion and Political Behavior in the United States*, ed. Ted G. Jelen. Westport, Conn.: Praeger.

———. 1993. "Religion, the Neglected Variable: An Agenda for Future Research on Religion and Political Behavior." In *Rediscovering the Religious Factor in American Politics*, ed. David C. Leege and Lyman A. Kellstedt. Armonk, N.Y.: Sharpe.

Kellstedt, Lyman A., and John C. Green. 1993. "Knowing God's Many People: Denominational Preferences and Political Behavior." In *Rediscovering the Religious Factor in American Politics*, ed. David C. Leege and Lyman A. Kellstedt. Armonk, N.Y.: Sharpe.

Kellstedt, Lyman A., John C. Green, James L. Guth, and Corwin E. Smidt. 1994. "Religious Voting Blocs in the 1992 Election: The Year of the Evangelical?" *Sociology of Religion.* 55:307–26.

Kellstedt, Lyman A., and Corwin E. Smidt. 1991. "Measuring Fundamentalism: An Analysis of Different Operational Strategies." *Journal for the Scientific Study of Religion* 30:259–78.

———. 1993. "Doctrinal Beliefs and Political Behavior: Views of the Bible." In *Rediscovering the Religious Factor in American Politics*, ed. David C. Leege and Lyman A. Kellstedt. Armonk, N.Y.: Sharpe.

Kellstedt, Lyman A., Corwin E. Smidt, and Paul M. Kellstedt. 1991. "Religious Tradition, Denomination, and Commitment: White Protestants and the 1988 Election." In *The Bible and the Ballot Box*, ed. James L. Guth and John C. Green. Boulder, Colo.: Westview Press.

Leege, David C., and Lyman A. Kellstedt, eds. 1993. *Rediscovering the Religious Factor in American Politics.* Armonk, N.Y.: Sharpe.

Marsden, George M. 1984. "Introduction: The Evangelical Denomination." In *Evangelicalism and Modern America*, ed. George M. Marsden. Grand Rapids, Mich.: Eerdmans.

———. 1991. "Fundamentalism and American Evangelicalism." In *The Variety of American Evangelicalism*, ed. Donald W. Dayton and Robert K. Johnston. Knoxville: University of Tennessee Press.

Miller, Arthur H., Christopher Wlezien, and Anne Hildreth. 1991. "A Reference Group Theory of Partisan Coalitions." *Journal of Politics* 53:1134–49.

Murphy, Cullen. 1981. "Protestantism and the Evangelicals" *Wilson Quarterly* 5:105–6.

Noll, Mark, and Lyman A. Kellstedt. 1995. "The Changing Face of Evangelicalism." *Pro Ecclesia* 4:146–64.

Roof, Wade Clark, and William McKinney. 1987. *American Mainline Religion.* New Brunswick, N.J.: Rutgers University Press.

Rothenberg, Stuart, and Frank Newport. 1984. *The Evangelical Voter.* Washington, D.C.: The Free Congress Foundation.

Sernett, Milton G. 1991. "Black Religions and the Question of Evangelical Identity." In *The Variety of American Evangelicalism*, ed. Donald W. Dayton and Robert K. Johnston. Knoxville: University of Tennessee Press.

Smidt, Corwin E. 1989. "Identifying Evangelical Respondents: An Analysis of 'Born-Again' and Bible Questions Used across Different Surveys." In *Religion and Political Behavior in the United States*, ed. Ted G. Jelen. Westport, Conn.: Praeger.

———. 1993. "Evangelical Voting Patterns: 1976–1988." In *No Longer Exiles*, ed. Michael Cromartie. Washington D.C.: Ethics and Public Policy Center.

Smidt, Corwin E., and Lyman A. Kellstedt. 1987. "Evangelicalism and Survey Research: Interpretive Problems and Substantive Findings." In *The Bible, Politics, and Democracy*, ed. Richard J. Neuhaus. Grand Rapids, Mich.: Eerdmans.

Smidt, Corwin E., Lyman A. Kellstedt, John C. Green, and James L. Guth. 1994. "The Characteristics of Religious Group Activists: An Interest Group Analysis." In *Christian Political Activism at the Crossroads*, ed. William Stevenson. Lanham, Md.: University Press of America.

Smith, Timothy L. 1980. *Revivalism and Social Reform.* New ed. Baltimore: Johns Hopkins University Press.

Smith, Tom. 1990. "Classifying Protestant Denominations." *Review of Religious Research* 31:225–45.

Stackhouse, Max L. 1982. "Religious Right: New? Right?" *Commonweal* 29:52–56.

Stark, Rodney, and William S. Bainbridge. 1985. *The Future of Religion: Secularization, Revival, and Cult Formation.* Berkeley: University of California Press.

Stark, Rodney, and Charles Y. Glock. 1970. *American Piety: The Nature of Religious Commitment.* Berkeley: University of California Press.

Stellway, R. J. 1973. "The Correspondence Between Religious Orientation and Socio-Political Liberalism and Conservatism." *Sociological Analysis* 14:430–39.

Stransky, Thomas. 1988. "A Look at Evangelical Protestantism." *Theology, News and Notes* 35:24.

Sweet, Leonard I. 1984. "The Evangelical Tradition in America." In *The Evangelical Tradition in America*, ed. Leonard I. Sweet. Macon, Ga.: Mercer University Press.

Wald, Kenneth D., Dennis E. Owen, and Samuel S. Hill. 1988. "Churches as Political Communities." *American Political Science Review* 82:531–48.

Wald, Kenneth D., and Corwin Smidt. 1993. "Measurement Strategies in the Study of Religion and Politics." In *Rediscovering the Religious Factor in American Politics*, ed. David C. Leege and Lyman A. Kellstedt. Armonk, N.Y.: Sharpe.

Warner, R. Stephen. 1979. "Theoretical Barriers to the Understanding of Evangelical Christianity." *Sociological Analysis* 49:1–9.

————. 1993. "Work in Progress toward a New Paradigm for the Sociological Study of Religion in the United States." *American Journal of Sociology* 98:1044–93.

Wells, David F. 1987. " 'No Offense: I am an Evangelical': A Search for Self-Definition.' In *A Time to Speak: The Evangelical-Jewish Encounter*, ed. A. James Rudin and Marvin E. Wilson. Grand Rapids, Mich.: Eerdmans.

Webber, Robert. 1976. *Common Roots*. Grand Rapids, Mich.: Zondervan.

Weber, Timothy P. 1991. "Premillenialism and the Branches of Evangelicalism." In *The Variety of American Evangelicalism*, ed. Donald W. Dayton and Robert K. Johnston. Knoxville, Tenn.: University of Tennessee Press.

Wilcox, Clyde, Ted G. Jelen, and David C. Leege. 1991. "Religious Group Identifications: Toward a Cognitive Theory of Religious Mobilization." In *Rediscovering the Religious Factor in American Politics*, ed. David C. Leege and Lyman A. Kellstedt. Armonk, N.Y.: Sharpe.

14

Religious Voting Blocs in the 1992 Election: The Year of the Evangelical?

Lyman A. Kellstedt
John C. Green
James L. Guth
Corwin E. Smidt

The 1992 elections were characterized by change: the defeat of an incumbent president, a strong independent candidate, upheaval in a scandal-ridden Congress, and a historic number of women elected to public office. But beneath the turmoil, more subtle changes were occurring in the basic building blocs of American electoral politics: significant alterations in the long-term connections between religious traditions and party coalitions. Indeed, because the election turned on economic problems, it provided a crucial test for the strength of ethnoreligious party alignments and for the continuing role of religion in electoral politics. And amid changes and continuities, there were harbingers of a new kind of cultural division.

Religious factors were largely ignored, however, in early accounts of the election by both journalists and scholars (Lipset 1993; Nelson 1993; Pomper 1993; Ladd 1993 is a clear exception). Preoccupied with campaign minutia and a stagnant economy, most observers missed the deeper impact of religion (Guth et al. 1993). The Christian Right's campaign activities were noted, of course, but primarily as tasteless and quixotic aberrations which cost George Bush some moderate votes. The voting behavior of religious groups was usually explained by reference to economic status, while the proclivities of more secular voters went unnoticed, or paradoxically, were assumed to be the social norm. Given the agenda of the mass media and the biases of social science, such interpretations are hardly surprising, but they are in need of correction nonetheless.

This article presents a different perspective on the election. In our view, the building blocs of contemporary American party coalitions are still ethnoreligious groups with their distinctive values. Economic questions represent, by comparison, transient forces that surge and decline within the channels provided by the cultural bedrock. Thus, we reverse the conventional wisdom on the primacy of electoral forces: cultural alignments come first, economics second. Economic issues and evaluations were indeed critical in 1992, as they often are, but the voters' response to economic stress is best understood against the baseline of fundamental cultural cleavages. Although ethnoreligious alignments have undergone substantial shifts in the past three decades, they are still the underpinning of American party politics.

Central to our argument is the political behavior of the major religious traditions in 1992. First, white evangelical Protestants solidified their support for the Republican party and replaced Protestant mainliners as the most loyal adherents to the GOP. This attachment reflects both their social traditionalism and, to a lesser extent, preferences for conservative economic policy. Second, white mainline Protestants loosened their GOP ties, with many defecting to Perot and Clinton. Although still within the Republican camp, mainliners are divided on both social and economic issues. Third, white Catholics returned to the Democratic fold, halting two decades of drift toward the GOP, but this reversal obscured serious rifts among Catholics over traditional values. Fourth, secular voters moved solidly into the Democratic coalition, where their consistent liberalism provided a sharp counterpoint to the across-the-board conservatism of evangelicals. Members of smaller religious traditions, including black Protestants and Jews, played an important role, but displayed remarkable continuity in their traditional Democratic attachments. For simplicity's sake, then, we will focus here on the largest traditions: evangelical and mainline Protestants, Catholics, and seculars. These groups not only constitute the overwhelming majority of voters, but were also those most subject to political change.

The 1992 election reshuffled traditional alliances and rivalries among religious traditions, already modified by emerging cultural disputes and by cross-pressures created by current economic problems. As in the past, voters with strong religious commitments often held most firmly to their religious tradition's long-term partisan attachments, while the less committed were more influenced by short-term forces. But there was a new wrinkle: the highly committed in all religious traditions were also more conservative on social issues, potentially linking them together in opposition to a similar combination of less committed and more liberal members. When superimposed on the widening gulf between evangelical Protestants and seculars, these trends suggest that a new kind of party alignment is emerging: a division between religious and nonreligious voters from all traditions, replacing the old ethnoreligious politics based on disputes between religious traditions (Green and Guth 1991).

In this context, evangelical Protestants play a special role: they are a fulcrum on which both present and future party alignments rest. Their key position in the GOP coalition comes at the end of thirty years of realignment and is now strong enough to persist even in a very bad Republican year. And the limits of their support for the party may not have been reached: there is still considerable "upside potential" for the number of evangelicals identifying with and voting for the GOP. In addition, their turnout is still rising toward the higher rates of mainline Protestants and Catholics. The partisan attachments of evangelicals are magnified by their large and, perhaps, growing numbers, bolstered by high religious commitment, and fostered by conviction that religion is relevant to politics. Their Republican proclivities are likely to be enhanced, at least in the short run, by further gains in social status. All told, future party historians may well label 1992 the "Year of the Evangelical."[1]

We support these conclusions with evidence from several sources. First, to provide some needed historical context, we examine the University of Michigan's National Election Studies (NES) for 1960 and 1988. Although NES religion measures before 1990 leave much to be desired, if used carefully they reveal the restructuring of party coalitions over the last generation. Second, we look at the National Survey of Religion and Politics conducted at the University of Akron during the spring of 1992 to establish a baseline on the eve of the campaign. This survey has the advantage of numerous highly detailed measures of religion. Third, we mine the Voter Research and Surveys (VRS) exit polls for data on election-day voters. While these surveys are marred by poor religious items, they offer valuable information on a massive sample of actual voters. Finally, we turn to the 1992 NES's improved battery of religious items for the post-election situation. To produce roughly comparable measures for all surveys, we employ two fairly simple variables: religious tradition (cf. Kellstedt and Green 1993) and church attendance, which will serve as a proxy for religious commitment (Wald et al. 1993). We should note, however, that more elaborate measures of religious affiliation, beliefs, and commitment, when available, produce even stronger results than those reported here.[2]

Religious Traditions and Party Coalitions 1960–1988

Since at least the mid-nineteenth century, American party coalitions have been comprised of competing ethnoreligious alignments, based on rival world views, life-styles, and negative reference groups (cf. McCormick 1986; Swierenga 1990). First the Whigs, and then the Republicans, were primarily the party of culturally dominant Protestants, the forebears of today's mainline churches, while the Democrats were a collection of cultural minorities, including Catholics, Jews, secular "free-thinkers," and interestingly enough, many sectarian Protestants, the spiritual predecessors of today's evangelicals. The exact makeup of these coalitions varied considerably by locale and over time, but their basic contours were still visible in 1992. Social scientists and survey researchers, however, have been slow to recognize these cultural patterns (cf. Swierenga 1990: 145–49 on this point). Not until the most recent eruption of religious politics during the Reagan era did political analysts pay much attention to measuring religious variables accurately (Wald and Smidt 1993). In fact, their initial confusion over the role of evangelical voters in the 1980s resulted from the deficiencies of religious measures in most polls (cf. Bruce 1988:95–103). Our analysis here has benefited from recent advances in this area (Kellstedt 1993).

Present-day party alignments result from a reshuffling of historic patterns since 1960, changes illustrated by data from the 1960 and 1988 National Election Studies, shown in table 14.1 (cf. Kellstedt et al. 1991). Perhaps the most significant shift from the old alignments involved evangelical Protestants: in 1960, fully 60 percent identified as Democrats, but by 1988 only 40 percent did, while Republican affiliation rose from only 32 percent to 48 percent among all evangelicals. The reaction to Roman Catholic John Kennedy's candidacy in 1960 foretold the trajectory of evangelical presidential voting, which by 1988 was decisively Republican. By the late 1980s, this Republicanism extended to offices down the ballot, such as the House of Representatives. In 1960, for example, while endorsing Nixon by a large margin, evangelicals gave only 41 percent of their votes to Republican House candidates; by 1988 this proportion was 52 percent. Note that all these shifts were magnified for regular church attenders, those most deeply engaged in their faith

TABLE 14.1
Religious Tradition, Church Attendance and Political Behavior,
1960 and 1980*

Religious Tradition & Church Attendance	Party ID		GOP Pres Vote	GOP House Vote	Vote Turn Out	% Pop
	Dem	Rep				
Evangelical Protestant						
1960 All	60	32	60	41	72	26
Regular Attenders	55	38	77	52	80	10
1988 All	40	48	70	52	64	26
Regular Attenders	36	53	72	63	77	12
Mainline Protestant						
1960 All	37	54	69	63	86	41
Regular Attenders	36	58	75	63	91	15
1988 All	36	55	65	51	79	27
Regular Attenders	33	62	69	56	92	8
Roman Catholic						
1960 All	73	19	18	19	89	20
Regular Attenders	77	13	14	18	93	15
1988 All	50	40	54	39	78	24
Regular Attenders	57	38	49	39	90	10
Secular						
1960 All	40	30	46	55	55	8
1988 All	41	37	41	37	62	9

Source: National Election Studies, University of Michigan, 1960 and 1988.
*All numbers in percent. See Appendix for further information.

and thus most receptive to religious cues. Of equal importance is the evangelical community's size: despite the massive social transformations of this era, they remained at one-quarter of the adult population, with regular attenders actually increasing slightly in "market share."

The evangelical realignment was not, however, a steady process. The definitive movement was quite abrupt, occurring during the 1984 Reagan landslide. The Nixon triumph in 1972 had produced an earlier high point of Republican voting (but not GOP identification), but the candidacies of Southern Baptist Jimmy Carter in 1976 and 1980 slowed the Republican trend. Thus, when analysts looked at "born again" voters, they variously concluded that evangelicals were tending to be Republican, were still largely Democratic, or were sharply divided (cf. Himmelstein 1990:109–28). With the benefit of hindsight, the pattern is much clearer: the changes rumored among evangelicals in the 1970s and 1980s were indeed under way, but not yet fully realized (Smidt 1993). Changes in identification and behavior among a voting bloc of this magnitude obviously had enormous ramifications for American politics (Dionne 1991:209–41).

The evangelical conversion finally united the two white Protestant traditions in the GOP. By 1988 evangelicals nearly matched mainline Protestants in Republican affiliation, and actually voted Republican more often in presidential and congressional elections. The political behavior of mainliners changed little over the period, but their numbers declined dramatically, decreasing by more than one-third overall and by nearly one-half in regular church attenders. Thus, by 1988 evangelical and mainline voting blocs were of equal size, but church-going evangelicals greatly outnumbered their mainline counterparts. Mainliners' sustained their historic prominence in the GOP coalition by a decreasing margin, largely on the basis of greater turnout (Kellstedt et al. 1991).

During this period Catholics were also on the move. Overwhelmingly Democratic in 1960, they shifted toward the GOP in both affiliation and voting at the presidential and congressional levels, but remained marginally Democratic in 1988. But unlike the situation among evangelicals, observant Catholics did not lead the exodus toward the Republicans. While some Catholic traditionalists, especially among younger voters, turned to the GOP on cultural and foreign policy issues (accounting for many "Reagan Democrats"), others remained loyal to their ancestral party; a similar division occurred among less committed Catholics (Kenski and Lockwood 1991). Over the period, Catholics gained in number, at least matching each of the Protestant traditions, but regular attenders declined by one-third, to a number roughly equal to that of church-going evangelicals. Catholic turnout rates closely paralleled those of the Protestant mainline.

Although Republicans benefited from such trends among evangelicals and Catholics, the Democrats increasingly depended on other traditions. Secular voters drifted toward the Democrats in presidential and congressional voting, and remained modestly Democratic in party identification, but their turnout lagged behind the other three major religious traditions (Erickson et al. 1989). According to the NES, they also became slightly more numerous. (We will see below, however, that precise measures of religious affiliation suggest much faster growth of secular voters.) The Democratic coalition was rounded out by two smaller traditions, black Protestant and Jewish voters. The former grew in size, Democratic affiliation, and turnout over the period (Wilcox 1991), while the latter declined in number, but remained solidly Democratic with high voting rates (Sigelman 1991).

What causes these shifts in party coalitions after 1960? At the risk of oversimplification, there were two important factors: social issue polarization and upward social mobility (Green and Guth 1993). Over this period, a powerful new divide opened on social issues, with defenders of traditional values and social arrangements fighting advocates of cosmopolitan values and new lifestyles. In many respects, foreign policy disputes paralleled this cultural divide. At the same time, however, the country experienced dramatic gains in socioeconomic status, with some historically disadvantaged groups, such as evangelicals and Catholics, gaining the most in relative terms. For evangelicals, these trends interacted to generate support for the GOP, the more conservative party on both counts, although cultural polarization clearly mattered most. These same trends cross-pressured mainline Protestants and Catholics, moving some toward the GOP and others toward the Democrats. Secular voters faced a similar situation, but as social issues such as abortion and gay rights became increasingly important more of them moved in a Democratic direction. Contemporary social movements surely played a role in fostering these new alignments, including the Christian Right and the pro-life movement on the one hand, and feminist, gay, and civil rights movements on the other, but the precise magnitude of their impact on the scope, form, and pace of these changes is far from clear (Wilcox 1992; Wuthnow 1989).

Thus, the ethnoreligious structure of party coalitions at the ascension of George Bush in 1989 was a variant of the historical pattern: the GOP was the party of (united) Protestantism, leavened with conservatives from other religious backgrounds, while the Democrats remained the party of cultural minorities, with increased numbers of secular voters, black Protestants, and a smattering of liberals from other traditions. During the 1980s, this alignment favored Republicans at the presidential level and Democrats at the congressional, but there were great tensions in both coalitions (Shafer 1991). First Ronald Reagan and then George Bush cemented their coalition with a careful mix of social, economic and foreign policy conservatism; congressional Democrats attracted votes with a skillfully wrapped package of tangible and symbolic benefits.

The Spring of 1992

Much had changed by the spring of 1992. The end of the Persian Gulf and Cold Wars robbed Republicans of key issues, a weak economy undermined Bush's popularity, and a primary challenge from Pat Buchanan damaged his credibility. The Democrats did not go unscathed, however, with scandals in Congress, accusations of gridlock, and the usual infighting in the Democratic primaries. Party alignments that seemed so solid four years before appeared to many observers to be in flux.

In table 14.2 we present a snapshot of the ethnoreligious composition of party coalitions prior to the fall campaign using data from the National Survey of Religion and Politics conducted at the University of Akron in the spring of 1992. This picture suggests continuity with 1988, rather than change. Although this portrait is based on more sophisticated measures of religious tradition and behavior than available in the 1988

TABLE 14.2

Religious Tradition, Church Attendance and Political Behavior, Spring 1992*

Religious Tradition & Church Attendance	Party ID		*1988 Bush Vote*	*1990 GOP Cong Vote*	*High Bush Eval*	*Plan Vote Bush 1992*	*% Pop*
	Dem	*Rep*					
Evangelical Protestant							
All	34	48	72	57	43	54	25
Regular Attenders	30	55	75	62	44	60	13
Mainline Protestant							
All	32	51	67	58	38	51	20
Regular Attenders	31	54	70	57	42	56	6
Roman Catholic							
All	41	40	63	43	35	43	24
Regular Attenders	46	38	65	44	35	43	12
Secular							
All	41	34	53	46	28	37	16

Source: National Survey of Religion and Politics, University of Akron, 1992.
*All numbers in percent. See Appendix for further information.

NES, the political patterns in table 14.2 are strikingly similar to those in table 14.1. The GOP allegiance of evangelicals had not wavered under Bush, and the relative positions of Catholics and secular voters remained static. All groups actually recalled more support for Bush in 1988 than table 14.1 shows, and in addition, reported higher support for GOP House candidates in 1990. Only mainline Protestants experienced a modest decline in Republican allegiance, but this may reflect better measurement of religious affiliation in the Akron study, with some erroneously classified "mainline" (and staunchly Republican) voters in previous analysis being moved to the evangelical tradition. Note that mainline Protestants, particularly regular church attenders, are markedly less numerous in table 14.2 than in table 14.1, while seculars are nearly twice as common. The reason is straightforward: the Akron study data in table 14.2 come from questions that minimize the social desirability effects of having a religious preference, encouraging people with no religious affiliation to report just that (Kellstedt and Green 1993).

Despite the basic continuity in alignments from 1988, Bush obviously faced some serious political problems in spring 1992. As table 14.2 shows, evaluations of his presidency were quite low, with far less than 50 percent in each group giving him "excellent" or "good" ratings. Worse yet, a much lower proportion of each group planned to vote for him in 1992 than reported voting for him in 1988. Still, evangelicals gave Bush the strongest support, followed in order by mainliners, Catholics, and seculars. And there were clear issue bases for this pattern. Table 14.3 demonstrates that evangelicals were the most conservative on abortion, gay and women's rights, with regular church attenders markedly more so. Mainliners and Catholics were less conservative, although regular attenders often leaned more to the right, especially on abortion and among Catholics. Seculars were by far the most liberal on social issues. These data suggest that the social issue conservatism linked to religious beliefs, religious traditions, and involvement clearly structured partisan and electoral choices. Indeed, the contrast between the more and less committed people in each tradition, as well as the sharp split between evangelicals and seculars, helps account for persistent rumors of a "culture war" in American politics (Hunter 1991).

Evangelicals were not only social conservatives, but more surprisingly, were also the most conservative group on economic and domestic issues, including aid to minorities, national health insurance, and environmental regulation, if only by small margins. Once again, regular church attend-

TABLE 14.3
Religious Tradition, Church Attendance and Issue Position, Spring 1992*

Religious Tradition & Church Attendance	Pro Choice	Pro Women Rights	Pro Gay Rights	Gov Aid Black Rights	Gov Health Insur.	Pro Envir.	Back Israel	Cut Defense
Evangelical Protestant								
All	46	52	35	35	55	56	42	45
Regular Attenders	29	45	26	34	49	54	48	43
Mainline Protestant								
All	72	59	57	40	59	63	26	47
Regular Attenders	59	55	52	45	61	63	29	51
Roman Catholic								
All	60	61	59	39	63	58	22	51
Regular Attenders	44	57	57	41	63	58	23	52
Secular								
All	86	60	62	36	63	65	21	58

Source: National Survey of Religion and Politics, University of Akron, 1992.
*All numbers in percent. See Appendix for further information.

ers were even more conservative. As on social issues, mainliners and Catholics were more liberal than evangelicals on these domestic issues, but here their regular attenders were modestly more liberal. And with the exception of aid to minorities, seculars resembled the Protestant mainline. This pattern of opinion on domestic issues had many sources: growing ideological consistency among both evangelicals and seculars; the upward mobility of religious groups, with evangelicals gaining middle class status and seculars flooding into the "new class" professions; and selective perception on the part of committed partisans, including Republican evangelicals and Democratic seculars. As one might imagine, foreign policy concerns were of little importance in early 1992, but support for Israel and cutting defense spending were emblematic of the past power of these issues: evangelicals were the most pro-Israeli and pro-defense, and seculars at the other extreme on both (Guth and Fraser 1993).

So, on the eve of the 1992 general election campaign, Bush faced serious difficulties: eroding support for his presidency across the board, but particularly among mainline Protestants, a key constituency in 1988, with parallel declines among Catholics, a swing vote four years earlier, and among seculars, who had backed Michael Dukakis. Looked at another way, evangelicals were Bush's strongest supporters, holding conservative positions on both social and economic issues. Furthermore, social issues offered access to pockets of traditionalists among other groups. Given his problems with the economy, it is easy to see why Bush chose to make social issue appeals a major part of his campaign. By the same token, these data also reveal the basis for Pat Buchanan's primary challenge from the right, and for Bill Clinton's "New Covenant" platform during the general election, combining social issue moderation with domestic policy initiatives.

Election Day 1992

How did the 1992 campaign affect ethnoreligious elements in party coalitions? Our first evidence on this point comes from the widely quoted network exit polls from Voter Research and Surveys (VRS), reported in tables 14.4 and 14.5. Unfortunately, VRS used very simplistic (and idiosyncratic) religious measures, and thus the results are not strictly comparable to other studies. As a religious tradition measure, VRS allowed voters the choices of "Protestant, Catholic, Other Christian, Jewish, Something Else, None." This permits no easy classification of evangelical and mainline Protestants, but fortunately, VRS also asked voters to check a box labeled "born-again Christian/Fundamentalist," if those terms applied. We used responses to this question in combination with the earlier one to produce evangelical and mainline categories. Of course, not all voters in the evangelical tradition respond positively to both "born-again" and "fundamentalist." Therefore, this operation produces fewer evangelicals and more mainline Protestants than the more accurate data reported in tables 14.2 and 14.6, even after accounting for differences in turnout. Still, the patterns we find are consistent with more sophisticated pre- and post-election surveys.

On election day, according to VRS, evangelicals were Bush's strongest supporters: 63 percent of all evangelicals and 70 percent of regular church-goers among them voted for the president, a very impressive showing for a three-way race. Considering only the two-party vote, the analogous figures were 74 percent and 79 percent, respectively, higher than in 1988. Overall, evangelicals provided more than one-quarter of Bush's 1992 vote and regular attending evangelicals were roughly as

TABLE 14.4
Religious Tradition, Church Attendance and Political Behavior,
Election Day 1992*

Religious Tradition & Church Attendance	Party ID		Pres Vote		GOP House Vote	% Pop
	Dem	Rep	Dem	Rep		
Evangelical Protestant						
All	24	56	22	63	67	15
Regular Attenders	21	58	18	70	73	11
Mainline Protestant						
All	33	44	38	37	51	32
Regular Attenders	31	49	33	46	56	11
Roman Catholic						
All	42	34	41	36	46	22
Regular Attenders	44	33	39	41	47	10
Secular						
All	65	14	71	17	22	16

Source: General Election Exit Poll, Voter Research and Surveys, 1992.
*All numbers in percent. See Appendix for further information.

important to Bush as black Protestants were to Clinton. In addition, evangelicals' GOP identification increased modestly from the spring, and they voted for Republican House candidates at *higher* rates than in 1988 and 1990. Southern Baptists Bill Clinton and Al Gore actually received a lower percentage of evangelical votes than Michael Dukakis did in 1988, despite mid-campaign press reports of possible inroads among conservative Protestants.

A much different result appeared among mainline Protestants, where Bush garnered less than two-fifths of the vote, and less than one-half even among regular church attenders. These figures paralleled declines in Republican identification and support for GOP congressional candidates. As we might expect, Catholics were even less supportive of Bush, although their behavior and party identification were not dramatically off the mark from previous elections. But a major shift did occur among secular voters: Bush received less than half the level of support that he enjoyed in 1988, while their party identification and congressional vote went solidly Democratic. By adding the customary huge Democratic majorities among black Protestants and Jews to his column, Clinton

TABLE 14.5
Religious Tradition, Church Attendance and Issue Positions,
Election Day 1992*

Religious Tradition & Church Attendance	Financial Situation Compared to 4 Yrs. Ago: Better	Worse	Pro Choice	State of Economy	Most Important Issues in Vote Decision: Abortion/Family Values	Deficit Econ Jobs	Other Domes Issues
Evangelical Protestant							
All	33	24	29	33	53	50	26
Regular Attenders	34	20	22	33	57	45	23
Mainline Protestant							
All	25	32	72	24	24	65	39
Regular Attenders	30	38	63	24	31	57	37
Roman Catholic							
All	23	36	62	19	22	66	39
Regular Attenders	22	35	47	19	27	63	39
Secular							
All	24	38	78	11	22	66	50

Source: General Election Exit Poll, Voter Research and Surveys, 1992.
*All numbers in percent. See Appendix for further information.

assembled a facsimile of the old New Deal religious coalition, but with some mainline Protestants and a growing corps of seculars replacing the departed evangelicals.

Ross Perot also absorbed some evangelicals dissatisfied with Bush who might have voted for Clinton. Overall, Perot received 15 percent from evangelicals, markedly less than from mainliners (25 percent) and Catholics (23 percent), but more than from seculars (12 percent). Clinton was the second choice among all groups of Perot voters, but least so among evangelicals (51 percent), followed by Catholics (58 percent), mainliners (61 percent), and seculars (78 percent). Perot supporters may have been a cross-section of the electorate in some respects, but not in religious tradition, or more significantly, religious commitment: in all traditions Perot voters attended church less regularly and were less involved religiously by almost any measure. This lack of religious commitment parallels their detachment from parties and other political institutions.

The VRS data also underscore the issue basis of the 1992 vote, presented in table 14.5. The economy was clearly the most powerful issue and it hurt Bush everywhere. Never more than one-third of any group gave the president "excellent" or "good" job ratings, markedly lower than in the spring, and a plurality in most groups claimed their personal financial situation had worsened since 1988. But as before, evangelicals consistently gave Bush the highest marks on the economy, significantly ahead of other traditions, and were also far less pessimistic about the future of the economy. An even starker contrast appears on the social issues: evangelicals were strongly pro-life and seculars as adamantly pro-choice, with mainline Protestants and Catholics falling in between. As before, regular attenders in all traditions were more pro-life than their co-religionists.

Similar patterns emerge for the issues that voters claim influenced their choice, revealing starkly different priorities across religious traditions. More than half the evangelicals identified abortion or family values as important, often twice the percentage of other groups. Indeed, social issue mentions decline from evangelicals to seculars, with the now familiar variations among regular church attenders. Something of an opposite pattern appears for those who mentioned the economy. Although evangelicals were concerned with these issues as well (50 percent mentions), the other traditions showed substantially more interest (average 66 percent mentions). Nonevangelicals also cited much greater concern for domestic issues such as health care, education and environmental regulation: only one-quarter of evangelicals mentioned these, compared to nearly one-half of seculars. These priorities clearly influenced votes: nearly 90 percent of regular attending evangelicals who named abortion as important voted for Bush, whereas 75 percent of seculars who named the economy as important voted for Clinton or Perot (data not shown).

Contrary to conventional wisdom, this evidence suggests that Bush's social issue appeals did *not* cost him the election. In fact, on balance social issues helped him. Among voters who supported Bush in both 1988 and 1992, just over two-fifths mentioned social issues as important to their vote, and an equal number named the economy. But of those who abandoned Bush for Clinton in 1992, only one-fifth mentioned social issues compared to almost three-quarters naming the economy. The numbers were even more lopsided for Bush voters who defected to Perot: about one-sixth mentioned social issues and more than four-fifths named the economy. All told, *the economy cost Bush more than four times as much support as social issues* (17 to 4 percent) among those who defected to Clinton or Perot. As one might imagine, these patterns were much stronger for evangelicals than for voters in the other traditions.

Clearly then, Bush held evangelicals and some other religious conservatives largely because of their views on social issues, aided by their less critical evaluation of the economy, while Clinton and Perot cashed in on economic discontent and domestic policy concerns among voters for whom social issues were less salient. Clinton's masterful focus on the economy, combined with Perot's erratic populism, effectively exploited the weaknesses in key Republican constituencies evident in the spring of 1992, expanding the Democrats' base of cultural minorities enough to win a three-way race. By the same token, Bush secured his base of cultural conservatives, but failed to assuage the economic worries of his key constituencies. Although social issue and economic appeals operated largely independently of one another, considerable polarization occurred between each party's core constituencies.

The Fall of 1992

Did these exit poll patterns persist after election day? The 1992 NES data allow us to confirm these findings and investigate further, with the help of more sophisticated measures of religion than are available in the VRS data (for further discussion of the new NES religion measures, see Leege and Kellstedt 1993). As table 14.6 confirms, Bush held evangelicals to a remarkable degree, lost ground among mainliners and Catholics, and was soundly beaten among seculars. Overall, the 1992 NES results are strikingly similar to the comparable pre-election data from the Akron study (compare table 14.6 to table 14.2), but reveal some important, if subtle, effects from the campaigns.

After the election, evangelicals still identified Republican, *but in even larger numbers* than in the spring. Furthermore, their turnout far exceeded that in 1988—but did not quite equal that of mainline Protestants and Catholics. Unlike the election-day VRS survey, which showed mainliners far behind evangelicals in Republican identification, the NES survey has mainliners matching evangelicals in that respect. The NES agrees with VRS, however, in finding much greater voting support for Bush and GOP congressional candidates among evangelicals. As in the VRS survey, Catholics and seculars in the NES identified more often as Democrats and supported Democratic candidates at a higher rate than did either Protestant tradition, although the NES shows Catholic churchgoers to be significantly more Republican in identification and behavior than nonattenders. As in the VRS surveys, seculars identify and vote heavily Democratic, but their turnout rate still lagged behind the other traditions.

TABLE 14.6
Religious Tradition, Church Attendance and Political Behavior, Fall 1992*

Religious Tradition & Church Attendance	Party ID		Pres Vote		GOP HR Vote	Vote Turn Out	% Pop
	Dem	Rep	Dem	Rep			
Evangelical Protestant							
All	38	51	28	56	53	76	25
Regular Attenders	31	61	22	70	61	81	14
Mainline Protestant							
All	34	53	38	37	49	84	21
Regular Attenders	31	63	35	42	59	91	7
Roman Catholic							
All	51	38	45	31	42	86	24
Regular Attenders	43	44	41	36	44	88	11
Secular							
All	50	32	55	20	35	65	15

Source: National Election Studies, University of Michigan, 1992.
*All numbers in percent. See Appendix for further information.

The issue basis of these post-election patterns seemed little changed from the spring. Table 14.7 provides information that parallels table 14.3. Although the topics are the same, question wording and format in the Akron study and the NES differ enough to make direct comparisons problematic. The relative differences among religious traditions were clearly maintained, however, and perhaps even extended. As before, evangelicals (especially regular attenders) were most conservative across the board, but particularly on social issues. Mainline Protestants and Catholics sustained their relative positions, with Catholics more liberal and regular attenders in both traditions slightly more conservative than their less observant counterparts. The only exception is on abortion, where Catholics as a group were less pro-choice than the mainline and regular churchgoers even more conservative. Secular voters, on the other hand, were the most liberal on all issues, often by wide margins.

All these data reveal considerable polarization along partisan and cultural lines, with a gulf widening between evangelicals and seculars. But this development was temporarily obscured by the salience of economic issues among mainline Protestants, Catholics, and especially

TABLE 14.7
Religious Tradition, Church Attendance and Issue Position, Fall 1992*

Religious Tradition & Church Attendance	Pro Choice	Pro Women Rights	Pro Gay Rights	Gov Aid Black Rights	Gov Health Insur.	Pro Envir.	Cut Defense
Evangelical Protestant							
All	42	64	44	13	41	53	31
Regular Attenders	25	52	32	12	34	43	29
Mainline Protestant							
All	77	75	59	17	42	56	50
Regular Attenders	66	73	53	15	38	48	44
Roman Catholic							
All	59	83	67	19	55	61	51
Regular Attenders	40	81	69	15	52	57	44
Secular							
All	83	85	69	26	61	70	53

Source: National Election Studies, University of Michigan, 1992.
*All numbers in percent. See Appendix for further information.

seculars. In fact, the 1992 election did not represent a rejection of social issue conservatism—any more than Reagan's election in 1980 represented an endorsement. Both elections largely turned on the economic failures of incumbent presidents. Even powerful economic concerns were filtered, however, through the ethnoreligious structure of the party coalitions. In 1980, both social and economic issues reinforced each other for evangelicals, while other groups responded to one or the other. But in 1992, social and economic issues moved in opposite directions, sweeping away part of the GOP's mainline and Catholic "economic" constituencies and revealing the cultural backbone of the party, much as Carter's defeat in 1980 lay bare the Democrats' core constituencies.

These patterns show the limitations of defining electoral alignments only in terms of short-term economic forces or even of long-term economic status. Evangelical and high-commitment mainline Protestants were generally less affluent and objectively most affected by the recession, and yet they stood most firmly behind Bush and the Republicans. Meanwhile, Jewish, secular and low-commitment mainline Protestant voters were generally more affluent and least burdened by hard times;

yet they backed Clinton in large numbers. Perot voters were the most disconnected from both American political and religious life, and thus "available" for mobilization on the basis of economic discontent. All this reminds us that economic forces work *within* the cultural context.

Thus, the principal effect of 1992 was to bind evangelicals to the Republican party, much as black Protestants were cemented to the Democratic coalition in the 1960s. A secondary result was the acceleration of secular voters' migration toward the Democrats, much as evangelicals were pushed toward the GOP in 1984. And a third impact was the loosened Republicanism of mainline Protestants, paralleling the weakened Democratic attachments of Catholics from the last two decades. The changes and continuities among ethnoreligious groups make several scenarios possible. The GOP may try to resurrect the Reagan coalition by recovering attractive economic policies to parallel social issue conservatism, but it may be equally possible for Clinton to bolster a traditional Democratic coalition by delivering economic growth. Ironically, as president, Clinton must highlight liberal social policies to hold the seculars, much as Bush catered to religious conservatives, but the core cultural constituency of the Democratic party may not be enough to sustain Clinton's legislative program (Cook 1993). Whatever the outcome, many of these developments also point to the emergence of a new kind of party alignment.

A New Kind of Coalition

Ethnoreligious coalitions have always been messy affairs, fraught with internal tensions often incapable of any final resolution. The management of these tensions, however, sometimes points toward new and more consistent—if not always more productive—party alignments. Just as political controversy over the New Deal's pragmatic experimentalism resulted by 1964 in ideologically consistent parties, one liberal on economic management and the other conservative, the present ethnoreligious alliances point toward a new divide based on the extent rather than type of religious belief. Although elements of the older alignment will persist, increasingly the party coalitions may include, on one side, believers who organize their lives and religious commitments, while the other side would attract nonbelievers and those for whom religion is unimportant (Green and Guth 1991).

Such a cleavage would be new in American history, but has been quite common in European democracies, where socialist parties have often been adamantly secular, and conservative parties have frequently defended religious establishments (Berger 1982). While many factors have made American religion particularly vigorous, over the last thirty years secularizing processes have generated growing opposition to the influence of religion. The growth in the secular population has been mostly at the expense of more accommodated churches, particularly mainline Protestants and, ironically, has had the least effect on sectarian bodies, including evangelicals, who seem to prosper in opposition to secularizing forces. The developing conflict between evangelicals and seculars has been paralleled by battles between "modernists" and "traditionalists" within mainline and Catholic churches (Wuthnow 1988), and new alliances have been given form by various "ecumenical" and "nondenominational" movements that span even ancient religious boundaries (Jorstad 1990). The net result is to reconfigure religious traditions, the stuff of party coalitions, along broader and less particularistic lines.

Although this new alignment has not fully emerged, it is prefigured by the underlying cultural polarization in 1992, both between evangelicals and seculars, and between the more and less committed members of the major religious traditions. This cleavage is already well-advanced among cultural elites (Hunter 1991), religious professionals (Guth *et al.* 1991), party contributors (Green *et al.* 1991), and interest group activists (Green and Guth 1990). And, whether intentionally or not, antagonists on both sides of the cultural chasm are digging it deeper. On the religious side, Christian Right groups such as the Christian Coalition, Concerned Women of America, and Focus on the Family are amassing impressive resources to mobilize evangelical voters. Although they have not yet overcome historic animosities within their own tradition, they can help solidify one element of a broader traditionalist coalition in the GOP. Organizations such as People For the American Way and the American Civil Liberties Union may have similar effects for the secular and less religious groups in the Democratic party.

At this juncture, the Christian Right has far more raw political resources than the "secular left," but the latter campaigns with media and educational elites on its side. Intense conflict over cultural issues could well push elements of other traditions toward such an alignment, but for the new divide to become dominant, it must reach beyond cultural questions to include economic matters as well. In 1992 only among evangelicals and seculars did we observe consistent conservatism and liberalism on both kinds of issues, and some evangelical activists, at least, believe that such a broad agenda is necessary and possible (Seib 1993). Given their new-found political unity and their strong institutional base, evangelicals are the logical place to look for expansion of the "culture war" to other fronts.

Thus, the dominant interpretive theme of 1992, "It's the economy, stupid" (attributed to Clinton adviser James Carville), fails to capture the full significance of that contest. What we see is the first rumblings of an electoral culture war. In one sense, 1992 may be remembered as the "Year of the Evangelical," in which activists mounted impressive grassroots campaigns among an Evangelical public more receptive than ever. It is safe to predict that this mobilization will continue or even intensify in future local, state, and national elections. By the same token, however, 1992 could be characterized as the "Year of the Secular," reflecting the growing importance of this often-underestimated bloc of predominantly liberal voters. The new role of evangelicals and seculars as the cultural cores of the Republican and Democratic parties, respectively, puts them in key positions to shape the ideological contours of those parties. Ironically, mainline Protestants and Catholics, long the centerpieces of the Republican and Democratic party coalitions, are now "swing" constituencies, in many instances most responsive to short-term economic conditions.

The 1992 election indeed resulted in significant changes in the religious traditions that have been the backbone of party coalitions for most of American history. At present such alignments still structure party politics and are quite potent even when economic issues come to the fore. They are likely to be even more important during times of peace and prosperity, perhaps evolving into a more comprehensive religious alignment. For good or ill, observers cannot afford to ignore the role of religion in politics.

Notes

This article was originally prepared for the annual meeting of the American Political Science Association, Washington, DC, September 1–4, 1993. The authors wish to acknowledge major financial support from the Pew Charitable Trusts, which made this study possible. Additional assistance was provided by the Institute for the Study of American Evangelicals at Wheaton College, the Research and Professional Growth Committee of Furman University, the Ray C. Bliss Institute of Applied Politics at the University of Akron, and the Calvin Center for Christian Studies.

1. George Gallup, Jr. first referred to 1976 as the "Year of the Evangelical," a phrase later adopted widely by both the religious and secular media (see Woodward 1976).

2. For detailed examination of the relative influence of a variety of religious, ideological and socioeconomic measures on political behavior, consult Kellstedt (1993). For discussion of our religious tradition measure, see the Appendix.

References

Berger, S. (ed.). 1982. *Religion in West European Politics.* London: Cass.
Bruce, S. 1988. *The Rise and Fall of the New Christian Right.* Oxford: Oxford University Press.
Cook, R. 1993. "Clinton struggles to meld a governing coalition." *Congressional Quarterly Weekly Report* 51:2175–79.
Dionne, E. J. 1991. *Why Americans Hate Politics.* New York: Simon and Schuster.
Erickson, R. S., T. D. Lancaster, and D. W. Romero. 1989. "Group components of the presidential vote, 1952–1984." *Journal of Politics* 51:337–45.
Green, J. C. and J. L. Guth. 1990. "Politics in a new key." *Western Political Quarterly* 43:153–79.
———. 1991. "The Bible and the ballot box," pp. 207–26 in Guth and Green, *q.v.*
———. 1993. "From lambs to sheep," pp. 100–117 in Leege and Kellstedt, *q.v.*
———. and C. R. Fraser. 1991. "Religion and politics among party activists," pp. 113–36 in Guth and Green, *q.v.*
Guth, J. L. and J. C. Green (eds.). 1991. *The Bible and the Ballot Box.* Boulder, CO: Westview.
Guth, J. L., J. C. Green, L. A. Kellstedt, and C. E. Smidt. 1993. "God's own party." *Christian Century* (Feb.):172–76.
Guth, J. L., J. C. Green, C. E. Smidt, and M. M. Poloma. 1991. "Pulpits and politics," pp. 73–93 in Guth and Green, *q.v.*
Guth, J. L. and C. R. Fraser. 1993. "Religion and foreign policy attitudes." Paper presented at the annual meeting of the American Political Science Association, Washington, DC.
Himmelstein, J. L. 1990. *To the Right.* Berkeley: University of California Press.
Hunter, J. D. 1991. *Culture Wars.* New York: Basic Books.
Jorstad, E. 1990. *Holding Fast/Pressing On.* New York: Praeger.
Keith, B., D. B. Magleby, C. J. Nelson, E. Orr, M. C. Westlye, and R. E. Wolfinger. 1992. *The Myth of the Independent Voter.* Berkeley: University of California Press.
Kellstedt, L. A. 1993. "Religion, the neglected variable," pp. 273–303 in Leege and Kellstedt, *q.v.*
Kellstedt, L. A. and J. C. Green. 1993. "Knowing God's many people," pp. 53–71 in Leege and Kellstedt, *q.v.*
Kellstedt, L. A., C. E. Smidt, and P. M. Kellstedt. 1991. "Religious tradition, denomination, and commitment," pp. 139–58 in Guth and Green, *q.v.*

Kenski, H. C. and W. Lockwood. 1991. "Catholic voting behavior in 1988," pp. 173–87 in Guth and Green, *q.v.*

Ladd, E. C. 1993. "The 1992 vote for President Clinton." *Political Science Quarterly* 108:1–28.

Leege, D. C. and L. A. Kellstedt (eds.). 1993. *Rediscovering the Religious Factor in American Politics*. Armonk, NY: Sharpe.

Lipset, S. M. 1993. "The significance of the 1992 election." *PS* 56:7–16.

McCormick, R. L. 1986. *Party, Period and Public Policy*. New York: Oxford University Press.

Nelson, M. (ed.). 1993. *The Elections of 1992*. Washington, DC: CQ Press.

Pomper, G. (ed.). 1993. *The Election of 1992*. Chatham, NJ: Chatham House.

Seib, G. F. 1993. "Christian coalition hopes to expand by taking stands on taxes, crime, health care and NAFTA." *Wall Street Journal* (Sept. 7):A16.

Shafer, B. (ed.). 1991. *The End of Realignment?* Madison: University of Wisconsin Press.

Sigelman, L. 1991. "Jews and the 1988 election," pp. 188–203 in Guth and Green, *q.v.*

Smidt, C. E. 1993. "Evangelical voting patterns," pp. 85–117 in M. Cromartie (ed.), *No Longer Exiles*. Washington, DC: Ethics and Public Policy Center.

Swierenga, R. P. 1990. "Ethnoreligious political behavior in the mid-nineteenth century," pp. 146–71 in M. A. Noll (ed.), *Religion & American Politics*. New York: Oxford University Press.

Wald, K. D., L. A. Kellstedt, and D. C. Leege. 1993. "Church involvement and political behavior," pp. 139–56 in Leege and Kellstedt, *q.v.*

Wald, K. D. and C. E. Smidt. 1993. "Measurement strategies in the study of religion and politics," pp. 26–49 in Leege and Kellstedt, *q.v.*

Wilcox, C. 1991. "Religion and electoral politics among black Americans," pp. 159–72 in Guth and Green, *q.v.*

———. 1992. *God's Warriors*. Baltimore, MD: Johns Hopkins University Press.

Woodward, K. 1976. "Born-again." *Newsweek* (Oct. 25):68–76.

Wuthnow, R. 1988. *The Restructuring of American Religion*. Princeton, NJ: Princeton University Press.

———. 1989. *The Struggle for America's Soul*. Grand Rapids, MI: Eerdmans.

Appendix: Variable Construction

Religious Tradition

The major difficulty in defining religious traditions is distinguishing between mainline and evangelical Protestants. Our classification is based on extended analysis of the history and beliefs of specific denominations. Briefly, mainline Protestants come from theologically moderate to liberal churches, such as the Episcopal Church, the United Church of Christ, the Presbyterian Church in the U.S.A., and the United Methodist Church, while Evangelicals identify with more theologically conservative bodies, including most Baptist, Pentecostal, and Holiness groups, along with many nondenominational churches, and a scattering of the smaller denominations from the Presbyterian, Lutheran, and Wesleyan families. Despite some similarities with both mainline and evangelical Protestants, black Protestants constitute a separate religious tradition, and because this tradition is often difficult to identify from survey data, our analysis here is of white voters only. Secular voters are those who have no denominational identification or, if they do, show no evidence of religious interest or involvement beyond that preference. For a more elaborate discussion of the criteria used in classification and a list of denominations, see Kellstedt (1993:300) and Kellstedt and Green (1993).

In tables 14.1, 14.2, 14.3, 14.6 and 14.7 we follow this denominational scheme as closely as possible. The National Election Studies prior to 1990 present difficulties for table 14.1 because of an outmoded denominational code, but the 1992 Akron and NES surveys in tables 14.2, 14.3, 14.6, and 14.7 utilize the new classification system. The VRS exit polls (tables 14.4 and 14.5) present special problems, as they do not ask for voters' denominational affiliation. Using questions available, we defined mainliners as Protestants and Other Christians who do not identify as "born again Christian/fundamentalists," and evangelicals as those who do so identify.

Church Attendance

Individuals who attend church once a week or more were classified as "regular attenders."

Political Variables

Tables 14.1, 14.2, 14.4, and 14.6 use standard NES party identification items, with independents who report feeling closer to one party treated as party identifiers (Keith *et al.* 1992). In table 14.2, the Bush evaluation is a five-point Likert scale, and the combination of the two highest points is reported ("excellent" and "good"). The 1992 vote intention item asked about voting for Bush, his "Democratic opponent," or "other candidate."

The issue questions in table 14.3 are five-point Likert scale items, with the exception of abortion, which was a four-point scale. In table 14.5, the abortion item was a four-point scale, the respondent's own financial situation was a three-point scale, and the evaluation of the economy was a four-point scale (the combination of "excellent" and "good" is reported). The abortion item in table 14.7 is identical to the four-point item in table 14.3; although the other items in table 14.7 parallel the topics in table 14.3, their wording and format differ, including both five- and seven-point Likert scales. Additional information is available from the authors.

15

Has Godot Finally Arrived?
Religion and Realignment

Lyman A. Kellstedt
John C. Green
James L. Guth
Corwin E. Smidt

Everett Ladd has noted that talk of party realignment is akin to "Waiting for Godot."[1] Does the stunning Republican victory in 1994 mean the wait is finally over? While GOP gains may prove ephemeral, exit poll data reveal that one kind of realignment is indeed under way: a religious one. Members of the nation's two largest religious groups, white Evangelical Protestants and Roman Catholics, show every sign of a fundamental reordering of political preferences. In 1994, Evangelicals entrenched themselves as the senior partner in the Republican coalition, while Catholics departed once again from their traditional Democratic moorings, after a brief visit home in 1992. Interestingly, the key GOP supporters in both groups were regular church attendees, the easiest to mobilize through such channels.

The Religious Vote in 1994

How did major American religious groups vote in 1994? Table 15.1 reports the GOP House vote for the three largest traditions among whites (Evangelical and Mainline Protestant and Roman Catholic), for those who claim no religious identification (seculars), and several smaller groups of whites (such as Jews and Mormons).[2] For purposes of comparison, the voting of nonwhite ethnic groups is also included.[3]

The 1994 vote had significant religious underpinnings. The strongest Republican vote came from Mormons, with 78% backing House GOP candidates. Evangelicals were a close second at 75%. The size of the GOP House vote may not be a record for Mormons, a small group concentrated in the West, but is probably a historic high for the more numerous Evangelicals, who not only dominate the South, but are a major presence elsewhere.

In contrast, Mainline Protestants, long the backbone of the GOP, gave Republicans just over half their votes, only modestly more than Roman Catholics, once the strongest pillar of the Democratic ethno-religious establishment. Note that among both Evangelicals and Catholics, regular church attendees were more Republican, a tendency long evident among Mainline Protestants, but which, ironically, almost disappeared among them in 1994. The remaining religious and ethnic groups were much less Republican, ranging from 44% of seculars to only 10% among black Americans.

The second two columns in table 15.1 summarize the religious composition of party electorates. Evangelicals provided almost three out of

TABLE 15.1
Religious Groups, Voting and Partisanship in the 1994 Elections

	GOP Vote	Party Coalitions (by 1994 Vote)		Party Identification		Party Coalitions (by Party ID)	
		Rep.	Dem.	Rep.	Dem.	Rep.	Dem.
White Mormons	78%	4%	1%	56%	12%	5%	1%
White Evangelicals:	75	29	11	52	21	30	12
Regular Church Attenders	78	(22)	(7)	56	17	(24)	(7)
Not Regular Church Attenders	68	(7)	(4)	42	30	(7)	(5)
White Mainline Protestants:	56	27	24	38	31	27	21
Regular Church Attenders	56	(9)	(8)	40	28	(10)	(7)
Not Regular Church Attenders	55	(18)	(16)	36	31	(17)	(14)
White Catholics:	53	22	22	33	38	21	23
Regular Church Attenders	57	(13)	(12)	35	37	(13)	(13)
Not Regular Church Attenders	49	(9)	(10)	29	38	(8)	(10)
White Seculars	44	9	12	27	40	9	11
White Other Religions	39	2	4	20	33	2	3
Hispanics	35	2	3	29	60	2	4
White Jews	25	1	4	12	62	1	5
Blacks	10	2	17	6	77	2	19

Source: 1994 Mitofsky International exit poll.

ten GOP voters; weekly attendees alone supplied more than one-fifth. Mainline Protestants contributed slightly more than one-quarter, Catholics, slightly less. Note that regularly attending Catholics actually outnumbered their Mainline counterparts among GOP voters. Taken together, all weekly church attendees constituted just over half the Republican electorate, highlighting both the salience of social issue conservatism and the great tensions it provokes among Republicans.

What about the Democrats? As one might expect, their coalition is more diverse. Mainline Protestants provided about a quarter of the total, while Catholics accounted for just over one-fifth, slightly more than did nonwhites. Seculars and Evangelicals each contributed slightly more than one-tenth, as did combined Jews, Hispanics, and whites of other religions. In contrast to the GOP, religiously observant whites provided less than a third of the Democratic coalition, helping to explain both the dominance of social issue liberalism and less attention towards religion within the party.

Historical Backdrop

The magnitude of change within religious traditions is more impressive when put into historical context. Surveys from the 1950s reveal Evangelicals and Catholics as fixtures of the Democratic House electorate, supplemented by small numbers of seculars and religious minorities, while Mainline Protestants were the core of the GOP. In the 1960s, Evangelicals moved away from the Democratic Party, first in presidential contests, then in down-ticket races, a process now well advanced but not yet complete.

Catholics drifted from their historic Democratic moorings as well, but the first defectors were often those with minimal religious attachments. By the late 1980s and 1990s, however, defectors were often the more religiously observant, especially among younger Catholics, replicating the Evangelical pattern. During the same period, Mainline Protestants were headed in the opposite direction. Many, but particularly the least religiously involved, were abandoning the GOP. Also, the steady growth in the number of secular voters since the 1950s provided an additional source of Democratic votes in House races.[4]

Anatomy of the 1994 Religious Vote

Thus, the 1994 vote had a significant religious component, reflecting a long-term realignment of important groups. What factors help explain these findings?

A good place to begin is with issues. Exit poll respondents were asked: "Which two issues mattered most in deciding how you voted for US House?" Not surprisingly, responses differ significantly by religious group and church attendance. Regular church attendees among Evangelicals were much more likely to name family values (47%) or abortion (29%) as most important, while nonattenders cited crime (31%), family values (28%), plus taxes and economic issues (both 25%). Among Mainline Protestants, church attendees and nonattenders were quite similar with crime the top priority (36% mentions for both), economic concerns (25% and 32%, respectively), and taxes (24% and 29%). Catholics in both groups resembled their Mainline Protestant counterparts in priorities, with the exception that regular attendees were considerably more likely to name family values (22%) or abortion (17%) as important vote determinants. Seculars put little emphasis on abortion or family values, stressing instead crime, economics and taxes as the most important issues, while giving education a higher rating than did voters in the major traditions. Mormon choices paralleled those of Evangelicals, while Jews and blacks responded like seculars.

What impact did issue priorities have on the vote? Table 15.2 shows the Republican House vote for those making each issue a priority. Three important patterns stand out. First, regardless of issue focus. Evangelicals were the most Republican and seculars the least, with Mainline Protestants and Catholics falling in between. Second, with few exceptions, regular attendees were more Republican than their less observant counterparts, regardless of tradition or issue focus. Third, there are some strong partisan/issue patterns. Republicans gained from concern with family values and taxes in all religious groups and attendance levels. In contrast, they gained markedly less from voters' worries on education, health care, or crime. Abortion was clearly the most divisive issue. Over 90% of regularly attending Evangelicals choosing it voted Republican, but only 20% of seculars for whom the issue was salient opted for the GOP. Mainline Protestants and Catholics were also sharply divided by abortion. For both groups, weekly attendees choosing the issue voted Republican while the less observant voted Democratic. Finally, emphasis on the economy and jobs had mixed effects: nonregular attendees among Evangelicals selecting this option were the most Republican, while seculars were the most Democratic.

The data also reveal some important interactions between religious tradition and demography in producing partisan choices. A staple of the New Deal Democratic coalition was support from working class voters. This classic alliance was undermined in 1994, at least among Evangelicals.

TABLE 15.2
Percentage Voting Republican: House Elections 1994

[Whites by: religious traditions, church attendance, issue salience, and selected demographic characteristics.]

	Evangelicals		Mainline Prot.		Catholics		Seculars
	RegCh	NotReg	RegCh	NotReg	RegCh	NotReg	
Respondents listing the issue as key for them:							
Abortion	90%	83%	56%	24%	65%	38%	20%
Family Values	88	74	70	69	73	67	60
Taxes	85	83	69	61	71	66	77
Crime	72	72	55	60	52	52	48
Education	67	58	48	44	49	28	31
Economy/Jobs	60	70	54	55	54	47	45
Health Care	59	49	44	42	36	36	24
Respondent's Education:							
High School	66	59	51	52	46	46	52
Some College	82	70	59	60	57	49	51
College Grad	87	80	66	62	61	58	37
Post Grad	78	81	47	46	65	42	36
Respondent's Income:							
Less than $30K	73	59	45	53	44	42	40
$30K - $75K	79	74	60	58	60	49	43
Over $75K	87	93	60	55	66	62	49
Respondent's Gender:							
Male	78	74	61	61	64	52	47
Female	78	65	52	51	52	48	38
Group's 1994 GOP Vote	78	68	56	55	57	49	44

Note: RegCh = Regular Church Attendance, NotReg = Less than Regular Church Attendance. The n's are small for some groups of "post graduate" education and high [$75 Thousand +] income.
Source: 1994 Mitofsky International exit poll.

As table 15.2 shows, large majorities of lower income Evangelicals went Republican, especially among churchgoers, voting their beliefs, not their pocketbooks. Among both Mainliners and Catholics, those in the low-income and low-education groups also voted Republican in substantial numbers.[5]

Similar exceptions to the classic New Deal pattern work in the other direction, such as the relatively strong support given the GOP by the least educated secular voters and the Democratic preferences of voters with post-graduate education among Mainline Protestants, nonobservant Catholics, and seculars. Perhaps this latter group constitutes a highly educated, politically liberal "New Class" of professionals which spans several religious traditions. Yet, the classic effect of education still holds among regularly attending Catholics, who become more Republican with every step up the educational and income ladders. In some cases, status and religion reinforce each other, as among high income Evangelicals, who were the most Republican of any demographic voting group in table 15.2.

One more demographic factor in table 15.2 is worth considering, gender. Many pundits noted the larger gender gap in 1994, reporting a massive male "backlash" against the Democrats. Indeed, men gave the GOP more votes than women in almost every religious group except for two. Among churchgoing Evangelicals, males and females voted Republican at exactly the same rate, and among faithful Mormons the gender gap was actually reversed. Clearly, Republican gains involved strong support from conservative, religious women, not just disaffected men.[6]

Considering these results, it is not surprising that statistical controls for various demographics have no impact on religious voting patterns, confirming the findings of other analysts that religion was more powerful than economics in 1994.[7]

Long-Term Effects?

Do these findings signal realignment? If realignment is conceived as a process involving changes in the partisan alignments of major groups, then Godot may well have arrived for white Evangelicals and Catholics.

We examined the impact of church attendance and age on the Republican House vote in 1994. GOP support was very high among churchgoing, younger Evangelicals (85%), so high in fact that its long-term persistence seems assured. Older church attending Evangelicals were strongly GOP as well (67%), but less than their younger co-parishioners. And younger non-attending Evangelicals voted just as Republican (68%) as older church attendees, but much more so than older non-attenders (53%).

Among Mainline Protestants, age had little impact on voting, with young and old voting Republican in roughly equal measure. Among Catholics, however, age mattered a great deal, with younger Catholics more likely to vote Republican. Among regular attendees, 58% of those under the age of 40 voted for the GOP, while 52% of those over 60 did the same. Among nonobservant Catholics the difference is even greater, with 53% of those under 40 voting Republican, while only 35% of those over 60 did the same.

Finally, what about party self-identification? Table 15.1 presents data on this much-watched indicator (independents are excluded for purposes of presentation). Mormons (56%) and Evangelicals (52%) are by far the most Republican, while Mainliners (38%) and Catholics (33%) exhibit deep partisan divisions, with the Mainliners marginally more Republican and Catholics slightly more Democratic. These figures alone suggest a fundamental change in party coalitions. Seculars are two-fifths Democratic, and the Democratic bias tends to increase for the remaining groups. Hispanics and Jews are more than three-fifths Democratic and blacks nearly four-fifths. Note that in the three largest traditions, church attendees are more Republican, although by varying margins.

The end result of these long-term changes in the parties' core constituencies can be noted in the two right hand columns in table 15.1. Among 1994 voters, Evangelicals were the largest Republican constituency, easily outnumbering Mainliners. Catholics constituted one-fifth of the GOP identifiers and all the remaining groups combined for one-fifth. Thus, Mainline Protestants are no longer the GOP's religious backbone. Catholics are still the largest Democratic religious constituency (23%), but barely edge out Mainline Protestants for top honors. Blacks are slightly less numerous, but when combined with other racial and ethnic minorities, account for more than one quarter of the Democratic total. The remaining one quarter is similarly diverse, with equal proportions of Evangelicals and seculars, plus Jews and other smaller groups.

Emerging Ethno-Religious Coalitions

The importance of these changes can hardly be overstated. The core groups of the New Deal coalition, namely white Evangelicals and white Catholics, have, to varying extents, deserted the Democratic Party. Evangelicals are now at the center of the Republican coalition, and Catholics are up for grabs. Thus, after years of gradual disintegration, the New Deal religious coalition is now in shambles, and with it the Democratic lock on congressional and state government. Although the GOP has gained substantially from partisan shifts within religious traditions, it has suffered some losses as well. Mainline Protestants have left the GOP in large numbers, and like Catholics, are now an electoral swing group. Democrats also have gained or maintained support with less observant members of the major traditions, among the growing number of seculars, and various ethnic minorities.

New forms of ethno-religious politics are emerging, with the GOP drawing the more religiously observant voters, at least among whites, and the Democrats attracting the least observant in the major traditions, seculars, and various minority groups. While it is unclear exactly how these trends will play out, the Grand Old Party has at least one short run advantage: as recent elections demonstrate, grassroots religious institutions can mobilize the Republican religious constituencies. There is at present no comparable set of institutions mobilizing less-religious Democratic voters. This Republican advantage can be erased, however, if religious mobilization goes too far, driving dissident groups to the Democrats, the traditional "party of diversity." Thus, religious realignment poses serious challenges for both parties as 1996 approaches.

Notes

1. Everett Carll Ladd. "Like Waiting for Godot" in Byron E. Shafer, ed., *The End of Realignment* (Madison: University of Wisconsin Press, 1991), chapter 2.

2. Exit poll data are difficult to categorize into religious traditions, although the 1994 Mitofsky International exit poll was an improvement over past efforts. Here, we classify as "Evangelical Protestants" respondents who checked the "Born Again/Evangelical Christian" box on the questionnaire and classified themselves as either "Protestant," "Other Christian," or "Something else." The label "Mainline Protestant" was assigned to non-born-again Protestants and Other Christians. Other religious categories included in the exit poll are Catholic, Jewish, Mormon and "Nothing in particular." The latter category serves as the basis of our "secular" group.

3. The exit poll data make it difficult to ascertain the religious characteristics of nonwhites, so we focus on blacks and Hispanics as unified groups.

4. For documentation of these trends, see Lyman A. Kellstedt, "Evangelicals and Political Realignment," in Corwin W. Smidt, ed., *Contemporary Evangelical Political Involvement* (Lanham, MD: University Press of America, 1989), pp. 99–117, and Corwin E. Smidt, "Evangelical Voting Patterns: 1976–1988," in Michael Cromartie, ed., *No Longer Exiles* (Washington DC: Ethics and Public Policy Center, 1993), pp. 85–117.

5. The distribution of education and income levels varies significantly across religious traditions. Nonregular-attending Evangelicals have the lowest levels of education and income of all the groups in the table, even lower than African Americans. Church attending Evangelicals trail Mainliners and Catholics only slightly in these respects, but both trail Jews. Thus, nonattending Evangelicals and blacks share lower social status, but differ sharply in political dispositions. Similarly, Jews, Mainliners and Catholics share high status, but vote very differently. Clearly, religious differences among these groups are central to their politics.

6. It should be noted that there is a higher ratio of women to men among the regular churchgoers than among less regular attenders in the Evangelical, Main-

line, and Catholic religious traditions. The lowest percentage of women is among seculars, 43%.

7. See, for example, the findings of Fred Steeper, cited in *The Washington Post*, National Weekly Edition, February 27–March 5, 1995, p. 23; and *Roll Call*, February 27, 1995, p. 8.

16

The Political Relevance of Religion: The Correlates of Mobilization

James L. Guth
John C. Green
Lyman A. Kellstedt
Corwin E. Smidt

When do citizens make conscious connections between their religious faith and political choices? What difference does such a linkage make? In recent years political scientists have made great advances in understanding the influence of religious variables on political attitudes and behavior (for a thorough review, see Leege and Kellstedt 1993a). The political effects of denominational affiliation, biblical literalism, or doctrinal beliefs often depend upon the strength of a person's religious commitment. Although religious commitment is sometimes an important predictor in its own right, it more often conditions the relationship between other religious variables and political choices. Still, even when measures of personal commitment are combined with belief and affiliation items, a great deal of variance often remains unexplained. Perhaps this situation reflects the failure of many religious Americans to make a conscious connection between faith and politics. As Leege (1993:11) has noted: "But surely it would be misleading to claim that all people who report a religious affiliation have their political views shaped in similar ways by that tradition. For some a religious affiliation is highly salient for politics. For others it is salient for salvation but little else." The same could be said about other aspects of religion. In a popular review of a national poll on American values, Patterson and Kim (1991) discovered that although many citizens claim strong religious attachments, markedly fewer see the relevance of religion to public life or political choices.

A few studies provide tantalizing hints that conscious linking of religious belief to political choices can greatly enhance the political impact of religion. MacIver's (1989) pathbreaking study of "religious politicization" in Europe provides important leads. Using a cross-national data set (the Eurobarometer series), MacIver found that in most European countries, half or more of the "subjectively religious" nevertheless claimed that their religious convictions played no role in forming their political preferences. Although the results varied by country, MacIver discovered some consistent differences between two groups of equally "religious" respondents. Those who saw religion as politically relevant "place themselves farther to the right than their non-religiously politicized compatriots" and were less likely to vote for a leftist party (119). Somewhat surprisingly, however, MacIver also found that on most of the few issue items available (which did not include moral questions), differences were minor, except for stronger "internationalist" leanings among the religiously politicized.

Other scholars have corroborated the possibility that perception of the political relevance of faith may influence the extent to which religious variables shape political choices. In a "direct approach" to religious politicization, Rothenberg and Newport (1984:114) asked their sample of "evangelical voters" how important their religious views and convictions were in making electoral choices in 1980, 1982, and 1984. Although they found an increasing tendency over those years for Evangelicals to say that their religious convictions would play at least some role in deciding how to vote, the authors emphasized the "half-empty" nature of their findings: that 40 percent of white Evangelicals reported that religion would be "unimportant" in 1984 presidential choices. Nor do they comment upon or analyze any political differences between "religiously politicized" Evangelicals and others.

In a secondary analysis of the Rothenberg and Newport data, Wilcox (1992:61) reversed the emphasis, discovering that "those evangelicals who perceive a strong connection between religion and politics were indeed more conservative than those who perceived a weaker connection." This relationship persisted even in multivariate analysis, especially on attitudes toward religio-political groups such as the Moral Majority. Although Wilcox's analysis was by necessity confined to Evangelicals, the results are certainly consistent with MacIver's European findings, based on the views of respondents from several Christian traditions.

Even these modest forays into the political consequences of religious politicization have not been matched by equal attention to explaining why some religious citizens make a conscious connection between faith and politics and others do not. MacIver (1989) tested two hypotheses: *organizational mobilization*, measured by church membership, and *cognitive mobilization*, tapped indirectly by items on education and political interest. She found organizational mobilization predominant, with education a secondary influence, but the results must be regarded as tentative, given the limited number of potentially relevant variables available. For their part, Rothenberg and Newport (1984:114) observed several influences on religious relevance among Evangelicals, finding that church attendance, general religious salience, biblical literalism, and self-identified fundamentalism produced reports that religion was extremely or very important to electoral choices. Unfortunately, they undertook no multivariate analysis, using either religion or other potential influences.

Thus, previous studies have adduced evidence that a conscious linkage between religion and politics may have important implications. In this essay, we explore the meaning of what we will call the *political relevance* of religion both by analyzing the factors that lead citizens to claim a connection between their faith and political choices and by evaluating the impact such claims have on political attitudes and behavior. In the first part of the chapter, we outline several perspectives about the location of political relevance. We will draw some leads from the studies mentioned earlier, but also derive hypotheses from a broader review of theories on the political mobilization of religion in the contemporary world. We assume that most such mobilizations are characterized by "consciousness-raising" about the connections between faith and the public order. Thus, we should be able to extrapolate from findings on which religious individuals are politically mobilized to hypotheses about individual consciousness of political relevance. We focus on four theoretical approaches, which argue in turn that political relevance is produced by (1) social mobilization, (2) agenda mobilization, (3) cognitive mobilization, and, finally, (4) organizational mobilization. Although many variables in each model are related to those in others, we find the division useful for heuristic and exploratory purposes.

Data and Methods

Our data are drawn from the National Survey on Religion and Politics, conducted by the Survey Research Center at the University of Akron in the spring of 1992. This study was designed to delineate relationships between detailed religious measures and contemporary political attitudes and behavior. As the survey was somewhat larger than most national polls (N = 4,001), we can look in detail at many American religious groups. Here, however, we restrict analysis to the three major American Christian traditions: evangelical Protestants, mainline Protestants, and Roman Catholics. Further, as religious traditions among African Americans and other ethnic minorities often have quite distinctive political meanings, we confine our analysis to whites, the overwhelming majority in all three traditions. (On the concept of religious tradition, see Kellstedt and Green 1993.)

We also limit the sample in one other critical way: *we include only respondents who say that religion is important to them.* Thus, the sample here incorporates only those who responded yes to the following standard National Election Study (NES) item, "Do you consider religion to be an important part of your life or not?" Those who claim religion is important in their lives were then asked a follow-up question: "Would you say that your religion provides some guidance in your day-to-day living, quite a bit of guidance, or a great deal of guidance in your day-to-day life?" We will refer to this as the *religious guidance* measure. Our dependent variable, *political relevance,* was measured by asking, "How important is your religion to your political thinking?" The response categories were from 1 ("very important") to 5 ("not at all important").

We find that subjectively religious people in the three Christian traditions differ significantly in their perceptions of political relevance, with Evangelicals having significantly higher levels (mean = 2.57, SD = 1.47) than mainliners (mean = 3.13, SD = 1.39) or Catholics (mean = 3.33, SD = 1.44). As the standard deviations (SDs) show, there is also significant variation within each tradition. Our basic question, then, is this: What factors predict the conscious connection of *subjective* religiosity to the wider political world? To answer this question, we turn first to the impact of social and demographic factors.

Perspective 1: Social Mobilization

One orientation to the emergence of new religious movements in politics stresses the role of social and economic factors, especially certain social transformations which take place during the modernization of traditional religious societies. Perhaps the best summary of this literature is Kepel's (1994) *The Revenge of God,* which posits that new political militancy (and presumably political relevance) among the religious is usually associated with higher education, upward mobility, youth, and residence in areas where tradition confronts modernity. Education, of course, has politicizing effects in most societies, producing greater civic competence, a sense of personal efficacy, and the cognitive tools for understanding the complex political world. Even more vital for our purposes, education also produces attitudinal constraint: well-educated citizens tend to connect the elements of their belief systems. Young people may be more open to efforts by religious elites to encourage political action on the basis of religious identities and beliefs. And, almost invariably, regions with large religious populations confronted with rapid socioeconomic transformations are likely to produce some citizens who connect religious and political worlds.

In the American context, then, we would expect to find those who see the political relevance of religion most numerous among religious people who are well educated and well off, young, and from the South, the nation's most "religious" section and the location of some of the most notable religious challenges to secularizing state authority. We also predict that traditional family structures should produce people with a greater sense of the political relevance of religion, although direct measures of traditionalist attitudes might be better predictors. Our expectations on other demographic traits such as gender are less clear, but we expect higher levels of political relevance among males, because of historically greater male involvement in political life. Table 16.1 shows both the zero-level correlations between sociodemographic variables and political relevance, and the results of multiple regressions, with all the sociodemographic variables entered simultaneously.

Unfortunately for social mobilization theory, none of the sociodemographic measures is very potent in predicting political relevance; some actually move in a direction opposite to that specified. In the full sample, education and income actually have modest *negative* relationships with political relevance. Among Evangelicals income has a small negative effect, whereas among mainliners and Catholics it is higher education that depresses relevance scores. In the full sample, contrary to our expectations, political relevance increases with age but, in conformity with our prediction, is higher among those in a traditional nuclear family (married and never divorced). Age is significantly associated with relevance in all three traditions, while traditional family structure matters most for Protestants, especially Evangelicals. Gender, however, is simply not associated with political relevance, either in the full sample or in any of the religious traditions. And although we expect that region should demonstrate some influence, the results are again quite modest. Across

TABLE 16.1
Sociodemographic Influences on the Political Relevance of Religion by
Religious Tradition

	All Christian (N = 2000)		Evangelical (N = 831)		Mainline (N = 497)		Catholic (N = 680)	
	r	*beta*	*r*	*beta*	*r*	*beta*	*r*	*beta*
Status Measures								
Education	-.09*	-.05	-.01	-.05	-.11*	-.07	-.13**	-.12*
Income	-.09**	-.05*	-.07*	-.10*	-.05	.00	-.05	.04
Personal Situation								
Age	.11**	.06*	.08*	.03	.09*	.08	.11*	.12*
Traditional Family	.08**	.07*	.12**	.13**	.09*	.07	-.02	.03
Male	-.01	-.01	-.03	-.03	-.01	.00	-.03	-.03
Residence@								
South	.10**	.07*	.05	.02	.02	.07	.08*	.10*
Midwest	-.01	-.01	-.03	-.02	-.01	.05	.05	.07
West	-.02	—	.00	—	-.05	—	-.03	—
East	-.10**	-.06*	-.03	-.04	.02	.05	-.10*	-.03
Adj. R²=	—	.03	—	.02	—	.02	—	.03

@ The West is the suppressed reference category for the multiple regresssion.
* p < .05
**p < .001

the entire sample, Southerners more often perceive a connection between their faith and political choices, but in the subsamples the relationship is significant only for Catholics, and not among the region's majority of evangelical and mainline Protestants. Midwestern and western residence has no effect, but living in the East produces a modest negative relationship with political relevance, but once again the bivariate effect is confined to Catholics.

A multiple regression using all the sociodemographic factors confirms their limited role, explaining very small amounts of the variance. In the full sample, education barely misses statistical significance, while income hangs in. A traditional family situation, age, and southern or eastern residence retain small but statistically significant effects. Among Evangelicals, only lower income and traditional family situation have significant impacts (which actually increase when other variables are controlled). Among mainliners, education, family situation, and age have modest predictive power, while for Catholics education, age, and southern residence are significant predictors of political relevance. In each subsample, as well, the variance explained is very small, which forces us to look to other explanations. Although demographic variables such as these are much more strongly associated with general importance of religion to individuals (see Guth and Green 1993), once that effect is accounted for, they are of little use in explaining political relevance among such "religious" people.

Perspective 2: Agenda Mobilization.

Another perspective on religious movements stresses what might be called agenda or issue mobilization (Verba, Schlozman, and Brady 1995). Although this view often subsumes the sociodemographic changes comprising the first model, it focuses on the emergence of religiously linked issues that directly trigger mobilization, often during the process of secularization. As religious influence over private and public realms is reduced all over the world, several issue complexes have repeatedly prompted religious movements. The most visible has been the revolution in gender roles, sexual moralities, and public policies concerning both. As Hawley (1994) has argued, sexual traditionalism has been critical to most "fundamentalist" movements around the globe. The mobilizing effect of abortion in the United States certainly reflects that pattern, but other issues such as equal rights for women, gay rights, and sex education no doubt have the same effect (cf. Bruce 1988; Jelen 1991).

Although we might anticipate that citizens concerned about "morality issues" will be more religiously politicized, this effect may be concentrated in traditionalist communities, such as evangelical Protestants. What issues might "politicize" religious mainline Protestants and Catholics? At least two possibilities emerge: first, theologically conservative members of these communities may respond to the same issues as Evangelicals. This reaction is especially likely for the "closet Evangelicals" among mainliners and conservative Catholics. Or, perhaps, committed mainliners and Catholics might respond to the primary agendas of their own elites. For example, both mainline and Catholic elites have preached, pronounced, lobbied, and demonstrated for racial equality (Findlay 1993). Support for the civil rights revolution of the 1960s and 1970s should thus produce more conscious connections between faith and politics in both traditions. According to other analysts, the racial revolution also politicized Evangelicals, but against programs benefiting minorities (cf. Carmines and Stimson 1989). Indeed, some critics see Evangelicals' recent affiliation with the GOP as due not so much to abortion, gender, and other social issues but rather to racial prejudice (Rosenberg 1989). If these theories are correct, then political relevance should be correlated with racial conservatism among Evangelicals and with racial liberalism among mainliners and Catholics. In a similar vein, the Social Gospel of mainline clergy and the Seamless Garment ideology of the contemporary Catholic hierarchy should produce higher political relevance among adherents of those traditions who favor social welfare programs, environmentalism, and reduction in defense spending—all important emphases of mainline Protestant and Catholic hierarchies over the past two decades.

We expect that at least some foreign policy questions influence political relevance, especially attitudes toward the (old) Soviet Union and the Middle East. We have no items on the former but do have a question on whether respondents favor Israel or the Arabs. As this item taps deep-seated evangelical theological orientations such as premillennialism, in which Israel plays a prominent role in the political future, we predict that pro-Israeli citizens will see more connections between their faith and political life. For Evangelicals taught that the Jews' return to Palestine is a harbinger of the Second Coming of Jesus, political events obviously have religious significance. As Boyer (1992) has recently pointed out, such theologically based views have extended into many Mainline Protestant congregations, a point that our evidence confirms (see Guth and Fraser 1993). Finally, we anticipate that political relevance also derives from more general perceptions that true religious values are being compromised in a society, under attack by secular forces or by new religious faiths or movements that the government has failed to curb. Jelen's (1991) work on religious particularism suggests that religious traditionalists may be politicized to the extent that they resist political encroachments by those who do not share their faith or actually adhere to clearly "deviant" perspectives.

How well does the agenda perspective fare in predicting perceptions of political relevance among the religious? On the whole, it provides some important insights. As table 16.2 shows, those who see the country afflicted by important moral or social issue problems consciously connect their faith to public life more often, but this effect results from a very strong relationship among evangelical Protestants, with virtually no bivariate effects among either mainliners or Catholics. Thus, perceptions

TABLE 16.2
Agenda and Issue Influences on the Political Relevance of Religion by
Religious Tradition

	All Christian (N=1864)		Evangelical (N=776)		Mainline (N=463)		Catholic (N=625)	
	r	beta	r	beta	r	beta	r	beta
Agenda Priorities								
Moral Problems	.12**	.03	.20**	.07	.02	-.01	.02	-.03
Economic Welfare	-.12**	.04	-.19**	-.06	-.04	-.02	-.04	-.02
Agenda Issues								
Pro-Life	.31**	.25**	.36**	.29**	.16**	.12*	.29**	.27**
Pro-Israel	.16**	.10**	.18**	.09*	.15**	.13*	.03	.01
Anti-Gay Rights	.15**	.08**	.13**	.00	.05	.04	.12*	.12**
Anti-Minority Religion	.11**	.04	.16**	.07*	.03	.01	.08*	.04
Anti-Women's Rights	.11**	.05*	.12**	.03	.07	.10*	.04	.00
Close to Blacks	.11**	.09**	.14**	.12**	.04	.02	.10*	.08*
Pro-Affirmative Action	.03	.03	-.02	-.04	.12*	.13*	.08*	.08*
Adj. R^2 =	—	.13	—	.17	—	.05	—	.10

* p < .05
**p < .001

that morality issues top the national agenda apparently produce political consciousness only among Evangelicals. What about social welfare problems? Does the historic Social Gospel emphasis of mainline Protestant elites and the liberal communal concerns of Catholics translate to perceived relevance? Apparently not. In the full sample, mention of economic and social welfare problems is *negatively* related to relevance, an effect once again accounted for primarily by the Evangelicals. Mentions of foreign policy problems, political process problems, and other kinds of issues have no discernible bivariate influence in either direction (data not shown).

The results of the agenda analysis lead us to expect that social issue *attitudes* may be stronger predictors of political relevance—and they are. Not surprisingly, abortion has the largest impact: pro-life respondents are most likely to see a strong connection between faith and politics, both in the full sample and in each religious tradition (although the association is much weaker for mainliners than for Evangelicals and Catholics). All this suggests that *Roe v. Wade* (1973) not only set off pro-life mobilization and, perhaps, the Christian Right movement but also that both issue and mobilization have heightened the political consciousness of many religious people.

Presumably, similar effects should be produced by other social issues, such as gay rights, equal rights for women, minority religions, and civil rights. Of these, gay rights has the strongest correlation with political relevance, having considerable impact among Evangelicals and Catholics, but not mainline Protestants. Attitudes toward women's rights are also correlated with political relevance, a tendency that declines from Evangelicals to mainliners to Catholics.

We also thought that political relevance would be associated with hostile attitudes toward religious minorities or "deviant" religions. We had no direct measures of this kind of particularism, but on reflection we concluded that an item on the Supreme Court's decision in *Employment Division v. Smith* (1990), the so-called "peyote" case, might serve as an acceptable surrogate. Presumably those who reject Native Americans' right to use peyote in religious exercises would be more sensitive to the connections between religion and public policy. This view was confirmed, but primarily for Evangelical Protestants and, to some extent, Catholics. (Ironically, most evangelical Protestant leaders fought hard for congressional reversal of *Smith* via the Religious Freedom Restoration Act.)

To test the impact of racial attitudes on political relevance, we used two indicators: a proximity item on how close people felt to African Americans and a policy item on affirmative action. The proximity question does predict political relevance but sometimes in the "wrong" direction: Evangelicals (and Catholics) who feel *close* to blacks more often perceive the political relevance of their faith. The evangelical results are puzzling at first, until we remember that the civil rights movement has become a very important positive model for evangelical political action, one repeatedly cited in leadership pronouncements (for one recent example, see Morgan 1994). On the other hand, as we expected, support for affirmative action policy is positively correlated with political relevance among both mainline Protestants and Catholics, but not among Evangelicals. Perhaps mainline and Catholic elite preachments have had some modest effect.

Our search for other issues eliciting political relevance was less successful. In foreign policy, results were mixed. Surprisingly, perhaps, defense spending attitudes show no significant impact, even at the bivariate level, despite the much publicized pastoral letters on war and peace from the Catholic bishops and many mainline Protestant bodies during the 1980s (data not shown). But a strong bivariate relationship does show up on one foreign policy issue: those who think the United States should back Israel over the Arabs more often perceive the political importance of faith. This result comports well with the potent "Christian Zionism" of evangelical Protestantism, based in premillennial theologies. Here the impact of pro-Israel attitudes on political relevance among mainliners is almost as strong as among Evangelicals—despite consistent pleas of mainline elites for a "balanced" Mideast policy. For Catholics, who lack premillennial theological direction, attitudes on the Middle East are not significant predictors.

Finally, we also considered other issues that might affect political relevance, especially given recent leadership cues provided the faithful in mainline and Catholic traditions, but neither liberal views on hunger and welfare policy nor proenvironmental attitudes had any appreciable influence on political relevance. In fact, the impact of economic and welfare policy was in a conservative direction among all three groups, with the bivariate relationship with political relevance approaching significance among Evangelicals (data not shown). The failure of environmentalism to produce greater relevance suggests that the "greening of Protestantism" (Fowler 1995) has not sunk very deeply into mainline political consciousness.

We concluded with multiple regressions using all the agenda and issue variables with a significant bivariate correlation in the entire sample or within one of the three traditions. The results are quite revealing. First, agenda priorities drop out, their effects absorbed by issue preferences in the multivariate analysis, although the coefficients remain close to significance for Evangelicals. Second, the potency of abortion is apparent in all three traditions: most for Evangelicals and Catholics, less for mainliners. Several other measures encourage political relevance among Evangelicals: proximity to African Americans, support for Israel, and sentiments against minority religions. When all else is accounted for, evangelical attitudes on gay rights and feminism do not add any explanatory power. Among mainline Protestants, a mix of issue tendencies predicts political relevance: conservative on abortion and women's rights, but liberal on affirmative action and pro-Israel on Mideast policy. For Catholics, antiabortion and antigay rights attitudes are joined by liberal racial attitudes to produce relevance. As the adjusted R^2 statistics show, all agenda variables in combination explain 13 percent of the variance in the full sample but are more successful among Evangelicals (17 percent), than among Catholics (10 percent) and, especially, among mainliners (only 5 percent).

Thus, the appearance of public policy questions closely connected to religious beliefs, worldviews, and elite emphases do seem to have "educated" at least some Christians to the political relevance of their faith. Most of this education, however, has had a conservative bias. Abortion, above all, has had this impact, but other elements of social traditionalism have contributed. The impact of liberal agenda issues, which might be expected to influence mainliners and Catholics, is much less, with the exception of race, in which liberalism is often associated with relevance, even among Evangelicals. Overall, the "agenda and issues effect" is much stronger among Evangelicals than among their mainline and Catholic brothers and sisters.

Perspective 3: Cognitive Mobilization of Religious Traits

Religious commitments, beliefs, identities, and sentiments toward other groups should also help shape political relevance. Although we are looking only at religious people, we still assume that the level of subjective salience or personal religiosity should have a straightforward influence on political relevance: the stronger the commitment, the greater the politicization (cf. Guth and Green 1993). Religious beliefs should play a major role, especially those that serve to mark off the boundaries of particular religious groups (Kellstedt and Smidt 1993; Jelen, Smidt, and Wilcox 1993). In the present case, we assume that items measuring "evangelical orthodoxy" will be strongly associated with political relevance, given the major efforts by conservative elites to activate such beliefs as "markers" of religious community. Similarly, we anticipate that both evangelical identifications and feelings of proximity to evangelical groups will be conducive to perceptions of political relevance in all religious traditions. Finally, we expect that political relevance will be associated with "foundational" religious views such as individualism and communitarianism. Theoretically, those with communitarian views should perceive more influence of religion on their politics but given the empirical evidence for individualism among evangelical activists, we suspect the real tendency will be in the other direction (Leege and Kellstedt 1993b).

We start with personal religious commitment. Remember that our analysis here is confined to those respondents who say that religion is important in their lives. Nevertheless, the extent of personal commitment is still a powerful influence on political relevance. As table 16.3 shows, both the NES religious guidance item and a personal devotion scale (made up of Bible reading, frequency of prayer, and sharing faith with others) are strongly associated with political relevance, across the full sample and in each Christian tradition (cf. Poloma and Gallup 1991). Once again, the bivariate associations are strongest for Evangelicals, with weaker links among mainliners and, especially, Catholics.

Political relevance is strongly correlated with religious belief as well. In table 16.3 we show that commitment to the inerrancy of scriptural authority, a marker of the conservative Protestant movement, produces higher relevance scores. Once again, the pattern cuts across religious boundaries but the effect is strongest for Evangelicals, weaker for mainliners, and least impressive for Catholics. Similar patterns appear on items on the historicity of Adam and Eve, the Virgin Birth of Jesus, and belief in premillennial doctrines on the End Times (data not shown). On the whole, then, one could summarize that both religious commitment and adherence to what might be called the elements of evangelical orthodoxy are strong predictors of political relevance, even in this disproportionately religious sample.

Basic religiosity and adherence to core beliefs are one measure of commitment to religious communities. Scholars have also argued that conscious commitment to religious movements or "in-group/out-group" assessments might well be associated with political consciousness. In American history, such "negative" and "positive" reference groups have played an important role in creating political alignments, with mainline Protestants gravitating toward the Republicans and Catholics, Jews, and other religious minorities preferring the Democrats. Presumably those believers who consciously identify with their own tradition and vigorously oppose others might be expected to demonstrate greater political relevance. In contemporary American politics, the old hostilities among religious traditions may no longer produce a sense of political relevance among their respective believers, but the new divisions between "orthodox" and "progressive" alliances produced by the "culture wars" may (Hunter 1991). One such in-group identifier may be "born-again" status, which has often been taken by scholars as a key marker of the American religious resurgence. Another example is identification with the several religious movements within the evangelical tradition, which are often seen as carriers of religious reaction to modernity (Wilcox, Jelen, and Leege 1993).

TABLE 16.3
Cognitive Influences on the Political Relevance of Religion by
Religious Tradition

	All Christian (N=2222)		Evangelical (N=936)		Mainline (N=547)		Catholic (N=738)	
	r	beta	r	beta	r	beta	r	beta
Religious Commitment								
Personal Devotion	.40**	.19**	.42**	.23**	.38**	.23	.25**	.10*
Religious Guidance	.35**	.15**	.35**	.11**	.33**	.15**	.30**	.17**
Religious Belief								
Biblical Inerrancy	.31**	.09**	.34**	.14**	.20**	.03	.16**	.04
Religious Identity								
Born-Again Christian	.32**	.07*	.29**	.01	.33**	.13**	.12**	.04
Evangelical Movement	.20**	.03	.21**	.01	.11*	.01	.11*	.05
Religious Proximities								
Close to Evangelicals	.30**	.11**	.31**	.14**	.17**	.05	.22**	.13**
Close to Catholics	.09**	-.02	-.02	-.07*	-.01	-.07	.19**	.08*
Close to Jews	.12**	.02	.17**	.07*	.02	.01	.08*	.02
Individualist Social Theology								
Salvation solves ills	.25**	.09**	.23**	.08*	.16**	.02	.27**	.14**
Church focus on Morals	.15**	.06**	.20**	.09**	.13*	.09*	.03	.01
Adj. R² =	—	.25	—	.28	—	.19	—	.16

* p < .05
**p < .001

In the full sample, self-identification as a born-again Christian is, in fact, associated with political relevance in all three Christian traditions. The relationship is actually a little stronger among mainliners than Evangelicals (who, of course, are more likely to take the label) and weaker, but still significant, among Catholics. The correlations between political relevance and affiliation with the fundamentalist, evangelical, Pentecostal, and charismatic movements are also positive and significant in both the full sample and in most instances in each tradition. (To simplify matters, in table 16.3, we report the correlations between political relevance and a dichotomous measure of movement affiliation: whether the individual identified with at least one of the movements.) The strongest association of affiliation with political relevance appears among Evangelicals and somewhat weaker ones show up in the other two traditions.[1]

The proximity data add interesting nuances to the self-identification information. In the full sample, respondents who feel close to the several religious movements within the Evangelical community are strongly inclined to see political relevance to their faith, as are those who feel close to Jews (once again tapping, no doubt, elements of premillennial and dispensational thought). This influence is, of course, strongest among Evangelicals but appears among Catholics as well. Interestingly, Catholics who feel close to their own church are more likely to see political relevance in their religion, but on the bivariate level proximity (or lack of it) to Catholicism has no major effect among Protestants.

Finally, we looked at "foundational" beliefs, especially the social theologies of individualism and communitarianism, measures of whether faith has primarily individual or social implications (Leege and Kellstedt 1993b). Our first item was a classic statement of Protestant individualist social theology: "If enough people were brought to Christ, social ills would disappear." This traditional evangelical perspective supposedly focuses the religious enterprise on conversion and denigrates collective social action. Another question asked whether the Church should focus on social reform or individual morality, tapping basic orientations toward the role of religious institutions. As table 16.3 shows, political relevance is associated with *individualist* perspectives: that conversion will solve social problems and that the church ought to focus on shaping morality, not social reform. The bivariate correlations are strong for both questions among Evangelicals and mainliners, but the conversionist perspective alone influences Catholics (cf. Leege and Kellstedt 1993b:224). In any case, perceived political relevance of religion is highest among those who see its role in classic individualist terms. This result may seem ironic, but it certainly comports with evidence provided earlier on social and moral traditionalism, both associated with individualist worldviews.

One fascinating pattern in the data is the tendency for aspects of evangelical Protestant theology and practice to influence elements in the mainline and Catholic communities. That many mainline Protestants are really "closet Evangelicals" and behave as such should not be surprising to any observer of American religion, but the frequent utility of "evangelical" items on Bible reading, witnessing, biblical inerrancy, and movement affiliation in distinguishing among Catholics calls to mind the "evangelically oriented Catholicism" discovered by Leege and Welch in the Notre Dame Catholic Parish Study (Welch and Leege 1991). Such Catholics are those most likely to respond to both the conservative cues produced by Christian Right leaders and the Catholic bishops (as on abortion and gay rights) and to some more liberal emphases of the bishops (as on racial justice.)

The multiple regressions allow us to sort out the relative influence of these various cognitive factors. For the full sample, personal devotion retains considerable power, along with religious guidance, belief in biblical inerrancy, born-again identification, proximity to evangelical movements, and individualist social theology. Among Evangelicals, personal devotion, religious guidance, belief in inerrancy, feeling close to evangelical movements, proximity to Jews (but distance from Catholics), and social individualism survive the regression. Among mainliners, many fewer variables shape political relevance, primarily personal commitment and guidance, born-again identity, and preference for a moral focus for the Church. Note, however, that proximity to evangelical movements— and distance from Catholics—almost reaches statistical significance. Among Catholics the religious guidance item is strongest, followed by strong salvationist orientation toward social ills, a feeling of closeness to evangelical movements, and personal devotion.

Our success in accounting for variation in political relevance once again differs by tradition. For the entire sample, cognitive factors explain over a quarter of the variance (25 percent), but more for Evangelicals (28 percent) than for mainliners (19 percent) and Catholics (16 percent). For Evangelicals, strong religious commitment combines with potent theological beliefs and moralistic social theology to produce political relevance. For mainliners and Catholics, personal devotion has the largest impact, along with feelings of identification with or closeness to some element of the evangelical tradition and adherence to individualist social theology. Once again, the combined effects are most powerful among Evangelicals.

Perspective 4: Organizational Mobilization

One of the most consistent findings of the religion and politics literature is that religious organization matters. Indeed, resource mobilization theories of social movements stress organization above all other factors. The literature on the Christian Right, for example, finds the movement based in preexisting religious communities and networks, in churches where clergy and lay activists "talk politics," and among those who pay marked attention to religious media, such as periodicals, religious TV, and religious radio (Wilcox 1992). These organizational contexts work in several ways. Those active in churches most often hear politicizing messages from religious leaders, are most likely to receive cues from other religious sources, including their denominational elites, and are more subject to reciprocal influence by members of their congregations (Wald, Owen, and Hill 1988). We expect, then, that political relevance will be directly related to church involvement, ministerial cue giving, and religious media use. Thus, we can test and perhaps elaborate upon MacIver's (1989) conclusion that organizational mobilization is a vital source of religious politicization. For heuristic purposes, we have divided organizational factors into three categories suggested by the literature: church involvement, ministerial activism, and religious media use. Although the items under each heading are closely related empirically and will later be reduced to single measures, we report each here because of their intrinsic interest.

Not surprisingly, in both the full sample and in each tradition, measures of church involvement have strong connections to political relevance. Frequency of attendance, size of financial contributions, and the proportion of close friends in the congregation all are statistically significant. Again, all the factors are most important among Evangelicals, less so among mainliners, and least useful in predicting Catholic attitudes. If deep personal involvement in religious communities heightens perceptions of the political relevance of religion, we would expect that cues from clergy should do so as well (Welch et al. 1993). And as Table 16.4 shows, political relevance is enhanced when clergy address electoral issues, abortion, and defense issues. But discussion of hunger (and, presumably, other "liberal" issues) seems not to have an effect, except among Evangelicals. All three of the former issues are associated with political relevance among Evangelicals and mainliners, but only election and defense preaching achieve significance among Catholics, although abortion sermons come close. (Almost all religious Catholics report hearing such sermons, so there is little variation on this item.) Thus, both church involvement and receiving political cues from clergy are tied to perceived political relevance.

Finally, we look at religious media use. We need not discuss the extensive literature suggesting that the electronic media has played a formative role in recent religious mobilizations (see Jelen and Wilcox 1993 for a review). Suffice it to say that our evidence supports those theories and suggests that heightened political consciousness was achieved in part through efforts of many evangelical media elites to convince otherworldly and politically passive Evangelicals of their political responsibility. Table 16.4 shows that political relevance is correlated with getting political information from religious periodicals, religious radio, religious TV, the local church, and religious direct mail. The relationships are generally strong, even among mainline Protestants and Catholics, although direct mail drops out of bivariate significance for these groups.

Once again we subject all the organizational mobilization variables to multiple regression. Generally, church involvement and religious media use are most important in raising political consciousness. Among Evan-

TABLE 16.4

Organizational Influences on the Political Relevance of Religion by
Religious Tradition

	All Christian (N = 2222)		Evangelical (N = 936)		Mainline (N = 547)		Catholic (N = 738)	
	r	*beta*	*r*	*beta*	*r*	*beta*	*r*	*beta*
Church Involvement								
Attendance	.31**	.18**	.40**	.22**	.24**	.15**	.21**	.15**
Contributions	.26**	.11**	.28**	.06	.25**	.17**	.12*	.04
Church Friends	.23**	.10**	.32**	.16**	.19**	.07	.17**	.08*
Clerical Activism								
Elections	.21**	.13**	.23**	.12**	.14**	.09	.20**	.13**
Abortion	.16**	.02	.24**	.04	.11*	.01	.07	.01
Defense/Foreign	.13**	.03	.14**	.02	.13**	.04	.12**	.04
Hunger	.04*	-.07**	.13**	-.04	.04	-.07	.00	-.07
Religious Media Use								
Periodicals	.25**	.10**	.27**	.10**	.23**	.13*	.24**	.13**
Religious radio	.25**	.09**	.26**	.12**	.13*	.01	.21**	.09**
Religious TV	.23**	.10**	.21**	.07*	.21**	.13**	.20**	.09*
Local church	.15**	.03	.16**	.03	.12**	.02	.14**	.05
Direct Mail	.08**	-.03	.15**	.01	.04	-.01	.04	-.05
Adj. R² =	—	.21	—	.25	—	.15	—	.14

* p < .05
**p < .001

gelicals, frequency of attendance and number of friends in church predict political relevance, whereas for mainliners commitments of time and money are most important. For Catholics, only church attendance and number of friends in the congregation matter. Religious radio, periodicals, and religious TV all matter for Evangelicals and Catholics, periodicals and TV for mainliners. When all else is accounted for, clergy mobilization is less important: only preaching on electoral matters influences perceptions of political relevance, both in the full sample and among Evangelicals and Catholics, while preaching on hunger issues actually is negatively associated with relevance, once other variables are taken into account. The total impact of organizational variables falls into a familiar pattern: while explaining 21 percent of the variance in the full sample, these items account for 25 percent among Evangelicals, 15 percent among Mainliners, and 14 percent among Catholics.

A Combined Model: Agenda, Cognitive, and Organizational Mobilization

At this point, we combine our models to provide a fuller picture of the causes of political relevance. Preliminary runs revealed that under all circumstances the sociodemographic variables (and many others) dropped out of the analysis. As a result, in table 16.5 we include only variables from the final three theoretical perspectives in the analysis and have omitted several that consistently showed no relationship in either the full sample or any of the three traditions. We have further reduced the number of variables by calculating several indexes and factor scores, following standard procedures. Thus, we convert religious guidance and personal religiosity from table 16.3 into a single religious commitment variable, and the church involvement, clerical activism, and media use variables incorporate the individual items in table 16.4. Although these reductions entail a slight loss of predictive power, the stability of the results and their interpretability are enhanced.[2]

In the full sample, religious commitment, media use, church involvement, proximity to Evangelicals, attitudes on abortion, and individualist social theology show the strongest effects. The pattern varies again by tradition: for Evangelicals, commitment is followed very closely by church involvement, pro-life attitudes, and religious media use as the most important independent factors, with many other items contributing something to explaining relevance. For mainline Protestants, religious commitment is the overwhelming influence, with religious media use and

TABLE 16.5
Combined Model for the Political Relevance of Religion by
Religious Tradition

	All Christian (N=2222)	Evangelical (N=936)	Mainline (N=547)	Catholic (N=738)
		Betas		
Agenda Mobilization				
Abortion policy	.12**	.16**	.01	.16**
Israel	.05*	.04	.11*	.02
Cognitive Mobilization				
Private commitment	.21**	.18**	.31**	.14**
Individualist social theology	.09**	.09*	.08*	.11*
Proximity to:				
Evangelicals	.12**	.09*	.08	.14**
Catholic Church	-.07**	-.06	-.09*	.02
Jews	.02	.09*	-.02	-.03
Organizational Mobilization				
Church involvement	.12**	.16**	.08	.06
Religious media use	.14**	.14**	.13*	.14**
Clerical activism	.07**	.08*	.04	.08*
Adj R^2 =	.30	.36	.21	.20

* $p < .05$
** $p < .001$

religious individualism significant but far behind in impact. For Catholics, pro-life attitudes and religious commitment have the largest impact, followed by elements of "evangelical-style" religiosity: individualism, proximity to Evangelicals, and religious media use. Note that clerical activism is statistically significant in the full sample but falls just short in the subsamples. Given that our study is confined to religious individuals in each tradition, the amount of variance explained is quite impressive—at least for Evangelicals. The model accounts for 30 percent of the variance in the entire sample, but much more among Evangelicals (36 percent) than among mainline Protestants (22 percent), or Catholics (20 percent).

The relatively modest results among mainliners and Catholics led us to consider the possibilities that the demographic traits dismissed earlier might interact with the other factors in producing political relevance. To test this hypothesis, we ran multiple regressions for each religious tradition, divided by education level and gender. Although we cannot report the full results here, they provide some additional insight into the ways these factors have produced political relevance. Among highly educated (at least some college) evangelical men, the belief variables have a very powerful impact and combine with high coefficients for the organizational mobilization factors to produce an explanation for fully 49 percent of the variance in political relevance; for highly educated evangelical women, private devotionalism and church activism alone make substantial contributions, explaining almost 35 percent of the variance (cf. Leege, Wald, and Kellstedt 1993). Obviously, one of the key factors in the successful evangelical political mobilization in recent years has been the recruitment of the growing numbers of well-educated men convinced of the political relevance of their faith.

Among well-educated mainliners and Catholics, as among Evangelicals, our models are much more successful in predicting political relevance scores among men than among women ($r^2 = .36$ versus .20 and .30 versus .23, respectively). For mainline men with high education, only doctrinal measures and religious commitment have any substantial effect; for their female counterparts, private devotionalism and religious media use overwhelm all other variables. For well-educated Catholic men, only abortion and personal commitment are significant, while for similar Catholic women, doctrinal orthodoxy, organizational mobilization, and abortion combine to produce political relevance. The results for respondents with no college education can be discussed more briefly. The amount of political relevance explained is much lower among those with more modest education and also lower among women than men. Even among these respondents, however, we can account for more of the variation in political relevance among Evangelicals: especially among men, levels of political relevance are explained primarily by the abortion issue and the three organizational mobilization factors. Thus, although highly educated evangelical men are in some sense cognitively mobilized by their own beliefs and attitudes, their less educated counterparts have been influenced by organizational involvement and institutional leadership. For less educated mainliners, the modest amounts of political relevance explained are accounted for primarily by private religious commitment and devotionalism. Among less educated Catholics, none of the variables explain a significant amount of the variance among either men or women; the only ones approaching significance are those encapsulated in evangelical-style religiosity.

Discussion and Conclusions

We have shown that a number of factors help explain perceptions that religion is relevant to political decisions. Political relevance is related strongly to religious commitment, evangelical Christian orthodoxy, religious individualism, organizational activity, and religious media use. As we have seen, the relationship between these variables and political relevance is by far strongest in the evangelical community but extends to other Christians as well. In conclusion, we wish to address two further issues raised by these findings. First, what are the attitudinal and behavioral consequences of political relevance? What difference does a high sense of the political relevance of faith make? Second, what accounts for the unusual patterns of relevance and its effects among religious traditions? In other words, why is political relevance so much more difficult to predict among mainline Protestants and Catholics, and why is its impact less evident?

What are the political implications of political relevance? Presumably one of the major empirical effects should be to produce stronger relationships between religious and political variables. In table 16.6, we examine the correlations between religious orthodoxy and political attitudes and behaviors within the three major Christian traditions. We confine our analysis to two groups within each: those who regard religion as politically relevant (scores 1 and 2 on the item) and those who do not (scores 4 and 5), with middle scores omitted for sake of comparison. (Comparing only the extreme categories produces even sharper results but in some cases reduces the number of respondents beyond a social scientist's comfort level.) To eliminate potential confounding effects of sociodemographic variables, we control for education, income, region of residence, age, and gender.

Close perusal of table 16.6 reveals consistent patterns among Evangelicals, but less interpretable ones for mainliners and Catholics. Among Evangelicals, there is a striking tendency for doctrinal orthodoxy to predict conservative political attitudes and behaviors among those who perceive religion as politically relevant. On the other hand, the relationships between orthodoxy and conservatism among those who do not see religion as relevant are confined to some "easy" issues (Carmines and Stimson 1989), in which the direct implications of religious belief may be

TABLE 16.6
Partial Correlations between Orthodoxy and Political Variables by Religious
Tradition and Political Relevance of Religion
(controlling for education, income, region, age and gender)

(N=)	Evangelical Relevant (495)	Not (239)	Mainline Relevant (173)	Not (205)	Catholic Relevant (214)	Not (317)
Issues and Alliances[@]						
Israel	.28**	.20**	.23*	.04	.04	.10
Abortion	.23**	.27**	.34**	.23*	.20*	.11*
Religious minorities	.23**	.01	.24*	.10*	.08	.04
Gay rights	.22**	.21**	.14	.19*	-.04	.16*
Defense spending	.19**	.02	.18*	.03	-.06	-.08
ALCU rating	.18**	.02	.24*	-.03	.04	.03
Women's rights	.17**	.01	.17*	.00	-.15*	.00
Feminists rating	.16**	.10	.19*	.12	.16*	.10
Environmental policy	.12*	-.11	.07	-.05	-.10	.05
National health plan	.10*	-.12	.07	.01	-.03	-.11*
Labor unions rating	.07	-.08	.07	.04	.13*	-.03
Hunger policy	.06	.15	-.03	-.03	-.08	-.06
Affirmative action	.02	.01	.03	.09*	-.12	-.11
Party and Ideology						
GOP House, 1990	.35**	-.13	.21*	.00	.11	.23*
Bush vote, 1988	.23**	-.12	.23*	.09	.00	.04
Bush vote, 1992	.20**	-.05	.10	-.08	.08	-.01
Ideology identification	.19**	.10	.26*	.09	-.05	.07
Party identification	.16**	-.11	.11	.04	-.05	-.03
Bush rating, 1992	.04	.03	.12	.08	.04	.01
Political Activity						
Political activity index	.05	-.18**	-.09	.00	-.03	-.05

[@] All variables are coded so that a positive correlation means a link
between orthodoxy and the conservative position. Negative scores represent
correlations of orthodoxy with liberal choices.
* p < .05
**p < .001

quite obvious to all members of the tradition, such as abortion, gay rights, and support for Israel. On "hard issues," on which the "correct" position may be more difficult to discern, orthodoxy predicts conservatism only among those with high political relevance.

Orthodoxy obviously produces different policy preferences among those who see religion as politically relevant, but it has other important effects on political behavior. Religious orthodoxy produces Republican voting in congressional and presidential elections and Republican identification only among Evangelicals for whom religion is politically relevant; among other Evangelicals, there is actually a slight but consistent tendency for orthodoxy to be correlated with Democratic choices (cf. Kellstedt et al. 1994). Orthodoxy leads to conservative ideological self-identification among both groups of Evangelicals, but the effect is much stronger for those who perceive faith as politically relevant. Finally, there is a slight (if nonsignificant) tendency for orthodoxy to be correlated with political activism among those who see religion as politically relevant. More important, perhaps, is the fact that orthodoxy is strongly linked to political *inactivity* among Evangelicals who do not see the linkage. In summary, then, among Evangelicals, perceptions of political relevance produce much stronger attitudinal constraint across religious/political spheres.

The results for mainline Protestants and especially Catholics are less impressive. For mainliners, orthodoxy does produce more conservative views among those who perceive the political relevance of religion, but the relationships tend to be limited to social issues and proximities and are sometimes slightly weaker than among Evangelicals. The ties of orthodoxy to Republican choices are also slightly weaker, but the link with ideological self-identification is stronger. Among Catholics, however, the patterns are seemingly random; only on abortion, proximity to feminists and to labor unions does orthodoxy produce conservatism among the subjectively relevant. But orthodoxy is tied to *liberal* attitudes toward women's and minority rights among these Catholics and to slight liberal tendencies on other issues such as defense spending, environmental policy, and hunger, which barely miss statistical significance. Conversely, orthodoxy is sometimes related to conservative choices among Catholics for whom religion is not subjectively relevant as well: on gay rights, Republican House voting in 1990, as well as abortion, but also to liberal positions on affirmative action. These results suggest some difficulty for those theorists who see an emerging "alliance of the orthodox" dominating the conservative side of the "culture wars" (Hunter 1991) and for political activists attempting to mobilize orthodox Catholics alongside evangelical Protestants and theologically conservative mainliners (Griffan-Nolan 1995).

Why the difference in the levels of political relevance in the three traditions and the degree to which the same factors explain political relevance? We must admit to some puzzlement here, although the patterns clearly mirror events in the real political world: a massive grassroots mobilization of evangelical Protestants has occurred, which has not been paralleled by similar activation of many Catholics (except for the abortion issue) or mainline Protestants (on any issue). Explanations for the differing perceptions of political relevance may lie in the fact that Evangelicals have simply been subjected to more reinforcing mobilizing influences than those in other traditions: they are especially sensitive to contemporary social issues, they are organizationally committed, and they are exposed to multiple and repeated leadership cues, in ways which mainliners and Catholics are not. But this explanation does not provide the entire answer.

At this point, connecting our analysis with another theme emerging in the contemporary sociology of religion may be useful: the growth of religious privatism. As many scholars have argued, often using different terminology, American religion is increasingly becoming a private, personal affair, which may not really have any systematic, patterned connections with the collective or public realm of social and political discourse. Whether characterized memorably as "Sheilaism" (Bellah et al. 1985), "personal autonomy" (Hammond 1992), or "lay liberalism" (Hoge, Johnson, and Luidens 1994), this religious perspective stresses lack of certainty about religious realities, universalism in belief, tolerance of all perspectives, and minimal commitment to religious community. This worldview, which may well be the dominant one among contemporary mainline Protestants and, perhaps, for the majority of American Catholics, hardly admits of any systematic communal statement of political relevance: religious tenets are purely subjective, are seldom held with any fervor, and do not admit of authoritative interpretation by clergy, congregation, or church. Nor is the objective or psychological commitment to religious institutions very strong: they are purely utilitarian service centers for ethical education for children or for other social needs. Few mainliners or Catholics exhibit the strong commitment to congregations exemplified by Evangelicals (see Olson 1993; for a portrait of one mainline congregation, see Dorsey 1995).

Some admittedly speculative evidence tends to support this argument. We looked at the political relevance scores among our 1992 respondents in what are sometimes thought of as the most "privatized" Protestant churches, namely the liberal Protestant denominations (Episcopalian, United Church of Christ, and similar groups) and nontraditional liberal groups such as the Unitarian-Universalists. If privatization and individuation of religious faith produces lower levels of political relevance, we should find it here. And that is exactly what we do find: among all religious Protestants, adherents of these churches and fellowships express the lowest levels of political relevance, despite the well-advertised political and social liberalism of their clergy and denominational elites. More direct evidence comes from a resurvey of our 1992 respondents that allowed us to test the plausibility of such speculations. In this resurvey, we used some of the same items on "lay liberalism" developed by Hoge, Johnson, and Luidens (1994) in their work on Presbyterians, hoping thereby to determine the political impact of this phenomenon. Not surprisingly, mainliners and Catholics are indeed higher than Evangelicals on lay liberalism; those who score high were also less likely to say that religion influenced their political choices, a tendency that was especially strong among Catholics.

Evangelical congregations and denominations are populated by individuals with lower scores on any privatism index. They still believe in objective religious truth, exclusivist theories of salvation, authoritative interpretations by community leaders, and commitment to institutional religion. On the whole, this portrait is one of a religious tradition that can be mobilized by appeal to shared doctrinal tenets and social beliefs, reached through organizational networks, and shaped into a coherent political movement. In comparison with the increasingly privatized and individualistic (and perhaps marginal) attachments of mainliners and Catholics, religion really matters for many Evangelicals; from there it may be simply a small step to convincing large numbers that it matters politically.

In historical perspective, of course, persuading Evangelicals that faith has implications for politics has been an enormous accomplishment. Since at least the turn of this century, Evangelicals have been tagged by Martin Marty's famous label as the "private party" in American Protestantism, devoted to personal piety while rejecting political engagement, in contrast to the mainline "public party," whose faith had obvious political relevance. The evidence presented here complements that of recent political events in demonstrating that the roles are now reversed: evangelical Protestantism, in both action and belief, represents a large proportion of those white Americans who join their African-American brothers and sisters in seeing that faith ought to inform political choices and identifications. That this is so helps explain their enormous recent impact on party alignments and electoral outcomes (cf. Kellstedt et al. 1994).

We conclude with a conceptual issue: Has the evidence here confirmed the utility of a political relevance question in surveys dealing with religion and politics? We can offer a guarded yes to that question. Certainly, those who are conscious of a connection between their religious faith and the political world do (at least among Protestants) seem to exhibit much greater ideological constraint across religious and political realms. As our data suggest, positive responses to this question tend to identify those most attached to the religious tenets of their faith, most attentive to events in the political world impinging on that faith, most involved in its institutions, and most subject to its cues. Our more modest success with mainline Protestants and Catholics may reflect the contemporary religious status of those communities, as argued here, or may in part be an artifact of inadequate measures of the religious variables relevant to those traditions. In any event, we strongly suspect that the religious relevance question does tap the relative extent of political mobilization within religious communities and identifies those whom religion has mobilized politically.

Notes

1. The proportion of religious people in each tradition who identify as born-again Christians varies, of course, from 71 percent in the evangelical tradition, to 37 percent among mainline Protestants and 11 percent among Catholics. Similarly, the number affiliating with predominantly evangelical movements also differs: Pentecostal (14 percent, 5 percent and 3 percent); charismatic (11 percent, 7 percent and 12 percent); fundamentalist (20 percent, 10 percent, and 8 percent), and evangelical (20 percent, 20 percent and 6 percent). In all, 55 percent of those in the evangelical tradition identify themselves with at least one of the four movements, as do 35 percent of mainliners and 25 percent of Catholics. And summing it all up: 82 percent of Evangelicals, 55 percent of mainline Protestants, and 31 percent of Catholics are born-again, identify with at least one of the four movements, or both. Thus, the mainline Protestant and Catholic traditions have substantial groups of religious members who identify with Evangelical labels and movements.

2. The combined variables were produced by standard procedures, most often as simple additive indices or as factor scores from a principal components analysis. In the latter instance, we used mean substitution for missing values, a conservative procedure that tends to reduce somewhat the coefficients and the amount of variance explained. The reliability coefficients for our combined variables (for "religious" members of the three traditions only) are as follows:

religious commitment (theta = .71), church involvement (theta = .57), clerical activism (alpha = .57), and religious media use (alpha = .62).

References

Bellah, Robert N., Richard Madsen, William M. Sullivan, Ann Swidler, and Steven M. Tipton. 1985. *Habits of the Heart: Individualism and Commitment in American Life.* Berkeley: University of California Press.

Boyer, Paul. 1992. *When Time Shall Be No More.* Cambridge, Mass.: Harvard University Press.

Bruce, Steve. 1988. *The Rise and Fall of the New Christian Right.* Oxford: Oxford University Press.

Carmines, Edward G., and James A. Stimson. 1989. *Issue Evolution: Race and the Transformation of American Politics.* Princeton, N.J.: Princeton University Press.

Dorsey, Gary. 1995. *Congregation.* New York: Viking.

Findlay, James F., Jr. 1993. *Church People in the Struggle.* New York: Oxford University Press.

Fowler, Robert Booth. 1995. *The Greening of Protestantism.* Chapel Hill: University of North Carolina Press.

Griffin-Nolan, ed. 1995. "Coalition Fishing for 'Pro-Family' Catholics." *National Catholic Reporter* October 27:5.

Guth, James L., and Cleveland R. Fraser. 1993. "Religion and Foreign Policy Attitudes: The Case of Christian Zionism." Paper presented at the annual meeting of the American Political Science Association, Washington, D.C.

Guth, James L., and John C. Green. 1993. "Salience: The Core Concept?" In *Rediscovering the Religious Factor in American Politics,* ed. David C. Leege and Lyman A. Kellstedt. Armonk, N.Y.: Sharpe.

Hammond, Phillip E. 1992. *Religion and Personal Autonomy: The Third Disestablishment in America.* Columbia: University of South Carolina Press.

Hawley, John Stratton. 1994. *Fundamentalism and Gender.* New York: Oxford University Press.

Hoge, Dean R., Benton Johnson, and Donald A. Luidens. 1994. *Vanishing Boundaries: The Religion of Mainline Protestant Baby Boomers.* Louisville, Ky.: Westminster/John Knox Press.

Hunter, James D. 1991. *Culture Wars.* New York: Basic.

Jelen, Ted G. 1991. *The Political Mobilization of Religious Beliefs.* New York: Praeger.

Jelen, Ted G., Corwin E. Smidt, and Clyde Wilcox. 1993. "The Political Effects of the Born-Again Phenomenon." In *Rediscovering the Religious Factor in American Politics,* ed. David C. Leege and Lyman A. Kellstedt. Armonk, N.Y.: Sharpe.

Jelen, Ted G., and Clyde Wilcox. 1993. "Preaching to the Converted: The Causes and Consequences of Watching Religious Television." In *Rediscovering the Religious Factor in American Politics*, ed. David C. Leege and Lyman A. Kellstedt. Armonk, N.Y.: Sharpe.

Kellstedt, Lyman A., and John C. Green. 1993. "Knowing God's Many People: Denominational Preferences and Political Behavior." In *Rediscovering the Religious Factor in American Politics*, ed. David C. Leege and Lyman A. Kellstedt. Armonk, N.Y.: Sharpe.

Kellstedt, Lyman A., John C. Green, James L. Guth, and Corwin E. Smidt. 1994. "Religious Voting Blocs in the 1992 Elections: The Year of the Evangelical?" *Sociology of Religion* 55:307–26.

Kellstedt, Lyman A., and Corwin E. Smidt. 1993. "Doctrinal Beliefs and Political Behavior." In *Rediscovering the Religious Factor in American Politics*, ed. David C. Leege and Lyman A. Kellstedt. Armonk, N.Y.: Sharpe.

Kepel, Gilles. 1994. *The Revenge of God*. University Park: Pennsylvania State University Press.

Leege, David C. 1993. "The Decomposition of the Religious Vote." Paper presented at the annual meeting of the American Political Science Association, Washington, D.C.

Leege, David C., and Lyman A. Kellstedt, ed. 1993a. *Rediscovering the Religions Factor in American Politics*. Armonk, N.Y.: Sharpe.

———. 1993b. "Religious Worldviews and Political Philosophies." In *Rediscovering the Religious Factor in American Politics*, ed. David C. Leege and Lyman A. Kellstedt. Armonk, N.Y.: M.E. Sharpe.

Leege, David C., Kenneth D. Wald, and Lyman A. Kellstedt. 1993. "The Public Dimension of Private Devotionalism." In *Rediscovering the Religious Factor in American Politics*, ed. David C. Leege and Lyman A. Kellstedt. Armonk, N.Y.: Sharpe.

MacIver, Martha Abele. 1989. "Religious Politicization among Western European Mass Publics." In *Religious Politics in Global and Comparative Perspective*, ed. William H. Swatos, Jr. Westport, Conn.: Greenwood.

Morgan, Timothy C. 1994. "NAE Reinvents Itself." *Christianity Today* April 4: 87.

Olson, Daniel V. A. 1993. "Fellowship Ties and the Traumas of Religious Identity." In *Beyond Establishment: Protestant Identity in a Post-Protestant Age*, ed. Jackson Carroll and Wade Clark Roof. Louisville, Ky.: Westminster/ John Knox Press.

Patterson, James, and Peter Kim. 1991. *The Day America Told the Truth*. Englewood Cliffs, N.J.: Prentice Hall.

Poloma, Margaret M., and George H. Gallup, Jr. 1991. *Varieties of Prayer*. Philadelphia: Trinity Press International.

Rosenberg, Ellen. 1989. *The Southern Baptists: A Subculture in Transition*. Knoxville: University of Tennessee Press.

Rothenberg, Stuart, and Frank Newport. 1984. The *Evangelical Voter*. Washington, D.C.: Free Congress Research and Education Foundation.

Verba, Sidney, Kay Schlozman, and Henry Brady. 1995. *Voice and Equality: Civic Voluntarism in American Politics.* Cambridge: Harvard University Press.

Wald, Kenneth D., Dennis E. Owen, and Samuel S. Hill, Jr. 1988. "Churches as Political Communities." *American Political Science Review* 82:531–48.

Welch, Michael R., David C. Leege, Kenneth D. Wald, and Lyman A. Kellstedt. 1993, "Are the Sheep Hearing the Shepherds?" In *Rediscovering the Religious Factor in American Politics,* ed. David C. Leege and Lyman A. Kellstedt. Armonk, N.Y.: Sharpe.

Welch, Michael R., and David C. Leege. 1991. "Dual Reference Groups and Political Orientations: An Examination of Evangelically Oriented Catholics." *American Journal of Political Science* 35:28–56.

Wilcox, Clyde. 1992. *God's Warriors: The Christian Right in Twentieth-Century America.* Baltimore: Johns Hopkins University Press.

Wilcox, Clyde, Ted J. Jelen, and David C. Leege. 1993. "Religious Group Identifications: Toward a Cognitive Theory of Religious Mobilization." In *Rediscovering the Religious Factor in American Politics,* ed. David C. Leege and Lyman A. Kellstedt. Armonk, N.Y.: Sharpe.

17

Religion and Foreign Policy Attitudes: The Case of Christian Zionism

James L. Guth
Cleveland R. Fraser
John C. Green
Lyman A. Kellstedt
Corwin E. Smidt

One of the most fascinating tasks confronting the analyst of American foreign policy is attempting to illuminate the characteristics of public opinion on international issues and its influence on the policy-making process. Since World War II, the conventional wisdom, couched in the "Almond-Lippmann consensus" (Holsti 1992), held that most Americans were uninterested in and ill informed about international events, that their orientation toward particular countries and issues lacked coherence and stability, and, therefore, that public opinion exerted little, if any, impact on the president and his foreign policy advisers in their pursuit of American interests.

Although much evidence suggests that the American public's interest in foreign affairs has not grown significantly (but see Aldrich, Sullivan and Borgida 1989), intriguing recent discoveries indicate that public attitudes on specific policy issues are determined by identifiable, and structured beliefs that are relatively stable over time. In studies of the mass public (Peffley and Hurwitz 1993), elites (Chittick and Billingsley 1989; Holsti and Rosenau 1990), and masses and elites (Wittkopf 1990; Chittick, Billingsley, and Travis 1995), analysts have uncovered rather complex attitude structures that provide heuristic frameworks for individuals to be the "cognitive misers" scholars have portrayed them to be. For example, in careful analyses of the quadrennial surveys of the mass public and elites by the Chicago Council on Foreign Relations, Wittkopf (1990) found that Americans organize their attitudes around two major dimensions: militant internationalism (MI) and cooperative internationalism (CI). Taking a slightly different approach and focusing solely on the mass public, Peffley and Hurwitz (1993) argue that individuals derive specific opinions from two general foreign policy "postures," militarism and containment. Finally, a recent article by Chittick, Billingsley, and Travis (1995) makes the case that masses and elites organize their opinions along three dimensions: identity, security, and prosperity. Thus, although the exact structure of foreign policy beliefs remains open to further debate, it is clear that many Americans are quite capable of forming distinct opinions on specific issues without relying on State Department memoranda, the *New York Times*, or marathon sessions with CNN or C-SPAN.

In this chapter we suggest that scholars need to consider another variable in their efforts to locate the determinants of foreign policy attitudes, one that has received little attention in foreign policy opinion studies: religion. Although recent intellectual advances in the measurement of religious variables have provided additional insight into problems of attitude formation, vote choice, and party alignments in domestic politics (Leege and Kellstedt 1993), researchers have made few efforts to connect religious variables with public attitudes on foreign affairs (but see Hero 1973) and even fewer using sophisticated religious measures (a notable exception is Jelen 1992). Still, there are hints that more careful measurement of the varied facets of religion might bear scholarly fruit. For example, clear evidence suggests that religion structured Cold War attitudes, with both fundamentalist doctrine and high religious commitment prompting citizens to hold anti-Soviet attitudes and support greater defense spending (Guth and Green 1993; cf. Wittkopf 1990:43–44; Hurwitz, Peffley, and Seligson 1993). Religiosity among American Catholics seems to have abetted the growth of anti-communist attitudes early in the Cold War era but reversed the effect during the 1980s, with the issuance of the Catholic bishops' letter on nuclear war (Wald 1992). Systematic efforts to connect religious worldviews with stances on either specific policies or the larger dimensions of public attitudes have been constrained, however, by the paucity of surveys with both sophisticated religious items and more than one or two foreign policy questions. Thus, the analysis of religion and foreign policy attitudes is in its infancy.

This chapter illustrates the payoff that careful employment of precise religious measures can have for students of public and elite opinion on a matter that has repeatedly preoccupied American foreign policy makers since World War II: the Middle East. We can offer at least two arguments for our specific research focus. In a recent discussion of American policy options in the wake of the Gulf War, Lewis (1992:108) notes that the United States was now the sole "predominant outside power" in the Middle East, and that "[t]oday the only serious restraint on the American administration is American public opinion." If so, it is imperative to understand the forces that shape that opinion. And that opinion may not conform to any of the established "dimensions." As Holsti (1992:450) has argued:

> [T]here is indeed rather persuasive evidence that attitudes toward some rather important issues cut across the main dimensions identified above. Trade and protectionism, an issue that is likely to become more rather than less contentious during the 1990s, is one such example; *questions revolving around Israel and American policy toward that nation appear to form another cluster of attitudes that does not fit neatly into the MI/CI scheme.* (emphasis added)

Thus, both the potential impact of public opinion on Mideast policy and the difficulty of explaining its origins justify our effort.

Public Support for Israel in the United States

One of the constants of the post–World War II period has been the staunch support that the United States has provided for the state of Israel (Curtiss 1986, appendix; Gilboa 1987), a policy rooted in relatively stable and long-term public backing for Israel in this country. A comprehensive survey over a fifty-year period has noted that "United States public opinion about the Middle East has followed a generally stable pattern of support for Israel but reluctance to get directly involved in conflict. Within this basic framework, opinions have changed somewhat in response to major events like wars and peacemaking attempts and the Palestinian uprising" (Page and Shapiro 1992:251). From the end of World War II to the late 1970s, a persistently high level of public support for Israel was the rule (Gilboa 1987). Since the early 1980s, the rapid ebb and flow of regional conflict and cooperation has been reflected in more volatile attitudes. Recent Gallup poll data reveal that support for Israel peaked in February 1991, when Iraqi Scud missiles were raining down on Israeli territory and the Israelis were exhibiting remarkable self-restraint in not retaliating. During this period, fully 79 percent of Americans held a mostly favorable or very favorable opinion of Israel; only 13 percent reported unfavorable opinions. This was a thirty-one-point improvement over October 1990, when only 48 percent of the sample was favorably disposed and 39 percent was not. By September 1991, when President Bush was feuding with the Israeli government over a $10 billion loan guarantee, a bare majority of Americans (56 percent) held positive views of Israel, with 34 percent giving unfavorable ratings. Indeed, by that time a large proportion of Americans (between 70–73 percent) favored the "land for peace" option (Hugick 1991b:6), and slightly more Americans felt closer to the Palestinians than to the Israelis (Hugick 1991a:28).

These trends also appear in the most recent (1994) Chicago Council on Foreign Relations survey. Conducted between October and December, 1994, the poll reveals a decline in various aspects of public support for Israel. As expressed on a "feeling thermometer" ranging from 0 to 100 degrees, Israel's rating is 54, equal to those of Russia and Brazil, lower than those of Germany and Mexico (57) and France (56), and only slightly higher than the ratings of Japan (53), Poland and South Africa (both 52) (Rielly 1995:22). This rather cool reading marked a seven-point drop since 1978. In the same vein, perceptions of Israel as a vital U.S. interest declined from 76 percent in 1986 to 67 percent in 1990 (Rielly 1991:23). In 1994, the proportion of the American public defining Israel as a primary interest declined again, to 64 percent. In contrast, the percentage of the leadership sample responding positively to this item rose from 78 percent in 1990 to 86 percent in 1994 (Rielly 1995: 20, 26). A majority (50 percent) of the elite sample and 44 percent of the mass sample also favored reducing or eliminating economic assistance. Interestingly, one area in which the American public dramatically reversed its trend of reduced support for Israel was on sending U.S. forces "if Arab forces invaded Israel." When asked in 1986, only 32 percent expressed willingness to go to the defense of Israel; by 1990, this figure had leaped to 43 percent, with an identical number opposed (Rielly 1991:21–24). Significantly these numbers did not change in the 1994 survey (Rielly 1995:26). Thus, while American public support for Israel remains fairly high, the public appears increasingly split over the extent of American commitments.

It is noteworthy, in the wake of recent historic events in the Middle East, such as the 1993 and 1995 Israeli-Palestinian agreements, and the November 4, 1995, assassination of Israeli Prime Minister Yitzhak Rabin, that the general orientations of the American public identified here have not appreciably changed. Indeed, other foreign policy issues, most notably U.S. participation in the Bosnian crisis, have moved Israel "off the scope" of pollsters and the American public. A series of NBC–*Wall Street Journal* polls illustrate this point. Asked to identify "the most serious foreign policy issue facing the United States today" in December 1993, only 12 percent of the public named relations between Israel and the Arab nations; a year later, this figure was only slightly higher at 16 percent (*National Journal* 1995:130). When the same question was asked at approximately the mid-point of this period (July 1994), only 8 percent considered Arab-Israeli relations to be a "front-burner" issue (Bowan and Ladd 1994:107.)

Religion and Public Attitudes Toward Israel

The American alliance with Israel has, of course, often been linked to strong support for Israel from the American Jewish community. Relatively little attention, however, has been paid to the ways theological perspectives in other faith communities have shaped Americans' attitudes. During most of this period, only the broadest religious categories (such as "Protestant, Catholic, or Jew") were available for analyzing differences in policy views. In a study of public opinion from 1945 to 1967, Hero (1973:77–78) found no significant gap between the positive attitudes of Catholics and Protestants toward Israel, although Protestants tended to be a bit warmer. This trend persisted in the two decades after the Six Day War in 1967 (Gilboa 1987:292). And little has changed in more recent studies. Gallup surveys for March and August of 1991 indicate that support for Israel among Protestants and Catholics is fairly high and that, on the whole, there is little difference between these two Christian communities (Gallup Poll 1991:40; Hugick 1991a:29, 32).

Of course, these crude measures may hide important differences within these religious categories, especially among "Protestants." As Stark and Glock (1968:56) noted long ago, "[W]hen we speak of Protestants, as we so often do in the social sciences, we spin statistical fiction." A few more specialized or local studies of opinion have sought to do better, suggesting that various doctrinal, social, or behavioral facets of religion may influence attitudes more than being "Protestant, Catholic, or Jew." In a study of rural residents in Wyoming during the 1973 Yom Kippur War, Griffin, Martin, and Walter (1976:107) discovered a strong positive relationship between "religious orthodoxy and the belief that the present state of Israel represents fulfillment of Biblical prophecy," but failed to find a significant relationship between either orthodoxy or church membership, on the one hand, and stances relating to U.S. economic aid, military assistance, or sending U.S. troops to Israel's defense, on the other. A few specialized studies have hinted that church attendance, doctrinal orthodoxy, or other religious factors may influence American Christians' attitudes toward Israel (cf. Stockton 1987).

During the 1980s, several scholars (Mouley 1982; Reich 1984: 204–6; and Curtiss 1986) and journalists (Blitzer 1985:193–201; Halsell 1986; Mojtabai 1986) have noted the strong support that Israel has received from one specific religious group: Protestant evangelicals. Perhaps the most visible support has come from Christian Right leaders, such as Jerry Falwell, speaking for many fundamentalists, and Pat Robertson, with his Pentecostal and charismatic constituency (Mouley 1982; Lienesch 1993:223–46). Although Israeli officials and Jewish leaders in the United States were initially quite suspicious of such professions of friendship, in some instances the Christian Right's stance has been acknowledged and appreciated (Simon 1984). Indeed, historian Marsden (1991:77) has argued that "although impossible to measure, perhaps evangelicalism's greatest political impact on American policy during the past fifty years has been its role in broadening the popular base for an almost unreserved support for the state of Israel." In fact, elite support for Israel in evangelical Protestant circles has become the subject of considerable intramural debate within that community. Still, the phenomenon of Christian Zionism is really nothing new, despite its seemingly recent discovery (see Stockton 1987, and Wagner 1992, for excellent summaries). It is embedded deeply in a powerful theological current that has had a profound impact on American evangelicalism: dispensationalism (Marsden 1980; Weber 1987).

Dispensationalism is a special variant of Christian premillennialism, which arose out of the ideas of Irish cleric John Nelson Darby (1800–1882), who argued that human history was divided into seven dispensations, eras in which God related to humans in different ways. This classification assisted Darby and others in accounting for the apparent variations in the portraits of God presented in the Scriptures and also helped to explain (and predict) developments in the world. For our purposes, the relevant ideas concern the last dispensation before the End Times, that of the Church. Like other variants of Protestant premillennialism, dispensationalism held a fundamentally pessimistic view of human society. According to its understanding of Scripture, the human race would become worse and worse as the time for Christ's second coming drew near. The postmillennial optimism held by many American Protestants in the 1800s—that Christian missions and social reform ventures could bring in the Kingdom of God—was rejected by dispensationalists as scripturally unsound and empirically untrue. Things would deteriorate until Christ returned for his church and took it out of this world ("the Rapture"), while on earth events quickly moved to the cataclysmic Battle of Armageddon foretold in the Book of Revelation, a core text for dispensationalists. Thus, eschatology (the doctrine of the "last things") was central to this theology.

Where does Israel enter the picture, other than as a site for the final battle? For most of the great expounders of dispensationalism, including Darby himself, the return of Jews to Palestine was a mark of the approach of Christ's return. Indeed, events leading to the establishment of the state of Israel in 1948 provided an enormous fillip to dispensationalist movements in American Protestantism (Fishman 1973; Weber 1987). But the Jews are not just a "leading indicator" of the End Times; they play an essential part in the events of that time. For the dispensationalists, unlike many Christian "supercessionists" (who saw the Church replacing Israel in God's redemptive plan), the Jews had always remained God's people, despite their rejection of Christ, and would in the End Times be restored to the land that God had promised them and would acknowledge Christ as Messiah at his Second Coming. Although there are many variations on this scenario, anyone spending time in a dispensational church can attest to the frequent, and powerful expression of these ideas and the fascination of dispensationalists with the state of Israel. Indeed, it is not too much to say that dispensationalism became the core of premillennialist thinking in a broad swath of the American evangelical community and that it is often difficult today to distinguish it from other brands of premillennialism (Weber 1987:11–12; Lienesch 1993:224–25).

As Boyer (1992) has demonstrated in convincing detail, these "prophetic" ideas have diffused widely into American popular culture, spreading far beyond their original conservative Protestant home. Consider only the best-selling book in America during the 1970s, Lindsey's (1970) *The Late, Great Planet Earth,* which in several editions and millions of copies introduced these theories to the larger religious public. As Weber (1987) has noted, central dispensationalist concepts have been adopted by many traditionalists in conservative Protestant churches and have influenced many mainline Protestant laity and even Catholics. The sky-rocketing sales of eschatological tracts during the Persian Gulf War and after Prime Minister Rabin's assassination confirm that there is a broad and continuing market for these ideas (Jorstad 1993:147; Scott 1995:B6). Thus, we might expect that support for Israel among Americans, both elites and mass public, would also be shaped by these theological perspectives.

Of course, doctrinal beliefs inculcated by generations of dispensationalist preaching are often activated and reinforced by the outspoken public support for Israel from prominent evangelical leaders. These public cues should be matched on the other side, however, by the visible stances increasingly adopted by mainline Protestant and Catholic officials, much more critical of Israel and increasingly supportive of Palestinian and Arab interests in the Middle East. Not only does Israel lack a preferred position in the theologies of these traditions, but the "liberation theology" and "social justice" emphases dominant among mainline Protestant and Catholic elites may actually produce greater sympathy for oppressed Palestinians. Indeed, the public statements and organizational activities of the National Council of Churches and most mainline Protestant denominations have reflected much less support for Israeli policies in the 1980s and 1990s (Kimball 1990). We would expect to see these actions affecting the views held by mainline clergy and lay activists but also to be reflected in these churches' lay membership. And, based on some poll data (and the absence of strong religious incentives or cues to support Israel), we expect secular citizens to be even more critical, when all other factors are taken into account.

Data and Methods

To examine the impact of religious variables on attitudes toward Israel, we draw on four surveys of clergy, religious activists, political party contributors, and the mass public. Fortunately, all have both detailed religious queries and items on Middle East policy. In the clergy, religious activist, and mass public studies, we have one or more specific theological items tapping dispensationalism directly. And although in the party activist studies we cannot identify exactly those holding specific dispensational or premillennial theologies, we have useful proxy measures.

In our analysis, we have sought to produce comparable analytic categories in each sample. Our general approach is as follows. First, we allocate our respondents into *religious traditions*, combinations of denominations and churches that represent broadly shared theological perspectives and historical experience. Here we follow our previous approach (Kellstedt and Green 1993), distinguishing several major American traditions on which we will focus our attention: evangelical Protestant, mainline Protestant, Catholics, and seculars. Where data are available and reliable, we will comment on other, smaller traditions as well. If religious tradition makes a difference in Americans' attitudes toward Israel, we expect that evangelical Protestants should be most supportive, mainline Protestants less supportive (and not too different from Catholics), with secular citizens likely to favor an "even-handed" or even pro-Arab position.

Although religious tradition should be helpful in analyzing support for Israel, there are enormous variations in theological perspectives within each tradition. For example, although Evangelicalism has been most strongly influenced by dispensationalism, some of its "subtraditions" have not. Similarly, while virtually all mainline Protestant churches officially reject dispensational notions, some clergy and many laity do not. Thus, our second religious variable is *dispensationalism*. Although we will not be able to make fine distinctions within the "premillennial/dispensational complex," if these ideas are correlated with support for Israel, both across and within religious traditions, then we have made an important discovery. Of course, these are not the only religious variables of possible interest to the student of foreign policy attitudes. In some surveys, we have additional measures of religious orientation. Given our desire for both parsimony and comparability across samples, we cannot incorporate all these in the analysis, but we will comment at points about promising leads for more detailed analysis and future research derived from such experimentation.

We will proceed as follows: First, we look at relationships between religious tradition, eschatology, and Christian Zionism among religious professionals (i.e., Protestant clergy). We should find a strong relationship here, given the attitude constraint typical of clergy (Hadden 1969; Quinley 1974; Guth et al. 1991). Next, we review the same variables among contemporary religious activists in politics, both clergy and laity, ranging theologically from fundamentalist to liberal. Among these politically conscious believers we should see the same patterns, perhaps less well-defined among the laity than among the clergy. Then we turn to a survey of political party activists, conducted in 1986–88, which provides a somewhat sterner test of the hypotheses, given that religious ideology is not always central to these activists. Finally, we undertake the hardest test of all, the mass public, with its notorious lack of attitudinal constraint and prolific "nonattitudes." If dispensational notions predict warmth toward Israel in the mass public, we have considerable confidence that Christian Zionism is an important contributor to pro-Israel attitudes.

To focus our attention on the key variables of religious tradition and dispensationalism, we use multiple classification analysis (MCA). In all instances, the analysis is restricted to whites: religious affiliation and beliefs often have strikingly different political meanings in minority traditions. We also control for the demographic and political variables that predict support for Israel in earlier studies. Gilboa (1987) reports that education, age, partisanship, and ideology are important correlates of pro-Israel attitudes. Americans who are young, well educated, and (after the 1970s) Republican and conservative are more supportive of Israel. Of these, Gilboa argues that education (and related status measures) are most powerful, although he reports no multivariate analyses. In any case, we have included these variables as simultaneous controls (covariates) in each analysis. As we report later, these variables often have little impact when included with precise religious measures in multivariate analyses.

Clergy, Activist Laity, and Christian Zionism

The importance of clergy to the acquisition of religiously linked attitudes is obvious. These professionals not only are key agents in religious socialization but help connect the normative ideas of their tradition to assessment of people and events in the political world (Hadden 1969; Quinley 1974; Guth et al. 1991). In addition, clergy may be key actors in the mobilization of religious movements in politics. They also exhibit highly constrained worldviews, combining theological, social and political ideas in a coherent ideological form. Thus, if religious tradition and dispensationalism have clear effects, these should be most evident among clergy. Here we use surveys of Protestant ministers in five major denominations, coordinated by one of the authors in 1988–89 (for details, see Guth et al. 1991). These surveys included a question on Mideast policy and detailed theological batteries.

The few previous studies of clergy attitudes on foreign policy usually found "complex patterns of responses" (Holsti and Rosenau 1984:149), a complexity that is largely an artifact of considering clergy as a single elite, without differentiation by religious tradition or theological perspective. We have aligned denominations in table 17.1 in two ways: First, we divide them into religious traditions, with the Assemblies of God (AOG) and Southern Baptists (SBC) in the *evangelical Protestant* tradition, and the United Methodists (UMC), Disciples of Christ (DOC), and Presbyterian Church in the U.S.A. (PCUSA) in the *mainline Protestant* camp (Kellstedt and Green 1993). Second, the order reflects the degree to which each has been influenced by dispensationalism and other

TABLE 17.1
Protestant Clergy's Support for Israel by Denomination and
Dispensationalism With Party Identification, Ideology, Age, and Education
Controlled Multiple Classification Analysis

Question: "A lasting peace in the Middle East will require Israel to recognize
some kind of Palestinian State."
[1 = Strongly Disagree, 5 = Strongly Agree. Grand Mean = 3.67]

	(N)	Unadjusted Mean Scores		Adjusted for Independent Variables		Adjusted for Independent and Covariables	
		Mean	Beta	Mean	Beta	Mean	Beta
Religious Tradition							
Evangelical							
Assemblies of God	(653)	2.80		3.13		3.28	
Southern Baptist	(711)	3.33		3.50		3.61	
Mainline							
United Methodist	(694)	3.89		3.81		3.76	
Disciples of Christ	(711)	4.06		3.89		3.77	
Presbyterian USA	(739)	4.19		3.97		3.89	
			.48*		.29*		.20*
Dispensationalism							
Very high	(419)	2.83		3.15		3.40	
High	(748)	3.10		3.39		3.57	
Moderate	(416)	3.56		3.56		3.68	
Low	(932)	3.96		3.80		3.72	
Very Low	(991)	4.22		4.03		3.81	
			.49*		.29*		.13*
Multiple R					.526		.562
Multiple R-Squared					.276		.316

* p< .001

Source: 1988 Clergy Surveys, conducted by James L. Guth, Helen Lee Turner,
John C. Green, and Margaret M. Poloma (see Guth et al. 1991).

premillennial theologies. Pentecostal and charismatic denominations are quite thoroughly rooted in dispensationalist theology, although they have modified the doctrine to remove many anti-Pentecostal elements stressed by fundamentalists (Blumhofer 1993:16–17). The Southern Baptist Convention has recently been captured by fundamentalist forces, among whom strict dispensationalists and other premillennialists are quite numerous, if not dominant (Turner and Guth 1989). Among mainline churches, United Methodists have at times been swayed by premillennial ideologies, while the Disciples of Christ and Presbyterians come from traditions where premillennialism and, especially, dispensationalism was early and forcibly rejected by the dominant elites—if not by all clergy and laity (Guth and Turner 1991). This denominational alignment, of course, also has a broader theological content, moving from theological traditionalism or orthodoxy to more liberal theologies. Thus, a finding that Assemblies clergy were more sympathetic to Israel than Presbyterians might reflect theological differences other than eschatology, such as orthodoxy—or perhaps the attention paid by clergy to authoritative or prominent spokespersons representing their denomination or religious tradition. To determine whether or not eschatology has an independent role, we construct our dispensationalism measure. In these surveys, three common questions tap core ideas of dispensational premillennialism: the inerrancy of Scripture, acceptance of a premillennial interpretation of Scripture, and adherence to dispensational ideas. We combined these items into an index and recoded it into five categories, ranging from the strongest dispensationalist to the completely nonpremillennial (see the appendix for wording and reliability). If Christian Zionism is a factor among clergy, support for Israel will vary directly with this index.

Our dependent variable is an item asking about the desirability of Israel accepting a Palestinian state. As the mean scores in table 17.1 reveal, both denominational affiliation and eschatology have effects. Assemblies pastors are most likely to reject a Palestinian state, followed by Southern Baptists, Methodists, and Disciples of Christ, with Presbyterian ministers most inclined to support the Palestinians. Within each denomination, ministers high on premillennial eschatology are closer to the Israeli position; those low on this scale are more pro-Palestinian, although premillennialism is more prevalent, of course, among Evangelicals. The differences are greatest among Southern Baptists, who have large numbers of clergy in each theological category. The MCA shows that denomination is seemingly more powerful when all variables including age, education, ideology, and party are taken into account. The covariates are all significant predictors but in this sample do not always run in the same direction as in recent mass public surveys. Support for Israel is *lower* among younger and better-educated clergy (especially among those with extended seminary training), although Republicans and conservatives do take the expected pro-Israeli stance. Most covariates have only minor effects, except for ideology, which accounts for somewhat less variance than dispensationalism (data not shown). As the multiple R^2 demonstrates, religious measures account for the lion's share of variance, with all six variables explaining a very respectable 31.6 percent.

We can confirm and elaborate on this pattern with data from the Wheaton Religious Activist Study. This 1990 survey of religious activists from eight political interest groups elicited almost five thousand responses, including those of one thousand pastors. Some of these are mainline Protestants and Catholics, but most are evangelical Protestants, which permits us a more detailed look at this diverse tradition (for details, see Guth et al. 1993). We asked respondents how close they felt to the state of Israel. Table 17.2 has the results for clergy, divided by religious tradition and dispensationalism (see the appendix for construction of the dispensationalism index used in tables 17.2–17.4). Not surprisingly, evangelical clergy feel closer to Israel than do mainline Protestants or Catholics, who are almost identical in their scores. Once again, in all three traditions, dispensationalists are significantly closer to Israel. And across this predominantly evangelical sample, eschatology is again the best predictor. Republican identification and conservative ideology are also associated with support for Israel but have only minor effects when entered simultaneously with religious tradition and dispensationalism. Neither age nor education has any significant effect when other variables are controlled. This probably reflects the nature of the sample, which includes primarily well-educated clergy from all traditions, with relatively few of the "called" ministers without seminary training, who are quite numerous in the AOG and Southern Baptist surveys discussed earlier. Nevertheless, the results are consistent with those in table 17.1: in two different samples, using slightly different measures of dispensationalism and of warmth toward Israel, we find that evangelical Protestant clergy and, more specifically, those of dispensationalist bent, are most likely to back Israel.

Do the four thousand laity in these groups behave the same way? Presumably such activists should be swayed more by their religious beliefs than the average citizen, should be more likely to pick up political cues provided by local clergy, and, finally, may be more attentive to the

TABLE 17.2

Clerical Activists' Support for Israel by Religious Tradition and
Dispensationalism With Party Identification, Ideology, Age, and Education
Controlled Multiple Classification Analysis

QUESTION: "How close do you feel to the State of Israel?"
[1 = Very close, 5 = Very far. Grand Mean = 3.01]

	(N)	Unadjusted Mean Scores		Adjusted for Independent Variables		Adjusted for Independent and Covariables	
	(N)	Mean	Beta	Mean	Beta	Mean	Beta
Religious Tradition							
Evangelical	(564)	2.73		2.97		3.04	
Mainline	(212)	3.54		3.13		3.03	
Catholic	(93)	3.49		2.97		2.78	
			.33*		.06*		.07*
Dispensationalism							
Very High	(166)	2.13		2.17		2.34	
High	(98)	2.41		2.45		2.56	
Moderate	(173)	2.80		2.81		2.88	
Low	(198)	3.40		3.39		3.31	
Very Low	(234)	3.70		3.67		3.51	
			.52*		.50*		.39*
Multiple R				.52		.555	
Multiple R-Squared				.27		.308	

* p< .001

Source: 1990 Wheaton Religious Activist Study, conducted by Lyman A. Kellstedt, John C. Green, Corwin E. Smidt, and James L. Guth (see Guth et al. 1993).

urgings of prominent national figures from their traditions, whether evangelical, mainline, or Catholic. Of course, even religious activists might not exhibit the strong attitudinal constraint seen in the clergy. Nevertheless, the findings for the laity subsample in table 17.3 are consistent with the clergy studies, with a few variations. Evangelical laity are much more pro-Israel than mainline Protestant laity, but Catholic

TABLE 17.3

Lay Activists' Support for Israel by Religious Tradition and Dispensationalism
With Party Identification, Ideology, Age, and Education Controlled Multiple
Classification Analysis

QUESTION: "How close do you feel to the State of Israel?"
[1 = Very close, 5 = Very far. Grand Mean = 2.90]

	(N)	Unadjusted Mean Scores		Adjusted for Independent Variables		Adjusted for Independent and Covariables	
		Mean	Beta	Mean	Beta	Mean	Beta
Religious Tradition							
Evangelical	(2177)	2.69		2.85		2.87	
Mainline	(647)	3.31		3.03		2.99	
Catholic	(348)	3.48		2.99		2.92	
			.25*		.06*		.04*
Dispensationalism							
Very High	(599)	2.08		2.12		2.28	
High	(524)	2.44		2.47		2.58	
Moderate	(876)	2.89		2.93		2.97	
Low	(672)	3.39		3.35		2.23	
Very Low	(501)	3.69		3.63		3.42	
			.44*		.41*		.31*
Multiple R					.441		.466
Multiple R-Squared					.195		.217

* p < .001

Source: 1990 Wheaton Religious Activist Study, conducted by Lyman A.
Kellstedt, John C. Green, Corwin E. Smidt, and James L. Guth (see Guth
et al., 1993).

activists are even less pro-Israel than mainline Protestants. Once again
the link between dispensational theology and sentiment toward Israel
holds, across the sample and within each religious tradition. The greatest
differences by eschatology occur among Evangelicals, where strong
dispensationalists are highly pro-Israel, while those lower on the eschatology scale are actually the group furthest from Israel in the entire

sample. (This statistical interaction between religious tradition and dispensationalism shows up as a significant and substantive effect in the MCA.) As expected, among lay activists the predictive power of the two religious measures is somewhat less than among the clergy, yet they account together for almost 20 percent of the variance (compared to 28 percent for the clergy in the Wheaton study). The control variables are all significant in this case, but the direction differs from expectations in some instances. Republicans and conservatives are again more pro-Israel, but, as in the 1988 clergy surveys, younger and better-educated respondents feel further from Israel, not closer. Although all four control variables have significant effects, their impact is modest compared to the religious measures (data not shown).

A comparison of clergy and laity within the two Protestant traditions and the constituent denominational groups uncovers some intriguing patterns. As tables 17.2 and 17.3 reveal, evangelical clergy and laity, in aggregate at least, are closely matched in their felt proximity to Israel (clergy mean = 2.73; laity mean = 2.68). The mainline clergy, however, are distinctly *less* friendly to Israel (mean = 3.53) than mainline laity (mean = 3.32). And, although the Ns are relatively small, the same pattern appears among activists from major denominational groups in each tradition. For example, mean scores of laity and clergy among Evangelicals are: nondenominational charismatic (2.04, 1.83); nondenominational fundamentalist (2.35, 2.41); Conservative Baptist (2.53, 2.37); Southern Baptist (2.55, 2.57); nondenominational Evangelical (2.69, 2.68); Christian and Missionary Alliance (2.73, 2.73); Nazarene (2.80, 2.68); and, Baptist General Conference (2.96, 2.78). Compare these to laity-clergy differences in mainline churches: United Methodist (3.04, 3.47); Evangelical Lutheran Church in America (3.35, 3.65); Presbyterian Church in the U.S.A. (3.37, 3.52); and, United Church of Christ (3.38, 3.72). Although the size of the subsamples leads us to be cautious, this pattern is suggestive. Several explanations are possible for both the similarity between evangelical clergy and laity, and the disparity between mainline clergy and their parishioners. First, popular dispensational ideas may indeed have the kind of influence Weber (1987) claims among some mainline laity, while mainline clergy are more attentive to, and influenced by, denominational positions favoring "balanced" Middle East policies. In addition, the higher level of clergy education compared to laity, or the special nature of seminary training in mainline institutions, may also be factors. That mainline Protestant laity are much less likely to attend church or regard their religious beliefs as very important may reduce the impact of theological ideas and clerical leadership on political attitudes. Whatever the reason, it is very tempting to find yet another example of the much-discussed political gap between mainline clergy and laity (Hadden 1969; but cf. Hertzke 1988). Whether such differences obtain on other foreign policy issues is a fascinating topic for future research.

As the observant reader has noticed, important differences obtain within the Evangelical camp as well. The Wheaton sample allows us to explore these differences by comparing activists from various Evangelical traditions. To maximize our Ns, we recombined the sample, including both clergy and laity. In table 17.4, we divide the evangelical tradition into denominational families: Pentecostal, nondenominational Evangelical, Baptist, Holiness, evangelical Presbyterian, European Free Church, and Reformed. Once again, we have arrayed the denominational families in the order of historic premillennial influences in general and dispensational impact in particular. Pentecostals are by far Israel's strongest supporters, with nondenominational Evangelicals (who include many fundamentalists and charismatics) next. Baptists, with strong historical ties to premillennial movements come third. Evangelicals with fewer links to Protestant millennialism such as the Holiness churches—or historic antipathy to such movements—as among the Presbyterian, European Free, and Reformed Churches—are much more distant from Israel. Note especially the strong "feel far from" score of the Reformed contingent, drawn from a tradition that has always rejected premillennial eschatology.

That this effect is connected to the eschatological orientation of these Protestants is illustrated by data for smaller groups not listed in the table. Members of the Churches of Christ, a restorationist group that has long opposed dispensational theology, also report feeling far from Israel, a result comporting nicely with Hailey's (1988) study of their clergy, who dissent strongly from a statement that the state of Israel has special theological standing (cf. Hughes 1991). Yet, many nondispensational evangelical churches have been influenced, at least among laity, by popular dispensationalist ideas. As table 17.4 shows, among evangelical Protestants, adherence to dispensational ideas predicts stronger support for Israel. The MCA confirms that the dispensational index is the most potent explicand of attitudes toward Israel, with denominational family retaining influence even when dispensationalism and the control variables are accounted for. Once again, religious variables explain attitudes much better than education (not a significant predictor in this evangelical subsample), age, or the political variables, although ideology and partisanship remain statistically significant and of some substantive importance.

TABLE 17.4
Evangelical Activists' Support for Israel by Religious Tradition and
Dispensationalism With Party Identification, Ideology, Age, and Education
Controlled Multiple Classification Analysis

QUESTION: "How close do you feel to the State of Israel?"
[1 = Very close, 5 = Very far. Grand Mean = 2.68]

	(N)	Unadjusted Mean Scores		Adjusted for Independent Variables		Adjusted for Independent and Covariables	
		Mean	Beta	Mean	Beta	Mean	Beta
Denominational Family							
Pentecostal	(302)	2.26		2.40		2.42	
Nondenominational	(843)	2.46		2.52		2.83	
Baptist	(662)	2.69		2.75		2.75	
Holiness	(297)	2.83		2.79		2.81	
Presbyterian	(126)	3.03		2.73		2.83	
European Free	(346)	3.07		2.95		2.86	
Reformed	(71)	3.92		3.23		3.21	
			.26*		.16*		.14*
Dispensationalism							
Very High	(714)	2.08		2.11		2.24	
High	(549)	2.40		2.44		2.52	
Moderate	(790)	2.80		2.82		2.81	
Low	(396)	3.38		3.33		3.13	
Very Low	(198)	3.73		3.56		3.30	
			.42*		.38*		.28*
Multiple R					.446		.480
Multiple R-Squared					.199		.231

* $p < .001$
Source: 1990 Wheaton Religious Activist Study, conducted by Lyman A.
Kellstedt, John C. Green, Corwin E. Smidt, and James L. Guth (see Guth
et al. 1993).

As we conclude our look at religious elites and activists, we should note that in each study we have additional religious measures that we have not used because they are not available in all samples. These measures not only reinforce our findings but, if incorporated, add to the predictive power of the models. For example, in both the 1988 clergy and the 1990 Wheaton activist samples, we use religious self-identification (Wilcox, Jelen, and Leege 1993). As one might suspect, clergy or activists identifying as Pentecostals or charismatics are most supportive of Israel, followed by fundamentalists and self-identifying Evangelicals. Mainline, liberal, and ecumenical Christians are much less supportive. Similarly, in the Wheaton study many religious items, especially items assessing views of the Bible and the born-again experience, have strong bivariate correlations with the Israel measure and add substantially to the power of multivariate analyses. The same can be said for some other doctrinal items. What all these measures have in common is close association with the characteristic emphases of Protestant premillennial theologies.

Political Party Activists and Christian Zionism

Do these influences extend beyond the circle of religious professionals and activists? What about political elites? Here we are at a mild disadvantage, not having the same detailed religious measures available in the surveys used to this point. Still, two surveys of 2,600 Republican and Democratic party contributors conducted in 1986–88 provide supporting evidence (for details, see Green, Guth, and Fraser 1991). We asked respondents whether the United States should seek closer ties with Israel and determined respondents' precise denominational affiliation. In table 17.5, we have again divided the combined sample into religious traditions, but this time we separated Evangelicals into Pentecostals, the prime support group for Marion G. "Pat" Robertson's 1988 campaign for the GOP presidential nomination (Green and Guth 1988) and "other evangelicals." Then we include mainline Protestants and Catholics, as in previous tables, and add two groups found only in small numbers in the earlier samples, but much more numerous among these wealthy, well-educated party elites: liberal nontraditional affiliates (primarily Unitarians, Quakers, and Humanists), and secular activists, those with virtually no "religious" traits, beliefs, or affiliations.

Unfortunately, we have no precise measure of dispensationalist beliefs. A logical proxy is a standard Bible item, asking respondents whether the Bible should be taken as the literal Word of God, the inspired but not

TABLE 17.5
Party Contributors' Support for Israel by Religious Tradition and View of
the Bible With Party Identification, Ideology, Age, and Education Controlled
Multiple Classification Analysis (Whites only)

QUESTION: "Should the U.S. seek closer ties with Israel or not?"
[1 = Much closer, 7 = Much more distant. Grand Mean = 3.78]

	(N)	Unadjusted Mean Scores		Adjusted for Independent Variables		Adjusted for Independent and Covariables	
		Mean	Beta	Mean	Beta	Mean	Beta
Religious Tradition							
Pentecostal	(57)	1.72		2.34		2.44	
Evangelical	(236)	3.38		3.65		3.67	
Mainline	(781)	3.78		3.78		3.76	
Catholic	(300)	3.78		3.72		3.75	
Liberal Nontrad	(75)	4.40		4.20		4.11	
Secular	(246)	4.46		4.20		4.22	
			.28*		.18*		.17*
View of the Bible							
Literal	(713)	2.72		3.04		3.12	
Inspired	(547)	3.75		3.74		3.74	
Fables, Legends	(786)	4.31		4.10		4.06	
			.28*		.19*		.17*
Multiple R					.319		.331
Multiple R-Squared					.102		.109

* p< .001
Source: Republican and Democratic Party Contributor Studies, 1986-1988,
conducted by John C. Green, James L. Guth, and Cleveland R. Fraser (see
Green et al. 1991)

literal Word of God, or as a collection of fables, legends, and moral
precepts (Kellstedt and Smidt 1993; see the appendix for exact wording).
From both historians' work and survey research, we know that dispensationalists and premillennialists have very high views of Scripture and
should dominate the first category, whereas more liberal or secular

respondents will comprise a large portion of those taking the third option, making the Bible question a useful surrogate for a direct eschatological item. Nevertheless, we should expect considerably weaker relationships, given both the different type of sample and some error in measuring dispensational attitudes.

Despite these limitations, the religious variables work. Table 17.5 shows that Evangelicals are friendliest toward Israel, with Pentecostals leading the way. Indeed, Pentecostal contributors *are more convinced of the need for closer ties than are the Jewish activists* (mean scores = 1.72 and 2.56, respectively). In a now-familiar pattern, Evangelicals are followed by mainline Protestants and Catholics, with liberal nontraditionalists and secular donors preferring more distant relations. Within religious categories, support for Israel declines as activists' view of the Bible falls. As the MCA shows, both religious tradition and view of the Bible have substantial effects even controlling for party identification, ideology, age, and education, accounting for 10 percent of the variance. An interaction effect is also present between religious tradition and view of the Bible, with the latter having greater impact on Evangelicals: Evangelicals with a literalist view are much more supportive of Israel than their counterparts in other traditions (data not shown). Surprisingly, neither party identification nor ideology has a significant effect in this highly political sample when entered with the religious variables. Once again, education has a small but significant effect that runs counter to those reported in mass public surveys (i.e., among activists the better educated are less pro-Israel). Age has a very small impact: younger activists are slightly more supportive of Israel, similar to the relationships reported in the mass public by earlier studies. In any case, the political and demographic variables pale in importance compared to the religious measures. Adding other items such as the political relevance of religion to the respondent, religious self-identification, and frequency of church attendance boosts the variance explained to almost 15 percent, although religious tradition and view of the Bible remain by far the most important predictors.

Christian Zionism in the Mass Public

Now we approach the most difficult task: determining whether religious variables assist us in understanding the American public's attitudes toward Israel and Middle East policy. For this purpose, we draw on data from our 1992 poll of 4,001 Americans, conducted by the Survey Research Center of the University of Akron. This survey was designed to chart the links among religious affiliations, beliefs, and behaviors and American political life (for details, see Green 1992). We included a direct measure of eschatology, asking about a belief central to dispensational-ism: "The world will end in a battle at Armageddon between Jesus and the Anti-Christ" (five-point scale, "strongly agree" to "strongly disagree"). Premillennialists of all sorts, but especially dispensationalists, should answer this question affirmatively (see Turner and Guth 1989). Our dependent variable is an item asking respondents whether the United States should back Israel rather than the Arabs in the Middle East.

We report in table 17.6 an analysis of responses by religious tradition and the single Armageddon question. Note once again the clear pattern of declining support for Israel when moving from Evangelicals, through mainline Protestants and Catholics, to seculars, with by far the largest gap appearing between evangelical and mainline Protestants. And, once more, we find that the Armageddon item distinguishes pro-Israel atti-tudes both across the sample and within religious traditions. Among laity, however, the range within the three Christian traditions between the dispensationally oriented and opponents is about the same, although the score support for Israel declines among "dispensationalists" with movement from the evangelical to Catholic traditions. As the MCA confirms, both religious tradition and eschatology have independent effects on views toward Israel. Indeed, in this mass sample, *only* the two religious variables have much impact. Party, ideology, and education fall short of significance, even with the large N, and younger citizens are only marginally more pro-Israel than older voters. The two religious variables together explain about 7 percent of the total variance. If the sample is confined to an "attentive" public, those who reported voting in the 1990 congressional elections, the variance accounted for increases to almost 11 percent.

The relatively small proportion of the variance explained in the mass public sample does not come as much of a surprise, of course, but it does lead to another question: do other religious variables add to our ability to predict support for Israel? Because of the Akron study's focus on religious measures, we have many items that tap religious identifications, beliefs, and practices. Considerable experimentation reveals that incorpo-ration of other beliefs often associated with conservative theology in-creases our predictive ability. The most powerful is a three-point item asking whether respondents considered themselves born-again Christians and whether that meant having a specific experience in time or gradual development in faith (Jelen, Smidt, and Wilcox 1993). Those with dra-matic experiences are considerably more pro-Israel, as are respondents

TABLE 17.6
American Public's Support for Israel by Religious Tradition and
Dispensationalism With Party Identification, Ideology, Age, and Education
Controlled Multiple Classification Analysis (Whites only)

QUESTION: "The United States should back Israel over the Arabs in the
Middle East."
[1 = Strongly Agree, 5 = Strongly Disagree. Grand Mean = 3.14]

	(N)	Unadjusted Mean Scores		Adjusted for Independent Variables		Adjusted for Independent and Covariables	
		Mean	Beta	Mean	Beta	Mean	Beta
Religious Tradition							
Evangelical	(707)	2.77		2.90		2.91	
Mainline	(500)	3.20		3.22		3.23	
Catholic	(629)	3.33		3.30		3.30	
Secular	(439)	3.40		3.21		3.21	
			.21*		.14*		.13*
Dispensationalism							
Very High	(396)	2.66		2.77		2.78	
High	(270)	2.88		2.93		2.94	
Moderate	(360)	3.09		3.09		3.10	
Low	(277)	3.27		3.24		3.24	
Very Low	(971)	3.39		3.34		3.33	
			.23*		.18*		.17*
Multiple R				.261		.268	
Multiple R-Squared				.068		.073	

* $p < .001$
Source: University of Akron Study of Religion and Politics in America, 1992,
conducted by John C. Green, Lyman A. Kellstedt, Corwin E. Smidt, and
James L. Guth (see Green 1992).

who consider themselves fundamentalists or charismatics, even after
other religious variables are taken into account. Following up an earlier
lead from the Wheaton study, we also broke the evangelical and mainline
traditions into their constituent denominational families. For the larger
families, the mean support for Israel from highest to lowest are as

follows: Pentecostal (2.46), Holiness (2.57), nondenominational Evangelical (2.67), Baptist (2.77), (and for the mainline) Presbyterians (3.12), Methodists (3.14), Lutherans (3.25), and United Church of Christ (3.54). Once again, the consistency of results among samples is striking. Finally, those who consult their religious beliefs when making political decisions are stronger supporters of Israel. Incorporating these additional variables in the MCA raises the variance explained to almost 12 percent for the entire sample, and to over 15 percent for congressional election voters.

One additional note is in order. Foreign policy attitudes may also be influenced by respondents' attitude toward domestic groups and policies. Although global measures such as ideology and partisanship may have relatively little impact, more specific variables may. As Hill (1993) demonstrates, for example, racial attitudes are by far the best predictor of Americans' attitudes toward South Africa. This suggests that Americans' support for Israel may be structured by their attitudes toward Jews. In fact, respondents' felt proximity to Jews is a solid predictor of attitudes toward Israel, even controlling for the religious variables (Evangelicals and dispensationalists also feel closest to Jews) and the covariates, although it does not match religious tradition or the dispensationalism in substantive importance. Thus, not surprisingly, many citizens do seem to evaluate psychologically distant foreign policy issues in part through the lens of more proximate domestic group likes and dislikes.

Discussion and Conclusions

We have argued that carefully constructed indicators of religious orientation are essential for providing a more complete view of American public opinion toward important foreign policy issues such as U.S.-Israeli relations. In this case, both religious tradition and religious doctrine influence attitudes. Evangelical Protestants are more favorable to the State of Israel than mainline Protestants, who in turn are more supportive than Catholics and secular citizens. Even within the evangelical tradition, some stark differences are noted, with Pentecostals and fundamentalist groups friendliest toward Israel. And within each Christian tradition, an eschatological doctrine—premillennial dispensationalism—predicts positive assessments of Israel. These patterns are remarkably consistent across several samples, in different populations, mass and elite, taken at different times, and using somewhat varied measures of both independent and dependent variables. And religious variables consistently outperform the demographic and political measures that have been cited in earlier studies as most influential in shaping opinion toward Israel.

These findings may be especially important in tracking the future of the American public's views on Middle East policy. As we noted earlier, public attitudes toward Israel have become more volatile over the last decade. Indeed, one could argue that American public opinion has passed through at least two "dispensations" in the postwar era: first, a period of very high and virtually unquestioning support for the Jewish state and, more recently, a period of reassessment and attitude instability. In the wake of Israel's activities in southern Lebanon, its involvement in the Iran-Contra affair, its repression of the Palestinian "Intifada," as well as its policies regarding settlements on the West Bank, the American public has had much greater difficulty in reaching a consensus about what our relationship should be with Israel. Israel's rapprochement with the Palestinian Liberation Organization (PLO) since 1993 further complicates matters. If Americans are increasingly confronted with diverse and often conflicting perspectives on Middle East policy, we would expect that among a large segment of the public, prophetic cues derived from the evangelical tradition would minimize the "cognitive dissonance" associated with this foreign policy issue and resolve it in Israel's favor.

Where do we go from here? Perhaps the most promising direction for further research is to determine whether these and other religious variables influence a wide variety of specific foreign policy attitudes and, perhaps more important, whether they help structure the general heuristic frameworks citizens use to think about foreign policy. The connection between religion and attitudes toward Israel may be unique, bound up as it is with a religious entity (Israel) and biblical interpretation. But there are indications that religious variables may in fact be linked both to a good many specific issues, such as defense spending or foreign aid (cf. Guth and Green 1993; Lumsdaine 1993: 44) and to the larger structures in which these attitudes are imbedded. Evangelical Protestants, for example, more often take hawkish defense postures, while mainline Protestants and Catholics (especially among elites) may be more amenable to foreign aid programs, reflecting their "social gospel" theological orientations. It is imperative to explore how and why religious variables locate individuals within the various opinion types identified by Wittkopf or Chittick and his colleagues. For at least some Americans religious beliefs may be primary determinants of political worldviews. If so, religious variables may be profitably introduced into hierarchical models of attitude constraint in foreign affairs (see Hurwitz and Peffley 1987, 1990; Peffley and Hurwitz 1993). Future research in this area will produce results if careful attention is paid to conceptualization and measurement of religion in all dimensions: affiliation, beliefs, and practices. After all, given the intense religious commitments of many Americans, no policy area will be altogether immune from religious influence.

Appendix

We use several measures of premillennial dispensationalism in this chapter. The questions used to construct each of these measures and the reliabilities are reported here for each index.

1988 Clergy Surveys (Table 17.1)

Five-point Likert items, ranging from 1, "strongly agree," to 5, "Strongly disagree."

"The Bible clearly teaches a 'premillennial view' of history and the future."
"I believe in a dispensationalist interpretation of Scripture."
"Scriptures are the inerrant word of God not only in matters of faith, but in all other matters as well."

For this measures, alpha = .83.

1990 Wheaton Religious Activist Study (Tables 17.2–17.4)

Five-point Likert items, ranging from 1, "strongly agree," to 5, "strongly disagree."

"I believe in the 'Rapture' of the church."
"The Bible teaches a premillennial view of history."
"Which of the following comes CLOSEST to your views regarding the Bible?

1. The Bible is God's Word, and is meant to be taken literally, word for word.
2. The Bible is God's Word, and all it says is true, but it is not meant to be taken literally, word for word.
3. The Bible is God's Word, and is authoritative for Christian faith and practice, but it is not intended as a book of science and history.

4. The Bible was written by men inspired by God, but it does contain some spiritual errors, often reflecting the limitations of its authors and their eras.
5. The Bible is a good book because it was written by wise men, but God had nothing to do with it.
6. The Bible was written by men who lived so long ago that it is worth very little today."

For our analysis, responses 5 and 6 were combined to produce a five-category item, for use in the scale.

For this measure, alpha = .74 for the clergy subsample and alpha = .70 for the laity subsample.

1986–88 Party Contributor Studies (Table 17.5)

"Which of the following comes closest to your view of the Bible?

1. the actual Word of God, to be taken literally, word for word
2. the inspired Word of God, but not all to be taken literally
3. an ancient book of fables, legends, history, and moral precepts."

References

Aldrich, John, John Sullivan, and Eugene Borgida. 1989. "Foreign Affairs and Issue Voting: Do Presidential Candidates 'Waltz before a Blind Audience'?" *American Political Science Review* 83:123–41.

Blitzer, Wolf. 1985. *Between Washington and Jerusalem*. New York: Oxford University Press.

Blumhofer, Edith. 1993. *Restoring the Faith: The Assemblies of God, Pentecostalism, and American Culture*. Urbana: University of Illinois Press.

Bowan, Karlyn, and Everett C. Ladd. eds. 1994. "Trouble Spots." *The Public Pespective*. September/October.

Boyer, Paul. 1992. *When Time Shall Be No More: Prophecy Belief in Modern American Culture*. Cambridge, Mass.: Belknap.

Chittick, William, and Keith Billingsley. 1989. "The Structure of Elite Foreign Policy Beliefs." *The Western Political Quarterly* 42:201–24.

Chittick, William, Keith Billingsley, and Rick Travis. 1995. "A Three-Dimensional Model of American Foreign Policy Beliefs." *International Studies Quarterly* 39:313–31.

Curtiss, Richard. H. 1986. *A Changing Image: American Perceptions of the Arab-Israeli Dispute*. Washington, D.C.: The American Educational Trust.

Fishman, Hertzel. 1973. *American Protestantism and a Jewish State.* Detroit: Wayne State University Press.

Gallup Poll. 1991. "Americans Favor 'Land for Peace' Solution in Israel." *Gallup Poll Monthly* 306:35–42.

Gilboa, Eytan. 1987. *American Public Opinion Toward Israel and the Arab-Israeli Conflict.* Lexington, Mass.: Lexington Books.

Green, John. 1992. *A Survey of Americans' Religious Beliefs and Politics.* Akron, Ohio: Ray C. Bliss Institute, University of Akron.

Green, John, and James Guth. 1988. "The Christian Right in the Republican Party: The Case of Pat Robertson's Supporters." *Journal of Politics* 50:156–65.

Green, John, James Guth, and Cleveland Fraser. 1991. "Apostles and Apostates? Religion and Politics Among Party Activists." In *The Bible and the Ballot Box: Religion and Politics in the 1988 Election,* ed. James Guth and John Green. Boulder, Colo.: Westview.

Griffin, Kenyon, John Martin, and Oliver Walter. 1976. "Religious Roots and Rural Americans' Support for Israel During the October War." *Journal of Palestine Studies* 6:104–14.

Guth, James, and John Green. 1993. "Salience: The Core Concept?" In *Rediscovering the Religious Factor in American Politics,* ed. David Leege and Lyman Kellstedt. Armonk, N.Y.: Sharpe.

Guth, James, and Helen Lee Turner. 1991. "Pastoral Politics in the 1988 Election: Disciples as Compared to Presbyterians and Southern Baptists." In *A Case Study of Mainstream Protestantism: The Disciples' Relation to American Culture, 1880–1989,* ed. D. Newell Williams. Grand Rapids, Mich.: Eerdmans.

Guth, James, John Green, Corwin Smidt, and Margaret Poloma. 1991. "Pulpits and Politics: The Protestant Clergy in the 1988 Presidential Election." In *The Bible and the Ballot Box: Religion and Politics in the 1988 Election,* ed. James Guth and John Green. Boulder, Colo.: Westview.

Guth, James, Corwin Smidt, Lyman Kellstedt, and John Green. 1993. "The Sources of Antiabortion Attitudes: The Case of Religious Political Activists." *American Politics Quarterly* 21:65–80.

Hadden, Jeffrey. 1969. *The Gathering Storm in the Churches.* Garden City, N.Y.: Doubleday.

Hailey, Mel. 1988. "The Political and Social Attitudes of Church of Christ Ministers." Paper presented at the annual meeting of the American Political Science Association, Atlanta.

Halsell, Grace. 1986. *Prophecy and Politics: Militant Evangelists on the Road to Nuclear War.* Westport, Conn.: Lawrence Hill.

Hertzke, Allen. 1988. *Representing God in Washington: The Role of Religious Lobbies in the American Polity.* Knoxville: University of Tennessee Press.

Hero, Alfred O. 1973. *American Religious Groups View Foreign Policy: Trends in Rank-and-File Opinion, 1937–1969.* Durham: Duke University Press.

Hill, Kevin. 1993. "The Domestic Sources of Foreign Policymaking: Congressional Voting and American Mass Attitudes Toward South Africa." *International Studies Quarterly* 37:195–214.

Holsti, Ole R. 1992. "Public Opinion and Foreign Policy: Challenges to the Almond-Lippmann Consensus." *International Studies Quarterly* 36:439–66.

Holsti, Ole R., and James N. Rosenau. 1984. *American Leadership in World Affairs: Vietnam and the Breakdown of Consensus.* Boston: Allen and Unwin.

———. 1990. "The Structure of Foreign Policy Attitudes: American Leaders, 1976–1984." *Journal of Politics* 52:94–125.

Hughes, Richard T. 1991. "Are Restorationists Evangelicals?" In *The Variety of American Evangelicalism,* ed. Donald Dayton and Robert Johnson. Downers Grove, Ill.: Intervarsity Press.

Hugick, Larry. 1991a. "Public Support for Israel Continues." *Gallup Poll Monthly* 311:26–32.

———. 1991b. "No Opinion Winner in Bush-Israel Clash." *Gallup Poll Monthly* 313:5–9.

Hurwitz, Jon, and Mark Peffley. 1987. "How Are Foreign Policy Attitudes Structured? A Hierarchical Model." *American Political Science Review* 81:1099–1120.

———. 1990. "Public Images of the Soviet Union: The Impact on Foreign Policy Attitudes." *Journal of Politics* 52:3–28.

Hurwitz, Jon, Mark Peffley, and Mitchell Seligson. 1993. "Foreign Policy Belief Systems in Comparative Perspective: The United States and Costa Rica." *International Studies Quarterly* 37:245–70.

Jelen, Ted G. 1992. "Religion and Foreign Policy Attitudes." Paper presented at the Conference on the Political Consequences of War, sponsored by the National Election Studies, the Center for Political Studies, and the Brookings Institution, Washington, D.C.

Jelen, Ted G., Corwin Smidt, and Clyde Wilcox. 1993. "The Political Effects of the Born-Again Phenomenon." In *Rediscovering the Religious Factor in American Politics,* ed. David Leege and Lyman Kellstedt. Armonk, N.Y.: Sharpe.

Jorstad, Erling. 1993. *Popular Religion in America: The Evangelical Voice.* Westport, Conn.: Greenwood.

Kellstedt, Lyman, and John Green. 1993. "Knowing God's Many People: Denominational Preference and Political Behavior." In *Rediscovering the Religious Factor in American Politics,* ed. David Leege and Lyman Kellstedt. Armonk, N.Y.: Sharpe.

Kellstedt, Lyman, and Corwin Smidt. 1993. "Doctrinal View and Political Behavior: Views of the Bible." In *Rediscovering the Religious Factor in American Politics,* ed. David Leege and Lyman Kellstedt. Armonk, N.Y.: Sharpe.

Kimball, Charles. 1990. "Protestant and Catholic Churches Show New Support for Palestinians." *The Link* 23:1–13.

Leege, David, and Lyman Kellstedt, eds. 1993. *Rediscovering the Religious Factor in American Politics.* Armonk, N.Y.: Sharpe.

Lewis, Bernard. 1992. "Rethinking the Middle East." *Foreign Affairs* 71:99–119.

Lienesch, Michael. 1993. *Redeeming America: Piety and Politics in the New Christian Right.* Chapel Hill: University of North Carolina Press.

Lindsey, Hal. 1970. *The Late Great Planet Earth*. New York: Bantam Books.

Lumsdaine, David. 1993. *Moral Vision in International Politics: The Foreign Aid Regime, 1949–1989*. Princeton: Princeton University Press.

Marsden, George. 1980. *Fundamentalism and American Culture: The Shaping of Twentieth-Century Evangelicalism, 1870–1925*. Oxford: Oxford University Press.

————. 1991. *Understanding Fundamentalism and Evangelicalism*. Grand Rapids: Eerdmans.

Mojtabai, A. G. 1986. *Blessed Assurance: At Home with the Bomb in Amarillo, Texas*. Boston: Houghton Mifflin.

Mouley, Ruth W. 1982. "Israel: Darling of the Religious Right." *The Humanist* 42:5–11.

National Journal. 1995. "Opinion Outlook: National Security." 27:130.

Page, Benjamin, and Robert Shapiro. 1992. *The Rational Public: Fifty Years of Trends in Americans' Policy Preferences*. Chicago: University of Chicago Press.

Peffley, Mark, and Jon Hurwitz. 1993. "Models of Attitude Constraint in Foreign Affairs." *Political Behavior* 15:61–90.

Quinley, Harold. 1974. *The Prophetic Clergy*. Berkeley and Los Angeles: University of California Press.

Reich, B. 1984. *The United States and Israel: Influence in the Special Relationship*. New York: Praeger.

Rielly, John E. ed. 1991. *American Public Opinion and U.S. Foreign Policy 1991*. Chicago: The Chicago Council on Foreign Relations.

————, ed. 1995. *American Public Opinion and U.S. Foreign Policy 1995*. Chicago: The Chicago Council on Foreign Relations.

Scott, Rebekah. 1995. "Rabin's Assassination Viewed as Milestone on Path to Armageddon." *Grand Rapids Press*, 18 November.

Simon, Merrill. 1984. *Jerry Falwell and the Jews*. Middle Village, N.Y.: Jonathan David.

Stark, Rodney, and Charles Glock. 1968. *American Piety: The Nature of Religious Commitment*. Berkeley: University of California Press.

Stockton, Ronald. 1987. "Christian Zionism: Prophecy and Public Opinion." *Middle East Journal* 41:234–53.

Turner, Helen Lee, and James Guth. 1989. "The Politics of Armageddon: Dispensationalism Among Southern Baptist Ministers." In *Religion and Political Behavior in the United States*, ed. Ted G. Jelen. New York: Praeger.

Wagner, Donald. 1992. "Beyond Armageddon." *The Link* 25:1–13.

Wald, Kenneth. 1992. "Religious Elites and Public Opinion: The Impact of the Bishops' Peace Pastoral." *Review of Politics* 54:112–43.

Weber, Timothy. 1987. *Living in the Shadow of the Second Coming: American Premillennialism, 1875–1982*. Chicago: University of Chicago Press.

Wilcox, Clyde, Ted G. Jelen, and David Leege. 1993. "Religious Group Identifications: Toward a Cognitive Theory of Religious Mobilization." In *Redis-*

covering the Religious Factor in American Politics, ed. David Leege and Lyman Kellstedt. Armonk, N.Y.: Sharpe.

Wittkopf, Eugene. 1990. *Faces of Internationalism: Public Opinion and Foreign Policy*. Durham, N.C.: Duke University Press.

Index

abortion, 1, 13, 15, 18, 275; Catholic stand on, 64, 282; as Christian Right core issue, 7, 24, 33, 34, 39, 65, 74; coalition lobbies against, 24, 67; Evangelicals and, 187, 255; fundamentalism and, 200, 209; as ideological indicator, 36, 90–91, 161, 182, 184, 187, 255, 308–9, 310, 323; in 1994 elections, 294; status as issue, 21, 32, 64, 120, 273, 280, 306

activism, conditions for, 103–4

affiliation, religious. *See* religious affiliation

AFR. *See* Americans for the Republic

alienation, 120

Alliance of Baptists, 163, 168

alliances: changes in, 267, 268, 270–71, 273, 284; historical religious-political, 63–64, 82–83, 177, 268, 270, 293–95; orthodox and progressive, 1, 2, 5, 312. *See also* Christian Right

American Center for Law and Justice, 67

American Family Association, 163, 165, 166

Americans for the Republic (AFR), 66–67

Americans United for Separation of Church and State, 163

Anabaptists, 69, 70

attitude constraint, 11, 304, 338

Bakker, Jim, 12, 13

beliefs. *See* religion

BFW. *See* Bread for the World

Billings, Robert, 14, 15, 17, 19

Bob Jones University, 24, 28n14

Bread for the World (BFW), 66, 68; membership and activism, 163, 165, 166

Bush, George, 267, 273; 1992 election, 275, 276–77, 280–81

Calvinist Protestants, 69–70

candidates: Christian Right support for, 105–7; ideological mismatch with constituents, 107, 111

capitalism, 63

Catholicism, evangelical elements in, 314–15, 221

Catholics, 258; affiliation, 181; as conservatives, 275–76; charismatic, 221; commitment of, 185; mobilizing issues, 306, 310; political activity, 69, 119; political alignment, 63, 233, 234, 268, 272, 291; political alignment change, 291, 293, 296; political relevance of religion, 304–26; relations with Christian Right, 24; social issues and, 64, 71; support for Israel, 342–44; voting behavior, 269, 278, 292, 293

CBF. *See* Cooperative Baptist Fellowship

charismatics, 5, 10, 24, 45, 83n8, 225, 236, 237n2; Pentecostals distinguished, 224–26; as political activists, 49; in Protestantism, 221, 237n5. *See also* Pentecostals; spirit-filled movements

Christian Broadcasting Network, 16–17, 52, 53

Christian Coalition, 3, 66–67, 146; membership and activism, 163, 165, 166, 168, 212

Christian Left, 3, 66, 75. *See also* Religious Left

Christian Life Commission (CLC), 163, 166

Christian Right: arena of activity, 154; blacks and, 24–25; candidate choice, 105–6, 111, 112; charismatics in, 221; clergy in, 11, 146, 168; congressional campaign involvement, 3–4, 19–22, 104–14; constituencies of, 5, 26; defined, 2; demographics, 31, 108–14; distinction from Religious Right, 125, 138; funding, 45–46; future of, 22–27; general appeal of, 98; internal disunity, 23–26, 46; issues of, 7, 21–22, 32, 33, 34–35, 49, 64, 89–91, 129; lobbying strategy, 18–19; locales of activism, 104, 110, 111, 112; membership data, 87; opposition to liberals, 19; organization of, 16–18; origins, 8–9, 31; other evangelical organizations and, 25; political activists, relationship to, 7, 30, 33, 40; political mobilization by, 19, 20, 285; political power and effect, 20–23, 30, 87, 99; political resources of, 45–46, 58–59, 105, 112–13, 285; politicization of, 13–16; relations with Catholics, 24; religious affiliations of activists, 109–10; Republican Party and, 4, 20, 59, 110, 113; resistance to, 26;

response to modernization, 104, 112; schools and, 14; social status in, 108; support for Israel, 335; targets of, 4; view of government's role, 75. *See also* Religious Right

Christian schools, 14, 18, 21, 22; tax credits for, 24. *See also* education

Christian Voice, 7, 15, 16–18; constituency of, 24; future of, 21, 23; Morality Rating of legislators, 18–19; spirit-filled in, 221; voter encouragement by, 20

Christian Zionism, 5, 310, 335; as foreign policy attitude factor, 338; in mass public, 350–53; political activists and, 348–50

churches, liberal. *See* liberal churches

citizen groups, 62–66. *See also* religious interest groups

civil rights, 306–7, 309

CLC. *See* Christian Life Commission

clergy: dispensationalism and foreign policy attitudes of, 339–41; evangelical, 11–12; moderates' views of political activity by, 151; as political activists, 11–12, 50–51, 71–72, 80, 119, 146–47, 169 (*see also* Southern Baptist clergy); as political mobilizers, 318, 339; as Robertson supporters, 51–52; PAC affiliations, 36; of SBC (*see* Southern Baptist Convention); support for Israel, 341–45

Clinton, Bill, 5, 278–79, 281, 284

Concerned Women for America (CWA), 66

conservatism: economic, 38, 49–50; mainstream, 33; political, 11, 12; religious basis of, 49

conservative Christians, 65, 70

conservative churches: activism by, 7; growth of, 9–10, 64; political differences among, 118–19

conservatives: education level of, 68, 73; fundamentalists as, 200, 208–9; liberal, 4; religious, 31, 35; religious affiliations of, 125; Robertson supporters, 49, 86–101; secular, 15, 138; social, 15, 35, 36; social change theories, 71; in spirit-filled movements, 231; support for Moral Majority, 34–35; views of clergy's political activity, 151; wealth of, 136. *See also* Christian Right

Cooperative Baptist Fellowship (CBF), 163, 166, 168

cultural defense movements, 8–9

culture wars, 1–5, 187, 285–86, 312

CWA. *See* Concerned Women for America

cynicism, 32, 35, 36, 130

Democratic Party: Catholic support for, 63, 291, 293; composition of, 272–73; liberals in, 130; 1994 elections, 293–97; 1992 elections, 274, 281; religious alignment with, 63–64, 268, 270, 272–73; religious vote correlations (1994), 293; secular voters, 268, 272–73, 281

denominations, 63, 176, 181; disunity, 64, 118–19

dispensationalism, 335–37, 338, 353

Dobson, James, 67

Dolan, Terry, 15, 17

economic issues, 35, 49–50, 63, 74, 268; in 1992 election, 279–81, 282–84; as political action motivator, 75, 89, 120, 129; religion's relevance to, 308; Republican policy on, 94; spirit-filled movement positions, 229–31. *See also* political issues; social issues

education: effect on religiosity, 38; as political issue, 1, 13, 14, 15, 18, 21, 39 (*see also* Christian schools); politicizing effect of, 304, 320

Elder, William, 24

elections: candidate recruitment, 19; 1994 religious vote, 291–93; 1992 voting blocs, 267–86

electoral opportunities, 105–6

electronic church. *See* media

environment, 74, 75, 310

Equal Rights Amendment. *See* women's rights

evangelical Protestantism, 9–12, 179, 188; churches in, 4; political activity and, 62, 68–69, 109–10; size, 181

evangelical Protestants: black, 231; as conservatives, 229, 268, 275–76; core issues, 307, 310; 1994 voting, 293; 1992 voting, 270–86; political alignment, 270–72; political alignment change, 270–72, 291, 296; political mobilization of, 324; political relevance of religion to, 304–26; race issues, 307, 309; Republican Party and, 234, 268, 269–72; as Republicans, 268, 269, 275, 281; support for Israel, 335, 337, 342–44, 346, 350; types of, 244; voting behavior, 277–78. *See also* spirit-filled movements

Evangelicalism, 4–5, 31; beliefs, 244–45, 248–49; defined, 4–5, 240, 243–44, 247, 260–61; history, 241–43; measurement of, 240, 249–50; membership, 241, 258, 260; movement affiliation and, 255–59; political attitude correlations, 250–55, 259; Protestant (*see* evangelical Protestants); religious affiliation and, 245–47, 249; religious commitment and, 245; religious traditions and, 246; survey, 247–61; traditions within, 194; trait distribution, 250. *See also* fundamentalism; Evangelicals

Evangelicals: apolitical bias of, 23, 46, 71, 147, 325; beliefs, 194; black, 24–25, 231; characteristics of, 10, 84n8; as conservatives, 182, 252; defined, 9, 240; demographics, 26; fragmentation of, xvii, 12, 64, 83–84n8; fundamentalists distinguished, 245;

issues, 252; liberals as, 259; linkage of politics and religion, 301; ministers, 11–12; numbers of, 9–10; as political activists, 13, 119, 148 (*see also* clergy; Southern Baptist Convention); political alignment of, 11, 21; political mobilization of, 59, 64, 75; religious commitment of (*see* religious commitment); Robertson support by, 46; social change theories, 71; voting, 4, 292–93. *See also* evangelical Protestants; Evangelicalism

Falwell, Jerry, 12–15, 17, 195; funding, 25; political activity, 19, 23, 51
family issues. *See* abortion; gay rights; political issues; social issues
Family Protection Act, 18
Federal Communications Commission, 13
Focus on the Family, 66, 67, 146; membership and activism, 163, 165, 166, 168
foreign policy, 18, 35, 50, 89, 91, 94, 120, 273; American interest in, 330; attitude determinants, 330–32, 353–54; as mobilizing issue, 276, 307, 310; support for Israel, 332–55 (*see also* Israel)
fund raising, 13, 17
fundamentalism, 5, 31, 245; beliefs, 194–95, 196, 198, 211–12; defined, 193–94, 196; denominations, 213n5; fragmentation of, 10, 12; future of, 195, 196–97; measurements of, 199–212; Moslem, 8, 21; political conservatism and, 200, 208–9, 210; separatism and, 195, 200, 206–8, 212; sexual traditionalism in, 306
fundamentalists, 24, 83n8; as activists, 12, 156; demographics, 202–3; Evangelicals distinguished, xvii, 46, 245; identifying, 197–99, 208–11; political activism of, 12; religiosity of, 199,

204–6; views of clergy's political activity, 151

gay rights, 13, 15, 16, 22, 32, 33, 275; as ideological indicator, 161, 168, 184, 309, 323; status as issue, 64, 65, 74, 273, 306
glossolalia, 10, 222–28, 236, 262n7
Godwin, Ronald, 14, 26
GOP. *See* Republican Party
government functions, 74
Grant, Robert, 16

Helms, Jesse, 16
Hendricks, John Stephens, 10, 12
Henry, Carl F. H., 12
homosexuality. *See* gay rights
Humbard, Rex, 12, 13, 23
Hunsinger, Jerry, 17
Hunter, James Davidson, 1–2

ideological congruence, 32
ideological constraint, 33
ideological mobilization, 160–62, 306
interest group activists. *See* political activists; religious interest groups
intolerance, 32, 35, 36, 65; political, 73
"invisible army," *See* Robertson presidential campaign
Israel, 276, 307, 310, 323; factors in attitudes toward, 337–39, 346, 351; support for, 5, 332–55 (*see also* foreign policy)

Jarmin, Gary, 15, 19
Jews, 122, 124, 181, 182, 185, 186, 244, 273; proximity to other religious groups, 353; support for Israel and, 334, 350
Jones, Bob, II, 23
JustLife PAC, 66, 67–68

LaHaye, Beverly, 66
Land, Richard, 163
Laxalt, Paul, 18

liberal activists, 119, 137–38; demographics, 120; religious activities, 131–32, 138
liberal Christians, 65, 70, 75; issues, 65, 75, 80, 117
liberal churches: activism by, 7, 117; political alignment of, 10, 64, 119
liberal politics, 3, 70, 316
liberals: Democratic Party and, 268; economic, 89; education level of, 68, 73; theological, 4 (*see also* religious interest groups); views of clergy's political activity, 151; wealth of, 136

materialism, 136
MCA. *See* Multiple Classification Analysis
McAteer, Edward, 15, 17, 21
media: as political mobilization tool, 120, 131, 316–17; radio, 12, 79; religious interest groups' use of, 79–80, 120, 197; television, 12–13, 22, 79–80
ministers. *See* clergy
modernization, 7–8, 31, 104, 112, 118, 137
moral issues. *See* abortion; gay rights; political issues; social issues
Moral Majority, 2, 7, 12, 17, 62; approach, 26; clergy's role in, 146; constituency of, 24; future of, 23; growth of, 21; ideological basis of support, 35–38; internal disunity, 26; issues, 33, 34–35; leaders, 14; lobbying by, 18; Republican Party and, 96; support for, 30–40; voter encouragement, 20
morality, 74–75
Moslem fundamentalism, 8, 21
Multiple Classification Analysis (MCA), 203–4, 338–39

National Association of Evangelicals (NAE), 25, 64, 84n8, 220

National Conservative Political Action Committee (NCPAC), 15
National Council of Churches, 64
National Organization for Women (NOW), 66
New Right, 15–16, 23, 33; Robertson campaign donors' alignment with, 96; social issues and, 36
NOW. *See* National Organization for Women

O'Connor, Sandra Day, 22
organized religion, distrust of, 31

PACs. *See* political action committees
Pentecostals, 5, 45, 83n8, 220–21, 237n2; charismatics distinguished, 224–26; as political activists, 49; support for Israel, 350. *See also* charismatics; spirit-filled movements
Perot, Ross, 279, 281
Phillips, Howard, 15, 17
political action: agenda mobilization of, 306–11; orthodoxy and, 323–24; social mobilization of, 303–6; theological bases of, 4
political action committees (PACs), 30, 32, 35–36
political activism factors, 303–4
political activists: charismatics as, 49; Christian Right and, 7, 30, 33, 40; Christian Zionism and, 348–50; citizen groups, 62–63; clergy as (*see* clergy; Southern Baptist clergy); conservatives as, 269; demographics, 120–21, 132–37; education levels, 134–35; Evangelicals as (*see* Evangelicals); fundamentalists as, 12; gender, 136; participation levels, 127; Pentecostals as, 49; personal resources, 157–60; religious alignment of, 3, 4, 118–39; in Religious Left, 124–25; religious donors as, 117, 127; Religious Right and (*see* Religious Right);

social integration of, 131–32, 138; socioeconomic status of, 135–36, 157; Southern Baptists as, 4; support for Israel, 338, 348–50; wealth of, 136. *See also* religious interest groups

political alignment: Catholics (*see* Catholics); evangelical Protestants (*see* evangelical Protestants); Evangelicals (*see* Evangelicals); liberal churches, 10, 64, 119; mainline Protestants (*see* Protestants, mainline); Protestantism and, 119; religion as factor in, 2, 118, 301; spirit-filled movement members, 233

political attitudes: correlation with religion, 177, 178, 186–87; relevance of religion, 303–4

political issues, 1, 7; abortion (*see* abortion); Christian Right core issues, 33, 34–35, 36, 65, 75, 80, 89; civil rights, 11; domestic, 275–76, 280; education (*see* education); environment, 74, 75, 310; Equal Rights Amendment (*see* women's rights); foreign policy (*see* foreign policy); gay rights (*see* gay rights); 1994 elections, 294; pornography, 13, 16, 22, 49; school prayer (*see* school prayer); secular issues, 18, 65; single-issue groups, 129; spirit-filled movement positions, 229–31; "trigger" issues, 9, 22, 33, 306, 308–10; war, 11, 18, 67, 331. *See also* ideological mobilization; social issues

political parties: alignment changes, 269, 273, 283–84, 291; composition of, 270, 273–75; discontent with, 120; ethno-religious basis of, 268–69, 270, 273–74, 284–85; evaluation of, 130; policy stances, 130; purists in, 86, 98; religious, 73. *See also* Democratic Party; Republican Party

politics, restructuring of, 137–38

pornography. *See* political issues

premillennialism. *See* dispensationalism

presidential elections: issues in, 268, 273; 1992, 267–86; Pat Robertson and (*see* Robertson presidential campaign)

protest candidacies, 104

Protestantism; black, 179, 181, 189, 189n1, 231, 249, 258, 273; conservative, 110; divisions within, 179–81, 188–89, 249; evangelical (*see* evangelical Protestantism); mainline (*see* Protestants, mainline); political alignments and, 119; social change and, 71; theology of politics, 160

Protestants, mainline, 148, 179, 181, 258; affiliations, 188–89; as conservatives, 275–76; mobilizing issues, 306, 310; 1994 voting record, 292, 293; political alignment change, 296; political relevance of religion, 304–26; religious commitment of, 185; Religious Left and, 124; Republican support by, 268, 272, 275, 281, 292–93; spirit-filled, 221, 233; support for Israel, 345; voting behavior, 269, 278

Quinley, Harold, 148, 149, 151, 158

racism, 8, 306–7

Reagan, Ronald, 273; campaign donors, 88–97; support by Christian Right, 20, 87, 106; support for Christian Right, 17

religion: American, 63; defined, 175; government regulation of, 22; linkage to politics, xv–xix, 1, 2, 7, 82, 117, 300–302; measurement of, 4–5; organizations (*see* religious organizations); organized, 31; political relevance of, 300–326; in political science, 174, 187, 267–68, 300, 331; in public life, 117; social embodiment of, 174–88; societal influence of, 5, 195–96

religiosity: education and, 38; of fundamentalists, 199, 204–6; measures of,

122–23; politicization and, 311; religio-political conflict, reasons for, 119–21, 128–37; Republican Party and, 92

religious affiliation, 175, 188; categorizing, 176–77; Evangelicals, 194, 245–46; fundamentalists, 195; political relevance and, 312–14; spirit-filled denominations, 223–28

religious commitment, 177–78; as conservatism indication, 269; effect on political relevance perception, 311–15; Evangelicalism and, 245; mainline Protestants, 185; measurement of, 183–85, 188, 269–70; political attitudes and, 184–87; religious tradition, relationship to, 185

religious communities, 175–78, 312

Religious Freedom Restoration Act, 309

religious interest groups, 64–65; ideological trends, 75–78; issues, 73–75; membership data, 66–70; political activity of, 78–82; religious differences, 68–70; support for founders' views, 75; view of political role of religion, 71–73

Religious Left, 4; ethnicity, 133–34; liberals as, 129; political activists in, 124–25. *See also* political activists

religious observance, decline in, 10

religious organizations, 62, 196, 315, 316. *See also* religious communities; religious interest groups

religious privatism, 324–25

Religious Right, 4; affiliations in, 123–25; conservatives as, 129; distinction from Christian Right, 125, 130, 138; ethnicity in, 133; success, 138. *See also* political activists

Religious Roundtable, 7, 15, 17, 21, 146; constituency of, 24; voter encouragement, 20

religious traditions, 176–77; connection to political parties, 267, 269, 286; defined, 4, 288–89; differences on issues, 280; as Israel support indicator, 338; measurement of, 179–82, 187–88, 277; political attitudes and, 182, 186–87; political behavior of, 268; political realignment by, 293; religious commitment, relationship to, 185

Republican Party: Christian Right and, 59, 96–97, 99, 110; conservative Christians' role in, 86–87, 91, 98–99; conservatives in, 130; denominations in, 63; divisions within, 96; donors to, 88–101; evangelical Protestants' support, 268, 291, 292, 297; Evangelicals and, 252, 269–72; issues, 89, 94; Moral Majority and, 38, 39; 1994 elections, 292–96; 1992 elections, 274; policy shift, 20; Protestantism and, 93; Protestants in, 268–72; religiosity of mainstream donors, 92; religious alignment with, 63, 270; religious vote correlations (1994), 292–93; Robertson candidacy support, 96–97; similarity to activist Evangelicals, 45; social differences within, 92–94; strength of attachment to, 94–98

Roberts, Oral, 12

Robertson, Marion (Pat), 12; as divisive candidate, 96, 98; 1988 presidential campaign (*see* Robertson presidential campaign); *700 Club* program, 16–17, 45–46, 58, 67

Robertson presidential campaign, 3, 44–59; AFR and, 66; clergy support, 50–52; donor geographics, 54–58; donor numbers, 53; donors compared to GOP donors, 88–101; donors' political experience, 95; donors as political party members, 97–98; effect on Republican Party, 86, 87, 96; effectiveness, 58–59; funding, 47, 52–53; issues in, 89, 90; religion of

supporters, 58, 92, 221; supporter
and worker demographics, 45,
47–50, 52, 92, 94
Robison, James, 12, 13, 17, 21

SBC. *See* Southern Baptist Convention
Schlafly, Phyllis, 17
school prayer, 7, 18, 21, 22, 32, 33;
conservative stand on, 49, 90; status
as issue, 64, 65, 74, 120
schools, Christian. *See* Christian schools
Schuller, Robert, 17
secular activists, 119, 120–21, 125, 137–
38; issues, 128, 130; political information sources, 131; social integration of, 131–32
secular left, 4, 285
secularization, 7, 118, 119, 123, 137,
139, 195–96; cultural polarization
and, 285; issues arising from, 120,
306; of public policy, 13–14
separation of church and state, 65
700 Club, 16–17, 45–46, 58, 67
Sider, Ron, 67
Simon, Arthur, 68
social class, 7
social issues, 36, 49, 63, 71, 74–75, 273;
in Bush campaign, 277, 280–81; in
1992 election, 280; as party realignment factors, 273; as political action
motivators, 120, 129; religion's relevance to, 308, 309; Republican policy
on, 94; secular stand on, 275; spirit-
filled movement positions, 229–31.
See also economic issues; political
issues
social theology, 71, 160, 314
social traditionalism, 32
Southern Baptist clergy: Christian Right
participation, 154; congregational influence on, 164–65, 166; as conservatives, 169; demographics, 157–59;
ideological mobilization, 160–62,
169; intradenominational activism,
163–64; issue attachment, 161–62,

168; liberal organizations and, 163;
organizational memberships,
162–63, 165–66; political activities,
reasons for, 156–68; political activity, views on, 148–52, 168–69; political involvement, actual, 147–48,
152–56, 169; political involvement,
forms of, 149–51; psychological orientation, 158–59
Southern Baptist Convention (SBC), 10,
25; Christian Right and, 25, 147; fundamentalists and, 195; funding for,
25–26; membership, 147. *See also*
Southern Baptist clergy
spirit-filled movements, 10, 219–37,
245, 262n7; denominational affiliations, 223–29; disunity within,
231–32, 236, 237; member identification, 222–27; partisanship of, 232–
34; political attitudes within, 229–32;
political participation, 234–36; political potential of, 219, 236–37; religious traditions and, 228–29, 231,
236; as Robertson supporters, 45;
size of, 223–28, 236; social issues
and, 230–31
Swomley, John M., Jr., 22

television, 12–13, 22, 79–80

values, traditionalist, 1, 58, 268; Repub-
lican-Democrat conflict over, 86;
threats to, 13–14, 22, 78, 110, 112,
307
Viguerie, Richard, 15
violence, 1
voters: behavior of, 267–68; evangelical,
199; religious groups, 267, 291–93;
secular, 268, 273, 278, 281, 282, 286

Weyrich, Paul, 15, 17
women's rights, 13, 15, 32, 33, 63, 120,
275; status as issue, 306, 309

Zone, Richard, 16, 20

About the Authors

Lyman A. Kellstedt is professor of political science at Wheaton College.

Corwin E. Smidt is professor of political science at Calvin College.

James L. Guth is professor of political science at Furman University.

John C. Green is director of the Ray C. Bliss Institute of Applied Politics and professor of political science at the University of Akron.

Cleveland R. Fraser is associate professor of political science at Furman University.

Kevin Hill is assistant professor of political science at Florida International University.